PBS

PBS

BEHIND THE SCREEN

Laurence Jarvik

FORUM

An Imprint of Prima Publishing

PRIMA PUBLISHING and colophon are registered trademarks of Prima Communications, Inc.

Library of Congress Cataloging-in-Publication Data

Jarvik, Laurence Ariel, 1956–
PBS : behind the screen/Laurence Jarvik.
p. cm.
Includes bibliographical references and index.
ISBN 0-7615-0668-3
1. Public Broadcasting Service.   2. Public Broadcasting—United States.
I. Title.
HE8700.79.U6J38 1996

384.54'4'0973—dc20   96-31422
                                                                                                    CIP

97 98 99 00 01 HH 10 9 8 7 6 5 4 3 2
Printed in the United States of America

HOW TO ORDER

Single copies may be ordered from Prima Publishing, P.O. Box 1260 BK, Rocklin, CA 95677; telephone (916) 632-4400. Quantity discounts are available. On your letterhead, include information concerning the intended use of the books and the number of books you wish to purchase.

Visit us online at http://www.primapublishing.com

Dedicated to my parents,
Drs. Murray and Lissy Jarvik

Contents

Foreword

During nearly two decades in commercial broadcasting I observed PBS with reactions that fluctuated between disbelief and envy. To a president of CBS News, PBS seemed to defy the laws of economics, gravity, the natural order—whatever the forces were that governed those of us flailing about in the rapacious marketplace. PBS reflected a gracious, eccentric community, remarkably insulated from the risk and turbulence and misanthropic scrutiny of the real world. It exhibited the easy assurance of a left-of-center professor with both a wealthy wife and a rock-solid tenure at an esteemed university of faded gentility.

Initially framed by short-sighted and remarkably ill-conceived planning, and warped by a series of tawdry political struggles, PBS has become a structurally, financially, and competitively challenged institution. In spite of this, the system manages to accomplish three things beyond the grasp of commercial television as we know it today.

First, and most important, is the children's programming, far better in quantity and quality than that available in the commercial marketplace. Second is the nightly one-hour news broadcast that is articulate, focused, and balanced—more balanced, in fact, than most offerings by the leading cable and network news divisions. And third is the programming PBS generates several times a year that is of such scope, ambition, and achievement it probably could not find a home anywhere else on the screen.

In this sense, at this time, public broadcasting is an asset. In regards to children, an imperative. But the real grief with PBS is not so much what it is, but what it is not.

By design and fierce internal commitment (though that is increasingly disputed if not eroding), PBS is a professional mendicant, living off the government dole, the largesse of a small percentage of the citizenry and a limited roster of foundations and program funders.

The fanatical attachment to the federal government—and the life, in effect, of a taxpayer-supported monopoly—stripped PBS of vision, initiative, and competitive capability. While there are contemporary efforts to change that, PBS seems a middlebrow entitlement frozen in a wedge of 60s Great Society Lucite.

Smothered in the government's embrace of money and restrictions, PBS's institutional vision grew so narrow that it couldn't focus on new programming and commercial opportunities, let alone potential ownership and ancillary revenues from existing programming. It is tragic that PBS did not create—or, at the very least, create and manage for others—its logical commercial progeny. Now, the Discovery Channels, the A & E's, and the Bravos—well-focused and ably managed competitors—will over time steadily diminish the PBS monopoly of upscale programming. And why should the nation's information and entertainment export be dominated by the frequently cheesy output of a few Hollywood studios? The United States should also be exporting to the world programs representative of the higher artistic and cultural aspirations of our society. But there seems little hope that PBS, stunted at its inception, will ever rise to this challenge.

On the local level, the paucity if not absence of community-related programming by public television stations, including those in some major metropolitan areas that generate huge revenues, is an unreported scandal. Journalists tend to treat PBS with a sufferance that borders on the devotional. Commercial stations, with rare exceptions, have abdicated virtually everything local beyond the most superficial news.

Based on my experience as president of KVIE, the public television station in Sacramento, the nation's twentieth-largest media market, it is clear that public stations should be celebrating and encouraging the cultural and artistic endeavors of their communities while providing more textured insight into the apprehensions and aspirations of those communities. What better way to justify their continued existence as we approach technologies that could render the PBS "network" stations obsolete. Those public stations that exist primarily as PBS retransmission facilities, housed in money-raising factories, should, and probably will, vanish.

And as a side note, it is worth mentioning that the government has licensed, and financially supported, far more public stations than necessary to provide a PBS signal to the entire nation. The commercial networks service the nation with approximately 200 stations, public television uses about 300, with the redundant stations drawing down federal or community money that could be far better applied elsewhere to achieve higher quality television.

In 1995, public broadcasting's total revenues were $1.9 billion. Yes, that's $1,900,000,000 for public radio and television. Can anyone say that we are getting nearly $2 billion worth of public broadcasting today? Hardly! If a group of rational people were setting out today to create a public broadcasting system for this nation, they would not come up with a structure and governance in any way similar to the preposterous scheme now in place.

Unless it can be changed, PBS will be totally marginalized over the next decade or so by the emerging technologies and the new upscale networks. The failures of PBS will probably preclude the development of a privately supported, nonprofit public broadcasting system operating without federal inhibitions. In other words, a system where local stations report to community leadership and not to distant bureaucrats.

Laurence Jarvik's book provides an engaging and insightful summary of how the Corporation for Public Broadcasting and PBS evolved into the operationally convoluted and internally conflicted institutions we know today. It also raises provocative and pertinent questions about some of the most hallowed PBS brand names. The mandarins of PBS will be outraged—but that is healthy for them. And us. Public broadcasting is far too important to be left entirely to the Washington time servers and the cultural grandees of the East Coast. Some of those people, with whom I have had the pleasure of working over the years, are self-sacrificing in their efforts to salvage public television. But one suspects the attempts to reform such a defective system fall painfully close to folly.

The core of this book is reportage—reportage by a veteran and unquestionably outraged observer of public broadcasting. Jarvik is avenging in his indignation, driven by the failures of PBS as an institution and what he perceives to be its almost institutionalized philosophical bias. One hopes this book, an exclamation of exasperation, will attract attention and, more important, broaden the debate about public broadcasting in America.

VAN GORDON SAUTER

Introduction

The bitter conflict between Congress and public broadcasting was precipitated by two films aired in the summer of 1991: *Tongues Untied,* which graphically celebrated homosexual sex, and *Stop the Church,* which advocated the disruption of Catholic worship services by AIDS activists. Tim Graham, writing in *Media Watch,* captured the reaction of political Washington to these broadcasts: "How ironic it is that the Public Broadcasting Service now perceives its mission not as serving the public, but as thumbing its nose at it, taunting the public for being backward and 'uneducated.' "

That fall, the resulting firestorm ignited by the broadcast of these two films finally forced congressional Republicans *and* Democrats to take a hard look at public broadcasting. Legislation to reauthorize the Corporation for Public Broadcasting (CPB)—the federally funded body that both finances and regulates the Public Broadcasting Service (PBS) and National Public Radio (NPR)—was put on hold by the congressional leadership. Senator Robert Byrd, at that time the powerful Democratic chairman of the Appropriations Committee, introduced legislation to require decency in broadcasting, which passed by a vote of 93–3. Republican Senate leader Bob Dole introduced balance and objectivity requirements, which were approved unanimously.

Most important, however, is that from that point on the federal subsidy to PBS was no longer sacrosanct. In fact, since 1992, Congress has whittled away at public broadcasting's annual appropriation, gradually cutting it from $315 million to $250 million. For the first time there was even serious talk, most notably by Speaker of the House Newt Gingrich, of "zeroing out" public broadcasting—eliminating the subsidy entirely.

Like any special interest, however, the public broadcasting establishment did not sit quietly on the sidelines.

Since it first came under congressional scrutiny after the broadcasts of the two controversial films, PBS has been running a hard-hitting advertising scare campaign. Its commercials for itself imply that reduced federal funding threatens the existence of PBS, and that some favorite programs might disappear from the airwaves. Public broadcasting spent some $2 million on these ads in the first year alone. They were produced by the Hal Riney advertising agency, which handled Ronald Reagan's 1984 presidential campaign, and have been running continually for more than three years.

Pledge-week broadcasts and program guides sounded the call. Computerized mailings were distributed to 5.2 million PBS station donors with the message that the network was in mortal danger. People for the American Way (a liberal lobbying group founded by *All in the Family* producer Norman Lear) sent out its own mass mailing with a large message on the outside of the envelope warning readers of a threat to "shut down public broadcasting."

Panicked by the scare campaign, alarmed viewers hoping to save PBS from the federal budget ax deluged congressional offices with mail and swamped their switchboards. One Senate staffer recounted a telephone conversation she had with an upset constituent, to whom the staffer tried to explain congressional interest in what was by that time called "Barneygate." The investigation, she told the caller, was intended to determine whether PBS could make it without taxpayer subsidy. There was no danger of a successful program like *Sesame Street* going off the air; its producers had millions in the bank and billions in grosses from sales of 5,000 licensed items. If PBS did not really need taxpayer dollars, why not save money and reduce the federal deficit?

But the caller was so persuaded by the propaganda barrage that she was no longer interested in the evidence. "I don't care how much money they make or what they do with it," the caller responded. "Just give the money to Big Bird."

Yet, viewers received only one side of the debate from the PBS propaganda machine. The system's public relations, advertising, and lobbying efforts made a mockery of its legal obligations (spelled out in the Public Broadcasting Act of 1967 and the Public Telecommunications Act of 1992) to provide balance and objectivity in matters of public controversy. If one set of laws has been broken in order to win political advantage, one can't help but wonder what else has been going on.

In program guides, in mailings, on pledge programs, and in advocacy advertising, PBS used the slogan "If PBS doesn't do it, who will?" But the question was a straw-man, because issues raised by the critics of public broadcasting were structural and financial; no critic of PBS—not Newt Gingrich, not Jesse Helms—ever threatened to take PBS off the air. They could not have done so even if they had wished to. PBS does not need CPB money to stay on the air; federal funding accounts for only about 14 percent of the $2 billion annual budget for public broadcasting.

I was struck during the long congressional debate by objections from ordinary citizens to routine congressional inquiries into reported financial shenanigans by public broadcasters. How could opening the books on the financing and operation of the system deal a death blow to PBS? Was the case for PBS so manifestly weak that it could not survive the same level of scrutiny undergone by other government programs? The fear of exposure was so high among public broadcasters—and, thanks to their public relations efforts, among sectors of the general public—that I became convinced there was mischief still hidden from public view that the public broadcasting lobby simply did not want to come out. The PBS position had an irrational quality about it that could not otherwise be explained.

If PBS is indeed a public trust, then (to paraphrase Ronald Reagan's translation of a Russian proverb) the public has a right to verify the system's claims of poverty and entitlement to federal funding. If these claims cannot be verified, then PBS does not deserve our trust, never mind our money.

In my opinion, public broadcasting has failed this test. It has not shown the disinterestedness and high-mindedness required of those who hold a public trust.

PBS: Behind the Screen is intended as a reply to the official PBS version of this controversy. It is rooted in my personal experience with public broadcasting. In 1992, as a Bradley Scholar at the Heritage

Foundation, I made a proposal to sell shares in the CPB to the American public. I believed this would help to reduce the federal deficit and balance the budget, while at the same time securing a future for cultural and educational programming in the marketplace. For the next four years I covered PBS for the journal *Comint*. As director of the Washington office of the Center for the Study of Popular Culture, and then as cultural studies fellow at the Capital Research Center, I testified repeatedly before Congress to ask for a thorough evaluation of public broadcasting's finances.

On an entirely different level, however, this book is also a response to the notions of men like former CBS News president Fred Friendly and former Ford Foundation president McGeorge Bundy. In *Due to Circumstances Beyond Our Control*, Friendly's 1967 memoir of fighting McCarthyism alongside journalist Edward R. Murrow, he claimed that ratings, commercials, and the profit motive were obstacles to first-rate television coverage of news and current affairs. Friendly made the case for what was then called National Educational Television. He told his readers that he had recently been hired by Bundy as a consultant for the Ford Foundation to devise schemes to help "public service" broadcasting develop in opposition to the principles of commercial television.

Bundy and Friendly—two men who probably had more influence than anyone else in shaping public broadcasting—were an odd couple. Friendly was an autodidact, a middle-class striver from Providence, Rhode Island, who never graduated from college yet ended up a professor at Columbia University. Bundy, on the other hand, was a true Boston Brahmin whose career had been in public service and education. Elite institutions had been integral to his upbringing. The grandson of Harvard president A. Lawrence Lowell, Bundy had been John F. Kennedy's elementary school classmate in Brookline, Massachusetts, and later dean of the Harvard faculty. He left Harvard to take up the post of JFK's and LBJ's National Security Adviser. From the Johnson administration, he went on to head the Ford Foundation, where, from 1966 to 1979, he authorized the expenditure of hundreds of millions of dollars—for projects selected and overseen by Friendly.

Like many of "the best and the brightest" (as author David Halberstam dubbed the New Frontiersmen) who came from Harvard Yard to staff the round tables of Camelot in the Kennedy administration, Bundy could not have helped being affected by one of the most influential books of the period, John W. Gardner's *Excellence: Can We Be Equal and Excellent Too?* (1961). Its arguments provided the intellectual justification for what would become a national program of cultural uplift.

In his book, Gardner argued that the American leadership class was not adequate for a great world power. Appalled by what he perceived as the middlebrow mediocrity of Eisenhower's America, Gardner, a Ph.D. in psychology with expertise in intelligence testing, was obsessed by the idea of "excellence" and the possibility of engineering it. He wanted to make a clean break with what he saw as middle-class values in order to properly organize America's "natural aristocracy." For the best and the brightest, PBS would serve this purpose.

In contrast to Friendly et al.'s call for control of television by an educated elite fighting market forces and deciding what is best for the American public, PBS: *Behind the Screen* argues for creative freedom in the marketplace of ideas.

Is the profit motive really, as the elitists who gave birth to public broadcasting maintained, inimical to quality? Or can marketplace mechanisms help? The stories told in the thirteen chapters that follow illustrate my view that the marketplace can create strong incentives for excellent and original educational and cultural television programming on PBS. They also contain counter-arguments to the notion that federal funding is a guarantor of programming excellence and give evidence that the danger of a government propagandizing its citizenry is a real consideration in the public broadcasting debate.

The public broadcasting system, which began with a $5 million appropriation in 1967, has grown into a multibillion-dollar worldwide multimedia empire. The CPB oversees the largest radio and television network in the United States, with more than a thousand NPR, PBS, and other stations. When measured by the number of affiliates, PBS is bigger than Fox, CBS, NBC, or ABC. In addition to their on-air activities, public broadcasters publish magazines and newsletters, classroom study guides and textbooks, and provide computer programs, online services, and sites on the World Wide Web. They host conferences; license toys, games, and clothing; stage live shows; run mail-order catalogs and retail stores; and distribute videocassettes and compact discs. From these activities, a large industry has grown that parallels commercial broadcasting.

Prior to 1992, when political deliberation over continued funding for the system began in earnest, the extent to which public broadcasting had developed into a vast, powerful, and wealthy establishment remained largely obscured from public view. As a result of subsequent years of debate and disclosure, there is now a bipartisan consensus in Washington that public broadcasting can be self-supporting, although this news has not yet gotten much past the Beltway. In 1996, Congressman Jack Fields, chairman of the House Telecommunications Subcommittee, introduced what he called the "Public Broadcasting Self-Sufficiency Act." While there have been serious concerns raised over the wisdom of a proposed $1 billion final remittance to CPB (as a "trust fund"), no one has come forward to publicly argue against the basic principle of self-reliance.

Indeed, the public now accepts that educational and cultural programming on PBS can be successfully supported by private revenue streams. A January 1996 public opinion survey commissioned by the CPB found broad support among the American people for PBS sales of videotapes and merchandise, commercials, retail stores, online computer services, and mail-order catalogs. Fifty-seven percent of those asked said "the more sales the better." Eighty-six percent agreed that "sponsorship announcements are okay because public broadcasting has to do something to raise money in face of the decreased support from the federal government."

The political issue of "zeroing out" federal subsidies is no longer a matter of "if" but of "when." For the evidence is clear and convincing: public broadcasting does not need tax dollars in order to do its job.

The complicated bureaucratic structure of PBS is overwhelming to describe. Former PBS president Larry Grossman said it was "a system no one in the outside world understands or can penetrate. It is a system that ensures that public television will remain mired in second-class status with a top-heavy, expensive, and stifling bureaucracy . . ." But in some ways it is like any other network. MacNeil/Lehrer Productions president Al Vecchione testified to Congress in 1988 that "all of the same functions, duties, and responsibilities that exist for commercial broadcasting also exist for public broadcasting. Commercial networks have a corporate division which does the allocating of money and establishes the priorities through policies; we have CPB. They have a network division which obtains, schedules, and distributes the national programming; we have PBS."

However, some of the incentives created by federal subsidies appear political and perverse to those who have examined them. Marilyn Lashley, a University of Maryland social science professor, conducted a study for the Brookings Institution and the National Science Foundation in 1992 titled *Public Television: Panacea, Pork Barrel, or Public Trust?* In it she noted, "Public television performance is greatly constrained by managers' need to dance to the myriad tunes played by Congress, the executives, and special interest groups." Lashley concludes the resulting programs are "tried and true as well as bland and elitist" and finds—in direct contradiction to the official PBS rationale for its subsidy—that those most dependent on federal dollars "take fewer programming risks."

Such criticism was elaborated on by the Twentieth Century Fund, a liberal Democratic think tank that put together a blue-ribbon task force in 1993 to examine the finances and practices of PBS (affiliate stations declined to open their books, so the researchers had to rely on what station managers reported). The panel included former PBS president Larry Grossman and current PBS president Ervin Duggan, business leaders, and scholars. The chief researcher was Richard Somerset-Ward, former head of music and arts programming for the BBC. It was chaired by Brown University president Vartan Gregorian, former head of the New York Public Library.

The final document, titled *Quality Time?*, makes a devastating diagnosis. Among its analyses is an unfavorable comparison of American public broadcasting with the BBC and the Canadian Broadcasting Corporation. Although public broadcasters often point to the lower dollar amount per capita spent on PBS than that spent on the BBC and CBC, *Quality Time?* explains that it costs just as much to produce a program for an audience of one as for an audience of one million, so per capita expenditure comparisons are false comparisons.

If one looks instead at total expenditures by the systems to determine how much money was available to produce television programs, then the $1.26 billion spent on public television in the United States in 1991 was roughly comparable to the CBC's $988.3 million and the BBC's $1.57 billion. But unlike PBS, which is watched by approximately 2 percent of the American public, the BBC is watched by approximately 50 percent of the British. On any given night, according to *Quality Time?,* the BBC "runs two full national networks, competing in the sports and entertainment fields as well as the informational and educational; it has regional networks and production centers in Wales, Scotland, and Northern Ireland (as well as five in England); and it is the actual producer of the vast majority of all the programs it transmits."

Although it opposes privatization, the Twentieth Century Fund calls for "substantial revision in the existing system" through centralization to make PBS more like the BBC. On the principle that "individual station operations should be supported by the communities they serve," however, Twentieth Century did recommend an end to all federal aid to local PBS stations, which currently receive three out of four federal dollars in the system. While the diagnosis of PBS's problems was a penetrating one, the task force's prescriptions were not implemented. Americans simply could not be persuaded to establish a version of the BBC, and, as this book argues, for very good reasons.

The negative findings of the Twentieth Century Fund with regard to PBS structure and finances were not an aberration. Contrary to the conventional wisdom and public perception, criticism of PBS is not confined to Republicans or conservatives. The liberal James Day, the last president of National Educational Television, former president of WNET, New York, and KQED, San Francisco, said in his book *The Vanishing Vision: The Inside Story of Public Television,* "Unfortunately, our national need cannot be met by fine tuning the system now in place, a system whose fragmented and multi-purpose structure makes it hopelessly resistant to reform." Former Carter administration State Department spokesman Hodding Carter, a liberal Democrat, once said, "It's the perfect American screwed-up system, combining the worst of both worlds—bureaucratic Washington and opportunistic capitalism."

Boston-based, Harvard-educated, award-winning independent documentary film director Frederick Wiseman *(High School)* testified to Congress in 1988, "Public television is a mess. The fact that it is a mess is not a secret. Everybody knows. What is strange is that nothing is done about it. People working in public television seem to be incapable of taking corrective action." *Harper's* editor Lewis Lapham, who hosted the short-lived *Bookmark* program on PBS (1989–91), complained in a 1993 essay titled "Adieu, Big Bird," "I'd encountered a complacent bureaucracy so frightened of new ideas that it no longer knew how to do anything except go to meetings." That same year, former NBC News correspondent Eric Burns said in his book *Broadcast Blues,*

> People at PBS are morons. . . . They are the biggest collection of hypocrites and frauds ever gathered under the logo of a single American corporation. They raise double dealing to a craft, incompetence to an art. No wonder the government doesn't give the sons of bitches any money. No wonder most viewers prefer commercial television, where the ruling classes might be schlockmeisters, but are at least honest about meistering their schlock. The bozos at PBS are con men and poseurs and worse.

It is no wonder, then, that presidential candidate Bill Clinton told Brian Lamb in a 1992 C-SPAN interview that he did not think more federal money was needed for public television and called for a freeze—the same position articulated by Senator Jesse Helms during Senate floor debates in the same year! In fact, in its first budget the Clinton administration *did* propose a funding freeze on CPB. Congress took note and made its first CPB funding recision before the 1994 elections. So, when Speaker of the House Newt Gingrich promised to "zero out" public broadcasting, he was actually making a reasonable policy extrapolation based on a bipartisan understanding of evidence that federal subsidies for PBS were unnecessary. The record showed that the federal share could be replaced by increased fund-raising from the private sector and improvements in management of the system to reduce duplication, waste, fraud, and abuse.

When Gingrich and Congress backed down in the face of the massive lobbying effort by public broadcasters (there is a station in every congressional district), it was not because of any demonstrated need by PBS for taxpayer dollars. According to Tim Lamer's analysis in *Media-Nomics Watch* of public broadcasting's reported fund-raising totals, after Congress cut the federal payment to PBS in 1995, overall revenues to local stations from private donors increased substantially—more than making up for the reduction in subsidy at no cost to the American taxpayer. The private sector was willing to replace the federal role.

PBS has also made a number of lucrative business arrangements since 1992, most notably a $75 million deal in which *Reader's Digest* is paying to produce new programs for the network, and an arrangement with Turner Broadcasting to distribute videocassettes. PBS program producers have also managed to come up with new projects to enhance their revenues: This year, Children's Television Workshop announced the start of a children's cable channel, for example.

Such enterprise was in keeping with personal comments attached to the report of the Twentieth Century Fund task force by Markle Foundation president Lloyd Morrisett, cofounder and chairman of the board of Children's Television Workshop. He suggested one possible solution to the PBS predicament that might encourage more creative freedom would be for "public broadcasting to forgo, entirely, federal support of national programming."

Investment banker David Burke, a former executive at CBS and ABC and former chief of staff for Senator Edward Kennedy, agreed. He pointed out "the true corrosive effect of federal dollars on the system— the extent to which editorial freedom has been stifled; initiative has been constrained; or the failure to be a more provocative voice in our society." After four years of debate in the press and Congress—and over $100 million in cuts to the CPB appropriation—this proposal by a former Kennedy aide was adopted as part of the Republican platform for the 1996 election.

Unfortunately, the congressional debate over PBS funding rarely examined public broadcasting as closely as was necessary. There was only a hint of what might have been the equivalent of the 1959 quiz show hearings, most notably in the "Barneygate" investigation. This inquiry was prompted by Senator Dole, who was outraged by reported profiteering (as detailed in a *Washington Post* article) by *Barney's* producers. The matter was pursued in bipartisan fashion in hearings that took place periodically through 1995.

Like other telecommunications giants, public broadcasting spends millions to lobby Congress for subsidies. And PBS lobbyists have been extremely active in trying to preserve the special advantages of direct federal subsidy that bring with them the imprimatur of official status. *Sesame Street* characters, Barney, and Mister Rogers have trekked to Capitol Hill to meet members of Congress and their families. Politicians have received copies of the book and video versions of the PBS blockbusters *Baseball* and *The Civil War*, as well as other trinkets. David Frost invited Speaker of the House Newt Gingrich onto his program and lobbied him for fifteen minutes about poor old PBS, as if Gingrich had proposed sending an elderly maiden aunt to the workhouse. Charlie Rose, too, used the occasion of a Gingrich appearance on his show to shamelessly plug the PBS legislative position.

At the same time, as part of a nationwide mobilization of schoolteachers, little children were told that Big Bird might be killed, and classrooms were organized to mail protest letters to Congress. (No doubt the youngsters carried the frightening message home to worried parents.) Advertising was purchased by PBS station WGBH, Boston, in a Capitol Hill newspaper in the name of organizations for the blind, who were said to be great fans of PBS shows. College professors and their students circulated petitions on the Internet to "save PBS." Santa Monica, California, NPR station KCRW repeatedly denounced individual senators by name for weeks at a time. A flood of calls generated by a Louisiana station temporarily shut down the phones of Congressman Robert Livingston, chairman of the House Appropriations Committee.

Meanwhile, to build support among Republicans in Congress, PBS gave Bush speechwriter Peggy Noonan a three-part series produced by Children's Television Workshop, in which she had the privilege of interviewing Bill Moyers. The network also aired a flattering one-hour program by filmmaker Michael Pack about the "Republican Revolution," returned conservative Democrat Ben Wattenberg to the schedule,

and put a cartoon series into the children's program pipeline based on
The Book of Virtues, the best-selling anthology edited by Republican
pundit William Bennett.

The multimillion-dollar public broadcasting lobby used all its on-
the-air and off-the-air prowess to pressure Congress into first dropping
committee investigations, and then entirely dropping the issue of public
broadcasting from its agenda.

Because of strong opposition from the PBS lobby, the investigations of
Congress were unable to expose the root problem of our public broadcasting system: PBS is yet another well-intentioned federal program gone
awry. Ostensibly designed to help the underprivileged, it has made a
group of well-connected insiders even richer.

Behind the pleas for funding are legions of high-paid executives making six-figure salaries, producers with private production companies, and
scores of corporations that market videocassettes, books, and other
merchandise promoted on the educational network. In some cases,
members of what *Civil War* producer Ken Burns has called the PBS
"family" have run federally subsidized for-profit companies literally as
family businesses. Yet during pledge drives, on-air hosts often plead
poverty. For a time the CPB, which at any given moment has approximately $100 million in the bank because of its advance funding, handed
out an actual tin cup as a memento. Public broadcasters have the mentality
of a beggar who turns out to be an eccentric with millions in the bank.

As I pursued my research into public broadcasting, the truth of
Adam Smith's observation became manifest: "By pursuing his own
interest [man] frequently promotes that of the society more effectually
than when he really intends to promote it. I have never known much
good done by those who affected to trade for the public good."
Conversely, those who have made a career for themselves at PBS uttering
platitudes about "the public interest" and "the public trust" have sometimes treated the network as a private fiefdom. Affecting a snooty
disdain for ordinary Americans and a pose of contempt for commerce,
many have, as this book documents, done very well for themselves.

Evidence of this conduct is not hard to find. In 1990, the president
of the Jacksonville, Florida, public television station was forced to resign

in an uproar over his personal misuse of auction funds. After the *Pittsburgh Post-Gazette* published a series of articles in 1993 detailing the hundreds of thousands of dollars WQED president Lloyd Kaiser (at the time a member of the CPB board of directors) received both from his station and from a for-profit company that had contracts with WQED, Kaiser resigned. The *Post-Gazette* reported that, when the CPB refused to release documents relating to a fraud complaint against Kaiser, then–CPB chairman Marshall Turner told a reporter, "There are some things the public doesn't need to know."

Sheldon Siegel, president of the Allentown, Pennsylvania, public television station, and four members of his board of directors also quit in 1993 after the press exposed bid-rigging during that station's auction and questioned his expense account. The *Lehigh Valley Express-Times* editorial noted that "while viewers of WLVT-TV were watching Domingo and Pavarotti belt out the final chorus of 'Nessun dorma' during Channel 39's Great On-Air Auction, someone back at the television station on South Mountain was shredding documents. Bids, that is. Phony opening bids. . . ."

In 1994, the *Seattle Times* ran an exposé about the local PBS station's pledge drive under the headline "KCTS Pleads Poverty While Sitting on Fat Wallet." The paper revealed that, although on-air announcers pretended the station was in dire straits, it had some $6 million in the bank.

And in 1995, the president of WTVS, Detroit, cashed in when, upon his retirement, the station awarded his production company a sweetheart deal for $2 million in contracts.

Since most of the PBS broadcast schedule is provided by the system's national program service, there is not much for the local station managers to do except raise money. And with so much coming in and so little to spend it on, temptations become enormous. Most PBS stations are, in the words of KVIE, Sacramento, board member David Townshend to the *New York Times,* "for all practical purposes just a very big satellite dish sitting on top of a building that does fund-raising." That the practice among local stations of raising more money than they can use, placing the surplus in stock and bond portfolios called "endowments," and paying large fees (and providing lavish perks) to executives is not considered scandalous by public broadcasters is a scandal in itself.

* * *

It wouldn't be possible in a book of readable length to discuss every PBS program shown over the past thirty years, and I have not attempted to do so here. Instead, after a first chapter detailing the early history of PBS and the legacy of politics on the shape and development of the network, I examine, in succeeding chapters, specific programs and personalities that, for better or for worse, have had a lasting impact on American culture.

In researching this book I not only watched PBS programs, I went behind the screen in person. I toured PBS stations. I attended public broadcasting conferences and more specialized assemblies in locations all over the country. I sat in on CPB and PBS board meetings. I talked with dozens of people at various levels in and around PBS. I obtained materials from presidential libraries, public broadcasting archives, and private collections. I attended congressional hearings and floor debates, and consulted with both Democratic and Republican staff in the capital. I've pored over stacks of reports commissioned by the CPB and PBS.

Unfortunately, there were some people essential to the history of public broadcasting who refused to talk to me. Bill Moyers was straightforward enough to write and say he would not meet with me, and I respect him for his frankness. However, *Frontline* producer David Fanning and WGBH chairman David Ives did not return calls. Neither Fred Friendly nor McGeorge Bundy (who died in September 1996) ever so much as acknowledged receipt of a single letter or phone call over a five-year period.

Luckily, many others were forthcoming. Among the stars and the behind-the-screen talent who were kind enough to talk to me or write to me (formally or informally) were Alistair Cooke, Diana Rigg, Russell Baker (an early correspondent), Sharon Rockefeller, Joan Ganz Cooney, Julia Child, Morley Safer, Ian Richardson, Stephen Fry, Robert Mac-Neil, Jim Lehrer, Al Vecchione, Ken Burns, David McCullough, Fred Wiseman, Jack Valenti, Erroll Morris, Milton Friedman, Roger Fisher, William Rusher, Alan Miller, Michael Dukakis, Alan Dershowitz, PBS president Ervin Duggan, and William F. Buckley, Jr. Many others, too numerous to mention, have been extremely generous with their time and expertise, and I am grateful for their consideration.

* * *

In the preface to the 1982 edition of his *Capitalism and Freedom,* Milton Friedman described the "tyranny of the status quo." He pointed out that it is extremely difficult by intellectual argument alone to persuade those with conventional opinions that there is a need for change, but that when a crisis occurs, circumstances make change necessary, and the change is "produced by experience, not by theory or philosophy." As Friedman concludes, "The actions that are taken depend on the ideas that are lying around." One develops alternative policies and makes them available knowing that one day "the politically impossible becomes politically inevitable."

This book is written with that end in mind.

PBS

1

In the
Beginning

On September 16, 1962, legendary broadcast journalist Edward R.
Murrow and Newton Minow, then–Federal Communications Commission chairman, crossed an American Federation of Television and
Radio Artists (AFTRA) picket line to attend the dedication of the new
flagship educational television station in New York City. Murrow hosted
the station's maiden broadcast, uttering the first words spoken on the air:
"Good evening. The name of this station is Channel 13, WNDT. My
name is Edward R. Murrow."

The premiere of WNDT (which stood for New Dimensions in Television) marked a watershed in the history of public broadcasting. It sig-
nified the transition of "educational television" from a straightforward
instructional medium for college extension courses in secondary broadcast markets to what would become, by the end of the decade, the
multifaceted PBS network we know today.

During that first New York broadcast by an educational station, Murrow sat in his trademark swivel chair before banks of television monitors,
previewing the lectures, performances, and documentaries that WNDT
would present in the future. He explicitly spelled out the parallel
between the task of the United States Information Agency (which he

then headed as President Kennedy's appointee) "in educating the world about America" and educational television's "duty in educating America about the world."

Newton Minow joined Murrow on camera during the broadcast. "We at the Federal Communications Commission take pride in having played a modest part in this achievement," he declared. Minow, also a Kennedy appointee, was a great believer in the power of educational television. Like his former law partner Adlai Stevenson, he was considered an "egghead." And like the President, he intended to use public television to pressure commercial programmers to improve the quality of their product.

Murrow and Minow were Democrats with strong records of support for organized labor, yet both had crossed the AFTRA picket line to attend the dedication of WNDT. (The workers were protesting the station's refusal to sign a union contract.) Minow had kept close tabs on the AFTRA dispute for months; in hopes of averting a protest, he had set up a meeting between the union and the WNDT board of trustees in July, but the encounter was to no avail.[1] That Murrow and Minow were unafraid to violate one of the most sacred taboos of Democratic politics by crossing the picket line gives some indication of the crucial status of WNDT's premiere.

The opening-night broadcast featured an hour-and-a-half documentary produced by the British Broadcasting Corporation (BBC). *Television and the World* was an explicit indictment of commercial television programming in America. The show denounced the sale of U.S. shows around the globe. (What the documentary did not tell viewers was that the BBC was American television's largest competitor in the international television sales market.)[2]

WNDT's debut lineup had originally included a lecture on comedy that actor Zero Mostel had given at Harvard; it was to follow Murrow's introduction, but the taping had been canceled when AFTRA set up its picket line. Mostel would not cross, since he was an active union member. The station's management issued a statement declaring that the union "fails to recognize that there is a difference between education and show business" and that WNDT must be free to operate "without regard to union or any other impediments to their freedom of expression."[3] What the station's managers did not admit was that they had booked Mostel's comedy act, disguised as education, precisely to liven up a dull evening; the union saw an opportunity and called them on their ploy. The strike lasted two weeks.

The rest of WNDT's maiden broadcast (which otherwise went ahead as scheduled) had the depressingly praiseworthy quality that would become a signature of PBS. The lineup included *Around My Way,* Stewart Wilensky's ten-minute documentary about children's paintings; a local news show called *Once Upon a Day;* and *Russian for Beginners.* Murrow announced that White House cultural consultant August Hecksher, another Kennedy political appointee, would host *Books for Our Time.* He then previewed a broadcast of *Master Class,* which featured Jackie Kennedy's favorite cellist, Pablo Casals, and a French film called *A la Recherche d'Albert Camus* (for the existentialists in the audience). To add to the Camelot mystique, Murrow promised to rebroadcast President Kennedy's press conferences in their entirety whenever they occurred.[4]

If this was egghead television, it was soft-boiled. Of that first broadcast, the *Saturday Review* lamented: "We wish we could report it an artistic success. Unhappily, the program was spotty, and in some instances, poorly conceived and edited . . . far from impressive . . . in dire need of cutting . . . pretentious . . . lacked the sense of excitement and newness that people have a right to expect at a premiere . . . taken as a whole, lacked balance and luster. In sum, noncommercial television in New York is off to a slow start."[5] This review was especially devastating because the *Saturday Review* was edited by Norman Cousins, a friend of Minow's and a board member of the National Education Television network (NET).

Unknown to the viewing audience, the WNDT premiere was the culmination of years of secret political machinations to wrest the channel from private hands. It was financed behind the scenes by commercial stations seeking to ensure that WNDT did not compete for advertisers. Yet publicly, the startup of WNDT had been preceded by a well-financed public relations campaign *against* commercial broadcasters that vilified them for excessive violence, lack of concern for children, and poor taste.

The maiden voyage of WNDT was symptomatic of what would become hallmarks of PBS: secrecy, political intrigue, and reliance on the BBC for programming and American commercial networks for its stars—

all promoted with a glossy rhetoric of public service and education, camouflaging the self-interest of its backers and disguising a creative vacuum. Most important, WNDT was organized as a "community" television station free of any ties to university, school district, or municipality. WNDT would be moving beyond the educational ghetto of the more provincial instructional stations that had laid the groundwork for NET, formed in 1958.

American public broadcasting is different from any other radio and television system in the world. It has been eclectically structured from its earliest beginnings as a mixed set of different systems. Some public television stations are owned by school districts, others by cities; still more are controlled by colleges and universities, and the remainder tend to be independent "community" stations. Because the first educational stations were established by colleges and schools, they naturally mirrored the structure of those institutions and depended on the goodwill of local governments, state legislatures, boards of regents, and philanthropists. Support came from lobbying groups like the National Education Association (NEA), the Parent-Teacher Association (PTA), and the AFL–CIO. Consequently, elected and appointed officials at both the local and national levels had—and continue to have—great influence over American public broadcasting.

While European countries established centralized state broadcasting systems before the advent of commercial television, or professionally structured Crown organizations (like the British Broadcasting Corporation), which were and are dependent on license fees, the American system began in a decentralized manner (like its commercial counterparts) as the province of teachers, professors, social-science researchers, students, private donors, and dedicated amateurs. Unlike establishmentarian systems such as the BBC (and other European state-supported television), which broadcast a variety of programming, including comedies, sports, soap operas, and talk shows, PBS evolved from the progressivist notion of perfection through education and scientific planning; it was utopian and somewhat puritanical in intent, established with the objective of making a better world through educational programs.

Rather like university agricultural extension services, educational broadcasting was originally established on radio in the 1920s for the straightforward and practical purpose of furthering the instruction of those who were unable, for whatever reason, to attend school in person.

The University of Wisconsin's radio station, WHA, considered the country's first educational broadcaster, officially went on the air in 1919, though it had actually started in 1917 as experimental station 9XM. The station's purpose was "to share with the people of the state the advantages of learning on the campus." After ten years, WHA came to specialize in three kinds of programs typical of educational broadcasting at that time: agricultural information for farmers *(The Farm Program);* domestic science for housewives *(The Homemakers' Hour);* and University of Wisconsin Extension talks for students. In 1931, the university established the "Wisconsin School of the Air," and two years later it began its "College of the Air" broadcasts, offering courses for credit. In 1921, Brigham Young University became the country's second educational broadcaster, its radio license granted to "the Latter Day Saints University." It brought instructional programming similar to the Wisconsin prototype to listeners in Utah. Between 1921 and 1936, 202 radio licenses were awarded to schools, colleges, and universities.[6]

The year 1929 saw the entry of philanthropies into the educational broadcasting arena. The Carnegie Corporation of New York, established in 1911 by the steel magnate Andrew Carnegie to promote education, and the Payne Study and Experiment Fund, a New York charity well known for its studies on the influence of motion pictures on juvenile delinquency, financed the Advisory Committee on Education by Radio. Its members had been appointed by Secretary of the Interior Ray Lyman Wilbur in June 1929 to come up with a federal policy for educational broadcasting based on a national survey of instructional radio. They concluded in their 1930 report that the government should reserve broadcast bandwidth for educational purposes; establish an office of education for radio in the Department of the Interior; set up a permanent advisory committee representing educators, commercial broadcasters, and the public; secure funding for educational programs; and inform the President of the United States of the importance of educational programming.[7] The Federal Radio Commission (FRC)—the predecessor to the FCC—attempted to follow this advice, taking the first steps toward creating the Corporation for Public Broadcasting.

In July 1930, the Rockefeller Foundation, based on the Standard Oil fortune of John D. Rockefeller and a major supporter of American educational institutions, financed the formation of the National Advisory Council on Radio in Education (NACRE). Made up of prominent citizens, including commercial broadcasters, this group again worked closely with Interior Secretary Wilbur and Commissioner of Education William J. Cooper. Unlike the Carnegie- and Payne-financed group, the Council eventually recommended that educational programming be integrated into commercial broadcasts. The reason was straightforward: money. Educators did not have the funds to finance their stations independently. By 1937 some 164 educational radio stations had allowed their licenses to lapse or be taken over by commercial broadcasters (no specified bandwidth had yet been reserved for educational stations). The NACRE closed up shop in 1938, but not before convincing NBC (headquartered in Rockefeller Center and partially financed by Rockefeller interests) to carry instructional broadcasts.[8]

In reaction against the probusiness suggestions of cooperation from the Rockefeller group, yet another committee was formed: the National Committee on Education by Radio (NCER). This organization was opposed to letting educational stations be taken over by commercial interests. Set up in 1931 by supporters of college and university stations, and paid for again by the Payne Fund, its goal was to reserve 15 percent of the available radio bandwidth for educational use. The NCER has been called a "committee of committees." Member organizations included the National Education Association, the National Association of State University Presidents, the National Council of State Superintendents, the Association of College and University Broadcasting Stations (which became the National Association of Educational Broadcasters in 1934, the National Association of Public Television Stations in 1969, and the current PBS lobby, America's Public Television Stations, in 1990), the National University Extension Associations, the National Catholic Education Association, the American Council on Education, the Jesuit Education Association, and the Association of Land-Grant Colleges and Universities. By 1938, the

FRC had agreed to set aside five radio channels for noncommercial use; by 1945, fifteen more radio stations had been added. At the request of the National Association of Educational Broadcasters (NAEB), and with the support of the U.S. Office of Education, the FRC decided that the FM stations would be reserved for educational use below 92 MHz (the same portion of the dial used by National Public Radio today). Most educational AM frequencies had been surrendered to commercial interests by this time due to the failures of educational broadcasting during the Depression.

Both the U.S. Army and Navy had begun making educational telecasts as early as 1945. In 1948 the FCC put a freeze on new television licenses. Officially this was because of a dispute between CBS and NBC over incompatible color broadcasting systems they were seeking to use (it was eventually resolved in favor of NBC). The net effect, however, was to preserve the advantage of the mostly Democratic broadcasting force, of which most members had received their television licenses in the Roosevelt and Truman administrations. This partisan advantage in broadcasting was seen as balancing the newspapers, whose owners were mostly Republicans. Taking advantage of the freeze, the NAEB retained the law firm of Leonard Marks and Marcus Cohn (both former FCC officials) to file for ten ultra-high-frequency (UHF) television channel reservations for educational use. UHF was a new television technology, analogous to FM in radio in that it promised better-quality transmission but at lower power and shorter range.

Soon after the end of World War II, commercial TV broadcasters had begun offering free airtime to educational institutions, because they did not have enough advertising to support a full schedule of paid programming. DuMont (the fourth and least profitable network, many of whose stations eventually became independent, and then became Fox affiliates when Rupert Murdoch set up shop in the 1980s) made a deal with the New York Board of Education to carry instructional programs for free in its unsold time slots, such as *You Be the Judge,* which featured reenactments of famous court cases. In 1947, the Annenberg Foundation (headed by Triangle publishing magnate Walter Annenberg), the University of Pennsylvania, and Philadelphia's WFIL-TV collaborated on their own "University of the Air," presenting lectures by Penn faculty.

In 1949, the Rockefeller Foundation funded a conference at the University of Illinois for educational radio station managers to take a serious look at the possibilities for educational television. In October 1950, the University of Iowa began broadcasting on WOI-TV, making it the first educational television station in the United States. At that time, the FCC had not yet decided to reserve a portion of the bandwidth specifically for noncommercial stations, so WOI began using a commercial frequency (and later became an ABC affiliate) and included commercial programming in its lineup.

The early fifties saw a major push led by Frieda Hennock to reserve channel capacity for educational television programming. In 1950 Hennock, who had been appointed to the FCC in 1948 by Truman, hosted a planning meeting in her home, which led to the Joint Committee on Educational Television, a formal lobbying group.[9]

An important element of Hennock's strategy was the out-and-out vilification of commercial broadcasters. Martha Gable, a Philadelphia educator and a hostess for one of Hennock's lectures, recalled telling Hennock that the local commercial stations were very helpful and should not be publicly demeaned. "Look, Frieda," she recalls saying to Hennock, "these stations here in Philadelphia are very generous. They are giving us time," to which Hennock replied, "I can't change my story. If I say anything nice about the commercial people, I'll lose my pitch for the FCC. I gotta keep lambasting them."[10]

Meanwhile the National Education Association and the American Council on Education, both Washington-based education lobbies, supplied funds to prepare FCC testimony in support of channel reservation, which the FCC had previously rejected. They joined in supporting the Joint Committee on Educational Television (JCET), which had been funded by the first grant from the Ford Foundation's Fund for Adult Education. Ford paid out $90,000 for legal expenses and testimony (a large sum in 1951).

The JCET hired Nuremberg war crimes prosecutor and former FCC general counsel Telford Taylor to prepare its case for reserved channels. Taylor was perhaps the most prominent attorney in the United States at the time. To the public at large, he represented high-mindedness. He was also very well connected among Washington regulators and politicians.

The JCET had compiled over seventy supporting statements from prominent educators. Taylor also presented the results of a Ford-funded NAEB study of violence on commercial television that documented 2,970 "acts of violence" in a single week, with 17 occurring during children's viewing hours. According to James Day, the last president of National Educational Television, the violence study "moved the FCC to reconsider its previous rejection of the educators' request for channel reservations."[11]

Ohio State University's I. Keith Tyler, director of the Institute for Education by Radio-Television, a Midwestern proponent of instructional television, became the JCET chair. He published articles in *The Nation* calling for channel reservation to garner support from its liberal urban readership. The AFL-CIO, the PTA, and numerous educators backed the cause.

An initial FCC offer of 209 channels was rejected by the JCET. Eight hundred formal statements were filed asking for more channels for education.[12] When the FCC freeze ended in 1952, the FCC granted America's educational institutions exclusive rights to 242 radio and television frequencies for the purposes of noncommercial instructional broadcasting. They were divided between 80 VHF stations and 162 UHF stations. The Ford Foundation now began in earnest its long-term effort to create a network of noncommercial American television stations. It funded the National Citizens' Committee for Educational Television with a $90,000 grant to lobby and do public relations. The Foundation also established a central organization in Ann Arbor, Michigan, the Educational Television and Radio Center, to provide programs to educational broadcasters. The grant was $1.35 million; a year later, the Foundation more than doubled its initial subsidy.

The House Committee on Un-American Activities investigations into the motion picture and broadcasting industries had revealed commercial interests to be highly vulnerable to patriotic pressure groups such as the American Legion. The widespread practice of blacklisting suspected Communists through publications such as *Red Channels* led to support for anti-Communist boycotts. Lawrence Johnson, owner of an upstate New York supermarket chain, helped finance Aware Inc., an anti-Communist group run by former FBI agents. Businessmen such as

Johnson, with the cooperation of the networks, combined to make liberals leery of any sponsorship for educational television from businesses. Educational broadcasting, although not overtly designed to fight McCarthyism, could be seen as lessening the power of the sponsor and, therefore, lessening the power of blacklisting. With no sponsor influence, educational broadcasters thought that in the tradition of academic freedom they could provide an alternative in which viewpoints that sponsors shunned might have a place. (Ironically, it was a commercial sponsor, the Aluminum Corporation of America, that had supported Edward R. Murrow's *See It Now* on CBS, the very program that finally helped bring down Senator Joseph McCarthy in 1954. Alcoa even permitted Murrow to excise commercial breaks from his broadcasts on occasion, although Murrow did dedicate an entire program to illustrating the process of making aluminum from bauxite, a half-hour infomercial for Alcoa.)

But it took the so-called quiz show scandals, not McCarthyism, to discredit commercial sponsorship in the eyes of the American public. While most people didn't like Communism, they hated being conned.

In 1958, Herbert Stempel, a very successful contestant on the TV quiz show *Twenty-One,* announced that the show was rigged. New York District Attorney Frank Hogan began a grand jury investigation of quiz shows in general, and congressional hearings were held. In 1959, Charles Van Doren, an English instructor at Columbia University (and son of the poet Mark Van Doren) who had been a featured contestant on the show, confessed that he had been given the right answers ahead of time by producer Albert Freedman, who had assured him that he would be doing a favor to eggheads by bumping off the unsophisticated Stempel. "He also stressed the fact," Van Doren said in his testimony, "that by appearing on a nationally televised program, I would be doing a great service to the intellectual life, to teachers, and to education in general, by increasing public respect for the work of the mind through my performances. In fact, I think I have done a disservice to all of them." (That the confessed perpetrator of quiz show fraud was an educator went unremarked-upon in the subsequent campaign to turn over television frequencies to professors.)

In 1960, Congress passed legislation explicitly prohibiting rigged contests and requiring notice of paid consideration for promotional announcements.[13] The networks responded with assurances that they would become more responsible. CBS president Frank Stanton announced a new series of documentaries called CBS *Reports*. But the taint on commercial broadcasting would linger long afterward.

Supporting educational television looked like a good way for commercial networks to relieve congressional pressure and transfer to a third party public service requirements demanded by the FCC and Congress. Thus, from its inception, what we now call public broadcasting has been the servant of several masters. It is the result of a deal struck in the 1950s that has not come undone—a pact between commercial broadcasters seeking to get Congress off their backs and educators seeking prestige, money, and influence—as well as the good intentions of social reformers.

For this reason, from its inception as educational television, American public broadcasting has not competed directly with the commercial sector. The National Association of Broadcasters has consistently supported PBS because of its valuable role in reducing competition for advertising dollars.

The Educational Television and Radio Center moved its headquarters from Ann Arbor to New York City in 1958, changing its name to the National Educational Television and Radio Center, which was later shortened to National Educational Television (NET). The major purpose of the organization was syndicating programs to educational stations through "bicycling" films and tapes from station to station. A grant from the Ford Foundation enabled many of the stations to purchase their first videotape recorders in exchange for using NET materials in their broadcasts. Thus there was no national schedule, and NET was not a genuine network in the manner of NBC, CBS, or ABC. From 1958 to 1969, NET was headed by John F. White, a former university administrator who had headed Pittsburgh's WQED and had become one of the leading figures in the campaign to create a national educational "fourth network." NET published a book in 1962 called *A True Fourth Network: Why and How,* which declared: "America must have a fourth network—a strong, free noncommercial network whose only purpose, whose very reason for being, is to supply in abundance, for people in every region of the country and at the most convenient viewing hours, the fine cultural and informational programming that goes out to their homes in such small quantity today."[14]

NET offered to its member stations a rich selection of series such as *News in Perspective,* featuring *New York Times* editors Lester Markel, Max Frankel, and Tom Wicker; *Heritage,* an interview program that focused on current artists such as Richard Rodgers and Edward Steichen; *Playwright at Work,* which profiled Lorraine Hansberry and Edward Albee, among others; *Contemporary American Composers;* and *Face to Face,* a series of television portraits of Carl Jung, Edith Sitwell, and Otto Klemperer. NET also broadcast *An Age of Kings,* a cycle of eight Shakespeare plays produced by the BBC and sponsored by Humble Oil (a precursor to *Masterpiece Theatre*), and NET *Playhouse,* which was produced in its New York studios in the style of CBS's *Playhouse 90.*

White was a booster, delivering speeches across the country (including one with the optimistic title "Educational Television: America's Fastest Growing Network"). In 1962 he published an article, "We Will Guide but You Must Push," in which he continued to boost his network but spoke out against federal funding. "Such direct support could only lead to a loss of freedom that is noncommercial television's greatest asset," White prophesied.[15]

White pushed for national programming instead of instructional fare. In an address at Harvard University in 1963, he told his listeners: "Ten years ago when it began, ETV had a choice. Was it to be a fringe activity . . . or was it to be a powerful force for social good and cultural enrichment? Two roads diverged in a wood, said Robert Frost—and ETV, like Frost, took the latter." This was a direction opposed by many of the local university stations, which had their own priorities. In 1968, White quoted Frost again in a speech to NET affiliates, saying "the middle of the road is where the yellow is." Yet when he resigned in 1969 to become president of Cooper Union, an art and engineering school in New York City, *Newsday* reported "some station managers have accused him of giving the network an eastern liberal tone and dissident young Turks have charged him with being representative of the conservative establishment."[16]

White's most important accomplishment while at NET was his establishment of an educational television station in New York City. In

1962, despite its reputation as a cultural center, the Big Apple didn't have a single educational noncommercial television station. White bet that a station located in New York, the nation's media center, was bound to help to promote the political cause of educational broadcasting in Congress. He was right. As television critic Martin Mayer said, "The breakthrough in noncommercial television came in 1962, when a self-perpetuating nonprofit corporation raised the money to buy channel 13 in New York. Educational television lost its state-college, school-system image and became something the New York–based national media started to discuss more seriously. Congress responded with the first appropriations to help build and equip noncommercial stations, and Ford escalated its support."[17]

White decided that in order to achieve the kind of visibility he was hoping for, NET's New York station would need to deliver its programming over a VHF channel, which had a more powerful signal than UHF, where many of the nation's educational signals were to be found. In the fall of 1959, White had quietly put together a group of prominent New Yorkers to begin planning the purchase of such a station. In the group were some of the wealthiest and most influential men in the city, including John D. Rockefeller III, New York University chancellor George Stoddard, New York Life chairman Devereux C. Josephs, and Corning Glass chairman Arthur A. Houghton, Jr.[18] In November 1960, White met with Howard C. Sheperd, retired chairman of First National City Bank; Henry G. Fischer, who later served as NET's FCC attorney; and Josephs. As a result of that meeting, Fischer asked Howard E. Stark, a broker, to make an offer on Sheperd's behalf for the purchase of station WNTA in Newark, New Jersey, which had come on the market. WNTA was owned by National Telefilm Associates, whose chairman was Ely Landau, a New York producer. Landau was not the only stockholder, however, and this would soon complicate the completion of the deal.

Meanwhile, unbeknownst to his partners—who, despite being among the richest people in New York, were not sure they could raise the cash—White had secured money from the Ford Foundation toward the purchase price. The Foundation's only condition was that NET not be identified with the station, because no one station should be perceived as more important to NET than any of the other seventy-nine stations then subscribing to the network—especially since the rural stations had begun to worry that NET might be "going New York" at their expense once headquarters shifted from Ann Arbor to Manhattan.

Stark offered Landau $4 million on February 9, 1961. The offer was too low. Although Stark made Landau promise secrecy, on February 17 Landau held a press conference to announce the station was now open for bids. Landau said at the time that he would put together a group of his own to buy the station outright, rather than sell it at what he thought was a lowball price. He had other bidders with deep pockets lined up. Among them was television producer David Susskind, who had a backer at Paramount Studios. Then, on February 23, newspaper reports revealed NET's connection to the bidding. White was very angry that his secret and anonymous bid had been made public by Landau.

With the new publicity, he no doubt feared the deal blowing up in his face. Shortly after the story broke, NET issued a formal statement to the press that "educational interests will fight to bring this about and will make every effort to purchase this station at a reasonable price." White was worried that Landau and Susskind were bidding against him, and if the price went too high, NET would lose the station. He asked the FCC to intervene in the purchase on NET's behalf and solicited support from the head of the state board of regents, the president of the New York City Board of Education, Cardinal Spellman (as head of the parochial school system), and the New Jersey and Connecticut state school superintendents. He also approached local commercial broadcasters, including CBS president Frank Stanton and ABC vice president Frank Marx. White, in fact, succeeded in getting pledges of financial help from a number of WNTA's commercial competitors, who were eager to see one less rival for local advertising dollars.

CBS was the first commercial network to offer financial support, with a pledge of $500,000. ABC was next, matching CBS's pledge. Finally, NBC joined in. Local stations, like WNEW, WNIX, and WOR, also offered to contribute money to eliminate a competitor. ABC soon reneged on half its $500,000 commitment, however. Then CBS announced it would only match what ABC gave. Then ABC denied ever making its original pledge, a statement White called "a damned lie." White met with ABC chairman Leonard Goldenson and brought along the transcript of an air check of

ABC's announcement of its $500,000 pledge. It did no good. But CBS finally chipped in $250,000 after ABC pulled out, and another $250,000 over the next three years.

Before the sale could be completed, White and his allies had to mollify New Jersey governor Robert Meyner, who was not happy to see his state losing the station to New York and attempted to stop the sale. Meyner had opposed Kennedy in his bid for the presidency and feared he was paying a price by having the only broadcaster located in his state summarily removed. The governor complained to the FCC, but Minow was pushing hard for the sale. Meyner threatened court action.

Meyner came around at a private meeting in the New Jersey governor's mansion in the summer of 1961 with NET representatives Norman Cousins; attorney Joe Iseman; Richard Heffner, whom White hired from CBS to run the educational station; and the FCC's Ted Meyers, appearing on Minow's behalf. The group got Meyner to give up by promising to reserve airtime for New Jersey, to place Meyner and up to two other Garden State representatives on the station's board, and to maintain crews and studio facilities in Newark. "Except for Meyner's spot on the Board," John F. White later noted, "none of these [promises] have been lived up to."

To avoid possible antitrust charges that setting up an educational television station was reducing competition for advertising dollars, White secured the services of Judge Simon H. Rifkind, of the politically powerful Paul, Weiss, Wharton, Rifkind, and Garrison law firm, who obtained assurances from the U.S. Department of Justice that there would be no antitrust difficulties stemming from the project. On March 30, 1961, a group of attorneys from the commercial networks and NET led by Lloyd Garrison of Paul, Weiss met with the head of the Anti-Trust Division of the Justice Department, and got the "all clear" for the deal. The price NET finally agreed to pay for its New York outlet was $6.5 million.

There is evidence that the sale of the station did reduce competition and that the Kennedy administration was simply turning a blind eye to the facts of the case for political reasons. Letters from WNDT (as the station was now called) to NBC promising not to compete for viewers in exchange for a $100,000 gift were leaked to the press and appeared in the *New York Times* and elsewhere when WNDT general manager Richard Heffner was fired in 1963. A complaint was filed that year with the FCC, but not acted upon.[19] A few days later, Samuel B. Gould, Channel 13's new president, declared that NBC had not attached any conditions to its gift. FCC chairman Newton Minow told the papers he would "decide if further steps are necessary." Not surprisingly, considering Minow's role in establishing WNDT, none were.[20]

Minow's involvement was crucial to the successful purchase of WNDT. "As far as I'm concerned," he warned Ely Landau at the time, "we're going to get a noncommercial station in there, one way or another. I don't know how yet, but I'm going to be very straight with you. I'm going to oppose any transfer to another commercial licensee."[21] In other words, Minow would force Landau to sell his station to the group he wanted by using his power as a regulator to delay other offers. To strengthen his hand, Minow tried to get the FCC to pass a rule requiring cities with seven VHF channels to set aside one for educational broadcasting, but the other commissioners wouldn't go along. They did, however, agree to put together a special inquiry into the question, which created a credible threat that the FCC might take action if the sale went the wrong way.

On May 9, 1961, at a meeting of the National Association of Broadcasters, Minow delivered what became known as the "vast wasteland" speech. "The public is your beneficiary," he told the assembled TV honchos. "If you want to stay on as trustees [of the airwaves], you must deliver a decent return to the public, not only to your stockholders." Minow went on to make distinctions between shows he considered worthwhile, including CBS *Reports, The Twilight Zone,* and Fred Astaire specials, and those he did not: westerns and police dramas, which he derided for their violence and lack of complexity. He also attacked the endlessly "screaming, cajoling, offending" commercials that paid for the programming. Television, he concluded, was a "vast wasteland"—two words that would influence public perception of commercial television for a generation.

Minow's speech, and a string of television appearances, radio interviews, and print articles, generated a great deal of hostile public opinion toward commercial broadcasters. He was, in a sense, following Frieda Hennock's script. After the quiz show scandals, this black eye from the FCC chairman was particularly painful. And Minow had mobilized the support of the intelligentsia against the entire concept of commercial television, not just an isolated scandal. It seemed the eggheads were being egged on against the networks by a government official.

To combat Minow's offensive, the Television Information Office, which had been established in 1959 by commercial broadcasters to promote their industry and help it recover from the quiz show debacle, conducted a public opinion poll. The results showed that 70 percent of Americans disagreed with the "vast wasteland" judgment and enjoyed network offerings.

The damage had been done, however. The justification for federal funding for educational broadcasting had been made clear to the American public by the chairman of the FCC and endorsed by President Kennedy in a public statement.

In September 1961, Hartford Gunn, then station manager of WGBH in Boston, sent Minow a document stamped "Confidential" titled "Proposal for Basic Financing for National Educational Television." Originally written for the Ford Foundation, it was a blueprint for a "national television service to meet the nation's cultural and educational needs." Gunn sent a copy to Minow because he felt that if the Ford Foundation would not dedicate its full resources to the project, "Congress may well be forced to authorize and finance" such a network and Minow could help.

Gunn had invited Minow to the first organizing meeting of WGBH's Eastern Educational Network in April 1961. Minow met with Ford Foundation officials, including president Henry Heald and vice president James Armsey, on a number of occasions to discuss educational television as well. On February 12, 1962, Channel 13's general manager, Richard Heffner, wrote to Pierre Salinger, JFK's press secretary, offering "if there is any way at all in which our facilities . . . can be used for the prime informational purposes you have been emphasizing for television, I hope you will let me know . . . please do call upon us for whatever service we might render." A copy was sent to Minow.[22]

In 1962, thanks in part to Minow's exertions, the federal government authorized $32 million in matching grants for the construction of educational television facilities.

With the assassination of President Kennedy and the ascension of Lyndon Johnson, himself a former schoolteacher, the education establishment found itself firmly at the center of the new President's "Great Society." Under Johnson, the structures were put in place for a federally subsidized public television service.

In 1964, Johnson's Office of Education sponsored a conference on long-range financing for educational television. The most significant result of that conference was the formation in November 1965 of the Carnegie Commission on Educational Television, which was assigned to examine public television financing issues. The commission's study was actually conducted by Minow's former FCC economist, Hyman H. Goldin.

Meanwhile, the Ford Foundation was changing its focus when former National Security Adviser McGeorge Bundy arrived in 1966, bringing former CBS News president Fred Friendly with him. (Friendly had left CBS after chairman William F. Paley had insisted on showing an episode of *I Love Lucy* instead of Senator William Fulbright's hearings on the Vietnam War, which were being carried live on other networks.) Where Henry Heald and John F. White were "institution-builders," Friendly and Bundy were more activist. Friendly saw NET's potential for coverage of news and "public affairs" (which really meant politics) that was freed from the need for ratings. The Ford Foundation was deeply involved in funding political activities to shore up liberal programs of the Great Society affecting race relations, the War on Poverty, and community action. Bundy had doubled the budget of the Foundation's Division of National Affairs to $40 million annually (depleting the investment portfolio of the Foundation to do so) and saw educational television as an outlet to promote "public discussion of issues which are controversial."[23]

Bundy and Friendly drew up ambitious plans for satellite programming distribution and the establishment of an impressive national network. At its peak, the Ford Foundation was pouring money into educational television to the tune of $100 million a year, sponsoring NET and instructional projects around the country and influencing the development of flagship stations for the network. What Ford needed now was to more clearly promote its liberal political agenda via the most powerful station under its control in the largest market in the country, WNDT.

In January 1967, the Carnegie Commission (which had its offices in Cambridge, Massachusetts, because chairman James R. Killian, Jr., needed to be close to his day job as head of MIT) delivered its report *Public Television: A Program for Action,* which called for, among other things, the establishment of the Corporation for Public Television, federal support of educational stations, the setting up of two production centers, and facilities for interconnection by telephone lines or satellite to make possible live broadcasts to the entire network—in short, the basis for public broadcasting as we know it today. Programming would come from the bottom up, not from the top down, a reaction against what the stations had felt was the high-handed manner of the Ford Foundation and NET in dealing with affiliates.[24]

Legislation was introduced in Congress to implement the Carnegie report's recommendations, and LBJ made a public statement supporting the passage of the Public Television Act. "I believe that educational television has an important future in the United States and throughout the world," he declared.

After congressional hearings, provisions were added to the legislation to prevent editorializing and to require balance and objectivity in programming content. The act was also amended to include educational radio and renamed the Public Broadcasting Act of 1967. The bill was signed by President Johnson on November 7, 1967, and the Corporation for Public Broadcasting (CPB) was born.

One of the early results of federal funding of public broadcasting through CPB would be the shrinkage of NET and its eventual disappearance into New York's WNET.

The appeal of public broadcasting to the Johnson administration has been attributed to LBJ's own experience as a Texas broadcaster.[25] He owned Austin radio station KTBC (eventually renamed KLBJ) through his wife, Lady Bird. Using his station profits, Johnson made lucrative investments in land and banking. At one time his television station in Austin was the affiliate for all three major networks: ABC, NBC, and CBS. According to Johnson biographer Doris Kearns Goodwin, who was a White House aide in his administration, Johnson had learned that television regulation "is built upon informal alliances and nonpublic agreements between members of Congress, members of interest groups, and members of the federal bureaucracy."[26]

Johnson's desire to forge a compromise between JFK's New Frontiersmen, who wanted "excellence" in broadcasting, and network executives, who wanted secure profits, led to the Corporation for Public Broadcasting as a way out. Creating a new, noncompetitive network could "satisfy demands for 'excellence,' without necessitating more public service or less popular (and less lucrative) entertainment on the commercial channels."[27]

Douglass Cater, formerly Washington editor of *The Reporter,* a liberal journal widely read in the nation's capital during the Eisenhower administration, was LBJ's special assistant for educational matters and called himself the "midwife" of public broadcasting. Cater, who considered himself an "institution-builder," says he wasn't concerned with the specific shows to be broadcast. "I always felt that what we needed to do," he recalled in an interview, "was to create a credible institution that would be capable of making those judgments in a way that the public and the politicians alike would accept it without feeling that they had to pull it up by the roots and redo it."[28]

Jack Valenti, another assistant to President Johnson at the time, says LBJ didn't know exactly what he wanted for public broadcasting. "He wasn't quite sure what that would be," Valenti says, "but he thought there ought to be alternatives, and they ought to be without advertising, and they ought to be the kind of thoughtful and—he didn't use the word 'intellectual'—more spacious-minded television presentations. Some of it would be educational, some of it would be historical and entertaining, but it would not be what you would find on the commercial television channels, without being pejorative about the commercial television channels. That was the concept."[29]

Cater agrees that Johnson didn't have a specific public television agenda, just a general sense that education "should be a new priority in the Great Society, and that broadcasting was part of that potential." According to Cater, the model for the CPB was the existing system of private higher education in the United States, which, not coincidentally, held a large number of the educational television licenses. "I had no basic predilection against public broadcasting doing some profitable things," Cater says, "which would then, since it had no private owners, be plowed into things which didn't make a profit." He adds that he kept his specific ideas about public broadcasting to himself once the CPB was established, because he felt "once you set up something like the CPB you should give it the maximum opportunity to make its decisions on its own." Cater turned down Johnson's suggestion that he serve as its first president, recommending John Macy, the former head of the Civil Service for LBJ and a trusted political ally.

During the drafting of the Public Broadcasting Act of 1967, Cater had great influence. Originally, the Carnegie Commission had recommended that half the CPB board be appointed by the President, the other half by the board members. Cater quashed that recommendation. "I felt, institution-building-wise, that was a bastard recommendation," he said. "That if you had a disposition to fill the half of them by the President for political purposes, they were going to probably replicate themselves."

Instead, Cater insisted that all CPB directors be appointed by the President and confirmed by the Senate. He felt this would increase the accountability of the President to the board and also allow for congressional scrutiny. He was delighted when Congress accepted his proposals. Though Cater did not remember encountering much congressional opposition to the legislation, Valenti says some legislators worried about creating a government-funded television network. "There were a lot of people then" who opposed the idea, Valenti recalls, finding it "a wasteful expenditure of public funds."

Cater says the structure of CPB was partly based on that of the National Science Foundation and of the Tennessee Valley Authority, the New Deal agency that brought electrical power to the rural South. Cater had hoped CPB would follow the TVA "yardstick principle," setting standards for the private sector and improving the lives of ordinary citizens, spreading educational uplift the way the TVA brought development to isolated villages and farms. Cater felt the key question facing proponents of the legislation was how precisely to structure federal funding:

"How do you transmit money from government to a specific area of enterprise without having it be direct government money? It's got to be, in a sense, laundered on the way. And the foundation model seemed to be the best way to do that."

LBJ was very much aware of these issues, and Valenti says the President developed a strategy to answer concerns of congressional critics that the CPB might become a propaganda tool or a patronage boondoggle: his choice of personnel would be above reproach. "Johnson's answer to all this was that he was going to appoint members to the board of such prestige and such stature and such demonstrated influence in the community that their wisdom and their good sense would prevail."

Valenti himself served on the first board of directors and seemed impressed by his roster of colleagues. He warmly remembers John D. Rockefeller III (who had been instrumental in purchasing Channel 13 in New York); Oveta Culp Hobby, a Johnson friend and owner of the *Houston Post*; and James Killian, head of the Carnegie Commission, as composing a most prestigious board. "I do not believe that successive Presidents have provided that board with the same caliber of membership," he declares.

Valenti helped select the first chairman of the CPB board, Frank Pace, who at the time was the head of General Dynamics and a supporter of the war in Vietnam. He says Pace, a former Secretary of the Army and a friend of Johnson's, was chosen because he understood Washington and how to get along with Congress. "He had political judgment," Valenti (now a lobbyist himself) says. "He understood how the great elephant walks and moves, and he understood its habitat." (Pace did not last long, however. He was out soon after Richard Nixon took the oath of office.)

One of the first orders of business for the newly formed CPB, which began with a $5 million federal appropriation, was to arrange to interconnect (through AT&T telephone lines) the 150 educational television stations then in operation. National broadcasts would begin January 5, 1969. Initially, half the weekly schedule would come from NET. The remainder would be provided by a combination of the *Public Broadcasting Laboratory*, a live experimental program originated from New York by Fred Friendly; the educational stations themselves; and various regional organizations such as the Eastern Educational Network, based at Boston's WGBH, which distributed Julia Child's *The French Chef* and Eleanor Roosevelt's *Prospects for Mankind*.

Opposition from both the Ford Foundation and Congress prevented the CPB from running its own network. The 1967 legislation had specified "diverse" programming sources to encourage multiple providers and, specifically, to reduce the relative power of NET. Cater recalls that President Johnson wanted the CPB to create an alternative to Ford Foundation funding. "To the degree we thought about it at all," he says, "Ford could go on funding whatever it wanted. But having the Corporation [CPB] as a major funder would, in some ways, diminish Ford's influence."[30]

Yet someone would have to be responsible for what went on the air. The compromise organization eventually became the Public Broadcasting Service (PBS), like NET independent of the federal government, but unlike NET owned and controlled by the local stations. PBS was incorporated on November 4, 1969, with Hartford Gunn as president. The board had five representatives from stations, one from NET, one from CPB, and two chosen by the other directors to "represent the public at large."[31] Initially designed as a mere routing system for program exchange, PBS would soon displace all the other contenders to control the national program schedule.

Well liked by the local stations, McGeorge Bundy's Harvard roomate, not "too New York," and with close ties to educators through WGBH's location on the campus of Harvard University's business school (where he had received his MBA), Gunn was the perfect compromise choice for a system looking for a low profile. Gunn was a systems analyst, not a television programmer, and PBS was a membership organization and "a political solution to a programming problem." Aware of his need for federal funding, and of the phasing out of Ford Foundation money, Gunn decided to locate PBS in Washington instead of New York, where NET and the other networks had their headquarters.[32]

With the inauguration of Richard Milhous Nixon in January 1969, public broadcasting faced a dramatic challenge to its liberal Democratic origins. Nixon had not initially opposed PBS in principle, so long as it fulfilled an educational mission. Indeed, the Nixon administration at first recommended an additional $5 million in its 1969 reauthorization for the 1971–73 CPB budget. There was one administration request, which was also in the interests of CPB's own expansion of power: to replace National Educational Television. This idea was consistent with suggestions made by the Carnegie Commission and the Johnson administration, which had also proposed phasing out the central role of NET.

However, the proposed funding contained a threatening condition for the public broadcasting establishment, to wit: "Government funding of CPB should not be used for the creation of anti-Administration programming or for the support of program producing organizations which used other funds to create anti-Administration programs."[33]

Clay T. Whitehead, who ran Nixon's Office of Telecommunications Policy, said the administration felt that a PBS network run by local stations would not be as liberal as one whose programs were selected from New York or Washington.[34] Whitehead, an engineer with a Ph.D. in management from MIT, was the administration's expert on the issue (one of his young assistants was Brian Lamb, who thought he knew a better way to cover public affairs than PBS and went on to set up C-SPAN). Whitehead's specialty was the use of the budget process to influence policies.[35] With Whitehead keeping tabs on the action in the way Cater had done for President Johnson, the CPB and PBS were negotiating a contract dividing responsibilities for funding and distributing programs to the stations, and the Nixon administration was cooperating in trying to secure appropriations from Congress.

Administration officials were simultaneously working to induce CPB to change its emphasis from political programming. The Ford Foundation had required as a condition of its grants to NET that 50 percent of its shows be devoted to "public affairs" (i.e., politics), and those programs were still in the pipeline. While the Nixon administration was not at first opposed to PBS, the practical result of White House staffers' watching PBS shows, as Alistair Cooke has said, was that soon "Nixon hated public broadcasting."[36]

And not only Nixon was displeased. Congress noticed in November 1970, when PBS broadcast the NET-produced documentary *Banks and the Poor*. At the end of the program a list of congressmen (Democrat and

Republican) who had received money from banking lobbyists scrolled by.[37] The clear impression was that they had been bought in exchange for contributions.

Responding to congressional complaints was White House aide Peter Flanigan, a Princeton graduate and former investment banker who had been deputy campaign manager for Nixon's 1968 presidential run.[38] Flanigan wrote a memo to CPB director Albert Cole, declaring the broadcast "clearly inappropriate for a government supported organization."[39]

An angry bipartisan reaction from Congress quickly followed as well, and Jack Valenti suggested at a CPB board meeting that all contracts specify that the "final cut" on all programming was the responsibility of CPB.[40] He was unable to prevail. The controversy over *Banks and the Poor* strengthened PBS at the expense of NET within the system. Congress and the administration had demanded someone take responsibility for programming decisions. PBS immediately became the dominant force and set up its own standards department to screen programs before accepting them for distribution. This transformed PBS's role from passive conduit to network gatekeeper and programmer.

Valenti now thinks PBS was a mistake. "The CPB board made, in my judgment, a bad decision," he says, "setting up another organization called the Public Broadcasting Service, with its own board of directors. But the lawyers told us we could not own the apparatus and the hardware—we the board—and we had to have a subsidiary to do this. I opposed it then. I oppose it now. It made it very difficult to manage. And as a result, you had two groups competing for turf. Bad decision."

According to Peter Flanigan, the differences between Nixon and public broadcasters were philosophical. "Nixon believed that public funds should be used for things that were not being done in private television," Flanigan says, "but should not be used for things that were being done by private networks. Not news, which the networks did, but educational programs."[41]

The Nixon administration had three interconnected goals in this regard to reduce the leverage of the liberal Democrats who dominated public broadcasting: ending public broadcasting's dependence on the Ford Foundation; replacing NET with alternative production centers; and replacing public affairs programming with cultural and educational programming.

At the same time, the Nixon administration was promoting the establishment of cable television, independent commercial networks other than the big three (ABC, CBS, and NBC), and changes in the prime-time-access rule to allow syndicated programming on network stations. The goal was, in the words of ABC's Leonard Goldenson, "curbing network power."[42]

At the National Association of Educational Broadcasters' convention on October 20, 1971, Nixon aide Clay Whitehead gave a speech accusing association members of forming a fourth network and deviating from the decentralized ideals of the Carnegie Commission. (In public television history it ranks second in importance only to Minow's "vast wasteland" declaration.) He charged that the Ford Foundation "is able to buy over $8 million worth of [public affairs] programming on your stations." Whitehead urged local stations to play a larger role in the public broadcasting system. "You have to care about these balances and you have to work for them," he told the group. In exchange for a system dedicated to decentralization, Whitehead offered White House help with long-range financing.[43]

This apparent olive branch was immediately rejected by the CPB staff. John Witherspoon, then the CPB vice president for television, interpreted Whitehead's offer as meaning, "Until public broadcasting shows signs of becoming what this administration wants it to be, this administration will oppose permanent financing. And if we yield to that—well, let's hope the next administration and the one after that agree with this one, because it will be well known that we can be had." Witherspoon managed to get the Public Television Managers Council to resist Whitehead at first. But he noted, "There were, however, real differences among the various parts of the system, and the tensions of the day only made them worse."[44] Over time, Whitehead's strategy was succeeding, and support for the public broadcasters' goal of permanent unrestricted federal financing, which early on they had hoped Nixon might favor, was beginning to unravel.

To those who had helped set up educational television during the Kennedy and Johnson years at the Ford Foundation, Nixon's vision of local educational programming was anathema. David M. Davis, a former WGBH station manager and Ford Foundation program officer, put it simply: "The Nixon administration wanted to kill public television," by returning it to the role of instructional broadcasting.

By 1972, the CPB board had started to agree with Nixon administration requests. It voted not to fund news, news analysis, and political commentary. However, Whitehead observed, this would have little impact, because the "offensive programs" were funded through the end of the fiscal year, and even the ones that CPB dropped could still find funding from other sources.

In March 1972, PBS and CPB signed an agreement on program standards to settle outstanding questions over who controlled the network and how political issues might be resolved—fallout from the crisis that began over *Banks and the Poor*. But it was not enough for the administration. Nixon vetoed the reauthorization bill for public broadcasting on June 30, 1972, noting that the CPB had violated the law's intent to prevent formation of a fourth network by serving as "the center of power and the focal point of control for the entire public broadcasting system." Afterward, CPB chairman Frank Pace, president John Macy, and vice president John Witherspoon resigned. They were soon followed by other top executives.

The CPB board hired former Voice of America director and United States Information Agency deputy director Henry Loomis as its president. Loomis was acceptable to both the Nixon and Johnson appointees on the CPB board. He had been an assistant to James Killian at MIT and Deputy Commissioner of Education for Johnson and had worked on the transition team for the Nixon administration, where he had befriended Clay Whitehead. Loomis's hobbies were hunting and riding, and he saw himself as an American aristocrat. In June 1972 Whitehead and his general counsel, Antonin Scalia (now a Supreme Court Justice), went to Loomis's farm in Middleburg, Virginia, to ask him to take the job.[45]

"When they installed Henry Loomis as the president of the Corporation for Public Broadcasting," David M. Davis recalls, "I remember him coming into our Ford Foundation office and telling Fred Friendly and me that everything they did on public television should have shelf life. That is, you should be able to run it year after year. Which meant no public affairs, if you interpret that correctly."[46] Davis felt that such a move would result in true "educational television"—not what Ford wanted. Davis and Friendly were horrified at the possibility that PBS might become a mere conduit for instructional programming instead of political shows, and they made their views known to their friends.

One friend of the Ford Foundation's Fred Friendly was Ralph Rogers, chairman of Dallas's KERA, whose program *Newsroom* introduced Jim Lehrer to television. Rogers was a millionaire who owned a concrete company and had been a major contributor to Nixon's campaign. With true Texas bravado, Rogers also claims to be the inventor of "this terrible disease of begging on the air" called pledge drives. "I created that here in Dallas one night," he recalls. "I said, if the public wants this station, they ought to support it. So I picked up my granddaughter, who was seven years of age that night, and we went down to the television station and I told the public they had to support it."[47] At Rogers's urging, PBS, in a move designed to broaden its political base and guard against Nixon, set up what was called a Lay Board of Governors, which generally consisted of people known to be socially, politically, and economically influential. PBS also established a separate Board of Managers to represent the system's professional station managers. Rogers became the first chairman of the PBS Board of Governors—a millionaires' club with many Republican members. His reorganized PBS would be a "greater heat shield" for the educational network than NET or the CPB had been.

Rogers says the fight with Nixon to control the CPB activated his efforts to build up PBS. "Mr. Nixon, like all Presidents of the United States since George Washington, did not consider the media . . . to be friendly. . . . Mr. Nixon, who had more enemies in the media than most Presidents had, couldn't do anything about your independent right to write things, [but] public broadcasting was asking for money from the federal government, and Mr. Nixon said, 'Well, now, we should have something to say about this.' And he was up against the CPB. What he did was, he got enough of his appointees on the CPB, so for all practical purposes, he controlled it."

Although a Republican, Rogers volunteered to help PBS with the administration. In the winter of 1972, he personally hosted a meeting in

Dallas of the public television family. "I made a mistake [at that meeting]," he says. "I said, 'Well, when Mr. Nixon wanted money to run for office, he never had any trouble finding me. I have been a Republican all of my life.' And I said I wouldn't have any trouble getting to him."

Rogers felt at first that Nixon was being manipulated by his staff and could not believe that the President would be personally hostile to his favorite television network, one with many Republican contributors (such as himself and John D. Rockefeller III). "No president of the United States would ever take the position that the air would be censored by the federal government," he says. "You wouldn't have any right to public affairs programming. I said, 'This is somebody with an eye on this, but the president of the United States certainly wouldn't do that.'" Rogers thought that, once he got around the staff, he could convince the President to change his position. He felt that Nixon owed him the courtesy of a meeting because of his campaign contributions.

"And since he could find me any time, if you want to find me, I won't have any trouble in finding him and straightening it out," he recalled telling the PBS representatives who came to Dallas. "So they said, 'Great, go ahead and do it.' Well, I couldn't get to Mr. Nixon." Rogers soon concluded that, in fact, Nixon knew exactly what he was doing. And he was using his staff people to run interference and keep Rogers at bay. This treatment angered and insulted him. He took it personally.

"We laymen decided we would act," Rogers says. He organized a public broadcasting lobbying effort in Congress and pushed through the 1972 authorization bill for the CPB over Nixon's veto, which strengthened the position of PBS. "We just took on the administration and we beat them. When the final vote came down, we lost seventeen votes in the House and we lost seven votes in the Senate. We got all the rest of the votes." Rogers said he created PBS as a powerful player with a strong board of millionaires precisely "in order to take on Mr. Nixon."

But for its part, the Nixon administration felt it had reined in public broadcasting by replacing CPB board and staff, reducing the role of the Ford Foundation and NET, and transferring sovereignty over the system to the local stations, which tended to be more conservative than the network. And in fact, for a time, it had.

* * *

With a solid foundation laid for public television, it was time to concentrate on producing quality shows. Among the first was a revolutionary children's program that was originally envisioned as a tool to help close the educational gap between inner-city and middle-class kids. What began as a lofty vision of the liberal elite, however, soon evolved into a multimillion-dollar "nonprofit" cash cow.

2

Lessons from
Sesame Street

Since our federally funded system of public broadcasting first went on the air in 1967, none of its offerings have been more popular or more profitable than its children's shows. There is no better example of the schizophrenic inner life of public television, an enterprise that is at once fabulously successful and yet desperate for public money. Today, PBS is watched by more kids than any other network in America, and characters like Big Bird and Barney are recognized all over the world. Children's programs are popular with legislators, as well. Big Bird, Ernie and Bert, Barney, and Mister Rogers are frequent visitors to Capitol Hill and the most effective lobbyists for PBS. While PBS executives denounce commercial networks for selling to children, the publicly subsidized "educational" programming they broadcast is making literally billions of dollars for a select group of insiders. The fact is, if you want to market toys, books, or videotapes to the toddlers of America, you simply won't find a more effective venue than PBS.

And recently the PBS panjandrums have attempted to reach into the pockets of the commercial networks, getting the FCC to use its regulatory powers to pressure commercial broadcasters into giving money to public television in order to meet their requirements for minimum educational content as a condition of license renewals. On June 25, 1996,

PBS president Ervin Duggan, writing on the op-ed page of the *New York Times,* suggested that the future of PBS was linked to the educational television requirements found in the Children's Television Act of 1990. What Duggan proposed was that commercial networks pay for PBS children's programming in exchange for regulatory relief.[1]

Three programs in particular exemplify the type of children's programming on which PBS has built its reputation and viewership: *Mister Rogers' Neighborhood, Sesame Street,* and *Barney.* Each show, in its own way, captured the feel and the educational fashion of the period in which it was conceived.

By the time *Mister Rogers' Neighborhood* caught the eye of NET programmers in 1967, the low-key Fred Rogers had been producing it for thirteen years. Originally called *Children's Corner,* the program first aired in 1954 as a local show on Pittsburgh's educational station, WQED. The program starred Rogers and his cohost, Josie Carey, as well as the puppets Daniel S. Tiger and Grandpère the Skunk, who are still well known to children today. Carey was the on-camera talent, and Rogers served as puppeteer and guest performer in a variety of roles. Financial support for the show came from the Sears Roebuck Foundation. In 1955, *Children's Corner* won the Sylvania Award as the best locally produced children's program in the country.

The show was picked up from NET in 1956 by NBC as a one-season summer replacement for *Winchell and Mahoney,* NBC's successor to the wildly popular *Howdy Doody Show.* Rogers and Carey commuted between Pittsburgh and New York to do two versions of the program each week for live television that summer. The program continued to air on WQED until 1961. Carey and Rogers split up after that, and Rogers completed his studies at Pittsburgh Theological Seminary.

In 1963, Rogers obtained his doctor of divinity degree and was ordained a minister in the United Presbyterian Church. His course of study had included child development classes at Benjamin Spock and Erik Erikson's Arsenal Family and Children's Center in Pittsburgh, a center for progressive education. Rogers would use the children at the center to test puppets and songs later utilized on his show, which would be his ministry.

After his ordination Rogers moved to Canada, where he began producing *Mister Rogers' Neighborhood* for the Canadian Broadcasting Corporation at the invitation of the head of children's programming. In 1967, the show was picked up by the newly established Corporation for Public Broadcasting in the United States. *Mister Rogers' Neighborhood* was among the first children's programs to be funded by the federal government for broadcast on National Educational Television.

Rogers's style is gentle and personal, and his show is, by today's standards, remarkably slow-paced. Dressed in a cardigan sweater, he holds conversations with puppets and speaks about things that concern his young audience: things like fear of the dark, going to the dentist, and difficulties with friends and family members. On occasion, he even touches on serious subjects, such as physical handicaps, illness, even death. Rogers is very much the reassuring male figure, like the patient fathers in 1950s sitcoms. His show's emphasis on neighborhood rather than family also recalls the suburbia of that era. (Rogers's manner has been judged by some observers to be cloying and off-putting, however. Writer Jeanne Marie Laskas recalls telling "tough-guy, cynical editors" at *Life* magazine that she wanted to do a profile of Rogers, only to be mocked.)[2]

In 1976, Rogers stopped taping new episodes of his program and started spending more time traveling and at his vacation home, Crooked House, on Nantucket. Reruns of the show continued to air on PBS. Then, in 1983, in response to popular demand, Rogers resumed taping about two dozen new episodes a year, which are intermingled with the older episodes in the PBS broadcast schedule. Rogers has also hosted a number of PBS prime-time specials aimed at children, including one called *Heroes,* broadcast in 1994. The heroes Rogers chose for that show were not soldiers or famous stars from the worlds of sports or science, but social workers, schoolteachers, and others in the helping professions.

Today, Rogers utilizes his celebrity to support his nonprofit Family Communications Inc., which grosses over $2 million a year from grants and the sales of videos and other merchandise and activities related to Rogers's TV show. The financial reporting forms available for public inspection do not make clear precisely what Mister Rogers does with most of his time or what other sources of income such as speaking or consulting fees he might have. Family Communications does send him all over the world on various missions, so much so that he might appear a self-promoter if he did not enjoy beatified status among America's parents. Revealing his powerful impact on his fans, Laskas has called Rogers "a godlike figure, a holy man put on this earth with the singular task of making me feel good."[3]

If criticism could be aired honestly, one might question his judgment in taping a message to America's children to discuss Senator Robert Kennedy's assassination in 1968 or a similar message during the Persian Gulf War in 1991. Was he not inserting himself into matters beyond his mandate and expertise?

A pacifist who opposed the Gulf War (and who also opposed the Bush administration's attempts to clean up the National Endowment for the Arts), Rogers nevertheless made his way—along with Bill Isler, general manager of Family Communications Inc.—to a $1,000-a-plate fund-raising dinner for the President at Pittsburgh's Duquesne University in 1992. Rogers refrained from mentioning Bush's name in the sermon he preached to the assembled Republicans, asking every member of the audience to think of God and "listen to the cries of despair in our nation." As he left, he told a reporter that his presence should not be seen as an endorsement of Bush.

As enduring as the program has turned out to be, *Mister Rogers' Neighborhood* was too much like *Captain Kangaroo, Romper Room,* and other similarly gentle children's programs already found on commercial networks in the late 1960s to truly distinguish public broadcasting from its commercial counterparts. Public television needed a genuinely innovative alternative to demonstrate that it could, in fact, provide viewers with distinctive programming the commercial marketplace could not. It needed something faster, hipper, a show that reflected the colors, textures, pace, and sensibilities of the times. It needed *Sesame Street.*

Sesame Street was the brainchild of Joan Ganz Cooney. In 1966, she was working as a documentary producer at New York's Channel 13. A former reporter with a bachelor's degree in early childhood education, Cooney had come to New York from Arizona in 1954. After an introduction to General David Sarnoff, the president of NBC (whose own career in communications began as the telegraph operator who reported the sinking of the *Titanic*) at a party, Cooney soon found herself working for NBC as a publicist.

Not satisfied with promoting other people's programs, she moved to Channel 13 in 1962 to produce her own television shows, most notably a political debate series called *Court of Reason,* a precursor to *The Advocates* (PBS's popular 1970s public affairs show, see Chapter 7). Cooney's version featured a panel of three judges and two advocates. Among those who appeared on the program as an advocate was Malcolm X, who championed Black Muslim separatism against a Christian minister defending integration. Cooney proudly notes she provided what was probably Malcolm X's second television appearance in the New York market.

Another program Cooney produced was a documentary about Martin Deutsch, a professor at the Institute for Developmental Studies at New York University who was teaching four-year-olds in Harlem. After airing on Channel 13, the film was purchased by the federal Office of Economic Opportunity to train Head Start teachers. Cooney said she produced a number of shows about educational programs for the disadvantaged because of her interest in "compensatory education for the poor."

Cooney was married at the time to Tim Cooney, who was then making his livelihood working with so-called community groups in Harlem as part of President Johnson's Great Society reform efforts, and both were active in what Joan Cooney called "reform Democratic" politics—others might call her positions representative of extremely liberal politics. In addition to her political connections, she had a powerful personality. NET president John F. White once said that Cooney "could sell tea to the Chinese."[4]

In 1966, Cooney won an Emmy Award for her work on the Channel 13 documentary *Poverty, Anti-Poverty, and the Poor.* To celebrate, she and her husband were joined for dinner by Lewis Freedman, her boss at Channel 13, and Lloyd Morrisett, a vice president of the Carnegie Corporation. Morrisett, who had dated a cousin of Tim Cooney's in California, had a doctorate from the University of California, Berkeley, in psychology and a strong interest in the potential uses of television to improve the learning skills of the disadvantaged. He believed in social science, he believed in President Johnson's Great Society, and he believed in television. At dinner, Morrisett suggested that Cooney conduct a feasibility study for the Carnegie Corporation on the use of television to teach poor preschool children. The purpose was to attempt to close the IQ gap between rich and poor.[5]

Cooney has said that Morrisett chose her for the study because he didn't like any of the children's programming then being produced on either commercial networks or educational television. "He wanted a cold eye brought to this," she said. "The traditional childhood people were very soft in how they thought it ought to be done. Carnegie was far more hawkish. They were on the cognitive side versus the affective side of the issue. There were a lot of people, particularly in the upper classes, who believed that what children needed was a sort of love-in environment on television—'I love you just the way you are.' But our purposes were different."[6] In other words, Carnegie wanted Cooney to come up with a show that emphasized skills rather than feelings (as *Mister Rogers* did).

Freedman had actually suggested that another staffer at Channel 13 conduct the Carnegie study, believing Cooney wouldn't be interested. "She's a news and public affairs producer," he said at the time.[7] But Cooney wanted very much to stay with the project, and she asked her husband to lobby Morrisett on her behalf for the job.

On March 14, 1966, Cooney and Freedman met with two specialists in early childhood education at Carnegie to begin planning the research effort. They discussed the possibility of getting financial support from the U.S. Office of Education and New York City's Board of Education. On April 27, there was another Carnegie meeting, this time with Morrisett present. At this session, Cooney and Freedman laid out the specifics of the program they were planning. It would contain taped sequences and filmed visits to remote locations, such as fire stations and zoos. It would use puppets, stories, and music. And, they hoped, it would be broadcast twice a day. They emphasized the importance of involving educational psychologists and educators in the planning of the show. They also proposed selling books, toys, and crafts related to the program.[8]

Morrisett suggested that Carnegie itself might fund the feasibility study as a first step in the realization of the project. On May 13, Cooney submitted a proposal for a fourteen-week feasibility study and, a month later, received a grant from Carnegie to conduct a separate one-year study of educational children's television. For the next year, Cooney would travel around the country speaking to educators about preschool needs in relation to television.

In October of 1966, Cooney submitted the completed fourteen-week feasibility study to Carnegie. It argued that nearly all conventional children's programming was affective, but what was needed was a program that would provide cognitive education for the nation's preschoolers. Cooney cited the research of the author of *Teaching Disadvantaged Children in Pre-School,* Carl Bereiter, who found he could teach four-year-olds to read by using "verbal bombardment." She asserted that this method—though it may have sounded unpleasant—would be a good model for reaching inner-city children. "I thought the situation was so dire for these children of poverty," she recalls, "that radical intervention was, indeed, called for, as long as it was done in a humane fashion."

Cooney also believed that teachers treated children differently if they believed they were not smart, and that knowing how to count and recite the alphabet would help impoverished preschoolers impress teachers, raising the image of inner-city students and, thereby, improving academic achievement. "It's not that we argued that the ABCs were necessary for literacy," Cooney says, "or even that they were a good thing for a four- or five-year-old to learn. We argued that it would make all the psychological difference in their success in school if [disadvantaged children] came in with the same kind of skills as a middle-class child."[9]

Even at this early stage, Cooney suggested that her television program have the pacing and style of commercial television, including an educational version of commercial advertisements themselves ("*Sesame Street* is brought to you by the letters C and J, and by the number 4"). Cooney had noted that her young nieces and nephews were singing jingles from beer commercials on television—clear evidence that television could teach through song and repetition.

Cooney's original proposal also suggested a complementary program for parents to watch along with their children. "We learned through research very early on," Cooney says, "that it was extremely helpful if the mother—this was in the olden days, when mothers were home with their children—would watch with the child and talk about the program afterwards." The program for parents never got off the ground.

Although little actual empirical data existed to back up Cooney's methodological assertions, she quoted Harvard psychologist Jerome Bruner to impress Carnegie with the urgency of the task and the need for speed rather than prudence: "We cannot wait for the right answers before acting," Bruner said; "rather, we should look upon the first year of broadcasting for preschoolers in the nature of an inquiry. There is no substitute for trying it, and evaluating its effects, if we wish to know if television can be a valuable tool for promoting intellectual and cultural growth in our preschool population." If the same program did not work equally well for middle-class and disadvantaged children, Cooney added, she would suggest creating a special television show for inner-city kids to remedy any deficiencies in the first program. As it turned out, like the parents' show, this project never came to fruition.

In May 1967 Cooney left Channel 13 to become a full-time "television consultant" to the Carnegie Corporation, where she would develop her proposal into a show called *Sesame Street*. She estimated the cost of her project would total $2 million, and she approached a variety of possible funders, including commercial networks and sponsors. No donations were forthcoming from outside sources. Initially, even the Ford Foundation was unwilling to put up any money. Its child development experts found her proposal lacking.

Morrisett, however, was pleased with Cooney's proposal and circulated it widely that summer. He contacted his old friend Harold "Doc" Howe, then Commissioner of Education in the Johnson administration, who became enthusiastic about the project. "At that time, the idea of using education to break out of the cycle of poverty and helping [kids] to become more successful as they grew up was an idea I believed in," Morrisett recalls. "I thought that if it was going to be done right, there had to be a big piece of federal money."[10]

According to James Day (the last NET president and a cofounder of Children's Television Workshop), Howe instructed his staff to "find a way—any way—to organize the government's financial resources behind [the project]." According to Cooney, Howe personally called McGeorge Bundy, president of the Ford Foundation, and asked him to contribute money to the project. Bundy had to overrule his own staff's recommendation against Cooney in order to fund *Sesame Street.* (Bundy's people wanted to concentrate on a targeted reading program designed for inner-city youth.)[11]

Howe turned the project over to his special assistant, Louis Hausman. A former executive at both CBS and NBC, Hausman favored using commercial producers for the show instead of staff from educational television stations. He thought Cooney's proposed budget, which had been based on educational television precedents, was far too low and recommended an allocation of $6 million for the first year—an enormous sum for a children's television program. Cooney recalled that it was her good luck—and *Sesame Street's*—that Hausman had "enormous contempt for public television," because it resulted in much more funding from the federal government, funding that enabled her to hire professional staff from CBS to get her show off the ground.[12]

James Day has written that timing was crucial to the success of *Sesame Street.* "[The proposal,] with its aim to serve the educational needs of the disadvantaged, came at a moment in the nation's life when our collective conscience was darkened with the injustice of inequality. Racial riots, lighting the night skies of Newark and Detroit months earlier, were still fresh in memory. . . . A stunned nation was ready for palliative measures. Perhaps the workshop offered one such measure. If it was a small remedy for a large ailment it had the virtue of being fast."[13]

In 1968, Cooney and Morrisett established the Children's Television Workshop to administer the *Sesame Street* project. Although originally using Channel 13 administration and loosely connected with NET, CTW maintained organizational independence. Morrisett had insisted on this so that CTW could raise its own money (from commercial sources if need be) and maintain its own production standards. Cooney was named the first executive director.[14]

The new organization received its first $1 million check from the Carnegie Corporation that same year. President Johnson's Secretary of Health, Education, and Welfare, John Gardner (later to head the liberal lobbying group Common Cause), approved federal funding for the children's series. Additional money was pledged by the National Endowment for the Humanities, the Office of Economic Opportunity, and the National Institute of Child Health and Human Development, for a total first-year federal contribution of $4 million. The project's first-year budget would eventually reach almost $8 million—$2 million more than even Hausman had projected. It had turned out that children's television was, politically, an easy sell.

The premiere event for the Children's Television Workshop was a press conference held at the Waldorf Astoria on March 20, 1968, announcing the first year's production schedule. Present at that event were Howe, Bundy, and Alan Pifer of the Carnegie Corporation—the titans of the American educational establishment at the time.

At the suggestion of CBS executive Mike Dann, former *Captain Kangaroo* producer David Connell was named executive producer of *Sesame Street*. According to James Day, Cooney promised Connell her support in any confrontation with academic advisers over programming. That is, once the funding had been secured, academic recommendations would play second fiddle to the values of show business.

Day quotes Cooney as saying, "If we err, we will err on the side of entertainment." Connell soon brought more *Kangaroo* alumni to the project: writer Jon Stone and producer Sam Gibbon. On the scholarly side, Harvard education professor Gerald Lesser was named head of the academic advisory board.[15]

Jim Henson was hired to do the puppets. The Henson Muppets had the look Cooney was going for, and they were a known quantity, having appeared in television variety shows and commercials for Royal Crown Cola, Community Coffee, Wilson's Certified Meats, La Choy chow mein, Purina Dog Chow, Ivory Snow, Gleem toothpaste, and IBM. Henson had also worked with Jon Stone on *Hey, Cinderella,* an ABC special.

Henson made several significant early contributions to the program, most notably the invention of Big Bird, who was described as an overgrown six-year-old intended to make childen feel comfortable with their clumsiness. In the first five test episodes, Henson's Muppets and the live-action characters were kept separated in different sequences. When producers discovered that children weren't paying attention to the humans in the street scenes, they decided to allow the humans to interact with the Muppets, in order to keep kids interested in every aspect of the show. Thus was born Big Bird, who could walk freely among the people and keep young viewers watching. (Big Bird was played by Carroll Spinney, who had also played the dragon in the La Choy commercials.)

Another popular *Sesame Street* character, Kermit the Frog, was already a familiar figure in Washington, D.C. The lovable green Muppet had debuted on Henson's *Sam and Friends* local Washington, D.C., television show, and a version of Kermit was also used in television commercials for Wilkins Coffee, a well-known brand in the nation's capital. Famous in Washington, the Henson puppet was no doubt reassuring to the small army of bureaucrats at HEW who were subsidizing the new children's show.

Cooney chose Joe Raposo to serve as the show's composer. He had worked previously with Henson and with songwriter Jeff Moss, a *Captain Kangaroo* alumnus who was also hired to write songs for *Sesame Street*. As far as the show's live actors were concerned, Cooney had only one firm rule: no stars.

With an ensemble company of unknowns, no single actor would dominate or become so important that he or she could not be replaced. Cooney did not want prima donnas. Part of Cooney's preference for unknowns may have come from an ideological commitment to collective and cooperative structures rather than competitive and individualistic ones. And, of course, it was one way of preventing escalating salary demands from the cast.

Matt Robinson, who played Gordon the first three seasons, had been one of the show's producers—until Cooney convinced him to act the part of husband to housewife Susan, played by Loretta Long. Only the storekeeper, Mr. Hooper, was played by an established actor, Will Lee. "No one person is going to own this show, so every time a contract comes up, a gun is held to your head," Cooney said.[16] From the beginning, the real stars of the show were Henson's Muppets—they were indispensable and would make Henson a multimillionaire.

Staff writer Virginia Schone is the person credited with naming the show. "Sesame" came from the magical command "open sesame" in the

Arabian Nights tale "Ali Baba and the Forty Thieves"; "Street" indicated the setting for the show, a city street. That particular environment was chosen over a more typical house or schoolroom in order to signal "this is for you, too" to inner-city youth.[17]

Throughout the fall of 1969, the *Sesame Street* producers worked to secure a uniform block of time from 9:00 to 11:00 A.M. on PBS stations across the country, persuading many stations to drop already scheduled instructional programming designed for classroom use. They created a pilot episode as a promotional piece, which they sent to the stations.

On November 8, 1969, *Sesame Street* premiered as a prime-time special on NBC, sponsored by Xerox. Two days later, the show had its first daytime broadcast on PBS. In New York City, it initially ran on WPIX, a commercial station owned by the *New York Daily News,* because Channel 13 did not want to disrupt the instructional programming it beamed to city classrooms. A commercial station also carried the program in Chicago.

During its first season, it was estimated, some 7 million children watched the show. A survey cited by the Children's Television Workshop claimed 90 percent of children in Bedford-Stuyvesant, one of New York's poorest neighborhoods, watched the program. To this day, *Sesame Street* continues to be among the most-watched children's programs among all Nielsen families.

The Carl Byoir public relations firm spent almost $1 million in the series's first year to generate favorable publicity. In 1970, the Markle Foundation—headed by Children's Television Workshop cofounder Lloyd Morrisett—gave a two-year $165,000 grant to the Boston-based advocacy group Action for Children's Television (ACT). Headed by Peggy Charren, a liberal Democratic activist who came from a labor union background, ACT's mission was to lobby the FCC and Congress to require the networks to broadcast more educational children's shows, limit commercials on children's programming, and place a prohibition on product-based shows. Although there was no direct connection between the two groups, ACT and CTW were supportive of each other's goals. One direct beneficiary of federal restrictions on commercial children's programming—and commercial sponsorship—was *Sesame Street.* It was competing for viewers (and production talent) with programs like

Captain Kangaroo. By opposing commercial programs for children, ACT was helping to restrict the ability of the private sector to compete with CTW for the children's market. Politics and regulation were being used to limit the choices available to parents for their children—and Morrisett was cleverly hobbling his rivals (no commercial children's programmer was attempting to restrict *Sesame Street*).

The FCC passed regulations banning host-selling, toy-based shows and limiting the number of advertising minutes in children's programming. Within two decades of ACT's initial efforts to regulate children's programs, such commercial favorites as *Wonderama, Shari Lewis, Sheriff John, Soupy Sales, J.P. Patches,* and *Captain Kangaroo* would be off the air, replaced by cheaper cartoons. Indeed, not until the arrival of Nickelodeon on cable in the 1980s, and the Reagan administration's more laissez-faire attitude toward FCC regulation, would PBS again face significant competition for youthful viewers from live-action shows like *Super Sloppy Double Dare.* By then, *Sesame Street* would be a billion-dollar behemoth, marketing over 5,000 licensed products from CTW.[18]

A year after its first broadcast, the Children's Television Workshop arranged for the Educational Testing Service (ETS) to conduct a study of the effectiveness of *Sesame Street* as an educational tool. The ETS study concluded that the show did improve the learning skills of children who watched. However, the favorable ETS results showed not only that the presence of an adult was required for any effect to be found, but also that the show did nothing at all to close the gap between "advantaged" and "disadvantaged" children.

Shortly after release of the ETS study, criticism of *Sesame Street* began to emerge. The Russell Sage Foundation, a New York educational philanthropy, conducted its own study of the program's effects and published its results in a 1975 volume, *Sesame Street Revisited.* The foundation claimed it could not replicate the ETS findings of educational benefit from watching the show. Like the ETS study, the Sage report found no improvement in the disadvantaged children for whom the program was intended and concluded that "one can reasonably doubt whether the program is causing large and generalized learning gains."

The Sage Foundation study was not the only negative response to the program. When CTW tried to export the show to Britain, Monica

Sims, head of children's television for the BBC, rejected it, saying it was "authoritarian" with an "emphasis on right answers" rather than on thinking problems through in a logical fashion. Sims also criticized *Sesame Street* for its use of slang, "hard-selling techniques," "philosophy of built-in, never-ending repeats," "passive box-watching," its role as a "substitute for actual contact between a child and his mother, his companions, or his teacher," and, echoing the Sage study, the show's failure to "bridge the gap between the advantaged and disadvantaged."[19] *Sesame Street* producers never could convince the BBC that their program was good for children. Cooney said she believed Sims kept the program off the BBC because it was American. *Sesame Street* was finally broadcast in Great Britain on the Independent (ITV) network's London Weekend Television, the BBC's commercial competitor, sharing the schedule with programs like *Thunderbirds,* a violent space adventure featuring marionettes.

Sims was joined in rebuking *Sesame Street* by psychiatrist Robert Coles of Harvard University. In a 1988 article in the *New York Times,* he stated that *Sesame Street* did not reach its intended audience of inner-city kids but instead attracted middle-class viewers who derived no educational advantage from the entertaining programming—a conclusion that agreed with the earlier Sage findings.

Other critics have argued that the show not only fails to help children learn but, as Monica Sims stated, actually harms them. Author Marie Winn, in her 1977 book, *The Plug-In Drug,* attacked *Sesame Street* on the grounds that its fast-paced segments were shortening children's attention spans, leaving them unable to concentrate in a slower classroom environment. Winn argued that the best solution for improving the scholastic performance of children was "no television ever," saying evidence showed that children raised in households without television sets do better in school overall and have better relationships with their parents.

In a similar vein, Jerome and Dorothy Singer of Yale University have conducted psychological studies showing that *Sesame Street* reduces concentration rather than increasing it. In a 1993 study comparing *Sesame Street* with *Barney,* the Singers concluded that the purple dinosaur encouraged children to "look forward to school as a positive experience" and told reporters that it had more teaching elements than *Sesame Street.*

Jane M. Healy devoted an entire chapter of her 1990 book, *Endangered Minds: Why Our Children Can't Think,* to criticism of the show. In "*Sesame Street* and the Death of Reading," she listed ten reasons she felt the program actually encouraged illiteracy among preschoolers and accused the Children's Television Workshop of hucksterism, concluding, "It can easily be argued that they have led an overly trusting public astray."

Neil Postman, a professor at New York University, shares the opinion that *Sesame Street* can be dangerous to a child's ability to learn. In *Amusing Ourselves to Death: Public Discourse in the Age of Show Business* (1985), he writes:

> We now know that *Sesame Street* encourages children to love school only if school is like *Sesame Street.* Which is to say, we now know that *Sesame Street* undermines what the traditional idea of schooling represents. . . . *The Little House on the Prairie, Cheers,* and *The Tonight Show* are as effective as *Sesame Street* in promoting what might be called the television style of learning. . . . If we are to blame *Sesame Street* for anything, it is for the pretense that it is an ally of the classroom. That, after all, has been its chief claim on foundation and public money. As a television show, and a good one, *Sesame Street* does not encourage children to love school or anything about school. It encourages them to love television.

Most recently, Kay Hymowitz, herself a former teacher, published an article titled "On *Sesame Street* It's All Show."[20] She took issue with a 1995 CTW-sponsored study unveiled at the White House by First Lady Hillary Clinton praising the program. (No publicly released CTW-sponsored study has found fault with *Sesame Street.*)[21] Hymowitz agreed with earlier criticism of the program and especially objected to the "cool," "ironic," postmodern sensibility of the program for undermining traditional warmth and stability in human relationships.

Some observers have criticized specific *Sesame Street* characters. Cookie Monster, for example, has been taken to task for glorifying "sweet and unhealthy foods" and for setting a poor example with his bad manners. Oscar the Grouch has been cited for similar reasons. Others have argued that the show's depiction of what are essentially furry "street people" desensitizes children to the tragedy of the homeless mentally ill. Along these lines, *Village Voice* writer Billy Tashman lambasted the show's psychobabble: "When I asked writer Norman Stiles what was the educational point of a recent (and very funny) segment that had Bert interrogating Ernie about an uneaten cookie, he replied that this fell under the curriculum goal of 'consequent events.' Problem is, Beavis and Butthead torturing a bird would fall under the goal of 'consequent events.' " [22] Like the Great Society programs of which it was a part, *Sesame Street* has delivered little more than the rhetoric of educational fads.

Not surprisingly, Joan Cooney has defended her show against all detractors. "No single television program is going to bridge the gap in education," she said. "What CTW hopes to accomplish with its programs is to move all children across the basic literacy line, which is key to education and later entering the mainstream of American life."[23] And yet, though 90 percent of American children have watched *Sesame Street,* functional illiteracy has been rising and SAT scores have been falling throughout the country since the show went on the air in 1969.

Cooney's reply also ignored the fact that there is little hard evidence her program has any direct effect on the disadvantaged. Gerald Lesser, chief academic adviser to CTW, responded to the criticism by claiming that the project never intended to reduce the gap between advantaged and disadvantaged children. But if this was not the goal, then what was? Cooney's successor at CTW, current president David Britt, wrote in the *Washington Post* in 1995 that "the millions of children who watch *Sesame Street* regularly go to school better prepared than those who do not." However, the only hard data on which all the scholars agree show that middle-class children who watch *Sesame Street* do better in school than poor children who watch *Sesame Street*. Both groups are doing worse in school than their counterparts of thirty years ago, who did not watch *Sesame Street* at all.

If *Sesame Street* does not, in fact, help inner-city or middle-class children to learn more than they otherwise might, what does it do? In addition to serving as a babysitter and an entertaining pastime, one thing the show does very well indeed is to sell toys, games, and other merchandise connected to the show—some of which are manufactured in China and other Asian countries with exploitative labor practices. While the FCC strictly regulates program-length commercials, toy-based programs, and indirect advertising to children on commercial TV, PBS is not subject to the same level of scrutiny. Essentially, *Sesame Street* serves as an infomercial for the 5,000-plus licensed *Sesame Street* products that gross over $800 million in retail sales around the world each year. Ironically, when she was first promoting her new program for children, Joan Ganz Cooney said, unequivocally, that it was "terribly wrong" to pitch products to the young. "It is like shooting fish in a barrel," said the founder of the most commercially successful children's television program in history. "It is grotesquely unfair." In some markets *Sesame Street* airs eighteen times a week on the various PBS stations—a saturation unheard of for any commercial program.[24]

The show also makes a lot of money for the people who produce it. CTW has seven subsidiaries—two of them for-profit corporations. It had $58 million in a stock and bond portfolio in 1992 and reported $70 million in that same portfolio in 1995, despite claiming to "plow back" its profits into new productions. Executive compensation at CTW peaked at $700,000 a year in 1992. Children's Television Workshop's 1994 IRS form 990 showed five executives receiving compensation higher than that of the President of the United States: Jan Stone, divisional vice president, $456,163; William F. Whaley, divisional president, $373,922; Nina B. Link, divisional vice president, $357,056; Franklin Getchell, divisional vice president, $356,651; and William Hitzig, vice president, $235,433.

Lobbyists are making out on the show, too. In 1989, CTW reported spending some $4 million annually on lobbying. After Senator Robert Dole read from their tax filings in a 1992 Senate debate over funding for public broadcasting, CTW changed the way it categorized expenditures so that this number dropped dramatically, but those familiar with the field think that lobbying expenses are now hidden in other categories.

In that Senate debate, Dole—in the longest floor speech of his Senate career—complained about the big money being made by public broadcasting producers, including the Children's Television Workshop, who were not returning a fair share to the taxpayers. (In 1992, newly arrived CPB president Richard Carlson changed a grant payback rule instituted by his Reagan administration predecessor, Donald Ledwig.)

Dole did not tell his listeners that he had been bombarded with letters—written by schoolchildren under the direction of their teachers—attacking him for wanting to "kill Big Bird" because he simply wanted to let the program pay for itself.

In the conclusion to his book *Children and Television: Lessons from Sesame Street,* Gerald Lesser quotes Cooney saying, "The provision of good programs for children must be removed from the free enterprise system and be made a public service. For the commercial networks, this would mean that they 'half-nationalize' themselves, with television for adults remaining free enterprise, but television for children becoming public interest. But this means that commercial broadcasters will have to decide by themselves to do this. Not likely."

Yet, CTW has licensed products since the day *Sesame Street* went on the air. CTW has at various times had holdings including cable television systems, theme parks, commercial radio stations, and educational software producers. If Cooney truly believed that selling to kids was wrong, how could such an enormous commercial enterprise have grown from her brainchild?

Nickelodeon's Cy Schneider has noticed this seeming contradiction in his competitors at PBS. "For do-gooders to point to *Sesame Street* as an example of how all commercial television should be," he says, "is to lose sight of CTW's unique position as a production company. First of all, they are tax-exempt because of the educational nature of their products. Second, what other company has had the advantage of over $100 million in funding without any obligation whatsoever to repay its debt? The people at Children's Television Workshop sound like adolescents; they talk about ethics and keep asking for money."

No discussion of *Sesame Street* would be complete without mentioning its bipartisan support. In 1974, when the federal government was contemplating reducing its support for the Children's Television Workshop, which was by that time also producing *The Electric Company,* Cooney paid a call on Senator Barry Goldwater. The way had been smoothed by her personal friendship with fellow Arizonan and FCC chairman Dean Burch, a former top Goldwater aide. She was there to try to bargain for time. "Give us five years," Cooney said to Goldwater, "in which we will keep stepping up our income from books, toys, whatnot, and phase out government support. Don't pull out." According to Cooney, Goldwater agreed. "I always like to say, 'Barry saved *Sesame Street*,'" she says. From that year until 1981, CTW had a line-item in the federal budget.[25]

If anything captures the difference between the spirit of the 1980s and that of the 1960s, it is the story of *Barney*. Like *Sesame Street, Barney* is a big moneymaker. In 1994, *Forbes* listed the purple dinosaur who sings love songs to children as America's third-richest entertainer, trailing only Steven Spielberg and Oprah Winfrey. The magazine estimated the giant reptile's take-home pay over its first two years to be approximately $84 million. Gross retail sales of *Barney* merchandise for those years totaled around $500 million. But there is where the similarities end.

Where *Sesame Street* cost the taxpayers millions to develop, *Barney* found its own way in the marketplace. The child of 1980s private enterprise, it began its phenomenal rise in the home video market, only later moving to PBS.

The purple dinosaur character was created by a Texas housewife, Sheryl Leach, in 1988, the result of her efforts to entertain her two-year-old with puppets. She thought her idea might appeal to other mothers and interested her father-in-law, Richard Leach, who was successful in the religious video and book business in Allen, Texas. With his help, she raised $1 million and found partners for a series of three videos. Barney was on his way to being a serious challenge to Big Bird.

In pace and style, *Barney* is more like *Mister Rogers' Neighborhood* than *Sesame Street*. Where *Sesame Street* emphasizes cognitive elements, *Barney* leans toward the so-called affective side of education, most notably in the show's signature song, "I Love You" (sung to the tune of "This Old Man"). Yale psychologist Jerome Singer has said it "has more teaching elements than *Sesame Street*."

To promote her videos, Leach gave away free copies to preschools and daycare centers near Toys-R-Us stores, along with notes saying the tapes were available for sale nearby. She also placed thirty-second ads on Nickelodeon. In 1990, Lawrence Rifkin, executive vice president of Connecticut Public Television, bought a *Barney* tape for his four-year-old daughter. He admired how the simple, homespun programs captured the fancy of his child "in a way I'd never seen anything else do."

Rifkin contacted the Lyons Group, the Leaches' production company, and asked whether they would be interested in producing a series of *Barney* programs for PBS. The network was looking for new children's programming to supplement the Children's Television Workshop line, which had fallen in the ratings after some twenty years on the air. To stay competitive with cable for children, PBS needed new product.

The Corporation for Public Broadcasting, eager to bring more children's programming to the network, gave Rifkin a $2.25 million grant to produce thirty episodes of *Barney*. As CPB executives never tire of pointing out, *Barney* was already popular before it was picked up by PBS. It was after PBS began airing the shows, however, that *Barney* videos and merchandise began flying off the shelves. This is really no surprise: the show was now reaching viewers of the channel with the largest children's audience in America, with time slots near *Sesame Street*'s and the PBS seal of approval.

In 1994, the Video Software Dealers Association's Video Scan survey reported that *Barney* was the second-best-selling children's video series, after *The Mighty Morphin Power Rangers*, with over 2 million units sold. That same year, Barney did a live show at Radio City Music Hall and had a prime-time special on NBC. Universal Studios announced that its Orlando theme park would install a 60,000-square-foot Barney attraction. Warner Bros. announced a feature-length *Barney* movie in 1995.

The success of *Barney* led to a series of articles in the press on the vast riches accruing to the producers of the PBS series (some suggest hostility on the part of competitors as a source of the negative publicity that greeted *Barney* early on). In 1993, Senator Robert Dole noticed an item in the *Washington Post,* reporting that at the same time public broadcasting was asking for increased federal appropriations, PBS shows were generating half a billion dollars in annual sales of related merchandise. The senator was outraged. "Now we know why Barney smiles so much," Dole said in the speech from the Senate floor in which he labeled the situation "Barneygate." "You see, Barney isn't just a dinosaur, he's a cash cow. The American taxpayer helped make Barney into a multimillion-dollar enterprise, but the Public Broadcasting System, supported so handsomely by the taxpayers, doesn't get a cut of the sales of Barney backpacks, Barney slippers, Barney socks, Barney lunchboxes, Barney videos, Barney bedside lamps, Talking Barney, or the scores of other Barney items available at a toy store near you."

Perhaps surprisingly, one of *Barney's* chief critics is Joan Ganz Cooney, who compares the show unfavorably to her own. "Listen," she said of the purple dinosaur's success, "you've seen enough television in your lifetime to know that the lowest common denominator often wins. . . . If you sit down with children and put on *Barney* and *Sesame Street* and a cartoon, you're going to find that *Sesame Street* demands more than *Barney* and a cartoon. It's hard work for kids to watch it, and that's why it skews a little bit older than *Barney.*" Cooney maintains her show is tougher—and therefore better and more educational—than its competitors for a reason: "School is hard, learning is hard."[26] Yet of course the original appeal of *Sesame Street* was that the program was fun and as easy to watch as commercial television. And despite her criticism, Cooney says she's glad *Barney* is on PBS and not a competing network. In a head-to-head fight, she believes *Barney* would beat her show in the ratings.

Senator Dole's concerns were given new substance when the *Wall Street Journal* carried an account in January 1994 of a new PBS children's show called *The Puzzle Place.*[27] Designed specifically to teach multiculturalism to young schoolchildren, the program was financed by a $4.5 million grant from the CPB. On news of the grant award, the production company, Lancit Media, saw its stock, which had been trading around $3, rise to an all-time high of $13. In the aftermath of the award, the company signed multimillion-dollar licensing agreements for merchandise spin-offs with Fisher-Price, and the *Journal* estimated the value of Lancit Media, headed by the husband-and-wife team of Larry Lancit and Cecily Truett, at $80 million.

Meanwhile, *Forbes* magazine put annual grosses from products related to Thomas the Tank Engine, a character on the PBS show *Shining Time Station,* at $250 million.[28] Other programs that have joined the PBS lineup since 1990 include *Lambchop's Play-Along,* with a complete product line; and Scholastic Inc.'s *Magic Schoolbus,* featuring the voice of Lily Tomlin as science teacher Mrs. Frizzle, in animated educational adventures based on Scholastic's children's book series by authors Joanna Cole and Bruce Degen.

Clearly the lessons of *Sesame Street* had been learned by the 1990s. They were not about reducing the educational gap between rich and poor children, a goal that seems to have vanished from everyone's list of priorities at PBS and the Children's Television Workshop.

Rather, PBS provided programmers with a unique venue that added measurable value in the marketplace. It served as a kind of Good House-keeping seal of approval, which translated into profits. What amounted to program-length commercials would not be interrupted on PBS by plugs for cereals or other competing products. PBS could deliver more kids than any other network in the country, and the taxpayer would subsidize the cost of advertising, promotion, production, and develop-ment as well!

"Barneygate" had revealed that children's programs on PBS were in-deed a big business making literally billions of dollars for a select—and very well-connected—few.

In September 1994, Democratic senator Daniel Inouye of Hawaii held the first congressional hearing in which "Barneygate" was exam-ined. Shortly after that hearing, an oversight committee headed by Democratic representative Ed Markey of Massachusetts began looking at charges of profiteering in public broadcasting. A headline in the *Hol-lywood Reporter* dated September 20, 1994, read "PBS 'Barneygate' Era: Critics Follow the Money; Bipartisan Concern over Service's Fiscal Fit-ness." In January 1995, a Republican Congress continued the investiga-tion when an appropriations subcommittee headed by Republican representative John Porter of Illinois held a day-long hearing into the management of public broadcasting. At that hearing, numerous wit-nesses cited the failure to recoup revenues from children's programming and related merchandise as a symptom of a system in trouble.

Republican senator Larry Pressler of South Dakota suggested that the profitability of programs like *Sesame Street* and *Barney* was a model for the rest of public broadcasting, showing that popular programming of an educational bent could pay for itself and generate additional rev-enues to support the system. He was soon joined by Jack Kemp, former Secretary of Housing and Urban Development, who wrote an article in the *Wall Street Journal* endorsing privatization. Privatization was actually supported in principle by the public broadcasting lobby in 1995—with the condition that Congress pay $5 billion to set up a "trust fund."

The success of *Barney, Sesame Street,* and, yes, even *Mister Rogers' Neighborhood* have revealed a secret dimension of public broadcasting: PBS is extremely lucrative for those able to get a place on its tightly controlled schedule. The very children's programs that were originally intended to demonstrate the unique nature of public broadcasting during the Great Society and serve as a justification for a taxpayer-financed system had revealed themselves to be, in fact, the best argument for its privatization.

3

Rev. Moyers

Perhaps none of its stars better embodies the ideals and aspirations of PBS than Bill Moyers. He has produced over a hundred hours of personal essays, interviews, and documentaries for the network since he joined it in 1971, and his specials raise a great deal of money for local stations when aired during pledge weeks. Moyers's signature stance combines a populist appeal to the concerns of the ordinary citizen with a lofty moralistic tone; compassion for the less fortunate with an interest in education and uplift. As an interviewer, Moyers is usually respectful, deferential, with an eagerness to empathize that seldom seems forced. His personal life appears to be without a hint of scandal. He is still married to his childhood sweetheart, Judith Davidson Moyers, a longevity unusual in the worlds of television and politics (she is his partner in his company, Public Affairs Television Inc.). After his brother died, he looked after his sister-in-law, nieces, and nephews as well as his own children.

No one who has seen his documentary on his boyhood home, Marshall, Texas, with its interviews of his former teachers, can fail to be impressed with his charm, insight, and delight in his origins.

Moyers has been the perfect poster boy for liberals, living proof that their ideals could be attractive to a greater portion of the country than just the Eastern establishment. A small-town Texan trained as a Baptist minister who achieved power in Washington, fame and wealth in New York, he never lost touch with his roots, his Texas accent, or his link to the "common man," yet his political opinions seemed to have evolved with experience and education to become more acceptable to foundation program officers than to the residents of rural Texas; and his original Baptist religious views likewise seemed to have expanded to accommodate a wide array of New Age outlooks probably not taught in Marshall, Texas, Sunday schools during Moyers's youth.

Moyers himself often touches on the theme of his own personal growth. Certain actions he carried out for Lyndon Johnson, during his tenure as Johnson's press secretary, are things he has not hidden from discussions with the press, and he has projected contrition for his past in several of his documentaries on American politics. Yet while Moyers sometimes acts the part of a sinner who has been saved by grace, the image conceals a reality that is far more complex. In a sense, Moyers's career can be seen not so much as a story of personal growth but as a brilliant example of triangulation: two sides of Moyers's character—the ambitious, left-of-center politician and the shrewd entrepreneur—are cleverly balanced by the moderate, understanding persona who hosts *Facing Evil, The Power of Myth,* and *Amazing Grace* and champions Robert Bly and the men's movement.

Throughout his career as a journalist and political operative, Moyers has followed a pattern of ingratiating himself with powerful figures, from whom he has later parted on bad terms. Lyndon Johnson was not Moyers's only patron who felt an angry sense of betrayal after their association came to an end. Like LBJ, or Harry Guggenheim, or William Paley, the public wooed by the gentle Moyers often fails to realize that it has to some extent been used by him: that, for example, Moyers often has a financial stake in figures such as Joseph Campbell, whom he presents in deferential soft focus.

And, too, Moyers often has a political stake in the other side of his oeuvre: the often very pointedly political documentaries he has produced throughout his career. Public television's historic pattern of meeting Republican objections to its liberal public affairs programming by claiming that it is presenting uplifting fare admired by all sides of the political spectrum is repeated in microcosm in Moyers's career.

Moyers is a brilliant bridge: a talented television evangelist but acceptable to progressive, nonreligious public television viewers who prefer sermons couched in the language of pop psychology rather than that of hellfire and damnation; a Baptist minister who hawks tote bags and cassettes instead of prayer handkerchiefs, books of mythology instead of the Bible, and faith healing based on the authority of science rather than revelation. Who, although stopping short of saying he will be called to meet his maker if viewers don't send in donations (as Oral Roberts once did), participates in equally high-pressure PBS pledge drives and political campaigns to "save public broadcasting." And all the while, Moyers continually increases his personal and family net worth through a complex series of interlocking business ventures, foundations, and subsidies.

A 1992 *New York Times* article by former CBS producer Jon Katz described Moyers as "the media's holy man." In keeping with the conventional wisdom about him, Katz declared: "Mr. Moyers has a politician's honed instinct for perceptions and a preacher's sense of propriety, agonizes over every criticism, eschews agents and Hamptons parties. His fans are among the most deprived viewers on television, the politically adrift of the 80's and 90's: liberals, academics, intellectuals, and old-fashioned do-gooders left in the cold by 22 years (with Jimmy Carter sandwiched in the middle) of Republicanism. To them, Mr. Moyers symbolizes what they think broadcast journalism should be."[1]

One person who doesn't accept Moyers's story of his own personal growth or his benevolent public persona is Morley Safer. In his memoir, *Flashbacks,* the still bitter *60 Minutes* correspondent devotes several pages to strong personal criticism of Moyers, though diplomatically expressed. Safer reminds his readers of the Texas "holy man's" collaboration with the FBI as Johnson's press secretary. He points out that Moyers was responsible for supervising the FBI's bugging of Dr. Martin Luther King, Jr.[2] Safer charges Moyers with leaking material based on this surveillance to foreign diplomats and the press. He also accuses him of spying on civil rights protesters attending the 1964 Democratic convention in Atlantic City. "Moyers was the conduit to J. Edgar Hoover," he says. "Bill, the darling of us liberals, was spying on King."[3] In his book, Safer blames Moyers for compiling requests to the FBI for dirt on Barry Goldwater's 1964 presidential campaign.[4]

Moyers responded to these and other charges in a letter printed as a two-page paid advertisement in the *New Republic* after writer Andrew Ferguson had repeated them in a 1991 article titled "The Power of Myth."[5] Moyers denied knowing that King had been bugged. He said he had only been interested in the FBI looking into security matters at the Atlantic City convention, not political ones. Moyers added that he did not tell the FBI what to do and that he was the FBI go-between for only six months following LBJ chief of staff Walter Jenkins's resignation in October 1964. Jenkins had been arrested on "disorderly conduct" charges in a Washington men's room. Moyers said LBJ thought Jenkins had been set up by Goldwater's campaign, and Moyers ordered the FBI to investigate because the President had asked him to do it. Moyers said he "forgot about the matter" until the FBI agent in charge told him "the suspicions could not be substantiated." Moyers continued, "I regret that we didn't tell Hoover to go fly a kite." He denied leaking any information to anyone other than "officials involved in national security."[6] Johnson's record in these sorts of cases is far less punctilious than Moyers admits, however. David Halberstam cites the former president terrorizing his aides by threatening those who crossed him that "two men were going to follow their ass to the ends of the earth": J. Edgar Hoover and the IRS director.[7]

But what clearly bothers Safer most about Moyers's activities for Johnson were those directed personally against him. Safer believes Moyers tried to "get" him for his August 1965 CBS News report about the burning of the Vietnamese village of Cam Ne by U.S. Marines. The famous story showed young soldiers setting huts on fire with Zippo lighters. It created a storm of outrage, undermining Johnson's prosecution of the war.

Safer recalls that LBJ called CBS president Frank Stanton and started his phone conversation by asking: "Frank, are you trying to f— me?" He says Johnson then proceeded to give Stanton a "tongue lashing." Stanton was asked to attend a meeting at the White House a few days later and did so, conferring with LBJ and Moyers in a small private office. Johnson told Stanton that he and Moyers "had the goods" on Safer, damaging information in the files of the FBI, the CIA, and the Royal Canadian Mounted Police (Safer is Canadian).

The angry President attempted to blackmail Stanton, declaring, "Unless CBS got rid of [Safer] and 'cleaned up its act,' the White House would 'go public' with information about [Safer's] 'communist ties.'" Safer, however, already knew investigations of his background had "produced nothing" and that "Johnson, with Moyers's help, was simply bluffing." So, convinced of Safer's innocence, Stanton and CBS News president Fred Friendly backed him against the White House, and he kept his job at CBS News.

There is documentary evidence to support Safer's suspicions that Moyers had been his eager adversary. In an undated personal memorandum from Moyers to Johnson, found in a presidential file for August 1965, the young press secretary declares he has "been working for the past few days on steps we can take to improve coverage of the Vietnam war." Moyers had asked for reports from Defense and State Department officials and said he would come to the President with some "hard proposals." Although "we will never eliminate altogether the irresponsible and prejudiced coverage of men like Peter Arnett [later a CNN correspondent] and Morris [sic] Safer, men who are not Americans and do not have the basic American interest at heart," he pledges to Johnson, "we will try to tighten things up." On the note, Johnson enthusiastically scrawled "Good!" followed by his first initial.[8]

"Bill Moyers's role in the affair has since made me feel slightly uneasy in his presence," Safer said in a telephone interview. When he later asked Moyers about the incident—twice—LBJ's former press secretary "laughed it off," explaining that he "was the good guy trying to play peacemaker." Safer said the Moyers version is "not quite true." And he believes that Moyers may have continued to smear him afterward, alleging ties to the KGB, charges attributed to others as "White House intelligence," which reached Secretary of State Dean Rusk and U.S. Ambassador to South Vietnam Graham Martin. The accusations that he was a Soviet agent continue to bother Safer because they involved his parents and family. He characterizes Moyers as "a gleeful retainer feeding the appetites of Lyndon Johnson . . . playing the role of Iago" to the President's tragically flawed Othello.[9]

The circumstances surrounding Moyers's departure from the Johnson administration are curiously marked by a similar bitterness and sense of betrayal. As LBJ biographer Merle Miller recalls, "Moyers was one of the few people Johnson was never reconciled with, who very much wanted to be reconciled." In many ways, Moyers had been like a son to Johnson: "None was quite so golden, quite so bright and willing, as Billy Don—and [Moyers's] resignation came as a great shock to [Johnson]."[10]

Like Johnson, Moyers had started life as an outsider. Billy Don Moyers was born June 5, 1934, to John Henry and Ruby Johnson Moyers in Hugo, Oklahoma, and grew up in the little town of Marshall, Texas—a place he would make famous on his PBS specials. Moyers first saw Lyndon Baines Johnson speak in 1948 in Marshall and was attracted to his powerful persona. "I couldn't really hear him," he later recalled. "I was in the back row. Fourteen years old. But I remember the sheer presence of the man. And I thought, 'That's what power is.' "[11]

He began college at North Texas State in Denton and graduated from the University of Texas, Austin, in 1956 with a degree in journalism. The young journalist won a Rotary International Fellowship to study at the University of Edinburgh in 1956–57 and then enrolled in the divinity program at Southwestern Baptist Theological Seminary in Fort Worth. After ordination in 1959, he did some circuit preaching.

Moyers first worked for Johnson as a summer employee of his radio and television stations while still a student at North Texas State in 1954, at the recommendation of Marshall *News Messenger* publisher Millard Cope, a friend of Lady Bird's (and employer of his brother James Moyers, a reporter on the paper). Johnson hired Billy Don as a full-time personal assistant for his senatorial office in 1959, taking him away from an offer to teach Christian ethics at Baylor University. Moyers hit it off with Johnson, rapidly rising to the job of executive assistant, directing LBJ's vice presidential campaign and acting as liaison with the Kennedy clan. He lived in Johnson's Washington basement while his wife, Judith, and their three children stayed in Texas.[12]

The Kennedys liked Moyers, too. His closeness to that family would later plant suspicions of disloyalty in the mind of Johnson as his presidency unraveled (after Moyers left LBJ's administration, he joined the board of trustees of the Kennedy Foundation).[13] In 1961 President Kennedy appointed Moyers associate and later deputy director of the Peace Corps, where he stayed until 1964, working closely with Peace

Corps director Sargent Shriver, the president's brother-in-law.[14] The Kennedys saw great promise in the young divinity graduate turned New Frontiersman who had "perhaps too much of the Bible in him." The Kennedys were confident "that would change."[15] They were right.

In November 1963 Kennedy aide Kenneth O'Donnell sent Moyers to Austin to do advance work for the President's trip to Texas and "mend political fences."[16] When Kennedy was shot, Moyers rushed to be with Johnson, chartering a plane to take him to Dallas. As LBJ waited in Air Force One to take the oath of office, Moyers passed him a note that said "I'm here if there's anything I can do." The answer came back, "There will be, just hang around." He did.[17]

David Halberstam points out that Lyndon Johnson, a believer in Texan machismo, divided the world into men and boys, and he categorized Moyers at that time as "a boy who was halfway to becoming a man, a writer who was moving into operational activities."[18] As Johnson's protégé, Moyers left his Peace Corps job to become a special assistant to the president and coordinate the Great Society task forces operating under Douglass Cater, Joseph Califano, Richard Goodwin, and Harry McPherson.[19] Yet his intimacy with Johnson did not spare him from the President's famous wrath. In 1964, LBJ was contemplating removing J. Edgar Hoover from the FBI and discussed it with Moyers. The White House aide immediately leaked the story to *Washington Post* editor Ben Bradlee, who printed it. In response, the furious President announced at a press conference that he was appointing Hoover permanently. Johnson then told Moyers, "Now call up your friend Ben Bradlee and tell him I said, 'F— you.'" Halberstam says that after this incident, Bradlee became known in the capital as "the man who got J. Edgar Hoover a lifetime appointment."[20] In fact, it was Moyers who had achieved that feat by leaking the story.

In his role as campaign adviser for Johnson in the 1964 presidential contest against Barry Goldwater, Moyers worked with New York advertising guru Tony Schwartz to put together the infamous "daisy" ad, which showed an idyllic scene of a little girl plucking a daisy, followed by an atomic blast and the exhortation that viewers vote for President Johnson, presumably to avoid a third world war. In his 1991 *New Republic* article about Moyers, Andrew Ferguson said this ad "was progenitor to the negative campaign spots that Moyers believes have 'trivialized' the conversation of democracy." Ferguson, who had been a speechwriter for President Bush, charged that in *The 30-Second President,* a Moyers documentary about political advertising, Moyers neglected to mention that he personally had pushed for the nuclear issue to be used in the campaign and approved the attack ad himself.

After the Johnson landslide that Moyers helped engineer, he was promoted to chief of staff in July 1965 and also named White House press secretary, making him among the most powerful presidential aides (he kept both titles until his departure in January 1967). Into his in-box flowed memos on everything from the Department of Health, Education, and Welfare to studies of religious voting patterns, birthday calls to President Truman, messages to a Polish-American convention, public opinion surveys, the disposition of Mrs. Johnson's personal motion pictures, mail protesting the President's showing his scar after gall bladder surgery in October 1965, nuclear nonproliferation, Vietnam, Appalachian legislation, and the Civil Rights Act of 1964.

One of the more interesting items Moyers handled was a memo dated November 25, 1963—three days after the Kennedy assassination—from Nicholas Katzenbach in the attorney general's office, which stressed the importance of convincing the American public that Oswald acted alone and not as a part of a Communist conspiracy (Oswald had Communist ties through the Fair Play for Cuba Committee and his years in the Soviet Union). The memo included the suggestion that the President establish a commission to investigate the assassination, the germ of the Warren Commission.[21] Clearly, Moyers was at the center of the Johnson administration.

Yet by the time Moyers left, he had already been marginalized and no longer had Johnson's trust. To some extent it may have been a generational conflict. Johnson did not like the counterculture. He resented "dissenters, discontents, long hairs, intellectual crazies, and domestic Communists all over the place, including the hoodlums in and around Lafayette Park who kept shouting, 'Hey, hey, LBJ, how many kids did you kill today?' "[22]

The 1960s lifestyle that disturbed LBJ had its attraction for Moyers, who was, after all, a young man. In May 1966, the Associated Press reported complaints from Iowa congressman H. R. Gross about a wild party attended by dignitaries from the Johnson administration. "I was amazed and shocked that they had a $75 to $100 per ticket dance at the Smithsonian with the Rev. [Bill] Moyers doing the watusi and frug and one woman sent home to get dressed because she was half naked."[23] The report of his antics, no doubt leaked to discredit him, was a symptom of a deeper split between Moyers and the White House—a split based on differences over Vietnam.

Moyers had become a secret dove and was working quietly to undermine Johnson's commitment to winning the war. One event that alienated the President was Moyers's clearance of a 1966 anti-Vietnam speech by Secretary of Defense Robert McNamara in Montreal without Johnson's knowledge or approval. "[It] would speed Moyers's own departure," David Halberstam noted. As well as McNamara's, who soon departed for a post at the World Bank. Not one to confront Johnson directly, Moyers had served as an interlocutor for George Ball, an Undersecretary of State who was a critic of the war. He passed Ball's critical memoranda to the President because Moyers "showed his own doubts on Vietnam largely by encouraging other doubters to speak and by trying to put doubters in touch with one another." Moyers was still too timid to lay himself on the line. Indeed, he tried to burrow further into the administration. When National Security Adviser McGeorge Bundy left LBJ in 1966 to join the Ford Foundation, Moyers offered himself as "a quiet candidate" for the post.[24] But he was passed over in favor of Walt Rostow, who had more enthusiasm for the Vietnam War and by now more of Johnson's trust as a house intellectual. Moyers had also been interested in an Undersecretary of State job when George Ball resigned, but Johnson chose Nicholas Katzenbach.[25]

As part of his exit strategy from a White House that no longer held a future, Moyers had found a useful surrogate father in Harry Guggenheim, owner of Long Island's daily tabloid *Newsday*. Moyers had written to Guggenheim after the publisher met with the President in 1965 to talk about Latin America, where Guggenheim owned mines. Moyers and Guggenheim exchanged numerous cordial notes.[26] "And thanks for those fine editorials," Moyers gushed in one handwritten message.[27] The elderly Guggenheim (seventy-five when he met Moyers) quickly took a shine to the young Johnson acolyte. Having disinherited his relatives in a series of nasty disputes, he was looking for an heir to run *Newsday*, which he had founded. Guggenheim admired Johnson and thought the President's press secretary would be quite a catch.

Unbeknownst to the Long Island newspaperman, Moyers's relationship with Johnson was already on the skids as the President came to believe Moyers was getting better press than the man he was supposed to be representing—another source of tension between them. Johnson also became fearful his press secretary was undermining him with the American public, and this deepened his distrust.

In 1966, a year after Guggenheim first raised the possibility of a job at *Newsday* for Moyers, the two had lunch at the exclusive Metropolitan Club in Washington, and Guggenheim made Moyers a firm offer. At first, Moyers declined. But then his brother, James (who had also joined the White House staff), committed suicide after being diagnosed with cancer. That event propelled Moyers out of Washington because, he later said, he needed more money to take care of his brother's family.[28]

John P. Roche, national chairman of Americans for Democratic Action in the 1960s and a special adviser to Johnson from 1966 to 1968, remembered how upset Johnson was with the way Moyers took his leave. On the day he announced his resignation to LBJ, Moyers had a very public lunch with New York senator Robert Kennedy at the fashionable Sans Souci restaurant. A news photographer was present, and the *Washington Star* ran a picture of the two of them on its front page. "Johnson just went up the wall," said Roche. "After that nothing would ever convince Johnson that Moyers really hadn't been on the Kennedy payroll for years and years."[29] Some Washington insiders, including columnist Drew Pearson, thought Kennedy had helped broker Moyers's job offer from Guggenheim.[30] Johnson and Moyers never mended their relationship. When he attempted to attend Johnson's memorial service in Washington on January 26, 1973, Moyers was hospitalized for chest pains and spent the time in Georgetown University Hospital's intensive care unit.[31]

But Guggenheim knew nothing of these strains. He treated Moyers like a prince, providing him with a rent-free house in Garden City, Long

Island, a five-year contract paying $75,000 a year (double what he had been making at the White House), and a company car. Moyers's first day as publisher of *Newsday* was February 15, 1967; Guggenheim organized a testimonial luncheon for nine hundred guests, including Senators Robert Kennedy and Jacob Javits, and Governor Nelson Rockefeller, two days later. "I've got a star," Guggenheim told a friend, delighted to be bringing the national spotlight to his otherwise low-profile operation. He wrote to Nobel Prize–winning author John Steinbeck, then working as a *Newsday* columnist, "Bill Moyers at long last is on the job, and is already everything I anticipated."[32] Like Johnson, Guggenheim was projecting his wish-fulfillment fantasy onto the eager and ingratiating young protégé. Like LBJ, Guggenheim would later regret that he had treated Moyers so royally.

In his new role of newspaperman, Moyers proclaimed that he was now above politics: "I don't believe a publisher should get involved in partisan politics," he told the *New York Times*.[33] However, the staff at *Newsday* began to resent the rumblings of Moyers's political ambitions that reached the newsroom. The *New York Daily News* reported that Moyers wanted to run for the Senate. Former New York governor Averell Harriman invited Moyers to his home and offered his support for a Senate run. So did Nassau County executive Eugene Nickerson. Secretary of Health, Education, and Welfare John Gardner tried to recruit Moyers to run the Urban Coalition (Moyers had Guggenheim write Gardner to decline, rubbing Guggenheim's nose in the fact that he was in demand). Robert Kennedy and Eugene McCarthy asked him to work on their presidential campaigns. Soon Guggenheim was annoyed. He resented Kennedy visiting Moyers. He didn't like the fact that Moyers flew alongside Kennedy to Martin Luther King's funeral.[34]

Once ensconced as publisher at *Newsday,* Moyers began to differ with Guggenheim over political coverage. Moyers was too liberal for Guggenheim, a Long Island Republican who supported Nixon. They disagreed over editorial endorsements for the 1968 election. The paper published a dissent from Moyers, with Guggenheim editorializing in Nixon's favor. Relations between surrogate father and son deteriorated rapidly.

On election night, Guggenheim became disturbed by the vocal disrespect he witnessed in the *Newsday* office when Nixon was declared the winner and by Moyers's failure to check it. Guggenheim sent a handwritten complaint to his publisher about the news operation: "The reaction of the people in my office last night confirms my worst suspicions. They were pathetically praying for the defeat of Richard Nixon and their deep-seated hostility toward him was obvious." Moyers wrote back defiantly, in a note that took the moral upper hand in a somewhat having-it-both-ways manner: "I did not notice the 'hostility' or 'dismay' in the group that watched the returns in your office. . . . If you want a paper that hews to any undeviating line on any President, I shouldn't be running it."[35]

Despite the rising tension between them, Guggenheim put Moyers down in his will for $100,000 plus 20 percent interest in his worldwide mining interests and in Guggenheim Brothers, the family investment firm on Wall Street. He may have overlooked Moyers's politics and management style because of his personal attentions to the ailing proprietor. Moyers had rushed to Guggenheim's estate when called in the middle of the night and arranged for him to be seen at the Mayo Clinic.[36] Moyers's increasingly active politics continued to worry Guggenheim, however, especially the way *Newsday* was changing. Moyers published a major series of corruption investigations targeting Republican politicians in local Suffolk County government. Guggenheim felt he had lost control of his own newspaper. One day he remarked to Sidney Gruson, a *New York Times* editor he had hired to help Moyers put out the paper, "Be careful of that city room—it's full of communists."[37] Gruson left *Newsday* shortly afterward to return to the *Times*.

Calling on his Washington connections, Moyers hired David Laventhol, editor of the *Washington Post* Style section, as his associate editor. Moyers himself replaced Guggenheim's handpicked editorial writer, Stan Hinden, who had penned pro-Nixon columns for the paper. "He charmed everybody out of their shoes, and later out of their jobs. What I resented about it was the way that he gave me the bad news by leaving a letter in my typewriter," said Hinden. Banished to the Washington bureau, Hinden stopped off to see Guggenheim on his way out of town to let him know what he really thought about Moyers. A distressed Guggenheim asked Hinden, "What is it that Moyers is trying to do?"[38]

On October 15, 1969, Moyers appeared at a Moratorium Day rally at Wall Street's Trinity Church to give a speech denouncing Nixon and the Vietnam War that echoed his comments in *Newsday*'s editorials. Guggenheim objected, repudiating the "left-wing city room," which had been "sucked into the deception perpetrated by the organizers of the moratorium." Guggenheim said *Newsday* had been wrong when it wrote that the protest was organized by young people. "They were merely dupes for known organizers, all of them not very young, who are trying to destroy our way of life on directions from outsiders." Moyers responded to Guggenheim's defense of the Republicans by running an exposé of Nassau County state senator Edward Speno's ownership of land in partnership with gambler Harry Soccoroso. Speno, a Republican, asked for a formal investigation by a state panel, accused Moyers of partisan motivation as a Democratic political operative, and issued a public statement "calling on Harry Guggenheim today to remove Bill Moyers as publisher of *Newsday*."[39]

Guggenheim soon stopped talking to Moyers altogether. He approached the Republican Chandler family of California, publishers of the *Los Angeles Times* and renowned anti-Communists, to offer them his paper out of respect for their conservative reputation at a bargain price of $31.6 million for his 51 percent of the stock. Guggenheim did not want to haggle and had only one condition for the sale: Moyers must go.

Learning of the deal from Guggenheim himself, Moyers scrambled to find another buyer in order to save his job and his political platform. He approached Chase Manhattan Bank, the *New York Times,* Time-Life, and even lawyer William Casey (later Reagan's CIA director). He leaked word of the Chandler deal to the *Newsday* newsroom. A story with the headline "Newsday Employees Seek to Block Sale of Paper" appeared the next day in the *New York Times*. The report (citing an anonymous source who stated Moyers's position in the dispute) said that the paper's staffers were hoping minority shareholders would help them maintain the paper's independence.[40] In April, Moyers left the country for Switzerland. Meanwhile, Guggenheim rushed through the negotiations to unload his property before Moyers returned. Moyers was not around on May 1 when the official announcement was made that the deal with the Chandlers had been closed. Guggenheim's final settlement with Moyers awarded him $300,000 and the right to continue living in his rent-free home. On May 8, Guggenheim took Moyers out of his will, transferring his share of the estate to a relative. Moyers announced his resignation on May 12. He recalls Guggenheim's parting words as, "I deeply admire the way that you and Judith are trying to bring up your children."[41]

Like President Johnson, Guggenheim felt used and betrayed by Moyers. But once again, Moyers had risen above and beyond his protector. In April 1969, Moyers had joined the board of the prestigious Rockefeller Foundation, an organization David Halberstam once characterized as the central committee of the Establishment.[42] In July, Moyers joined the board of directors of EDP Technology Inc., a data processing corporation with government contracts.[43] The outsider from Marshall, Texas, now had clout on Wall Street. (In 1980 Moyers produced *The World of David Rockefeller* for PBS, a glowing portrait of the billionaire.)

Cushioned by his settlement with Guggenheim ($300,000 was a very generous sum in 1970), Moyers moved on to his next frontier, the world of letters. Willie Morris, then editor of *Harper's,* commissioned a long article from him about the mood of the United States. The essay was published in book form in 1971 under the title *Listening to America: A Traveler Rediscovers His Country.* The year he took to write it, and the 13,000 miles he traveled, conveniently kept Moyers away from New York and *Newsday* for a decent interval. Interestingly, many of the supposedly ordinary Americans Moyers visited as he traveled around the country were Democratic Party operatives (some of them radical agitators). His interview subjects ranged from ward bosses in Texas who organized migrant laborers, to Yale students who supported the Black Panthers, to Anne Wexler—today a prominent Washington lobbyist—and her husband, Joseph Duffey—then a Democratic candidate for Senate, who became President Carter's chairman of the National Endowment for the Humanities and is today director of the Voice of America. The book was both a bestseller and a critical success. Moyers now had intellectual cachet in Manhattan.

But where would he go next? The answer was the West Side institution of public television. After public affairs program production had been stripped from NET in 1971 by the Corporation for Public Broadcasting and the Ford Foundation and transferred to National Public Affairs Center for Television (NPACT) in Washington, Robert Kotlowitz, a WNET vice president and former *Harper's* editor, invited Moyers to host *This Week*, his station's new pared-down public-affairs discussion program. The weekly show would allow Moyers to reassert himself in the public arena, providing a platform to replace *Newsday*. Despite telling the *New York Times* that he "did not know how long he would remain in television," he had found his permanent calling.[44] He was paid $75,000 a year by WNET, his salary at *Newsday*.

This Week had the signature elements of Moyers's work today: a focus on the moral dilemmas of the issues at the top of the liberal agenda and filmed location interviews. Like the subjects of Moyers's bestseller, the show's guests were eclectic and political: the first set of programs included one about Cesar Chávez's attempt to recruit organizers for his farmworkers' union and another that spotlighted *New York Times* columnist Russell Baker and *Washington Post* humorist Art Buchwald.

In 1972 Moyers, saying he felt uncomfortable with the standard television format, suggested a more personal approach to interviewing and a new name for his show: his name. So the next year, *Bill Moyers' Journal* made its debut. The season featured Washington columnist Joseph Alsop, historian Barbara Tuchman, foreign policy expert George F. Kennan, World War II hero and Kennedy adviser General Maxwell Taylor, author Lewis Mumford, and historian Samuel Eliot Morison.

To complement this parade of famous names, Moyers produced theme shows. One, "Civil Rights—Today," featured Julian Bond, who had worked with Martin Luther King; Stokely Carmichael, a black nationalist who later changed his name to Kwame Toure and became an anti-Semitic speaker on college campuses; and Charlayne Hunter-Gault, the first black woman admitted to the University of Georgia (and since 1983, coanchor of the *MacNeil/Lehrer NewsHour*). Another theme show was headlined "Dorothy Day: Still a Rebel." Day was a Socialist who had founded the *Catholic Worker* as a radical newspaper and missionary movement of the Catholic church. She was the darling of the antiwar set.

When Robert MacNeil refused to anchor the 1972 Republican convention for PBS, Moyers stepped into the breach and hosted the gavel-to-gavel coverage. But Moyers soon found himself under scrutiny from the Nixon-appointed board of the Corporation for Public Broadcasting because of his ties to the Democrats. The *New York Times* called *Bill Moyers' Journal* "a prime candidate for cancellation." Indeed, the CPB stopped funding Moyers shortly after the *Times* story was published.

At the time, Moyers had told the *Times* he would not mind a cutoff of federal funds, declaring that "the Government should not be funding news and public affairs if that would mean Government interference with content." Moyers added that Lyndon Johnson had used an old Texas proverb to explain things: "He who hands out the dough slices the bread." Moyers felt "news and public affairs should be funded by contributions directly from the public and other sources."[45] But Moyers was not off the air for long.

While his television programs featured farmworkers and Catholic Socialists, in private life Moyers was not reluctant to avail himself of capitalist opportunities featured on Louis Rukeyser's *Wall Street Week*. In March 1973 Moyers joined the Wall Street brokerage firm of Mitchell, Hutchins & Company as a director. The firm was instrumental in backing Data Resources Inc., an econometrics firm headed by former Johnson administration officials in which, according to a 1975 *New York Times* account, Moyers at that point owned some 6,250 shares valued at $16 a share.[46]

Seeing that the Watergate hearings had weakened Nixon's attempts to control public broadcasting, in June 1973 the Ford Foundation announced it would make up funding for Moyers's weekly broadcast that the CPB had eliminated. MacNeil and Lehrer had done the heavy lifting by covering the Watergate hearings night and day (see chapter 4), and now Moyers delivered the coup de grâce to the collapsing presidency of Richard Nixon.

Moyers's "Essay on Watergate" was a scathing indictment of the Nixon administration for the October 31, 1973, season premiere of his suddenly revived series. James Day, then head of NET, recalled the return of *Bill Moyers' Journal* with satisfaction, saying the program was "the best that he has ever done." Moyers spoke for all of public broadcasting as he cheered Nixon's downfall (just as his *Newsday* newsroom had jeered Nixon's election). Of the President's failed attempts to cling to office,

Moyers opined: "It was close. It almost worked. But not quite. Something basic in our traditions held . . . believing what is best about this country doesn't need exaggeration. It needs vigilance."[47] Moyers called Watergate "the worst scandal in our history" because while others were about "money or sex," Watergate was "a way to tunnel under and around the protocol of law." Moyers made no mention of his own work as go-between for LBJ and the FBI (or, for that matter, his attempted smear campaign against Morley Safer).

Once Nixon had resigned, Moyers appeared to be searching for new venues. He announced that his programs would henceforth concern themselves with foreign affairs and that he had received pledges from the German Marshall Fund (essentially a public relations operation of the German government) and IBM as well as CPB for a new series called *Bill Moyers' Foreign Report*. But it never took off. Instead, what seems to have followed is Moyers's quest for an outlet on one of the commercial networks. He had helped bring down Nixon, and now it was time to cash in.

Although before Nixon's resignation Moyers said he had twice turned down an offer to cohost NBC's *Today Show* in order to stay at PBS because "it is much more fun to build an institution than to go with a settled one," in May 1974 Moyers declared that he would cancel his PBS show and move to Aspen, Colorado. There he would vacation and teach at the Aspen Institute, a liberal think tank funded by Arco. Moyers's title was to be Arthur Morse Fellow; Morse had been a longtime producer on CBS *Reports* with Edward R. Murrow. Murrow had helped bring down Joseph McCarthy, and Moyers had helped bring down Richard Nixon. The symmetry between the two men's careers did not go unnoticed at CBS.

Moyers's show was replaced on the PBS schedule by *American Chronicle,* a hodgepodge featuring *Newsweek's* liberal columnist Shana Alexander, Chicago radio personality Studs Terkel, author and civil rights activist Maya Angelou, and token conservative George Will.

In September 1974, *Newsweek* proclaimed that Moyers would take over Stewart Alsop's regular column, but his print career was short-lived. In October 1974, Moyers was back once again on PBS, hosting WNET's *Behind the Lines*, a series giving "the story behind the story." Finally, in

1975 *Bill Moyers' Journal* returned to PBS. Apparently, Moyers was angling for some sort of better financial package, and the various announcements to the press were a method of conducting negotiations. In 1976, it finally became clear what Moyers was up to. He was going to CBS News. Moyers had acquired another patron in William Paley, founder and chairman of the network, who had also been Murrow's patron. After seeing his "Essay on Watergate" and other PBS programs, Paley had personally made the decision to hire Moyers (who had been preparing a weekly PBS series called *Front and Center,* which he was to cohost with George Will).

Moyers's toehold at CBS was, to be sure, a little tenuous. On April 27, 1976, the network affirmed Bill Moyers would become the new host of *CBS Reports*. He replaced Dan Rather, who was moved to *60 Minutes* at producer Don Hewitt's invitation (when Harry Reasoner left for ABC News). Mike Wallace had persuaded Rather that he would be a fool to stay at *CBS Reports,* whose obsolescent hour-long documentary format was plagued by low ratings now that the magazine format predominated. "If you were a KGB agent looking for a place to hide you couldn't find a better place than *CBS Reports,*" Wallace told Rather. "Dan, Dan, Dan! Even Ed Murrow couldn't make *CBS Reports* fly. Come on. Don't be an idiot."[48]

But Paley liked the idea of Moyers in the old Murrow slot. He thought Moyers was "classy." Like Harry Guggenheim, Paley was generous to him and ordered his employees to give Moyers whatever he asked for. Paley's enthusiasm for Moyers, David Halberstam wrote, was such that he thought Moyers was "what network television executives dream about, someone so smart, so intuitive, and yet so subtle that he could deal with the most explosive of subjects in a strong and intelligent way without tearing the house apart."[49] CBS was so committed to hiring Moyers that the company agreed to his demand for a unique exception to its famously strict guidelines on conflict of interest for its journalists. As a condition of taking the job, Moyers had insisted on keeping his seat on the board of the Rockefeller Foundation, despite the foundation's activities in international development, population control, environmental programs, and domestic affairs. He got CBS News to ignore this clear conflict of interest and thus retained his seat on the Central Committee of the Establishment. Once again, however, as at the White House and *Newsday,* his farewell would be less cordial than his welcome.

Moyers worked as an analyst for CBS News during the 1976 presidential campaign. At CBS *Reports* he was paired with producer Howard Stringer. Among their films was "The Fire Next Door," a critically praised examination of the burned-out buildings of the South Bronx—many of them torched for insurance money.[50] Neoconservative Ernest Lefever complained about Moyers's 1978 broadcast titled "The Battle for South Africa," saying it was "one-sided and simplistic."[51] But Moyers's 1977 two-hour documentary "The CIA's Secret Army" was among his most explosive. It documented the training and supply of Cuban émigrés in Florida. At CBS it was esteemed as second only to "The Selling of the Pentagon" (a 1971 film that criticized military junkets). Whether Moyers became too hot to handle after CIA criticism, as some have suggested, or whether he merely "was having trouble adjusting to the rigid policies of a huge commercial network," he did not last long in his first tour of duty at CBS. In January 1978 he told CBS News president Richard Salant he would leave the network unless he got a regularly scheduled time slot. But the top brass was more excited by *60 Minutes* than CBS *Reports,* and Moyers lost out to producer Don Hewitt for the affection of network management, who didn't care whether Bill Moyers remained at CBS or not.[52] Paley's ardor had clearly cooled.

So in 1979, *Bill Moyers' Journal* returned to PBS. Moyers did not mention any disputes with management as reason for his departure from CBS, stating that scheduling had been the problem—the same cover story Fred Friendly had used when he left CBS in 1966 in his bitter fight with Paley over coverage of the Vietnam War. Moyers merely told the press he had not had "the satisfaction or the impact I want from television through irregularly scheduled broadcasts, no matter how good they might be."[53] However, Moyers must have been eager to return to CBS even on an episodic basis. He reappeared in 1980 as an election news analyst because, according to CBS News president William Leonard, "he has one of the keenest political minds in America and has the ability to analyze complicated political issues in clear and incisive language." In September 1980 Moyers moderated the first presidential campaign debate of the season between John Anderson and Ronald Reagan (President Carter had refused to participate).

Although Moyers could not express his own opinions as a moderator on CBS, that very same week PBS aired "God and Politics," his attack on evangelical Christian supporters of President Reagan. It was his most serious political program since "An Essay on Watergate." Moyers mocked candidate Reagan's pronouncement to his Christian fans: "You may not endorse me, but I endorse you." Moyers then took what many regard as a cheap shot at the faith of Southern Baptist Convention president Bailey Smith, who testified to his belief in Jesus Christ with the statement: "God Almighty does not hear the prayer of a Jew, for how in the world can God hear the prayer of a man who says Jesus Christ is not the true Messiah? It's blasphemous." Moyers did not emphasize the fact that President Carter had been elected on the strength of his own Southern Baptist background. Others quickly picked up Moyers's coded attempt to play up public fears of theocracy. Anthony Lewis, the influential *New York Times* columnist, chimed in with the liberal perspective. He warned of "the terrible danger of intolerance" posed by "political religion." Lewis repeated Moyers's commentary in his documentary: "Our democracy cannot agree to a 'moral majority' that makes sectarian doctrine the test of political opinion. You may have that only where all are alike in thought and root and intent, which America is not." Moyers had preached a good sermon. He put forward the liberal party line to respond to the defection of Christians from Carter, and the media congregation responded.

Despite the failure of *Bill Moyers' Foreign Report* to materialize, Moyers never did give up his interest in foreign affairs, which dated from his service to LBJ. The jobs Moyers had coveted but failed to obtain in the Johnson administration were the foreign policy positions of National Security Adviser and Undersecretary of State. And in questions of foreign affairs, from his opposition to the war in Vietnam onward, Moyers has attempted to declare foreign conflicts the result of misunderstandings, not substantive disagreements. This approach, the product of both deeply religious impulses and a conventionally liberal political outlook, has resulted in his maintaining a number of curiously naive positions masquerading as sophisticated interpretations of international developments. When Moyers dealt with foreign affairs, he revealed he was out of his depth.

In 1980, a Moyers program on the Iranian hostage crisis tried not to take sides. Moyers reprised the "moral equivalence" argument often used by liberals to characterize both sides of the Cold War and here applied it to the Iranian students and their American hostages. In his commentary Moyers declaimed that "this may be the final lesson of Iran. Captives and captors alike were victims in this long ordeal between our two countries: victims of cultural illiteracy, of ways of seeing that *stare* across gaps of culture, language, history, and perception, and *staring,* do not connect with the other reality on the other side. It is the oldest lament of all, and the most likely to persist and to bring us to grief—that mankind has not the gift to see ourselves as others see us, or others as they are." This undermined President Carter's position, which initially had been to rally the country in support of the hostages, as well as conflicting with Reagan's call for a restoration of old-fashioned national pride.

Moyers went beyond simple moral equivalence on at least one occasion to argue that America was worse than the Soviet Union and to defend a double standard. Early in the Reagan years, Moyers hosted a televised debate for PBS on what he called the "New Cold War" and invited Georgi Arbatov, an Americanist member of the Central Committee of the Communist Party, to participate as an in-studio guest. There was a production hitch, however: Secretary of State Alexander Haig had withdrawn Arbatov's visa. His reasoning was that since the Soviets would not allow Americans to debate on Russian TV, he would not permit Arbatov to stay for the Moyers debate. Moyers denounced Haig for interfering with his show: "It's why one hates to see General Haig and his lieutenants infect every transaction between the two countries—journalistic, cultural, educational, scientific—with the fever of cold war. That happened in the fifties and left a poison in our lives which lingers to this day. No Russian *anywhere* can say *anything* to damage this republic as much as we injure ourselves when we forget *who* we are, and *why.*"

Shortly after his attack on Haig, Moyers again left PBS, giving a bottom-line explanation for his departure for greener pastures. "I've carried the *Journal* about as far I can with the existing resources. I simply felt there were more opportunities at CBS," he said.[54] Indeed there were.

It was quite clear that a Republican administration would not long tolerate taxpayer-subsidized television attacks from a partisan Democrat. President Reagan had slashed the public broadcasting budget and was arguing for its elimination when he took office. Moyers was an embarrassment to the system and a potential liability in budget negotiations. But at CBS, Moyers joined the "millionaires' club," a select group of talent making at least $1 million a year, which included Walter Cronkite, Dan Rather, Mike Wallace, and Don Hewitt.

What is so interesting about Moyers's checkered career with CBS is that although he refused to do lighter stories there in the name of journalistic integrity, when he eventually owned his own production company at PBS he ended up promoting pop psychology, spiritualism, and faith healing—a far more tabloidesque record than that compiled by *60 Minutes* in the same period.

Moyers was, perhaps unknowingly, in the wrong place at the wrong time to conduct Murrow-style exposés. CBS had changed. During his second tour of duty, the network was in the throes of defending itself against a libel suit brought by General William Westmoreland over a *CBS Reports* documentary called "The Uncounted Enemy: A Vietnam Deception." Leery of more legal hassles, and with Moyers already perceived as a controversialist, the network felt it could not afford to give him the freedom and time slots he wanted.

Even his nightly commentaries in Eric Sevareid's old slot as the conscience of the network and the nation were provoking negative reactions. Almost immediately Moyers began to make waves, which rocked the office of Ed Joyce, CBS News's executive vice president. Affiliate stations had started to complain. Some didn't like the change in style. Instead of restricting himself to spoken commentary, Moyers was going out into the field and filming segments on topics such as the misdeeds of political action committees. Others objected to Moyers's past as LBJ's press secretary. "How could he be fair to Republicans?" they asked Joyce. Finally, he offended the Reagan administration, and word got back to Joyce through the affiliates that Moyers was going too far, in one case exaggerating the impact of Reagan's budget cuts on American families. Joyce called in producer Howard Stringer, an Oxford-educated Briton who had worked with Moyers on *CBS Reports* and was now in charge of the nightly news broadcast, and who Joyce felt had "the ability to bring out the best in Moyers."

Joyce strongly defended Moyers, believing that "any commentator worth listening to inevitably generated protests." He would stand up for Moyers against critical affiliates and in conferences with Van Gordon Sauter, then president of CBS News, whom Moyers found difficult to talk to. Joyce liked Moyers because "Bill gave the broadcast an intellectual edge." He thought Moyers's commentaries "may have been tough [on Reagan], but they were not unfair." Sauter took the criticism of Moyers's bias more seriously than Joyce did, however, and Howard Stringer once told Joyce, "Van is so outspoken about being a right-winger in a sea of liberals I think Bill would stop listening and just get bloody-minded." Moyers was already known to disapprove of Sauter's attempts to jazz up CBS News's previously staid image, and Joyce had tried to keep Sauter and Moyers apart ever since his talk with Stringer about the tension between them.

In 1982, protests against Moyers surfaced at the CBS affiliates' meeting in Palm Springs, California. One station owner told Joyce, "A lot of our viewers think Bill Moyers is trying to stop the President from reducing the budget," and approving murmurs filled the meeting room. That year, in addition to his nightly commentaries, Moyers had presented "People Like Us," an hour-long profile dramatizing how Reagan's cuts in federal spending adversely affected ordinary Americans. Joyce fielded the inevitable request from the station owners about their new star: "I think a lot of us here would like to know what can be done to make sure he's fairer in his reports." In response to this question, CBS News president Sauter (himself critical in private) defended Moyers to the crowd, declaring "Bill Moyers is a man of integrity." He then added that CBS News had added a review process for Moyers's commentaries to ensure that they would "be fair and balanced." Joyce said the affiliates came away happy.[55]

But at the next affiliates' meeting there were again complaints against Moyers. This time he had been invited to make a speech. In it he promised to be fair and said he tried his hardest, but that "even with the best of intentions he knew there were times when he would fail." Apparently his words soothed the angry crowd, with the skill of "the

Baptist preacher he had once been." Ed Joyce recalled the occasion as one in which the station owners "were getting a firsthand glimpse of the best side of Moyers, a man who understands the power television gives to a handful of people and feels the burden of that responsibility." But Moyers left before dinner, declining to break bread with the distrustful station owners—because of a scheduling conflict, he said.

In December 1982 Moyers met with Sauter and Joyce to plan a new series of documentaries for 1983. He told them he wanted to revive *Bill Moyers' Journal*. No, they said. The network wanted Moyers to share a weekly hour with Charles Kuralt as coanchors of a magazine show. But Kuralt declined to cohost with Moyers. Instead, CBS assigned producer Andrew Lack (now president of NBC News) to Moyers and gave him a half-hour documentary series called *Our Times with Bill Moyers*. The other half-hour was given to Kuralt for *On the Road*.

When Moyers presented his schedule to Sauter, the CBS News chief got a sinking feeling. Instead of riveting human-interest stories or interviews with celebrities (precisely what Moyers would produce later on PBS), the first set of programs was to be unrelenting political criticism seemingly designed to embarrass the Reagan administration. One show was about the collapse of Gadsden, Alabama, a once prosperous rubber and steel town, now in decline. Moyers interviewed residents who declared "the American dream is floating out the window." Another show, titled "Toxic," detailed the involvement of organized crime in the waste disposal industry. Yet another segment, "The Pentagon Underground," attacked military procurement. It featured a woman who "unofficially monitors the effectiveness of defense spending and then leaks her findings to the press." She complained that the M-1 tank needed five gallons for each mile (a fact that must certainly have been more shocking before one saw how well the M-1 performed during Operation Desert Storm). Still another segment, titled "AIDS," visited a shooting gallery where infected addicts were to be found. A grim and glum America was Moyers's vision of the country under a Republican administration.

There was only one show that tickled Sauter's imagination, a look at the high divorce rate in California's Silicon Valley. "That story should go in the first broadcast," Sauter declared. Moyers disagreed. He had decided that his series would open with a program documenting moral problems faced by the atomic workers who live in Los Alamos, New Mexico. Sauter dug in his heels. "Let me play the whore," he told Moyers, advising him to include some lighter fare to "strike some spark of general interest." On hearing Sauter say "Let me play the whore" a second time, Moyers grew silent and stared at the floor. Moyers later told Joyce, "I never thought the day would come when I would hear a president of CBS News say, 'Let me play the whore.'"

Sauter recalled that he had meant the meeting with Moyers as a pep talk. "CBS News was urging him to undertake a series of prime-time broadcasts. He was, as ever, ambivalent, inclined ultimately to convince himself that a cabal of network executives, advertisers, and affiliates would scuttle his journalism. I disagreed and suggested to Bill that he list the most aggressive stories on his wish list and I would prove that his stories would transcend even the most crass and compromised standards." Sauter intended to do whatever he could to see to it that Moyers's programs "would get on the air and find an audience." Instead, after the session, Sauter found that Moyers lashed out at him. "He had taken an isolated moment of role playing, the purpose of which was to expand his work and audience, and turned it into a symbol of conspiratorial corruption and wickedness."[56]

When the first installment of *Our Times* eventually aired, Moyers had added to his lineup a film of Arthur Miller's visit to China to stage *Death of a Salesman.* Sauter declared it "dreadful," Joyce recalled.[57] *Our Times* was not renewed after its first ten weeks.

CBS News replaced it with *American Parade,* which Moyers and Kuralt were to coanchor in a magazine format much like *60 Minutes.* They would be joined by Diane Sawyer, Bill Kurtis, and Andrew Lack in his debut as correspondent. Again, Sauter and Moyers crossed swords when Moyers wanted to do his first piece on the Brazilian banking crisis. Sauter responded, "We need the kinds of names *People* magazine would put on their cover." Shortly afterward, Moyers came to Joyce's office and read him a letter of resignation. "*American Parade* is not my kind of journalism. I don't believe in it and I can't do it. It's that simple." Moyers said he was offended by the "entertainment ethos" he was confronting— meaning Van Gordon Sauter. Moyers objected to the celebrity lineup of

Woody Allen, Michael Jackson, and star photographer Annie Leibovitz scheduled for the program. At Joyce's urging, Howard Stringer persuaded Moyers to remain at the network as commentator on the CBS Evening New through the 1984 elections. And, Joyce noted with some satisfaction, *American Parade* was "a disaster."[58]

Moyers's final CBS series, *Crossroads,* was a compromise. He cohosted with Charles Kuralt, as the network had originally wanted. It was produced by Andrew Lack, Moyers's producer. The lineup featured segments on the terrorist bombing of the Marine barracks in Lebanon, problems with the Reagan administration's "Star Wars" program, and an investigation of the "covert war" in Nicaragua.[59] *Crossroads* was abandoned after one season, replaced by Lack's *West 57th,* a glitzier magazine show without Moyers (which also failed).

And Moyers once more was a commentator for CBS's election coverage in 1984. When the network refused to air Reagan's convention film, Moyers gave an on-air critique of the proceedings with Bill Plante and Dan Rather. (NBC showed Reagan's film and its ratings went up while CBS ratings dipped during the discussion.) *USA Today* blasted CBS for treating Reagan's piece like "pornography."[60]

Finally, Moyers found a series that did give his talents a suitable venue. In 1984, he hosted *A Walk Through the 20th Century with Bill Moyers.* Originally produced for the now-defunct CBS Cable, the nineteen-part history program was finally made available for airing on PBS. It was compelling television, expertly produced, although occasionally the Moyers bias was discernible. One episode, "The Arming of the Earth," dealt with the history of warfare. In the words of *New York Times* critic John Corry, it was "making the case for disarmament"—a swords-into-plowshares sermon from the Reverend Bill Moyers.

In 1985 Moyers used his commentary slots on the *CBS Evening News with Dan Rather* to host a six-part miniseries on African politics and its effect on hunger in the Sudan and Ethiopia. He also did a historic *CBS Reports,* produced by CBS veteran Perry Wolff (who had produced the legendary *Air Power* for Walter Cronkite), on the debate over immigration, which was well received. And he left the network on a high note. Moyers's documentary "The Vanishing Family: Crisis in Black America," also produced by Wolff and shown in 1986 on *CBS Reports,* was among his best. In the film, Moyers detailed the destructive effects of the welfare cycle on a group of black unwed mothers in Newark. This was perhaps Moyers's most memorable CBS production, setting off a glacial shift in public opinion about welfare that has continued to this day. Reacting to the message of the program, which could have come across as racist in less sensitive hands, reviewer John Corry called the choice of Moyers to host "prudent." He pointed out that Moyers, as a certified liberal, had credibility on the issue that conservatives did not. "George Will reporting the story, for example, would be discredited in advance," Corry wrote. The partnership with Wolff really did bring out the best in Moyers, as did his decision—finally—to abandon the liberal party line.

There is some evidence that the repudiation of the welfare state had not been Moyers's intended message when he recorded the broadcast. Perhaps it was more Wolff than Moyers. Once more, *New York Times* correspondent Anthony Lewis played interpreter to Moyers, spelling out the message of the film in print (as he had done in the case of Moyers's slashing attack on the Southern Baptists): The Reagan administration, not the welfare state, was to blame for the plight of the black family. Lewis argued that what Moyers had done was to draw attention to "Reagan's message: We don't care." The conclusion Moyers wanted the audience to reach, according to Lewis, was that "Attorney-General [Edwin] Meese is fighting to destroy the modest, long-existing effort to bring excluded blacks into the economic mainstream."

Thus the target had not been welfare after all, it had been Reagan. No one need worry. Moyers had not left the reservation. Moyers, expert in his use of public relations, had again achieved an echo chamber effect, his message reverberating through the media to shake the Republican administration. As he had done with his "Essay on Watergate" and "God and Politics," Moyers had planted a story in the mainstream media through his television program, and now it was beginning to flower.

But this flower was not the same one Moyers thought he had planted. Reagan was not Nixon, and his Teflon coating remained unscratched. The public did not blame Reagan for the plight of the black family—it blamed Bill Moyers's own Great Society programs, which set the stage for acceptance of social science theories such as Charles Murray's *Losing Ground*.

In September 1986, Loew's Corporation chairman Laurence Tisch (whose brother Preston Tisch was Postmaster General in the Reagan administration) and retired CBS chairman William Paley forced corporate executive Thomas Wyman from his job as CBS president—after a stock-buying campaign called Fairness in Media led by Senator Jesse Helms to fight the network's liberal bias and "become Dan Rather's boss" had put CBS stock into play and attracted the interest of Ted Turner (at that time considered a conservative Southerner). Moyers briefly returned to PBS in 1986, reestablishing his ties with WNET by recording a three-part series of panel discussions on Jewish identity as wraparound segments for Abba Eban's series *Heritage: Civilization and the Jews,* perhaps to ingratiate himself with the increasingly high-profile Tisch, an active supporter of Israel. It was not enough.

The anti-Reagan bias Moyers had come to represent had caused a major upheaval for CBS. With Tisch and Paley consolidating control, Moyers resigned from CBS News. He had repeated, in a more subtle variation, the scenario he had played out with Harry Guggenheim. Paley, who had adored Moyers to begin with, was now attempting to regain control of his enterprise, in part because of the political tendencies Moyers represented. Once more, Moyers had to go. In January 1987, Tisch became CBS president.

After his departure, Moyers formed his own privately held production company, Public Affairs Television Inc., and raised some $10 million through WNET from General Motors, Chevron, the John D. and Catherine T. MacArthur Foundation, PBS, and the Corporation for Public Broadcasting. His producer, Joan Konner, was named president of his company (today she is dean of the Columbia University School of Journalism). Moyers, used to being a prima donna at CBS for whom Paley had bent the rules on conflict of interest, was not prepared when this effort to expand with a commercially sponsored business venture was repulsed by PBS. He had wanted a piece of *The MacNeil/Lehrer NewsHour.* Literally. Three minutes. The concept, called "News Minutes," was intended to celebrate the bicentennial of the Constitution, with segments reporting the development of the document scheduled at the end of each broadcast in a "You Are There" approach. The logical outcome would be a permanent niche for Moyers after the constitutional celebration had faded away.

However, MacNeil/Lehrer Productions balked at someone else selling time on their program—even three minutes—for content independent of their editorial control. Moyers had insisted on the slot because that is what his underwriter General Motors wanted, he told the *New York Times.* When their preferred time slot turned out to be unavailable, General Motors withdrew its support for the project. And *MacNeil/Lehrer* had found Roger Rosenblatt, an editor of the *New Republic* who wrote essays for *Time* magazine and had taught at Harvard, and made him a regular essayist to forestall any future attempts by Moyers to get onto the broadcast. Later they would add other commentators, but they never did permit Bill Moyers to deliver an on-air commentary on the *The MacNeil/Lehrer NewsHour.*

Moyers's producer, Al Perlmutter, finally found another sponsor, the brokerage firm of Paine Webber, which agreed to air the program on its own as *Moyers: A Report from Philadelphia,* in other time slots.

By the time the show aired, Moyers had produced a ten-hour marathon called *Moyers: In Search of the Constitution.* Among those he interviewed were conservative American historian Forrest McDonald; Supreme Court Justices Harry Blackmun, William Brennan, and Sandra Day O'Connor; and a number of professors, including liberal legal theorist Ronald Dworkin, who attacked Attorney General Ed Meese's position regarding "original intent." Moyers was using a program of historical interest about the Constitution as a venue for attacks on the Reagan administration's claims of constitutional justification for its policies.

Moyers had more in store. In 1987 he once more attacked the Southern Baptists, in a one-hour documentary titled *Moyers: God and Politics.* Warning about an "alliance between Baptist conservatives and Republican conservatives in the White House," he seemed shocked anew, although he had reported the same story six years earlier.

To raise the stakes against the administration even higher, in 1988 Moyers hosted *Facing Evil,* which featured black poet Maya Angelou talking about how she suffered from racism and historians Raul Hilberg and Philip Hallie discussing the Nazis' mass murder campaigns during World War II. Curiously missing from the list of evil were horrors from the Communist world. The unspoken message: Reagan had been wrong to call Russia the "evil empire"—racism, particularly American racism, was the evil Reagan should have been facing. Truly facing evil would have required Moyers to criticize Black Panthers as well as Southern racists; Stalin, Mao, and Cambodia's Pol Pot as well as Hitler.

Moyers's first blockbuster financial success, a series whose spin-off books, videos, and related merchandise were worth millions, arrived in 1988. The show was *Joseph Campbell and the Power of Myth,* a six-part series that aired Monday evenings at 10 (a prime Nielsen "households using television" time), starting May 23. Campbell, a professor at Sarah Lawrence College, had made the study of comparative mythology his life's work. His book *The Hero with a Thousand Faces* is said to have influenced George Lucas's *Star Wars.*

But while *The Power of Myth* was popular with both critics and the public, it and a series Moyers did on the Arab world three years later elicited some complaints that Moyers had turned an amazingly blind eye to Campbell's anti-Semitism and to some darker sides of the Arab position.

The Arab World, a five-part PBS series hosted by Moyers in spring 1991 sparked charges that Moyers had not confronted his guests with the uglier aspects of Arab attitudes toward Israel. Letters arrived at PBS stations pointing out that while Moyers had not shown any anti-Israel bias in the past, in this series he had—in four out of the five episodes—failed to quote from one of the most basic documents in the Middle Eastern conflict: the charter of the Palestinian Liberation Organization, which called for "the destruction of the Jewish state," "expulsion of all Jews," and if the Jews would not leave, the threat to "kill them." (Only in the last segment did Moyers interview Arab scholar Charles Issawi, who spoke of problems in the Arab world.) Those who complained saw Moyers's deference to his interview subjects and accommodation of anti-Israel propaganda as troubling.

One of his interview subjects was Edward Said, the provocative Palestinian professor of English at Columbia University and author of *Orientalism,* a well-known book about Western perceptions of the Arabs. Moyers failed to note that Said was also at the time a member of the Palestinian National Council active on behalf of the PLO. During his interview, Moyers left unchallenged Said's charge that Israel was the cause of militant Arab nationalism. (In fact, Arab nationalism predates the creation of the State of Israel and was encouraged by the British as a means of dismantling the Ottoman empire and securing access to Arabian oil; Arab nationalism is one of the factors accounting for Arab hostility to the creation of Israel in 1948 by the United Nations.)

When Moyers interviewed former senator James Abourezk, an Arab-American activist, he chose not to contest the senator's claim that Israel's record in the Middle East resembled that of Iraq as one of territorial conquest and annexation. Moyers did not point out that in the past Abourezk had said the Jewish state had been the aggressor in 1948, when the Arabs vowed to drive the Jews into the sea. And Moyers never mentioned that Abourezk had on past occasions compared Israel to Nazi Germany, nor that the former senator had opposed the Camp David peace accords.

One protesting letter writer concluded with the observation that he was disappointed Moyers did nothing to defend Israel against a torrent of false charges. He had expected more from someone who represented moral conscience to the television audience; he was disillusioned that someone "who had registered his disgust at attempts to foster hatred and thereby justify genocide at earlier times [in *Facing Evil* and *A Walk Through the 20th Century*] was silent as the same tactics were rolled out again! As lie after lie was spoken, I felt certain: 'He'll call them on that one.' Silence. More lies . . . more silence."[61]

The charges against *The Power of Myth* came to light in a September 28, 1989, article in the *New York Review of Books*, in which longtime *New Yorker* architecture critic and essayist Brendan Gill accused Campbell of having been an unapologetic anti-Semite. Gill said he had personal knowledge of this fact because of conversations they'd had at the club they both belonged to. By implication, Moyers had covered up this dark side to Campbell's character. The news rocked the worlds of education and journalism. It was ironic that Moyers, who in television programs designed to tar Ronald Reagan had insinuated that Southern Baptist supporters of Israel were anti-Semitic, had unquestioningly given a national platform to an accused anti-Semite, even if unknowingly. Certainly, a man who had come to be called television's conscience should have known better. To prevent further erosion of his image, Moyers agreed to debate Gill on the issue.

One month later, New York's WNET broadcast a heated debate over the question of Campbell's anti-Semitism between Moyers and Gill. The television program, far from settling the matter, was so incendiary that it occasioned an analysis by Richard Bernstein, a cultural reporter for the *New York Times* assigned to sort out complicated and important cultural issues, especially those dealing with Jewish history and accusations of anti-Semitism.

What were the charges against Campbell? According to Gill, when American astronauts landed on the moon Campbell "made the repellent jest" that "the moon would be a good place to put the Jews." Carol Wallace Orr, a professor at Sarah Lawrence College who had worked with Campbell, charged that he was a racist as well. "In addition to anti-Semitism, I remember in particular his vexation over blacks being admitted to Sarah Lawrence," she told the *Times*. And Roy Finch, another professor at Sarah Lawrence, characterized Campbell as more than a mere social anti-Semite. He was, Finch charged, a "cryptofascist." Campbell had become interested in heroic myths as a way of countering the "decadence" of civilizations based on the Old and New Testaments. Finch pointed out that Campbell was an admirer of Nietzsche, Spengler, and Pound, all of whom were fascist favorites. And, indeed, National Socialist mythology as propounded by Goebbels was self-consciously designed to allude to the Nordic myths and Eastern legends Campbell recounted with equanimity. The symbol of the swastika had been taken from Hinduism.

Although some scholars sprang to Campbell's defense in the letters page of the *New York Review* and elsewhere, Bernstein concluded that "underlying the feelings of Mr. Gill and other Campbell critics is the notion that a rather vague, imprecise and largely unexamined philosophy has, through the power of television, gained a wide following." As Finch told Bernstein, "If Bill Moyers, who is an otherwise intelligent person, just sits there awestruck and gives the impression that what we're listening to is of great spiritual significance . . . this is the most serious problem."

What viewers didn't know at the time was that Moyers, his producer and business partner Al Perlmutter, and Campbell's publisher had signed a partnership agreement giving all three parties a share in the proceeds generated by the series. Moyers was counting on selling Campbell's books and tapes publicized by the broadcasts to enrich himself. (On June 10, 1985, as detailed in the Campbell estate's filings in the lawsuit "Erdman Campbell Trust and Joseph Campbell Foundation, Plaintiffs, vs. Bill Moyers, Alvin H. Perlmutter, Joan Konner, and Apostrophe S Productions, Inc., Defendants" [94 Civ 3314], Bill D. Moyers, Joan Konner, and her husband, Alvin Perlmutter [as Apostophe S Productions], and Alfred van der Marck [as Campbell's publisher] signed a business agreement setting up a joint venture on Apostrophe S Productions letter-head. It declared that "the above three entities will be referred to as 'The Group.'" The Group would share equally in the "preparation and production" of the shows and "have one-third ownership of the results of the taping and the subsequent programs." The agreement also called for the payment of fees "mutually agreed upon" and for any "unusual costs relating to marketing" to be "approved in advance by each member of The Group." The Campbell estate charged that Moyers and his partners did not live up to this agreement. The suit was settled out of court.)

Although Moyers later admitted to Bernstein that Campbell may have had "shadows," he defended his stance as host of *The Power of Myth* and maintained that Campbell showed "no evidence" of bigotry. But any journalist aware of "shadows" should dig deeper and bring them to light, for according to the code of ethics of the journalists' professional organization, Sigma Delta Chi, "there is no excuse for inaccuracies or lack of thoroughness." *Joseph Campbell and the Power of Myth* did not present any "shadows." And because he was his business partner, it was not in Moyers's financial interest to cast Campbell in anything but the most hagiographic light. The fact that Moyers was selling Campbell's mythologies for his own personal profit was not disclosed to the viewing public during the broadcast, to the press, or in Moyers's own filings with PBS (which is responsible for maintaining the journalistic integrity of its broadcasts). Such a financial arrangement might have been judged a violation of PBS guidelines for journalistic integrity and might have led PBS to drop the series.

More shocking was the fact that although profits from the books and tapes would go to Moyers, Campbell's estate, and their business partners, the production costs of the six-part series were paid by public broadcasting itself—that is, by the American taxpayer. PBS contributed $40,000 from a "post market fund" and $620,986.50 from a "challenge fund." CPB put up another $620,986.50 to match that. The John D. and Catherine T. MacArthur Foundation contributed $200,000, according to the PBS record, and the PBS program acceptance form (which is filed with every show accepted for distribution by PBS) states "additional funds (estimate to completion)" of $100,000. However, the source of these additional funds is not manifest in the PBS documents. And despite the fact that almost the entire production budget for the series came from public broadcasting, Bill Moyers's company would *not* "license audio-visual rights to PBS Video." To this date, Mystic Fire Video, a private, for-profit company with a private distribution deal not open to public scrutiny, handles *Joseph Campbell and the Power of Myth*.

How successful were the series spin-offs? In 1989, the *Los Angeles Times* reported: "*The Power of Myth* had 570,000 copies in paperback and 35,000 in hardcover, according to Jacqueline Deval, Doubleday's publicity director. 'We were printing them as fast as we could ship them and wish we could have printed more. It's been on the *New York Times'* bestseller list since May,' Deval said." By 1992, the *New York Times* called Moyers "the pastor of public affairs television" and declared "his six hours of conversation with the mythologist Joseph Campbell transformed a professor into something of a religion; 750,000 books based on the interviews are in print."

In his 1991 *New Republic* article, writer Andrew Ferguson denounced Moyers for succumbing to "the lure of spiritualism and pop psychology." He blasted Moyers for promoting Campbell's mythological meanderings "with none of the skepticism he applied, say, to the rise of evangelical Christianity." Moyers told Ferguson of his interest in pop psychology: "That's just one of the beats I cover as a journalist. I'm aware that the life of the spirit and the quest for self-transformation is a big story, and the press is ignoring it." While Ferguson's article pointed out that Moyers had made a great deal of money from the Campbell program, at that time Ferguson did not know of the business arrangements between the Campbell estate and Moyers.

This covert deal was distinctly at odds with Moyers's public posture as a moralist who believed in full disclosure. He had hosted a program called *The Truth About Lies* on PBS in 1989 in which he showed clips of Oliver North and Lyndon Johnson and interviewed experts to demonstrate that concealing and withholding information was a form of lying and almost as bad as declaratory falsehoods. "Public lies diminish your power and mine as free men and women to make informed choices," Moyers concluded. "We seem to prefer the comfortable lie to the uncomfortable truth. And we punish those who point out reality while rewarding those who provide us with the comfort of illusion. Reality is fearsome, but as we've learned in this series, experience tells us more fearsome yet is evading it."

Moyers had declared in print that he was not involved in public broadcasting to make money, that it was a labor of love. *Joseph Campbell and the Power of Myth,* he claimed, "did prove a big hit, but the revenues were divided among the producers (of which I was only one of three), the publishers, the distributors, CPB and PBS, and Joseph Campbell himself. My own share of those revenues over the six years since the series aired would not be enough to produce a single documentary."[62] But Moyers had settled not one, but two multimillion-dollar lawsuits resulting from the production. The first had come from Stuart Brown, a psychiatrist and Campbell admirer who charged he had prior film rights to Campbell's work. The second suit was filed by Campbell's estate. According to sources close to the latter case, Moyers's company paid out over $1 million in settlement and legal fees for both sides, to get his accusers to drop the claim that Moyers had shortchanged the Campbell estate. (Moyers denies any settlement money was paid.) Published court documents sketch out the kind of dealings one would associate with Hollywood studios, not public-minded public television journalists. The Campbell suit originally charged that "Moyers et al. did not use their best efforts to audit the expenses related to the tapings, many of which had been incurred by Alvin H. Perlmutter Inc. and PAT [Public Affairs Television, Moyers's own company], to ensure that they were reasonable, that they were accurately reported to the partners, and to correct any errors made in inter company transfers (for instance, between Alvin H. Perlmutter, acting for Apostrophe S, and Alvin H. Perlmutter, acting for Alvin H. Perlmutter Productions, Inc., a company controlled by Alvin H. Perlmutter which performed most of the production services, and to which large, unexplained amounts of money have been paid)."

According to the documents, many of these payments seemed designed to reduce any recorded profits—for example, an expense of $28,000 for the rental of two nineteen-inch television sets by Moyers and his partners. The Campbell estate also complained about extravagant charges from luxury shops: for example, bills dated 1993 and 1994 for $1,855 from "The Seafood Shop"; for $515.15 from "Bermuda Party Rentals"; and $1,003.63 from the "Sagaponack General Store." According to court documents, Perlmutter has a home in Sagaponack, Long Island.

When the Campbell estate asked for "further and full accounting information, as well as payment of its fee," they discovered that "Moyers et al. still to the present day refuse to release much of the key accounting information, including tax records of Apostrophe S [despite being charged one-third of the taxes due!], invoices supporting attorney's fees . . . bank statements . . . and records related to certificates of deposit in which were deposited the profits of the Joint Venture (including, without permission, the share belonging to the Trust.)" The estate complained that they had also been denied access to "any of the relevant books and records of either Alvin H. Perlmutter Inc. or PAT." Moyers and his partners settled the case out of court, avoiding a public trial.

The lawsuits and settlements received little media coverage, even though Joan Konner is now dean of the Columbia journalism school and Al Perlmutter has worked in public broadcasting since the days of *The Great American Dream Machine*. It remains unclear precisely what happened to all the money made from *Joseph Campbell and the Power of Myth*. Unfortunately, the complete financial data is still not available to the public who largely made the series possible in the first place through their tax dollars and donations to PBS. Moyers continues to enjoy 50 percent of the royalties from the Doubleday book of the series, edited by Jacqueline Kennedy Onassis.

The success of the Campbell series was a revelation. Middle-class professionals who were not likely to have a Bible on public display proudly placed their Moyers books and cassettes on their coffee tables and bookshelves. Moyers quickly cranked out a successor to the Campbell programs:

A World of Ideas, volumes I and II. Like *Joseph Campbell and the Power of Myth,* these two PBS series spawned tie-in books from Doubleday. Moyers even went back to revisit historians Barbara Tuchman, Forrest McDonald, and Henry Steele Commager, whom he first interviewed in the 1970s. But that had been before the advent of the videocassette recorder and the refinement of such PBS marketing techniques as on-air 800 numbers for instant credit card sales. The combination of PBS merchandising power and Moyers's ownership of the copyright gave him a veritable gold mine. The videotapes of both volumes of *A World of Ideas* were bestsellers of over 100,000 copies.

Like the Campbell series, *A World of Ideas* featured an interview with a professor whose extremist views were not acknowledged during the broadcast. MIT linguistics professor Noam Chomsky was identified as a political activist dedicated to social change. But when the recorded discussions touched on the Vietnam War and international relations, Moyers never challenged Chomsky on his long-standing defense of the Khmer Rouge's reign of terror in Cambodia or his support for the French historian Robert Faurrison, who made his name denying the existence of the Nazi extermination of European Jewry, or his support for the Palestinian Liberation Organization and his stance against Israel, positions he had for years articulated in print and in lectures.[63] The interview with Moyers burnished Chomsky's public image, according him legitimacy as an expert on issues of public policy, without ever engaging him in a debate on the premises of some of his most controversial public positions.[64]

Chomsky was treated with the same respect Moyers showed toward author Isaac Asimov, management expert Peter Drucker, and historian James MacGregor Burns. Moyers accepted Chomsky's charge that Columbus had committed genocide. Moyers even rejoiced that "the upcoming celebration of the five hundredth year of Columbus's 'discovery' [sic] of the Americas will also be met by a counterdemonstration, by descendants of those millions of people who were wiped out after the Europeans had arrived."[65] But Moyers did not ask Chomsky whether he thought the Aztecs or the Inca or the Blackfoot or the Sioux had murdered or enslaved anyone before the white man came. He let Chomsky pass through his examination with far less scrutiny than he had given to

Ronald Reagan or Ollie North. As with *The Power of Myth,* a book deal gave Moyers every incentive not to discredit his interview subjects. Perhaps profit was coming before principle.

Moyers was on a roll. He continued to churn out hit series and specials. His PBS special *Amazing Grace,* which told the story about the Christian hymn, became a bestselling video, with 48,000 sold. It was used for fund-raising during pledge weeks. *A Gathering of Men with Robert Bly,* one of the first shows to promote the men's movement, sold over 48,000 units at $39.95. Moyers's lecture fee was estimated at some $20,000 a talk. He was perhaps the most influential "thinker" on American television, thanks to PBS.

In 1991 Moyers attended a retreat at the country estate of Pamela Harriman near Middleburg, Virginia, to advise top Democratic Party officials on strategy for the 1992 presidential campaign. As if on cue, for the election year Moyers produced *The Secret Government: Constitution in Crisis,* which accused Ollie North and the Reagan administration of undermining the Constitution in the Iran-Contra controversy. That same year, Moyers hosted a special called *America: What Went Wrong?* that charged George Bush with betraying the American people. Moyers also anchored a weekly program on PBS covering the elections, called *Listening to America* (the same title he had used for his first book).

Moyers kept his business ventures going full force as well. He again exercised his superb salesmanship with *Healing and the Mind,* a 1993 show about traditional Chinese medicine and faith healing. It too became a bestselling book and videocassette and caused one old schoolmate of Moyers's from Marshall, Texas, to shake his head and mutter, "It seems Billy Don Moyers has gone into faith healing now."[66] (Indeed, it is estimated that Moyers has made more on *Healing and the Mind* than on any of his other projects to date, although some of this reflects simple increases in the sales price of books over time.) Other successful series in this mold included *The Language of Life* about poets and *The Wisdom of Faith,* with the Berkeley professor of religion Huston Smith in the Joseph Campbell role.

In addition to direct sales, Moyers has had other ways of making money from public broadcasting. He claims to have raised $15 million for his private company since 1986. In his *New Republic* article, Andrew Ferguson stated that in 1989 Moyers received $2.5 million from the

MacArthur Foundation and $850,000 from the Charles Stewart Mott Foundation for his television shows. That same year, CPB gave him $1.25 million. IRS documents for 1988 state that Public Affairs Television Inc. received $3 million from the Florence and John Schumann Foundation—which only gives out some $3.5 million a year. At the time, the Schumann Foundation was headed by William Mullins, a Democratic ally of Moyers from his Peace Corps years. When Mullins died in 1990, Moyers became president of the foundation and awarded an additional $300,000 to his corporate landlord, WNET, for the series *Environment: Your Own Backyard*. Later, Moyers stepped down as president of the Schumann Foundation—eventually to be replaced by his son, John Moyers.

When Ferguson asked Moyers about his success at raising corporate money as well as foundation support, Moyers told him: "We can leverage the funds very well. You get a dollar from MacArthur, say, and you go to a corporation for a matching grant. You get another dollar there and then you go to public television and ask for money based on that. I've raised four dollars for every one I've raised from public television." Among Moyers's backers from corporate America: Paine Webber, Chevron, Weyerhauser, General Motors, and Johnson & Johnson. Moyers's main corporate sponsor has been Mutual of America, an insurance company whose board included William Aramony, who resigned in disgrace from the United Way after a financial scandal.

In 1995 Moyers announced that he would be leaving PBS for a slot as commentator on *The NBC Nightly News with Tom Brokaw,* repeating the migrations of the 1970s and 1980s between PBS and commercial television. His producer would be Andrew Lack, who had been his producer at CBS in the 1980s. But before leaving PBS—and Moyers said he would still produce the occasional special, as he did last time he left—he appeared as an interviewee with former Reagan–Bush speechwriter Peggy Noonan in *Peggy Noonan on Values* on PBS. Noonan was perhaps trying to take over the niche that Moyers had filled so well: talking about "values" with an array of thinkers from various perspectives. But Noonan's series was short-lived, and NBC suspended Moyers's commentaries after a few months, following published complaints about his political bias.

Perhaps the closest to a confession Moyers has ever come was in a conversation with ethicist Michael Josephson in *A World of Ideas* about his values. In a way, the dialogue sums up the tradeoffs Moyers has made in his quarter-century in public broadcasting. Like any successful TV preacher, he has tried to pursue both power and principle, wealth and good works, success and salvation. Even Moyers does not know whether he has succeeded; his conscience still bothers him:

JOSEPHSON: . . . the fact of the matter is that a good conscience is the best pillow. Living a good life is the most important thing for us.

MOYERS: Yes, but I find every day is a constant struggle to decide between right and wrong in small ways that nobody ever sees. I win one day, and I lose the next day—so at nights, my pillow is often like stone. What was it Plato said? That virtue does not come from money, but money comes from virtue.

JOSEPHSON: I believe that can happen.

MOYERS: I was a beneficiary of the way the game is played. I was a beneficiary of rules that favored a white male growing up in the postwar era, in an economy carrying me buoyantly upward, and of patrons who plucked me out for scholarships and sent me to school and backed me and befriended me.[67]

In 1996 PBS announced that Steven Spielberg's Righteous Persons Foundation would finance a television series based on the biblical story of Genesis. The host would be Bill Moyers. After forty years of wandering, Bill Moyers was coming home to the circuit preaching he had done after graduating from his Texas Bible college. He was, after all was said and done, just one more televangelist.

4

The *NewsHour*

Considered even by Republican critics to be among the most balanced and objective programs on PBS, *The MacNeil/Lehrer NewsHour* (as of 1995, *The NewsHour with Jim Lehrer*) represents the best public broadcasting has to offer in news coverage. It has won every major award, including Emmys, Peabodys, and Columbia-DuPonts. But more important, in form and content it has shown, for twenty years, just how public broadcasting can adapt to criticism with integrity and attempt to remain true to a mission of public service (although some conservatives feel the show still tilts to the left).

Most viewers today don't realize that the show PBS president Ervin Duggan has called "the flagship news program of PBS" is actually an artifact of a nasty political struggle between the public broadcasting establishment and the Nixon administration. The daily presence of the anchor team of Robert MacNeil and Jim Lehrer—and the continuing efforts of Lehrer—were and are a living reminder of Watergate and its intricate relationship with the history of public television. Indeed, there is no better example of the influence of domestic American politics—both congressional and presidential—on the content of PBS programming than the *NewsHour.*

Since the program first went on the air in 1975, PBS has broadcast some 5,000 *NewsHours*, at a rate of about 260 a year. The original half-hour show, *The MacNeil/Lehrer Report,* was in 1983 expanded to an hour, and the name was changed to *The MacNeil/Lehrer NewsHour.* At that time, producers entered a short-lived joint business venture with the Gannett newspaper chain. In exchange for an undisclosed sum, Gannett became the production company for the show. However, the program did not produce the profits Gannett sought. Three years later, Gannett opted out of the partnership, and ownership returned to hosts MacNeil and Lehrer and original executive producer Al Vecchione (who retired as president of MacNeil/Lehrer Productions in 1996). Yet the *NewsHour* remained a desirable property because of its prestige. In 1995, Liberty Media, a division of the Colorado-based Tele-Communications Incorporated (currently the largest cable television company in the United States), purchased two-thirds of MacNeil/Lehrer Productions Inc. for an undisclosed sum.

The *NewsHour* operates on an annual budget of about $25 million, only one-quarter of NBC's news division budget. Nonetheless, it is the most costly regular series on PBS. At fifty-seven minutes, the show is more than twice as long as its competitors; the nightly network news broadcasts last only twenty-two minutes. The cost of producing a minute of the *NewsHour* is around $1,350; a network news minute costs more than ten times that. The *NewsHour* is less expensive to produce largely because of its greater number of in-studio interviews and less on-location coverage.

In the beginning, the program was intended to complement the nightly network news. When *The MacNeil/Lehrer Report* first went on the air as a production of New York's WNET in 1975, it was just a half-hour, scheduled immediately following the network news broadcasts. Its purpose was to analyze the major story of the day rather than to report breaking news. The producers assumed viewers had already seen the network coverage and were offering some depth. In this sense, the program continued the tradition begun in the 1960s by WNET's *News in Perspective,* hosted by *New York Times* editor Lester Markel.

That half-hour, one-story-per-night format was copied by ABC's *Nightline* in 1979 during the Iranian hostage crisis. *Nightline* also adapted the technique of live, long-distance interviewing, little used on network television since the days of Edward R. Murrow's *Person-to-Person.* Credit for the development of the single-issue approach belongs to MacNeil and Lehrer, but they owe their inspiration to the BBC's prestigious current affairs program series *Panorama.*

In public opinion polls, the *NewsHour* has consistently ranked with the most trusted nightly news broadcasts, among both the general public and other journalists. The series is also a favorite of television critics because, in the words of ABC News commentator Jeff Greenfield, "Talking heads, complexity, all of the values shunned by most local news broadcasts are permitted here." Others regard the program as a television equivalent of the *New York Times,* the newspaper of record.

The thoughtful, slow-paced, and unusually sober format of the *NewsHour* (gray like the *Times* itself) attracted loyal viewers among opinion leaders from the start. Author David Halberstam (*The Best and the Brightest; The Powers That Be*) told Robert MacNeil that the program had served a real purpose for him, both because it was so reserved and because in the early days it concentrated on only one story at a time. "All I need," Halberstam said, "is for someone, anyone, every few weeks to tell me what I need to know about Angola and then leave me alone until something important has changed and I need to know again."[1]

One of the reasons the *NewsHour* is so universally admired and respected is its demonstrated commitment to fairness and honesty. "Our stock-in-trade is giving a number of views of an issue simultaneously," Robert MacNeil explained in his 1982 memoirs, *The Right Place at the Right Time.* "It is perceived we do not quote people out of context, as many Americans believe all the news media do: we cannot, because our interviews are live and unedited; our guests create their own context." MacNeil and Lehrer have adhered to that credo since 1975, as have their cohosts Charlayne Hunter-Gault, Judy Woodruff, Kwame Holman, Margaret Warner, Elizabeth Farnsworth, and Roger Mudd, who joined them when the show expanded to an hour in 1983.

Although he is well known today for his impartiality, and his program even has a reputation among some for being "boring," Robert MacNeil (whose friends call him Robin) established his early reputation as a fiery, crusading journalist opposed to the Vietnam War, an outspoken reporter whose name appeared on President Richard Nixon's enemies list. Not surprisingly, documents from the Nixon White House reveal serious concerns about the fledgling PBS network's choice of MacNeil to anchor its new news program when The National Public Affairs Center for Television (NPACT) was established by the Ford Foundation and CPB in 1971.

MacNeil was born in Montreal in 1931. His father served in the Royal Canadian Mounted Police and commanded a Royal Navy cruiser during World War II. The younger MacNeil began his journalism career working for the Canadian Broadcasting Corporation and moved to England in 1955 for jobs with Independent Television (ITV) News and the Reuters news service. While working in London, he became a correspondent for NBC News and was transferred to America in 1963 to work for NBC's Washington bureau. MacNeil was soon moved again, this time to New York, where he first anchored a local news show. He later coanchored the national NBC weekend news with Ray Scherer. This marked also the first time his name appeared in a show's title, though he drew second billing on what was then called *The Scherer-MacNeil Report.*

By 1966, MacNeil was so well respected and successful on weekends that he was in line for a first-string position as a replacement for longtime anchor Chet Huntley or David Brinkley, should one become necessary. Brinkley had refused to cross an American Federation of Television and Radio Artists picket line in 1967 in a public dispute with Huntley, who defied the union, arguing that newsmen did not belong in the same union with entertainers.[2]

In his memoir, MacNeil says NBC wanted to send him to Vietnam to cover the war for six months to build up his experience as a correspondent and season the naive Canadian for the eventual anchor slot that awaited him. He declined, he says, because he felt such an assignment was a step down from anchoring the weekend news. He would also lose extra fees for other television projects he was doing on the side in New York. "Perhaps," he admits, "I was also a bit nervous about being killed." The decision was to mark the beginning of the end of his career in commercial network television. MacNeil had refused to get his ticket punched.

He had shown an independent streak by editorializing against the Vietnam War in 1967 on the NBC radio network in a three-times-a-week segment called *Emphasis.* Perhaps because he was Canadian, he felt free to attack American foreign policy in Southeast Asia. In his commentaries MacNeil criticized "the absurdity of American men dying to protect democracy in a land whose government trampled on democratic freedoms."

"[T]he U.S. Army must have had optimism packaged in aerosol cans," he concluded in one broadcast, "because every official who went out there full of doubts appeared to have been sprayed with optimism before he came home."[3]

In 1967, MacNeil left NBC News for England and a job with the BBC, no doubt because his commentaries had disturbed his superiors at NBC. Upset with what he perceived to be overly positive American media coverage of the war, MacNeil penned a broadside called *The People Machine* that strongly condemned what he described as the triviality and distraction offered by the mainstream media in the United States in the face of a brutal war in Southeast Asia. In his book, published in 1968, MacNeil blasted sound bites, twenty-two-minute network newscasts, and the lack of analysis of rapidly developing events—criticisms still made today by many pundits. In many ways, MacNeil's published call for longer and more in-depth news coverage was the blueprint for what would become the style of *The MacNeil/Lehrer Report.*

The People Machine criticized commercial networks for having been too easily manipulated by the Johnson administration and too susceptible to pressures from advertisers. It argued for the establishment of a public television corporation modeled on the BBC that would be dedicated to "public service" instead of profits. MacNeil had kind words for Ford Foundation consultant Fred Friendly's NET series *Public Broadcasting Laboratory,* regarding it as a prototype for the kind of television he was talking about. PBL, a weekly, "experimental" program broadcast live on Sunday evenings, covered controversial topics, such as race relations and the Vietnam War. What MacNeil didn't emphasize in his book was that PBL was a major client of the BBC and, in fact, purchased and aired BBC *Panorama* productions featuring MacNeil, then a BBC employee working on the weekly series. Nor did MacNeil overtly comment that his own argument against network television was not original. It echoed the sentiments of PBL's founder, Fred Friendly, in his

1967 book *Due to Circumstances Beyond Our Control,* which also argued for public broadcasting.

One of MacNeil's more controversial reports of that period, aired on PBL, was an impassioned anti-Vietnam documentary originally produced for the BBC. The show featured the burial of a fallen soldier from New Hampshire named Ronald Keller, intercut with footage of 1968 presidential primary campaigns of Lyndon Johnson, Eugene McCarthy, Richard Nixon, and George Romney. MacNeil was a McCarthy supporter at the time. He later explained, "If you felt as I did then about the war, McCarthy's was the only voice of sanity, putting Vietnam squarely where it belonged in the center of the political arena."

MacNeil's report clearly expressed his viewpoint: In one scene he juxtaposed a shot of the soldier's coffin being lowered into the ground with an excerpt from a Johnson campaign speech: "The Communists in Vietnam are watching this primary closely. Now is not the time for weakness or indecision. On Tuesday, March 12, let's show Hanoi that Americans back their boys in Vietnam and support their commander-in-chief." The scene was such an emotional indictment of the President that even the editors of PBL excised the closing shot of a bulldozer filling the grave with dirt. MacNeil says he intended the shot as a sign of Johnson's "contempt, or indifference."

"It went too far," MacNeil later said of the piece. "The irony I intended was too heavy. The film was a political statement more than a piece of journalism. I think it is the farthest I have ever been led into pure advocacy journalism."

Among those who disliked the show was MacNeil's then-wife, whom he described in his memoirs as "very unhappy about the way I had depicted America to the British." Although it bothered his wife, and he regretted it later, this strong anti-American statement established MacNeil's reputation in public broadcasting. He was now a "made" man, having taken on LBJ.

MacNeil produced another special in 1968 sure to annoy the American political establishment. This time his subject was the riots at the Chicago Democratic convention. MacNeil's account once more aired on PBL and again took the side of the Eugene McCarthy forces against Lyndon Johnson's choice, Hubert Humphrey. The report included a statement by Richard Goodwin (a staffer for the 1959 quiz show hearings, speechwriter for President Kennedy, and husband of regular MacNeil/Lehrer guest Doris Kearns Goodwin): "In a couple of years, we're going to take the country away from the Connallys, the Meanys, and the Daleys." (Texas governor John Connally was wounded as he rode in the presidential limousine when John F. Kennedy was killed in Dallas, George Meany was head of the AFL–CIO, and Richard Daley was Chicago's mayor and head of possibly the most powerful Democratic machine in the country at that time. Daley had ordered the Chicago police to disperse the antiwar protesters at the convention, and the ensuing melee was characterized as a "police riot" by liberal commentators at the time.)

MacNeil himself later declared in language typical of the sixties, "The savagery of the Chicago police was a bellow of indignation from the lower middle class against the kids of the McCarthy crusade who seemed loose in their morals and deficient in patriotism." In hindsight, it seems that the police—and Mayor Daley—may have been correct in their view that the protesters had been there to disrupt the convention and provoke the police. Todd Gitlin, one of the SDS student leaders who organized the protests in Chicago, wrote in his memoirs that he had planned some of the Chicago confrontations while on a trip to Cuba with other radicals.[4]

The next year, an increasingly outraged MacNeil produced a documentary on the Vietnam protest known as the Moratorium. MacNeil again chose to use the dramatic story of a dead soldier as an emotional hook. This soldier, Richard Genest, had been killed eight weeks earlier, just after the birth of his son. The program featured an interview with his twenty-one-year-old widow, Brenda, and featured her reactions as she watched President Nixon on television. Brenda Genest also provided tapes and letters from her fallen husband for use in the film. "His messages to her were sweet and intimate," MacNeil said of the letters, "a little embarrassed when he came close to verbalizing what he longed for sexually. Played like this, when we knew he was dead, of course made them heavily poignant." And clearly anti-Nixon.

In 1970, MacNeil produced a show for the BBC's *Panorama* about the Nixon presidency, a program that would serve as a preview of the format of his own nightly newscast. As part of that report, he and his BBC producer arranged for Perle Mesta—known as the "hostess with the mostest" during the Truman administration and the subject of a hit Broadway musical—to throw a fashionable Washington dinner party, which MacNeil and his crew filmed. The guest list included, among others, Chuck Stone, "a militant black journalist"; Democratic senator Charles Goodell of New York, an antiwar activist who had taken Robert Kennedy's place in the Senate; Kennedy aide Peter Edelman, later a top Clinton administration official at the Department of Health and Human Services; journalists Peter Lisagor and Richard Scammon; Senator Howard Baker, who later became ranking Republican on the Senate Watergate Committee and President Reagan's chief of staff; and Congresswoman Margaret Heckler, a liberal Republican.

With the guests seated around the dinner table, MacNeil led a series of discussions of topical issues including Vietnam. In a sense, one might see in this report a prototype for the *NewsHour,* which often has the feel of a dinner party for inside-the-Beltway notables.

But there was more to the program than just the dinner conversation. Like the *NewsHour* would, his BBC show featured taped "packages"—edited essays to make strong editorial points. In a segment called "Nixon Incorporated," MacNeil focused on the President's relationship with the press and described the White House public relations operation headed by press secretary Ron Ziegler as "a spectacle worthy of Cecil B. de Mille." In order to diminish his stature, MacNeil identified Ziegler as a former tour guide at Disneyland, a job Ziegler briefly held in his youth. The BBC crew also managed to film Vice President Spiro Agnew arriving at Andrews Air Force Base to a red carpet reception and the Marine band. The scene, MacNeil said, "cried out for spoofing." So he used the scene to end the film, pairing it with Ethel Merman's rendition of "There's No Business Like Show Business," which continued over the closing titles.

It was an unsubtle, clearly ironic statement critical of the President, and it was manifestly from MacNeil himself. "I had to decide which side I was on," he said at the time, "free press or repressive administration." The segment was not shown on NET, but the *Washington Post* carried an uncomplimentary account from its London reporter, criticizing the film for its cheap shots at the President. Again, though, harsh criticism of Nixon would not hurt MacNeil's journalistic career.

MacNeil returned to Washington in 1970 for the BBC, this time to cover protests against the Nixon administration's incursion into Cambodia and the Kent State tragedy. Although he says that he kept his personal feelings about Nixon out of his reporting MacNeil's anti-Nixon perspective is obvious in his own account and was widely shared by many in the media at the time (Dan Rather had become famous for rudeness during presidential press conferences, echoing the demonstrators who were becoming increasingly familiar on the nightly news).

In his own view, MacNeil had been unfairly targeted by Nixon since he had not actually attacked the President directly. MacNeil's account is either a masterly piece of mock innocence or a case of self-deception: "[I]n 1971, I got personally drawn in. The Nixon White House began a campaign that directly threatened public television and my own career. It reached a point where I felt obliged to throw off my own objectivity and resist. It became my personal corner of Watergate." MacNeil had been pounding Nixon for years. He should not have been surprised when Nixon became angry.

A September 23, 1971, "confidential eyes only" memo from Nixon's assistant Jon M. Huntsman on the subject to Peter Flanigan, who handled telecommunications, stated that the choice of Sander Vanocur and Robert MacNeil to anchor the 1972 election-year political coverage on PBS "greatly disturbed the President, who considered this the last straw. It was requested that all funds for public broadcasting be cut immediately. You should work this out so that the House Appropriations Committee gets the word."[5] But why had MacNeil been chosen for the job?

Precisely because of his hard-edged reporting on American politics and overt hostility to the Nixon administration. Executives at the Ford Foundation and NET's Washington bureau were so impressed with his work that when the Ford Foundation agreed with the Corporation for Public Broadcasting to open the National Public Affairs Center for Television (NPACT) in Washington to cover politics, MacNeil was hired as anchorman—at the direction of his old colleague from PBL, Fred Friendly. The opportunity to anchor a news program in America appealed to

MacNeil, so he took a leave of absence from the BBC for one year and moved to Washington to try his luck.

NPACT was the result of a 1969 agreement between the Nixon administration, the CPB, and the Ford Foundation to reduce NET's role in public broadcasting to zero over a period of three years. It was set up on paper as an independent corporation, supplying programs on a contract basis to PBS through WETA, Washington's educational station. "The new organization would, in fact, be NET's Washington bureau, divorced from NET and independently administered," NET chief Day recalled. "I found the decision to place public television's sensitive public-affairs operations cheek-by-jowl with the sources of its government funding much more worrisome than the loss of NET's news division." What Day did not comprehend was that the network news headquarters in New York are "cheek-by-jowl" with their source of funding—that is, corporate headquarters.

Moving the news division to Washington was to acknowledge the primacy of the CPB as funder. An angry James Day declared NPACT, the fruit of "Ford–CPB machinations," to be "an ill-starred and short-lived organization" whose "institutional ties" to WETA were to "create more problems than they solve[d]."[6] Eventually, NPACT was folded into WETA, after Nixon's resignation.

Jim Karayn, NPACT's executive vice president (and NET's former Washington bureau chief), chose MacNeil to anchor the NPACT-produced PBS coverage of the 1972 elections and asked Edwin Newman to cohost, but Newman declined. Unfortunately, his next choice, former NBC correspondent Sander Vanocur, was well known to President Nixon as a friend of John F. Kennedy, and the president was angrier about Vanocur than MacNeil.[7]

Nixon held a grudge against Vanocur for insulting him during the 1960 presidential campaign out of what the Nixon camp felt was his personal loyalty to the Kennedy campaign. During the debates, Vanocur had asked Nixon about Eisenhower's failure to remember a single important decision in which Nixon had participated. The result was that Vanocur became JFK's "golden boy," widely regarded as his favorite among the press corps during "Camelot." Vanocur had been Kennedy FCC chairman Newton Minow's college roommate at Northwestern University.

That public broadcasting had chosen two anti-Nixon correspondents to host coverage of the 1972 elections was viewed as a hostile act by the White House, which objected to what it saw as arrogant anti-administration politicking by a broadcasting system that depended on taxpayer subsidies from citizens on all points of the political spectrum. *NewsHour* host Jim Lehrer later noted, "The Nixon people saw Vanocur as a Kennedy-lackey leftist of the worst order. Memos and tapes released after Watergate show that the idea of Vanocur's covering the campaign, and being paid out of public money to do so, absolutely incensed Nixon et al."[8]

Soon the administration leaked the $85,000 and $65,000 salaries of Vanocur and MacNeil, respectively, to the press. Members of Congress, whose salaries had been capped at $42,500 in 1972, began to object. Seeing his income in print disturbed MacNeil greatly. "It was very upsetting," he later wrote. "I had no reason to be ashamed of what I was earning. It was what I had made in my last year at NBC, five years earlier. I was perfectly comfortable at the BBC, and $65,000 was my price for giving that up. But having it published, the subject of gossip among our friends and neighbors, was a very painful invasion of privacy."[9] (Of course, the salaries of all U.S. representatives, senators, and administration appointees in Washington are traditionally matters of public record.)

In January, Vanocur and MacNeil began broadcasting their weekly series of shows called *A Public Affair—Election '72.* MacNeil said he made a special effort to be fair and balanced. "I was determined not to give the Nixon people any ammunition. That editorial sensitivity was inhibiting but not paralyzing."

However, this "editorial sensitivity" didn't stop MacNeil from documenting antiwar congressman Pete McCloskey's New Hampshire challenge to Nixon. While the man MacNeil called "the arch Red-baiter of old" made his historic trip to China, opening the largest nation in the world to diplomatic relations with the United States, MacNeil was filming McCloskey watching the event on television in his motel.

"How do you compete with that?" he asked McCloskey.

"You didn't," MacNeil later wrote, answering his own question, "and that was the point."

MacNeil felt the eyes of the White House on him. "That I had even to consider what the reaction might be when the piece was viewed in the White House was to some degree inhibiting," he recalls. "Why were we devoting a half-hour to McCloskey's challenge? they might ask. Were we not magnifying his chances to make a dent in Nixon's advantage? Were we exaggerating the importance of McCloskey, and therefore of the antiwar movement itself? Those were all legitimate questions for us to ask ourselves; it was oppressive to be asking them over and over because of what we thought the effect might be in jeopardizing the wider future of public television."[10]

Meanwhile, MacNeil donned another hat at PBS: In addition to hosting the election specials, he became the moderator of *Washington Week in Review,* succeeding Lincoln Ferber, who had followed Washington lawyer Max Kampelman. Among the regular panelists was journalist Peter Lisagor of the *Chicago Daily News,* who had been at MacNeil's BBC dinner at Perle Mesta's. According to MacNeil, the Nixon administration was particularly aggrieved by Lisagor's anti-administration comments on the program and demanded his removal, but MacNeil and producer Jim Karayn stood firm, and Lisagor remained a commentator on the show until his death.

Perhaps mindful of growing White House interest in PBS programming and not wishing to give offense to the Nixon administration, NPACT did not provide gavel-to-gavel coverage of the 1972 Democratic convention, which nominated George McGovern. It did, however, air full coverage of the Republican convention. "We couldn't get the logistics mastered for the Democratic convention," recalls Al Vecchione, former president of MacNeil/Lehrer Productions, "and some people at the time thought it would be politically smart to throw a bouquet at the Republicans and do gavel-to-gavel. But MacNeil and Vanocur didn't want to do it, because it was unbalanced, and withdrew. Bill Moyers stepped in."

MacNeil and Vanocur had done half-hour wrap-ups of the Democratic convention and said that's all they would give the Republicans. PBS and NPACT disagreed. Today, Vecchione says he regrets siding with Moyers on the matter: "[MacNeil and Vanocur] were right—we should have done them both the same way or not done them at all."[11]

Meanwhile, MacNeil continued to host his weekly election series with Vanocur. They concluded their coverage with a segment showing a campaign visit by Nixon to Atlanta as staged, reminiscent of MacNeil's earlier dig at Agnew. Nixon's canned displays of popularity are what MacNeil said explained "the awful dilemma of America's Democrats, following their heads and not their hearts and dismissing McGovern for Nixon."[12] In other words, Democrats were voting for Nixon instead of McGovern because of the sophistication of the Nixon campaign machine's accomplished public relations techniques. To support Nixon was a rational decision, however, according to MacNeil's analysis. He didn't mention the large number of Democratic votes Nixon had received in 1968, especially from working-class voters, after the riots at the Chicago convention, which would have been evidence that McGovern did not have their hearts, either.

In November 1972, shortly after the CPB, at the suggestion of the Nixon administration, voted not to fund any more news and public affairs programs, MacNeil and Vanocur went on the air courtesy of the Ford Foundation's resurgent generosity. MacNeil recalls saying before the election that he thought Nixon was a pretty good bet for reelection. "Scarcely the conclusion of a hostile commentator out to get the President," he later wrote. (But he didn't say he was happy about his prediction.)

Nixon's 1972 landslide hardened MacNeil's resolve to "fight back." When the CPB declined to continue to pay for *Washington Week in Review* after Nixon's victory in 1972, MacNeil went on the air and announced that his funding was in jeopardy. He appealed to viewers "to write what they felt" about the matter. Some 13,000 letters soon arrived at his offices.

MacNeil also appealed to the Consumer Federation of America (CFA), a group traditionally allied with the liberal wing of the Democratic Party, for help in mobilizing a pressure campaign. In a speech to a CFA convention, MacNeil responded to the administration's charges that his show was biased against the President. "I strongly denied bias," he later said of his speech. "Bias in their minds is apparently any attitude which does not indicate permanent genuflection before the wisdom and purity of Richard Nixon." MacNeil went on to attack the President for attempting to "strangle the national public broadcasting network," and he urged the membership of the CFA to write letters to Congress. Thousands more flooded in.

Nevertheless, the CPB remained firm in its decision not to fund *Washington Week in Review.* By March, Sander Vanocur had resigned from NPACT, "partly out of personal wounds at the vendetta against him, partly to remove himself as a provocation," according to MacNeil. MacNeil himself remained, launching a new series with a young PBS programming executive who had come to the network. Their weekly magazine show was called *America '73.* The executive's name was Jim Lehrer.[13]

Lehrer had come to PBS in Washington in 1972 after an on-camera stint on Fred Friendly's Ford-funded *Newsroom* series on KERA, the Dallas educational station. A former Marine and editor at the *Dallas Times-Herald,* Lehrer was seen as more conservative than Vanocur because of his background and his ties to Ralph Rogers, the millionaire Republican chairman of the board of KERA and of PBS who tapped Lehrer for the national job.

According to *NewsHour* producer Al Vecchione, Lehrer was brought in "to impose a professional journalism standard" at PBS as public affairs czar. In Vecchione's view, despite initial fears by some in public broadcasting Lehrer did his job with great distinction. The reputation for integrity Lehrer established in this role was vital to his selection as cohost of the coverage of the Watergate hearings.[14]

Lehrer's job of coordinating programming was brand new and arranged in part by Rogers specifically to mute administration criticism of liberal bias at PBS. "I was told mostly just to do my coordinating through the enforcement of a new code of standards and practices for such programming that the Nixon assault had frightened public television into adopting," Lehrer recalls.[15]

Lehrer had helped write the rules for PBS along with a consulting committee headed by Columbia University School of Journalism dean Elie Abel and BBC newsman David Webster. "There was nothing in the final product that any working journalist could or would object to," Lehrer says. "And none did."

In fact, Lehrer's first confrontation was with then–PBS president Hartford Gunn. When Alabama governor George Wallace was shot on

Lehrer's first day on the job, the new public affairs czar arranged for MacNeil and Vanocur to interrupt the live broadcast of an opera performance for news bulletins. The next day, Gunn upbraided the new executive for cutting into another program. Lehrer remembers being "screamed at" by Gunn, who told him, "That opera had been in the works for months! You ruined it! And for what? News! We are not in news! We are in public affairs!"

According to Lehrer, this was "one of the key mantras of survival against the Nixon onslaught. I had just been clued in on my second day on the job."

Lehrer's first assignment at PBS was to review *VD Blues,* a program about sexually transmitted diseases that was hosted by Dick Cavett and produced by Don Fouser, who had been on the staff of the controversial *Great American Dream Machine.* Lehrer writes in his memoirs, *A Bus of My Own,* that the show featured a theme song about gonorrhea called "Don't Give a Dose." "There was only one thing worse than broadcasting *VD Blues,*" Lehrer recalled. "And that was not broadcasting it. . . . I had to figure out a way to get *VD Blues* on the air in a way that did not bring down the house of PBS."

Taking advice from PBS veterans, Lehrer set up a bureaucratic process to approve the program as worthy and to make as many people as he could within PBS share responsibility with him for the decision. He certified that the program did not violate standards and practices, sent a notice to the station managers that there were some questions of taste they might want to know about, and arranged a closed-circuit screening of the rough cut.

"And it worked," Lehrer notes. "There were complaints and screams of anguish and alarm . . . but no storms."

The next day, CPB president Henry Loomis showed up to ask Lehrer how "that VD program" got on the air. Lehrer explained the "process" and Loomis moved on to other issues, leading Lehrer to conclude years later, "He had been had. And we had won. For now. In order to raise hell, Loomis had to disagree with all TV critics and most of the people who ran and who watched public television. In order to change things, he would have to change everything." Which meant Loomis could, in effect, change nothing.

Sander Vanocur's resignation after the 1972 election was a stroke of good luck for Lehrer, who was teamed with MacNeil on *America '73,* presumably to keep an eye on him for the public broadcasting bureaucrats. (It was less good for Vanocur, who said he was "blacklisted" for years as a result of the NPACT controversy, and who eventually turned to writing and now is a host on cable's History Channel.)

Lehrer had hated being a "coordinator" and was delighted to return to reporting. At first, however, his lack of on-camera experience held him back. "MacNeil could open up an encyclopedia to any page and read it to the camera so it sounded like something important," Lehrer said in his memoirs. "My reading of an encyclopedia would sound like the reading of an encyclopedia—or worse. . . . I was truly awful. . . . Thank God for the Watergate hearings."[16]

PBS's gavel-to-gavel coverage of the 1973 Senate Watergate hearings gave Lehrer a chance to get accustomed to appearing on television.

Not surprisingly, Robert MacNeil was among those who advocated that PBS cover the hearings in full. No commercial network had agreed to cover them, so he saw it as an important opportunity for PBS. "The way was open for public television to win the kind of credibility that the new ABC network had by preempting all daytime programs to cover the Army–McCarthy hearings in 1954," he said.[17] Presumably television could do to Nixon what it had done to McCarthy.

Jim Karayn, who was head of NPACT at the time, says he had to spend months lobbying Hartford Gunn to persuade him to authorize the Watergate coverage. Gunn objected, telling Karayn, "You are trying to destroy public broadcasting." Karayn says he had to seek help from PBS board chairman Ralph Rogers, who took him to meet with Gunn.

Al Vecchione, then NPACT general manager, recalls how reluctant the PBS executives were to broadcast the hearings, no doubt fearing that further antagonizing the Nixon administration would hurt their federal funding. He said his production team provoked a stormy confrontation with top brass at PBS to get Watergate hearings on the air.

"I was with Robin and Jim every step of the way," Vecchione remembers. "The issue was how to get PBS airtime. All the powers that be in public broadcasting were feeling a lot of heat under the collar. Myself, Jim Karayn, Martin Clancy [who line-produced the Watergate

coverage, now at ABC News], and Lehrer were at a PBS meeting on behalf of NPACT making the case to PBS vice presidents Sam Holt and
Gerry Slater." At first, PBS held firm against televising the hearings, but
Vecchione, MacNeil, Lehrer, and the NPACT group persisted. "Coming
down to the wire, one hot steamy session lasted till eleven P.M.," Vecchione remembered. "There were threats of one or all five of us quit-
ting—or of calling a press conference saying PBS would not allow
Watergate coverage to be put on the air."

This threat seemed to have some effect on Gunn, who finally
agreed. But he did not want to take personal responsibility for the decision and so insisted on a poll of the 100 member stations. Vecchione
concurred, thinking that support from the stations would strengthen his
hand during any ensuing controversy.

Lehrer recalls that PBS vice president Gerry Slater got the hearings
on by posing a slanted "Should we do it?" type of question to the membership. "[It] would have done any professional pollster proud. It was
geared to get a yes answer, and it got that from a small but deciding majority." Small was right. Watergate got on the air by only a whisker.[18]

When the PBS stations voted on the proposal to cover the Watergate
hearings gavel-to-gavel, only 52 percent approved of the idea. So it was
important to get Ralph Rogers's personal blessing, as a prominent Republican and chairman of the PBS board, which he gave, though he was
said to have his own doubts about the enterprise.

And then the deed was done. NPACT ran the hearings twice a day,
morning and evening, for three months straight, all summer long. Former *Firing Line* producer Neal Freeman remembers the atmosphere as
"incredible, just wall-to-wall Watergate." After live afternoon broadcasts,
MacNeil and Lehrer hosted evening repeats, beefed up with expert
analysis, and alternated the closing commentary with each other à la
Huntley–Brinkley. They had become stars.

MacNeil recalls the public response as overwhelming.

For the first time in its brief history, it seemed the entire nation knew
what public television was. Viewers spontaneously sent money and took
out memberships. The memberships of some stations, like WNET in New
York, trebled because of the hearings. But the coverage served another,
deeper purpose: it revealed to doubters that public television journalism

could be vital, fair, and trenchant when dealing with the most sensitive political material. Perhaps the most important people to discover that were the managers of local stations who had long doubted that we should be in the news business at all.[19]

Lehrer feels the event was a watershed for the system. "As programming, the Watergate broadcasts were a terrific hit with the audience and the stations and established once and for all that real public affairs programming had a permanent place on public broadcasting. That was what Robin and I claimed, at least. As justice, it was pure delicious. We were being bailed out by the sins of a president who was trying to do us in. He and his minions were so distracted with the crumbling of his presidency that the plan to crumble us was abandoned and forgotten."[20]

And without PBS, it is unlikely that the networks would have covered what might have seemed like arcane proceedings. PBS's decision to broadcast the Watergate hearings convinced the commercial networks of their newsworthiness. "Watergate changed the history of this country," Al Vecchione says. "Public broadcasting, in its totality, did things that others don't do to set the standard. A couple of things I'd like to see on my gravestone: I helped get MacNeil/Lehrer going, and I'd like it to be remembered that we had something to do with forcing that initial decision to air the Watergate hearings." Vecchione later produced New York's 1976 Democratic convention (which nominated Jimmy Carter) for television. He turned down offers of political appointments in Carter's administration, though he served as a consultant to the President.

According to Lehrer, had it not been for the Nixon administration's early hostility to PBS over what the President perceived as anti–Nixon programming and PBS's revenge in the ensuing Watergate scandal, there would probably be no public broadcasting today, for lack of public passion. "It is an absolute certainty, there would be no anything called MacNeil/Lehrer. So for the record let me say . . . Thank you, Nixon. Thank you, Messrs. Liddy and Hunt, Dean and Colson, Haldeman and Ehrlichman. We could not have done it without you."

The broadcasts also forged the partnership of MacNeil and Lehrer. "Watergate got me on the air sitting next to Robert MacNeil," Lehrer says. "By example and by quiet words of advice, he taught me how to be what I was already paid to be: a television correspondent. . . . The most important happening during Watergate for me, of course, was that Robin and I had become friends."

Lehrer and MacNeil developed a philosophy of journalism that was to become the credo of the *NewsHour*. "Getting It Right is the first rule of journalism," MacNeil taught Lehrer. "And the second, the third, the fourth, and all the way to the tenth. Sloppiness with little facts, items as little even as middle initials or titles, leads to sloppiness with the big facts, the big ideas, and most everything else."[21] Together, immediately after the success of their Watergate coverage, the team proposed that PBS do a daily news show for which they would serve as anchors and maintain editorial control.

Approval for their proposal was not forthcoming, however, perhaps out of a fearful recognition by PBS brass and PBS chairman Ralph Rogers (still a registered Republican) that MacNeil and Lehrer might topple a sitting President.

So MacNeil returned to the BBC, because, he later said, "I had been marinating in the politics of public television for nearly two years, and my whole being began to smell of it. I could not face another year of that bickering." He found himself once again covering Nixon on *Panorama*. (Among other stories, he later covered Nixon's resignation and the inauguration of Gerald Ford for the program.)[22]

The House Judiciary Committee impeachment efforts soon came along to rescue Lehrer. In MacNeil's absence, Lehrer partnered with Paul Duke, MacNeil's replacement at *Washington Week in Review*. But the chemistry was not the same.

While MacNeil was back in London, Lehrer stayed at NPACT doing public affairs shows during the Ford administration—programs he characterized as the kind "nobody much watched except the blood kin of those who appeared on them." One was called *Washington Connection,* another was *Washington Straight Talk*. He spent his time interviewing Beltway insiders, such as Democratic National Committee chairman Bob Strauss and Republican National Committee chairman George Bush, as well as journalists like *New York Times* bureau chief R. W. Apple, Jr., and the *Baltimore Sun*'s Jack Germond. Lehrer felt he was in over his head. "The worst thing about it," he recalls, "was that I knew I was not doing well. . . . MacNeil was not there to counsel me."[23]

While Lehrer and MacNeil waited to be reunited, the PBS system was enjoying its victory over Nixon. James Day, former president of NET, characterized Jim Karayn's NPACT as "up off the deck and back in the fight again." *Bill Moyers' Journal* (sponsored by a Ford Foundation grant) had reappeared on the October 1973 public broadcasting schedule. Moyers's first show was called "An Essay on Watergate." Unlike MacNeil and Lehrer, Moyers hit Nixon when he was down and nearly out for the count.

After Nixon's resignation in August 1974, Jim Karayn was forced from his job at NPACT, and the operation was folded into WETA. Karayn believes PBS president Hartford Gunn had it in for him because Karayn had fought to air the Watergate hearings and Gunn held him responsible for the aftermath. According to Karayn, Gunn did not like political controversy. Karayn produced the 1976 presidential debates for the League of Women Voters and then went on to head up Philadelphia public station WHYY.

Lehrer went to London after Nixon's resignation to film a two-hour documentary about Vietnam called *The End of the Ho Chi Minh Trail*. His producers on that project were Al Vecchione and Linda Winslow, who would later become producers of *The MacNeil/Lehrer Report*. While he was working in England, Lehrer met up with MacNeil again. His former coanchor was about to return to the States to do a nightly half-hour news show for WNET in New York. It would focus on one story each night, in depth, as a supplement to the commercial networks' evening news. *The Robert MacNeil Report* was now "politically possible"—Nixon was gone.

With an initial budget of $1.4 million, MacNeil had the resources to hire Lehrer as Washington correspondent for the New York–based series. The project was initially opposed by Ward Chamberlin, Jr., then president of WETA, who felt it would compete with his Washington operations, but he relented after an understanding was worked out that shows like *Washington Week in Review* would remain, and Lehrer came aboard.

All agreed the show would play by a set of rules that would differentiate it from other programs. "We decided as an article of faith and practice that all guests were in fact guests and would be treated as such,"

Lehrer recalled. "We would help them get their positions or opinions out in a coherent and understandable form, so the audience could decide weight and merit. We would not beat up on our guests or embarrass them."[24]

The first broadcast of *The Robert MacNeil Report* aired on WNET October 20, 1975. It focused on New York City's fiscal plight. The next evening's program was about the Middle East. Within six months the program had been picked up for nightly national distribution by PBS, with the encouragement of then–PBS president Lawrence Grossman, who had succeeded Hartford Gunn in December 1975. And the program acquired a new name: *The MacNeil/Lehrer Report.* The set for the program, designed by Robert Wrightman, had a background recalling the box sculptures of American artist Louise Nevelson. A special horseshoe table was installed to facilitate discussions in the round, so that guest and host could sit comfortably without regard to camera placement. Instead of a traditional network news structure, which consists of highly paid correspondents who move from story to story, *MacNeil/Lehrer* hired young reporters and assigned them beats in which they would become expert. Rather than emphasizing visuals, the program concentrated on human faces, because, in MacNeil's view, "The human head is almost the only thing that appears on television close to life size. The TV screen is perfectly adapted to carrying the talking head."[25]

The two-host format, inspired by *The Huntley-Brinkley Report* and MacNeil's own role on *The Scherer-MacNeil Report,* allowed for some visual variety. Another advantage of the two-host format was, as MacNeil put it, "One can listen and think while the other is on." Instead of being introduced all at once, guests were introduced as their subject matter came up, as in a television documentary or newspaper article.

Famous already as a result of Watergate and his nightly news broadcasts, MacNeil was hired by the Mobil Corporation to serve as host for its syndicated Mobil Showcase Network, which ran on commercial stations from 1976 to 1983. Like Alistair Cooke on *Masterpiece Theatre,* MacNeil conveyed authority and class in his introduction to British dramas such as *Edward and Mrs. Simpson* and the Royal Shakespeare Company's *Nicholas Nickleby.* MacNeil's prestige had so grown that he was now sought after by Mobil for protection from an angry Congress concerned about the rising price of oil—at one point Senator Edward Kennedy had introduced legislation to nationalize the American oil industry. MacNeil's association with integrity would rub off on Mobil.

In 1983 *The MacNeil/Lehrer Report* expanded to one hour, changing its name to *The MacNeil/Lehrer NewsHour.* In marked contrast to the opposition of the Nixon administration and the CPB of the 1970s, CPB chairman Sonia Landau, a Republican who had been appointed to the CPB board by President Reagan, championed the expansion. It was a tribute to the program's reputation for balance and integrity; MacNeil and Lehrer were respected both by liberals like Larry Grossman and conservatives like Landau. Lester Crystal left NBC news to produce the expanded broadcast.

Charlayne Hunter-Gault, the first black woman to attend the University of Georgia and a *New York Times* reporter who had started filling in for MacNeil and Lehrer while the show was still a half hour long, was named national correspondent in 1983. She was given great freedom to pursue her own story ideas, "to follow my instincts," which tended to focus on stories concerned with human rights or international relations. During the Gulf War, Hunter-Gault received praise for her interviews with American soldiers. Afterward, though, she came in for criticism of her coverage of the Palestinians from the Committee for Accuracy in Middle East Reporting in America, a pro-Israel watchdog group based in Boston. She complained about their efforts in 1993. "They've launched a whole campaign against the work that I did in the West Bank and Gaza because they see it as being biased and stuff. But it wasn't." Hunter-Gault admitted that her Palestinian interview subjects "were allowed to say things that on the record aren't that way or may be not true. But it's their peception, and that's what's important when you're trying to help people understand a complex situation." She also covered apartheid in South Africa, famine in Somalia, and race relations in the United States.[26]

In 1983, MacNeil/Lehrer Productions began producing documentary specials for PBS and the other networks. These were different from the evening broadcasts, in that they gave the anchors a chance to add a personal perspective to the news, in much the way MacNeil had done for the BBC prior to his PBS days. The subject matter of these documentaries ranged widely. *The Heart of the Dragon* was a twelve-hour series about China, which PBS aired in 1985. *My Heart, Your Heart* grew out of Jim Lehrer's heart attack and detailed his bypass surgery at Georgetown University Hospital in 1984.

In 1986, MacNeil hosted a nine-hour documentary coproduction with the BBC, *The Story of English,* which traced the history and development of the language from Scotland to India to the isolated community of Tangier Island off the coast of Maryland. Thomas Edison was the subject of a 1988 one-hour biography. That year also saw the production of a six-hour series on American education, *Learning in America.* Parts I and II aired in 1988 and 1989; Part III of the series aired in 1992 under the subtitle "Education on Trial." It was taped in a courtroom in Denver, with lawyers presenting the case for and against America's public schools before an actual judge. Education was a subject MacNeil cared deeply about. In 1991, the company produced a five-hour special about President Reagan's surgeon general, C. Everett Koop. Health was of special interest to Lehrer after his heart attack, which no doubt led to *Eat Smart,* a television guide to sensible dieting.

At Christmastime 1994, MacNeil/Lehrer Productions branched out into new areas with the production of a staged adaptation of Charles Dickens's *A Christmas Carol.* Called *Bah, Humbug!,* the production recalled MacNeil's love affair with Dickens, as recounted in his early autobiography, *Wordstruck.* (A planned series on Shakespeare still remains in need of funding.) There was some poignancy to the event, broadcast from the Morgan Library in New York City. For on October 11, 1994, MacNeil had announced he would retire from the *NewsHour* on the program's twentieth anniversary. The 1995 season would be his last. He told the *Washington Post,* "I don't want to stay on the air until I start to drool." It was announced that Lehrer would succeed him as executive editor, and that MacNeil would concentrate on his writing and personal projects, such as a sequel to *The Story of English.*

While the *NewsHour* has been praised by liberals and conservatives alike, it has not been without its share of controversy. There have been occasional protests from gay groups like ACT-UP. Members of the organization once disrupted MacNeil's New York segment to protest what they claimed was a lack of interest in AIDS. The program's producers were forced to switch awkwardly to Lehrer in Washington until they had cleared the studio in New York. MacNeil later gave an interview to the *New York Times* in which he announced he had a homosexual son and supported his way of life.

Fairness and Accuracy in Reporting (FAIR), a left-wing organization best known for promoting the Super Bowl wife-beating hoax, issued a "study" that claimed the program was too "conservative" because it is hosted by white males and features government officials (many of whom are, in fact, extremely liberal). In response, the program added Erwin Knoll, editor of *The Progressive,* to its editor's roundtable.

There have also been attacks from highbrow conservative intellectuals, such as literary critic Bruce Bawer, over the presumed "middlebrow" status of the *NewsHour.* "The show is a mishmash," Bawer wrote in the *New Republic,* "a headline roundup that's notable for neither depth nor breadth and 'in-depth' coverage that too often resorts to unilluminating face-offs between familiar ideological extremes."

Such complaints don't bother Al Vecchione. He puts it somewhat directly: "Our approach has always been to take on the serious and important issues that we think people need to know about, not the ones that will titillate them. . . . We dare to be boring."

The very lack of flashy style reinforces the solemn purpose of the enterprise, as do the austere sets and the understated suits worn by the anchors. In his autobiography, Jim Lehrer calls this the "Skivvy Shirt Rule." The viewing public, Lehrer observes, would notice if they were to read the news in their underwear, and this costume would distract from the content of the news story. So the anchors of the *NewsHour* are committed to the proposition "Nothing should be noticed or absorbed except the information. Nothing else should be memorable. There is no such thing as a pretty slide, a zippy piece of music, a trendy shirt, a dynamic set, a tough question, or anything else, if it deflects even a blink of attention from the information." In other words, a puritan ethic and aesthetic for news programming.[27]

The result of this ethic, says Susan Jane Labaschin in her dissertation on television news, is a rational place to look at an irrational world.

The overall sense of the world conveyed by [the *NewsHour*] was that the world is highly complex but that thoughtful people can and do manage the complexities—basically by creating and supporting good laws. The role of the anchors in this is crucial: their function is to mediate between opposite opinions on frequently controversial and complex issues. The task of viewers is to decide for themselves what position to adopt. Clearly, despite the world's irrationalities, thoughtful and responsible human beings are deemed to make a difference. Moreover, even the viewer is encouraged out of a position of dependent passivity and is encouraged to become an active player in a fight to manage and rationalize the world.[28]

Such was MacNeil's prestige that when he retired in 1995 he was not replaced. The anchor's mantle fell to Lehrer alone, with a rotating crew of secondary hosts: Charlayne Hunter-Gault, Kwame Holman, Elizabeth Farnsworth, and Margaret Warner. After MacNeil's retirement, the New York studios were closed and production consolidated in Washington.

The second-longest-serving coanchor, Charlayne Hunter-Gault, was not fully happy with this arrangement. Passed over for a permanent anchor slot on the nightly news program in 1993, she began hosting *Rights and Wrongs,* a more overtly leftist series about human rights produced by former ABC News executive Daniel Schecter (not affiliated with MacNeil/Lehrer Productions). The series was rejected by the PBS national program service and syndicated to local stations. Hunter-Gault later told oral historian Mary Marshall Clark, "When a big and important job [opens up], for example . . . it still goes to the white man. . . . I think at a certain point the racial thing presents a greater challenge and difficulty than gender."[29] Yet her complaints have been relatively muted, and she has continued to appear on *NewsHour.* With the approval of both Democrats and Republicans, Lehrer was asked to moderate the 1992 presidential debates; anchor 1992, 1994, and 1996 convention and election coverage for NBC News; and host PBS's 1996 election specials.

It is clear that with the *NewsHour,* Jim Lehrer continues to do what he had managed to accomplish with Robert MacNeil, provide what the Carnegie Commission Report of 1967 called upon PBS to provide: "A civilized voice in a civilized community."

5

This Is *Frontline*

The current affairs documentary series *Frontline* is easily one of public television's most popular and prestigious offerings. Over six million viewers watch each episode, according to originating station WGBH, Boston.[1]

Since its debut in 1983, the only regularly scheduled documentary hour on the national PBS feed has won a shelf of honors, including Emmys as well as Polk, Peabody, DuPont/Columbia, and Robert F. Kennedy journalism awards.

Coproduction partners have included the BBC, *Time* magazine, Columbia University's Seminars on Media and Society, and San Francisco's Center for Investigative Reporting. Among the guest correspondents have been Bill Moyers, Hodding Carter, Garry Wills, Roger Wilkins, Shelby Steele, William Greider, Seymour Hersh, Richard Reeves, and James Reston, Jr. Former *TV Guide* reporter Don Kowet has said that executive producer David Fanning deserves a place in the "pantheon" of the most powerful people in national television news, alongside Peter Jennings, Dan Rather, and Tom Brokaw.[2] Series executive editor Louis Wiley, Jr., came to WGBH to work on *The Advocates* after graduation from Yale University and Georgetown University Law School in 1970. Senior producer Martin Smith had worked with Moyers on *Our Times* at CBS News before joining *Frontline*. Series editor Marrie Campbell was a Moyers alumna as well, having spent time as a researcher on *Bill Moyers' Journal* at WNET.

121

Yet despite its reputation for excellence, a close examination of *Frontline* reveals a pattern of political bias and shoddy journalism. Even *Mother Jones* magazine declared the series to be "knee-jerk liberal, but very influential with the educated elite."[3] Disturbingly, the series that is considered by many to be a crown jewel of PBS current affairs coverage has given significant airtime to demonstrably anti-Israel productions, casting overall doubts on PBS's credibility and offending some of the network's most loyal donors.

Frontline was the brainchild of Lewis Freedman, one of the pioneers of public broadcasting. Originally a producer for CBS's *Camera Three,* a cultural program, Freedman had produced *New York Television Theatre* for Channel 13 then joined Fred Friendly on *Public Broadcasting Laboratory* in the late 1960s and later headed up *Hollywood Television Theatre* at KCET in Los Angeles. Among his productions were *The Andersonville Trial* and *Steambath,* both critical and ratings successes. He left public broadcasting in 1972 to return to CBS, where he produced a miniseries on the life of Benjamin Franklin "and made Bill Paley happy" by producing the "Bicentennial Minutes" in 1976.[4]

Freedman returned to public broadcasting as an executive at the Corporation for Public Broadcasting, assuming the position of director of the program fund in 1979. "They wanted somebody experimental, with a little sense of daring," he recalled. Fearful of the effect Republican CPB appointees (half the board, as required by law) might have on public broadcasting, liberals on the CPB board such as Sharon Percy Rockefeller (wife of Senator John D. Rockefeller IV, whose father sat on the first CPB board) and Geoffrey Cowan (a former lawyer for Ralph Nader and the son of Louis Cowan, who had resigned as CBS president in 1959 in the wake of the quiz show scandals) established a "program fund" at the CPB to replace the previously freewheeling system whereby CPB directors would simply suggest programs to be funded. "Our mandate was to cater to independent producers," Freedman said. "It came from the board of CPB."

By establishing a unit headed by Freedman—a veteran of NET and the Ford Foundation—the CPB board transferred its authority to staff members and outside producers. He was a safe choice. The board promised Freedman that he could create a series with his signature and that there would be no interference with his programming choices.

The purpose of this bureaucratic move was political, namely, to insulate public broadcasting's establishment from any change and obscure the responsibility for programming decisions. Once the precedent had been set, it would be difficult for presidential appointees to undo decisions without an open revolt. Canceling a series against the will of CPB executives could be portrayed as "political" in a way that establishing the series in the first place would not. And by establishing the "principle" of separation between programming staff and the CPB board of directors, even as staff were following the instructions of the CPB board in establishing *Frontline* and other series, Cowan and Rockefeller and their compatriots on the CPB board provided an argument to preserve the status quo.

"The board expected me to recreate *Sesame Street,* because word had gotten out that I was involved in the original discussions," Freedman said. He established two public affairs series, *Matters of Life and Death* and *Frontline.*[5] The first series folded after one season, replaced by the equally short-lived *Crisis to Crisis,* but *Frontline* endured.[6]

Frontline, as Freedman conceived it in 1980, was a weekly documentary program, a reliable outlet for the work of the best independent filmmakers. By locating it at a PBS station and arranging a consortium of stations to support it, Freedman had also insulated the program against critics in advance—which may have encouraged careless reporting.

Frontline is a true child of the PBS system. Although it is based at Boston's WGBH, the program is coproduced by a consortium of four other stations: KCTS in Seattle, WNET in New York, WPBT in Miami, and WTVS in Detroit. *Frontline* is entirely paid for by the CPB and PBS. It depends on no corporate sponsor that could pull its funding unexpectedly. The series operates on an annual budget of over $11 million, airs on some 300 PBS stations, and reaches 97 percent of U.S. television households. Like many PBS offerings, *Frontline* is dependent on British sources, especially the BBC's *Panorama,* for material, some of which is "reversioned" at up to $100,000 per show with American voice-overs to mask its foreign origin. These are sometimes called "coproductions."

David Fanning, executive producer since the program's debut in 1982, first visited the United States in 1964 as an eighteen-year-old high school exchange student from South Africa. During a stopover in New York City, he saw television for the first time (it had been slow in coming to South Africa). Fanning eventually returned to his homeland, where he attended the University of Cape Town. He later worked as a newspaper reporter and then began a stint as a freelance documentary filmmaker for the BBC. He produced two anti-apartheid films in the early 1970s, *Amabandla AmaAfrika* (1970) and *The Church and Apartheid* (1972). In 1973, he talked his way into a job as a producer for KOCE, the public TV station in Huntington Beach, California. Since there were no staff positions available, Fanning worked for free until the station could hire him.[7] A low-budget documentary Fanning produced on the war in Angola caught the eye of Peter McGhee, the former executive editor of *The Advocates* who had risen to become director of national programming at WGBH. In 1977, Fanning left KOCE and moved to Boston to work for McGhee as the producer of an international documentary series called *World.*

"The [WGBH] general manager had wanted to hire somebody from commercial television who would be reassuring to the stations," McGhee recalled. "I thought David had some interesting ideas about documentaries. He was willing to gamble, and so was I." Fanning has called McGhee the most intelligent man in public broadcasting for securing foreign money to pay for his station's programs, including *Frontline's* many coproductions with British and other television networks.[8]

As *Frontline* after it would, WGBH's *World,* which ran for five years, depended heavily on BBC's *Panorama* and other imported documentaries for its content. In 1980, *World* aired "Death of a Princess," a docudrama cowritten and coproduced by Fanning and his British partner, Antony Thomas, working for Independent Television's ATV (a commercial British television company). Its broadcast would lead to *World's* eventual cancellation—after a decent interval.

"Death of a Princess" was based on a 1977 story Thomas said he read in newspapers and "heard as gossip from a friend." According to Thomas, the young princess in question, Mishaal, was the favorite granddaughter of the Saudi king's elder brother. She had met her lover at a university in Beirut. She was married at the time, but her husband had abandoned her. So when she brought her commoner lover home, she did not expect any trouble. When she was taken before a judge, she refused to deny her actions. After she was found guilty of adultery, she was wrapped in black, taken to a crowded parking lot, and shot. Her lover was beheaded.

Thomas thought the tragic love story symbolized the dangers of Islam for an oil-dependent West after the OPEC boycott. The Saudis saw PBS as an official government channel; federal sponsorship in this case led to an international incident. The Saudi government complained to the U.S. State Department that the film was offensive and inaccurate and demanded immediate cancellation of the broadcast; they expelled the British ambassador when the program aired in England (before the PBS broadcast). A multimillion-dollar libel suit was also filed on behalf of all Muslims, but it was later dismissed as frivolous.

The Saudi protest was delivered to the State Department by Ambassador Faisal Alhegelan, who gave Warren Christopher, at that time Acting Secretary of State, a letter outlining the Saudi objections. The ambassador asked that the letter be forwarded to PBS with a note from Christopher. One U.S. diplomat said afterward, "Because of the great importance we attach to having a strong relationship with Saudi Arabia, we have taken its concerns under review."

Christopher did write to PBS president Larry Grossman, urging that the system give "appropriate consideration" to the Saudi position. In the letter, Christopher said he was certain PBS would make sure that "viewers are given a full and balanced presentation." At the same time, the Acting Secretary maintained that the federal government "cannot and will not attempt to exercise any power of censorship" over the network.[9]

Republican senator Charles Percy of Illinois, father of CPB board member Sharon Percy Rockefeller, told President Carter, "There would be support in Congress should the President make a determination that the showing of the program would not be in the national interest." In the House of Representatives, Clement Zablocki, a Wisconsin Democrat, and William S. Broomfield, a Michigan Republican, urged that the film not be shown.[10]

The Mobil Corporation, a partner in the Arabian-American Oil Company (ARAMCO) and a major supporter of public broadcasting, notably as the underwriter of *Masterpiece Theatre* (see Chapter 11), also protested the docudrama with an advertisement in the *New York Times* headlined "A New Fairy Tale," four days before the scheduled broadcast. In the ad, WGBH's largest financial contributor publicly took PBS to task for the program, saying the broadcast threatened America's relations with Saudi Arabia. PBS president Larry Grossman has said he thought

Mobil may not have minded on its own account. Grossman noted, "Mobil was just going through the motions to please the Saudis," and claimed that the only effect of the published complaint was "to increase the ratings of the show, because once they ran the ad, PBS had to run the show."[11] WGBH president Henry Becton agrees with Grossman's assessment. "[Mobil] built up our viewership for the program by their criticism of it. But I never once had a phone call or comment directly from anyone at Mobil telling me 'Please don't run this program.' Nor any threats that it would affect our funding for *Masterpiece Theatre*."[12]

Others, however, note that Mobil's leverage was so great it didn't *need* to ask WGBH to do things. Curiously, although "Death of a Princess," which aired May 12, 1980, followed by a half-hour panel discussion, was the highest rated dramatic program ever shown in the history of PBS,[13] WGBH has never aired any reruns of it.

Criticism of the film focused primarily on its re-creations. The Saudis said they were wholly false, but Fanning maintained that they were backed up by "painstaking research."[14] Mobil's "New Fairy Tale" advertisement in the *New York Times* charged that PBS's airing of the film "raises some very serious issues." Mobil questioned the obligations of a free press and the role of the government in supporting public TV. But it was a portion of the ad headlined "The Reality of Docu-drama" that most angered Fanning and Thomas. It was based on a letter to the *New Statesman,* a British magazine, from Penelope Mortimer, who had worked as a writer on the "Princess" project.

Mortimer is quoted directly in the ad: "Every interview and every character in the film is fabricated." She claimed that the producers had made "no effort" to check certain facts. In response, Thomas claimed that Mortimer had left the project long before the film was finished, and he declared that "every line" was accurate. He said the film's facts were based on transcriptions of interviews with dozens of people with knowledge of the actual event.

Fanning charged that Mobil "almost threatens public television, 'If you want our continued support.'" WGBH's president, David O. Ives, characterized Mortimer as a "disaffected employee." Her protest, therefore, had to be "discounted to that extent." He added that since Mobil did business in Saudi Arabia, its protests were self-serving.[15]

A coproducer of the show, Michael Solomon, was said to have worked out a deal that kept "Death of a Princess" from being shown in Japan, Germany, Italy, and France for four years in exchange for $20 million from Saudi representatives. "It's not blackmail," Solomon told a reporter at the time. "I'm not blackmailing them. I'm putting a price on a film that I co-produced and own." At the time, Fanning said of the proposed deal, "We [he and coproducer Anthony Thomas] would oppose it absolutely."[16]

A little more than two years later, WGBH permitted *World* to disappear from the schedule. Among the last broadcasts was another coproduction with British producer Antony Thomas, this one profiling rogue CIA agent turned international arms dealer Frank Terpil, called "Frank Terpil, Confessions of a Dangerous Man." It won an Emmy in 1983.

Even as *World* was winding down, David Fanning moved into new territory as producer of the *Frontline* series. Almost immediately, he found himself accused of having joined the Establishment; independent filmmakers, who were used to a more open system of documentary commissioning, worried that Fanning's series might be a new barrier to limit their access to documentary funds. Fanning does rely on what he calls his "repertory company" of "filmmakers and journalists who had worked in a journalistic tradition."[17]

To host the program Fanning chose the glamorous young NBC weekend anchorwoman Jessica Savitch over veteran newsmen Charles Kuralt and Daniel Schorr, because he wanted an "audience getter, a popular figure who could convince mainstream viewers to turn their channels to public broadcasting." Savitch was lured to PBS with the promise of increased visibility as she attempted to climb to the nightly news anchor post at NBC. She received $91,000 annually for her part-time work taping introductions in Boston from Sunday nights through Monday. WGBH also paid for a full-time secretary, a credit card, prepaid expenses, first-class accommodations, and cash advances. Savitch demanded a writing credit as well, although the films had actually been written and produced by others: as Savitch biographer Alanna Nash commented, "to someone who didn't know how television fit together it looked like she was doing most of the work herself."[18]

Savitch was subject to violent mood swings and looked "disheveled" when not on camera. One staffer who found her one day on a couch looking like "one of the street people" with matted hair and rumpled clothes wondered "whether the drug rumors were true." Savitch had been known to use cocaine; Nash reports that the *Frontline* host told the staff "nothing like that is going on anymore," but in fact "it did not appear to be so."[19]

Frontline's premiere episode on January 17, 1983, was probably intended to be relatively uncontroversial compared with "Death of a Princess." "An Unauthorized History of the NFL" was about pro football, an alleged gambling scandal in the National Football League, and the strange death of former Los Angeles Rams owner Carroll Rosenbloom. Football must have seemed an easy target for a producer based on the campus of Harvard University. But unfortunately for Fanning, there was once again some uncertainty about what was true and what wasn't.

The program strongly suggested that Rosenbloom had been murdered by the Mafia in Florida in 1979. Savitch's ominous narration called him "perhaps the first NFL owner whose underworld ties led to his death." The producers had paid an anonymous informant to give testimony against the dead Rosenbloom, who not only was in no position to clear his name but whose bloated and waterlogged corpse was featured in close-ups in order to symbolize the intersection of professional football, gambling, and organized crime. The charges were not proved by the evidence presented in the show. *Frontline* was accused of checkbook journalism; members of the advisory board were "embarrassed." *Los Angeles Times* television critic Howard Rosenberg called the premiere broadcast "appallingly shoddy."[20]

Sports Illustrated published a rebuttal by William Taafe headlined "Unfounded Findings," which accused the producers of ignoring evidence that Rosenbloom had drowned accidentally. Taafe condemned the producers for paying a bookie's runner $1,500 "to repeat underworld gossip" while failing to interview any of the eyewitnesses listed in the police report or mention the recorded ocean conditions. *Sports Illustrated* had contacted five members of *Frontline*'s editorial advisory board: newspaper columnist Ellen Goodman and University of Massachusetts professor Lawrence Pinkham said they had not seen the broadcast;

Kennedy School of Government professor Jonathan Moore and WGBH producer Michael Ambrosino refused to comment. Only Richard Salant, former CBS News president, admitted to having seen the show and having concerns. From the beginning of the series, then, credibility has been a problem for *Frontline*.[21]

The 1983–84 season featured the liberal subjects that would recur during the series. It included "88 Seconds in Greensboro," James Reston, Jr.'s, report on a violent 1979 clash in North Carolina between Nazis and Communists that left five of the latter dead; "In the Shadow of the Capitol," which showed the poverty of Washington, D.C., and profiled Mayor Marion Barry; "God's Banker," an exposé of the Vatican Bank scandal surrounding the death of Roberto Calvi in London; the anti-military "Pentagon, Inc."; a call for gun control, "Gunfight USA"; "A Journey to Russia," sympathetically portraying the Soviet Union; "Daisy: Story of a Facelift," which followed a fifty-five-year-old woman through her surgical makeover; "Space: The Race for the High Ground," a critical look at what would become known as Reagan's Star Wars program; the intimate world of "Abortion Clinic"; "Crisis in Zimbabwe"; "Looking for Mao," which detailed the aftermath of the Chinese leader's death; "Israel: Between the River and the Sea," which told the story of an Arab reporter working for Israeli television; "In Our Water," about the story of contaminated drinking water in a New Jersey suburb; "Vietnam Memorial," on the dedication of the now-famous wall; "The Russians Are Here," a portrait that gave the impression that the émigrés had been better off before they came to America (A Washington Post review said the show highlights drawbacks to Capitalism: "the fact that nobody is responsible for you, that the state doesn't take care of you in the all-embracing way the Soviet state takes care of its own");[22] an attack on the Reagan administration's attempt to crack down on fraud in "Who Decides Disability?"; "Crossfire in El Salvador," critical of the anti-Communist government; "Sanctuary," favorably portraying those who helped Guatemalan refugees; "Moneylenders," a critical account of banks that had made loans to Brazil and Mexico; and "Klaus Barbie: The American Connection," which accused the United States and its intelligence agencies of working with the former Nazi.

After Savitch's own mysterious drowning in a car accident in 1983, television journalist Judy Woodruff began moonlighting as series host, keeping her "day job" at the *The MacNeil/Lehrer NewsHour* for the six years she hosted *Frontline*. At the time, Fanning told a reporter: "I appreciate that Les Crystal [executive producer of *MacNeil/Lehrer*] was able to spare her. I think it's a good chance for us to connect with the other part of PBS public service programming. It's a much better idea than for us to grab someone out of commercial television."[23]

Woodruff tried to make her role more than that of a spokesmodel. "We have an agreement," she said, "that if there's something in the program I for any reason am not comfortable with, it will be redone or else I wouldn't do the program. That's pretty standard for someone in my position." Fanning, however, insisted on limiting her role to the introductory segments. "This is not *Bill Moyers' Journal*," he said. "We're looking for someone to be a collaborator. We will certainly hear her opinions editorially. It will be up to her to craft and shape what's been said, and it's an opportunity for her to essay somewhat. . . . [But] we're not trying to find any individual to take over the show."[24] In 1992 Woodruff left *MacNeil/Lehrer* and *Frontline* to take a job with CNN as nightly news anchor.

Two senior producers joined Fanning to strengthen the *Frontline* team. In 1987 Michael Sullivan, previously chief of the investigative section at WCCO-TV (a commercial station) in Minneapolis, arrived. Sullivan had coproduced four *Frontline* documentaries, the last being "Death of a Porn Queen" (1987), about a young Midwestern girl who lived and died in the haze of Hollywood's X-rated-movie world. His other *Frontline* contributions include "AIDS: A National Inquiry" (1985) and "Vietnam Under Communism" (1984). Martin Smith, who joined the *Frontline* team in 1990, specialized in international productions. He was responsible for "Inside Gorbachev's Russia" that year and had supplied "The Real Life of Ronald Reagan" as an independent producer in 1989.

In any given year the series treats a wide variety of topics, only some of them overtly political. In 1992, for example, *Frontline* presented twenty-eight hours of new programming on subjects ranging from a biography of Soviet dissident Andrei Sakharov to an investigation of the federal government's bungling of the savings-and-loan bailout. One program in that year's lineup looked at the financial empire of the Unification Church; in another, the lives of a psychiatrist and a former patient of his were examined in intimate detail as the patient pursued a malpractice suit because the doctor had become her lover. Political reporter William Greider worked with *Frontline* as a correspondent on a series deploring the supposedly sorry state of American democracy.

Within PBS, Fanning operates with considerable autonomy. The series board of directors representing the five stations meets quarterly to approve the budget and make other administrative decisions. But Fanning and the staff at WGBH are the ones who come up with the ideas for the documentaries they produce. Board members do not officially approve the topics or preview the documentaries. The purpose of this setup is a process insulated from everybody, even from the board of directors. Previews of finished programs are offered only as a courtesy, producers say.

However, despite these claims of insulation and independence, Fanning has been accused of bending under sufficient pressure. In 1988 he pulled from his schedule two shows critical of the Reverend Pat Robertson—programs that had been produced by his partner on "Death of a Princess," Antony Thomas. Liberal groups complained of censorship when these films were axed from a season that had already included a broadcast attacking Jim and Tammy Faye Bakker (*Frontline*'s second season had included a devastating profile of Jimmy Lee Swaggart). Fanning must have realized that three anti-Christian shows in a row might have cost him his series. The shows were eventually aired on WGBH outside the series.[25] During the Gulf War, Fanning bowed to concerns about a pledge-week rebroadcast of "High Crimes and Misdemeanors," an episode about the Iran–Contra scandal that included unsubstantiated accusations of treason against Presidents Bush and Reagan, and agreed to cancel it. But when asked by the *Washington Post* whether he was rallying behind the President because of the war, Fanning replied, "I can't say strongly enough that that's the last thing in our mind."[26]

Not only did *Frontline* drop shows, it added them. In 1985 Fanning inserted a four-part miniseries into the *Frontline* schedule called "Crisis in Central America." The program included a segment favorable to American policy in El Salvador by conservative producer Austin Hoyt with the help and advice of Neal Freeman, William F. Buckley's former assistant and former member of the CPB board. Fanning needed considerable persuasion before he put the miniseries, which Hoyt characterized as "fair" and "balanced," in his *Frontline* schedule—previously known for pro-Sandinista offerings.[27]

Nevertheless, Fanning strikes a pose of independence and has often waxed philosophical about the superiority of *Frontline,* sometimes disparaging other documentary shows while blowing his own horn: "You can make intelligent television, but I fear for it. I think TV people don't believe in it. . . . *60 Minutes* rips off print investigation. That's what they do. There is a widening gap between print press and TV journalism. So we have an obligation to make every one of those films as thorough as we can make it."[28]

Despite the highly political nature of some of the programming Fanning produces, he feigns indifference to American politics. "Having grown up in the caldron of South African politics," he says, "I tend to be skeptical of establishments. But I've never had any political agenda. I'm not vain or arrogant enough [for that]."[29] Yet *Frontline's* reporters have often been the advance scouts on such highly charged political stories as the so-called "October Surprise," Carter National Security Adviser Gary Sick's charge that the Reagan campaign had delayed release of the Iranian hostages in 1979 in order to win the 1980 election. The October Surprise was the center of the April 16, 1991, program "The Election Held Hostage," reported by Robert Parry. As the Media Research Center's David Muska notes, "even after the *New Republic, Newsweek,* and even the ultra liberal *Village Voice* pronounced the story fraudulent, *Frontline* devoted another full hour to the charge a year later"[30]—the April 7, 1992, "Investigating the October Surprise," also reported by Parry. Not only journalists refuted *Frontline's* claims of Republican perfidy—a congressional committee controlled by Democrats came to that same conclusion after extensive investigation. Yet *Frontline* never corrected the record.

A pattern that apparently began with Fanning's "Death of a Princess," continued in "An Unauthorized History of the NFL," and reappeared in "The Election Held Hostage" is still in evidence today in numerous *Frontline* productions. In 1986 *Frontline* aired a twelve-part series sympathetic to the Soviet Union called "Comrades."

Muska argues that the pattern is found even in *Frontline*'s official account of its story selection process, which lists two significant criteria for programming decisions made collectively by the five senior producers on the editorial committee: a major social, political, or economic issue and a strong storyline with a human dimension. "Nowhere in the three-page document do the words 'objectivity' or 'balance' appear," Muska points out. He quotes a statement by Fanning that the purpose of his series is "to raise consciousness." No wonder, then, that in Muska's analysis of seventy-three programs produced between 1990 and 1993 he could find only two that could be considered conservative.[31] From 1993 to 1996 the pattern continued, with liberal programs criticizing Newt Gingrich, Rush Limbaugh, and Rupert Murdoch scheduled along with a favorable account of "Hillary's Class" at Wellesley College and a worshipful biography titled "The Pilgrimage of Jesse Jackson" that glossed over his history of anti-Semitism and blamed Jewish groups for calling attention to his notorious "Hymietown" remark.

A dramatic case of what Muska called "advocacy journalism" involved "Journey to the Occupied Lands" (1993), condemned by the Anti-Defamation League of B'nai B'rith for anti-Israeli bias in testimony to the Corporation for Public Broadcasting.[32] The controversy is interesting because it repeats themes that emerged twenty-two years earlier, when *The Advocates* dealt with similar material (see Chapter 7). Indeed, *Advocates* alumnus Peter McGhee, now responsible for *Frontline,* had been the producer who had placed a man Alan Dershowitz called "a phony" on the witness stand to represent the Palestinians in 1971. McGhee's program would be accused of fraud in this case as well. Louis Wiley, *Frontline*'s executive editor, began his career at WGBH working for McGhee on *The Advocates.*

Anti-Israel programming is unfortunately something of a tradition in public broadcasting. While the commercial networks air the occasional nightly news segment provoking the ire of friends of the Jewish state, they balance them with sympathetic accounts of the plight of a small nation surrounded by hostile neighbors. For every sympathetic *60 Minutes* interview with PLO leader Hanan Ashrawi or Yasser Arafat there has been a profile of an Israeli statesman such as Shimon Peres or Abba Eban.

But while PBS has aired sympathetic accounts of Holocaust victims and one series on the Jewish contribution to Western development (*Heritage: Civilization and the Jews,* with Abba Eban—paid for by the Israeli Bank Leumi), when it comes to current affairs the public network seems to believe that a vibrant and progressive Jewish state is not to be praised. Andrea Levin, executive director of the Committee for Accuracy in Middle East Reporting (CAMERA), has explained this strange inconsistency by pointing out, "PBS likes dead Jews, it just doesn't like living ones."[33]

David Bar-Ilan, a columnist for the *Jerusalem Post* and now an official in Israeli prime minister Benjamin Netanyahu's government, has written:

> In its treatment of the Arab–Israeli conflict, no commercial network in the U.S. is as guilty as PBS of conscious prevarications, outright falsehoods, and contempt for the most fundamental journalistic ethics. The network's anti-Israel bias dominates the choice of productions to the exclusion of virtually any other considerations. Films produced by PLO propagandists are accepted without question. In the network's search for Israel-damning material, values like probity, professional standards, rules of evidence, and basic fairness are cast to the winds.[34]

It is not just Israelis who object to what they see on PBS. American Jewish leaders are likewise disturbed. Ruthellen Harriss, executive director of the Jewish Community Relations Council of greater San Jose, California, is among those who have commented on the situation. She told a reporter, "There is a great sense in our community of anti-Israel bias by NPR and PBS in its Middle East coverage." Herb Brin, publisher of *Heritage,* a Los Angeles–based Jewish newspaper, characterized PBS documentaries as "yellow journalism" that was "hostile to the Jewish people."

Jerry D. Isaak-Shapiro, associate director of the San Francisco Jewish Community Relations Council, analyzed twenty-four programs dealing with Israel that had aired on KQED, the Bay Area PBS affiliate, since the mid-70s. Although these programs were not all necessarily broadcast nationally, Isaak-Shapiro's analysis provides clear evidence of partisanship at one PBS station. The study found that nineteen of the twenty-four KQED broadcasts promoted an Arab or Palestinian perspective. Among them were shows with titles like *Letters from Palestine* and *The Faces of Arafat.* Only two programs were critical of the Arab position vis-à-vis the Jewish state: *Sword of Islam* and *The Arming of Iraq.* Two programs were pro-Israel:

Heritage: Civilization and the Jews, which was historical in nature, and *Search for Solid Ground: The Intifada Through Israeli Eyes.* Of the twenty-four shows, the analysis found only one since 1981 that could be called fair and balanced: *Arab and Jew: Wounded Spirits in the Promised Land.*

A group of seventeen documentaries aired on the PBS network relating to the Arab–Israeli conflict have been analyzed by CAMERA as "damning Israel with distorted or false charges." The films included *Days of Rage* (1989), a puff piece on the PLO-led intifada, a film that was funded indirectly by Arab groups and eventually disowned by PBS. So pronounced was the propaganda element in this film that the PBS executive responsible for commissioning it was let go. Another case involved a film called *The Women Next Door* (1993). Using a feminist angle to chip away at the legitimacy of the Jewish state, the show blamed Israeli "oppressors" for causing increased miscarriages among Palestinian women through use of tear gas, a charge refuted even by a U.S. General Accounting Office study conducted at the urging of Berkeley congressman Ron Dellums. Yet another anti-Israel tract given the PBS seal of approval was *Struggle for Peace: Israelis and Palestinians* (1992), paid for in part by ARAMCO. This program focused on Israeli women who demonstrate against the government's policy in the occupied territories in solidarity with the PLO.[35]

"Journey to the Occupied Lands" centered on Sabri Gharib, a Palestinian farmer who claimed his land had been taken from him by the Israelis. Through this story, the film charged that Israel forces Arabs to live in "ghettos," that Arab villages are not allowed to grow, and that Israel keeps Gaza from becoming a "bustling commercial center." The film also claims that Arabs have been tortured by the Israeli military.

Despite the obvious removal of the wall that separated the Jordanian and Israeli armies from 1948 until reunification in 1967, and unlimited access to holy places by people of all faiths, the film claimed that Jerusalem, "a city that was supposed to be united in 1967, is as divided as ever." The film further alleged that Israel will not allow Arab workers suspected of "political or trade union activity" to enter the country. This claim flies in the face of published reports to the contrary by the International Labor Organization. The film even asserted that Israel "altered the balance" between the Jewish and Arab populations to ensure that

Jerusalem "will never be anything but a Jewish city"—despite over two hundred years of a Jewish majority or plurality.

The producer of "Journey to the Occupied Lands" was Michael Ambrosino, who had been associated with WGBH for over a quarter of a century in a variety of capacities and whose work could be said to represent all that public broadcasting documentaries were meant to be. Trained at the BBC as part of a transatlantic exchange with WGBH, he was one of the original producers of the highly praised science series *Nova.* He hired a number of BBC veterans at the Boston station. Ambrosino eventually left *Nova* to form his own private production company (called Public Broadcasting Associates, reflecting his close historical ties with the institution), through which he continued to produce shows for PBS, including the science documentary series *Odyssey* and *The Ring of Truth.* He was and is extremely highly regarded by PBS insiders. One retired public broadcasting official, Donald R. Quayle, wrote that he was glad to "have been able to make decisions regarding funding which have supported [Ambrosino's work]" because it is "characterized by his insistence on careful and painstaking research for accuracy, his passion for truth, his caring for the well-being of others. . . . Above all is his compassion for the human condition. All this was reflected in his 'Journey to the Occupied Lands.' " In other words, in his life and work, Ambrosino reflects the values public broadcasters share.[36]

Some outside observers to public broadcasting, however, see this particular example of Ambrosino's work very differently indeed. Writing in the *Jewish Advocate,* Jerold S. Auerbach called the film "as predictable as a grade-B Hollywood Western" with "Palestinian good guys" and "Israeli bad guys." He characterized it as straddling "science fiction and Palestinian agitprop." Auerbach especially objected to the use of stereotypes in the film:

> Once the focus of conflict is squeezed into the pat Palestinian formula of Israeli conquest and colonial occupation, Ambrosino can introduce all the usual stock characters. In the familiar starring role as pitiful victims are the Palestinians. Every Palestinian feeling, no matter how hallucinatory, is taken at face value. If they "feel" they are "descended from the original inhabitants of Palestine," who is Ambrosino to question it? If they "say" the land is theirs, because *muhktars* or goat droppings support their claim, it

must be true. When they attribute all sources of their misery to Israel, Ambrosino gently prods them: "This is what occupations are like, aren't they?" At the very least, this is what gullible filmmakers are like.[37]

Auerbach concludes that the initials PBS might be thought of as standing for the Palestinian Broadcasting Service. Or, as David Bar-Ilan put it in the *Jerusalem Post*, "the closest imitation of the old Soviet propaganda machine in the western world."

Outraged by "Journey to the Occupied Lands," CAMERA's head of research, Alex Safian, put together a detailed account of the program's factual flaws and presented it at the organization's 1993 annual conference, later publishing it as a monograph, PBS *and Israel: A Pattern of Bias*.

Ambrosino issued a rebuttal to Safian's report, which Safian quickly countered with a detailed 144-page study that is perhaps as revealing an indictment of PBS fraud as that which greeted "Liberators" (see Chapter 6).

Safian uncovered *Frontline* executive producer David Fanning's history of anti-Israel productions, among them "The Arab and the Israeli" (1984), which promoted a tour sponsored by the anti-Israel American Friends Service Committee; "Israel: The Price of Victory" (1987), which presented the triumph in the 1967 war as a cause of Israel's moral and spiritual decline; and "Israel: The Covert Connection" (1989), in which ultraleft, anti-Israel activists Andrew and Leslie Cockburn—son and daughter-in-law of British KGB agent Claud Cockburn—blamed the Jewish state for the Iran–Contra scandal, among other real and imaginary accusations.

Safian's research also turned up the facts that Ambrosino's senior researcher, Marty Rosenbluth, was a participating member of an activist on-line computer network called Palestine Net and a signatory to three separate anti-Zionist newspaper advertisements published in Great Britain in 1989 and 1990.

Ambrosino's film was originally titled "Justice in the Promised Land." This title turned out to be extremely significant, because it linked the production to an outside cause. Safian discovered that the case of Sabri Gharib had been at the center of a coordinated Palestinian propaganda campaign to smear Israel as an unjust society. The campaign had been waged since at least November 21, 1986, by the Palestine Human

Rights Campaign (PHRC), which was based in Chicago. On that date, the pro-PLO group had issued an urgent "Action Alert!" with the headline "Help us keep Palestinians on their land and in their institutions." The alert contained this passage:

> Our Jerusalem colleagues in the Committee Confronting the Iron Fist have called for PHRC's *immediate assistance* in two human rights cases. . . .
> *CASE #1: Palestinian Farmer Loses His Land:* [case of Sabri] presents a typical land case, but one that cries out for our immediate assistance to redress a gross injustice. . . . The family of 15 persons, including 12 children, have lived by farming their 112-dunum plot [1 dunum equals ¹/₄ acre] in the village of Beit Ijza [15 kilometers northwest of Jerusalem]. The farm was surveyed and has been in the Ghuraib family since the Ottoman occupation. Since 1979, Sabri has resisted the total theft of his farm from a nearby settlement, Hadasha, which bulldozed 25 dunums for a road. An Israeli Military Objections Committee upheld the settler theft in a 1982 ruling despite Sabri's ownership documents. *On April 15, 1986, the Israeli High Court of "Justice" upheld the Military Committee ruling which favored the settlement's actions and declared Sabri's farm "State land."*

It is obvious from the preceding passage that the case of Sabri Gharib (spelling varies) had been at the center of an anti-Israel propaganda campaign for at least seven years before the airing of "Journey to the Occupied Lands." There is little doubt that Ambrosino intended the original title, "Justice in the Promised Land," to be a mocking one, just as the PHRC "alert" put ironic quotation marks around the word "Justice." In any case, it is difficult to believe it a mere coincidence that the storyline of Ambrosino's film followed the script of the PHRC "alert" about the matter.

Interestingly, in "Journey to the Occupied Lands," Ambrosino goes beyond the assertions even of the PHRC, which admitted that the Israeli courts found the land claims unjustified. The film's narration states that "Gharib . . . did win an official decision to get most of his land back." Safian located the court records in Israel, translated them, and discovered that Ambrosino's claims, like Gharib's, were false.

Safian also revealed falsified satellite photos used in the film as evidence to support the claim that Israelis were oppressing Arabs by preventing their towns from growing. Ambrosino claimed to have 1973 satellite photos and 1986 and 1992 SPOT Image photos proving Israeli oppression. Strangely, all the satellite photos had the same resolution. But genuine 1973 Landsat photos were more primitive. Safian documented their resolution of 80 meters, while later, more sophisticated SPOT photos had a resolution of 10 meters. In other words, the 1986 and 1992 pictures were eight times clearer than the earlier pictures due to advances in technology. Safian obtained testimony from satellite experts that such different types of genuine images could not possibly appear to be identical. The experts concluded: "Either the '1973' image is not really from 1973, or there has been gross manipulation." Like McGhee's phony PLO fighter on *The Advocates, Frontline* had used fraudulent evidence against Israel to promote the Arab cause.

After the release of Safian's report, CAMERA requested that PBS publicly withdraw Ambrosino's film from circulation. "That PBS continues to endorse the accuracy of 'Journey to the Occupied Lands,' despite proof to the contrary published by CAMERA, and continues to sell the videotape which it promotes as an educational tool to students and educators, is a violation of its own program policies, which required fairness, accuracy, objectivity, and balance," Safian stated.

In response to CAMERA's criticism, PBS had asked Ambrosino and his researcher, Marty Rosenbluth, to conduct their own investigation. Not surprisingly, the investigation found that Ambrosino and *Frontline* had done nothing wrong. Sandy Heberer, PBS's director of news and information, wrote that Safian's report was "nothing new" and that "we stand by the fairness and accuracy of our Middle East coverage." She attributed Safian's concerns to the fact that the Arab–Israeli conflict is "such an emotionally charged issue" and that viewers like Safian "see that coverage through the distinctive lens of their own perspectives."

Heberer went on to accuse Safian, saying he had

> substantially overstepped in attacking the personal integrity of producer Michael Ambrosino. PBS has had a long and productive relationship with Ambrosino, creator of the highly respected science series "Nova," as well as the "Odyssey" and "Ring of Truth" series, the latter an examination of scientific process and proof. In keeping with his professional interests, Ambrosino is extremely meticulous in his research methods. We have seen nothing—including your paper—to make us doubt the factual

accuracy of "Journey to the Occupied Lands." On the contrary, the information provided by Ambrosino in response to your charges leads us to conclude that your report is an irresponsible and truly questionable piece of research . . . there is no place in that debate for baseless, ad hominem attacks on a man of Michael Ambrosino's professional reputation and character.[38]

Safian replied to this: "No doubt, when substantive questions have been raised about the quality and accuracy of a PBS program, it is appropriate for PBS to request documentation from the producer. But PBS's program policies speak very clearly on this issue: 'By placing its logo on a program, PBS makes itself accountable for the quality and integrity of the program.' Reviewing documentation from the producer should be the first step in the process, not as you would have it, the one and only step. By adopting Mr. Ambrosino's investigation of the accuracy of 'Journey to the Occupied Lands' as its own, PBS has invited a clear conflict of interest. How can PBS hold itself 'accountable for the quality and integrity of the program' if it simply accepts, as the last word, the producer's investigation of his own work?"

Stymied at PBS, Safian and CAMERA president Andrea Levin met with WGBH's Peter McGhee, the executive who supervised *Frontline* for the station. In a letter dated July 21, 1994, McGhee said he had asked an unnamed former staff member to investigate Safian's charges. In January 1995, when WGBH vice president Jean Hopkins was asked about the investigation, a report of which had yet to be made public, WGBH had concluded the Ambrosino show had only "minor errors."

Ambrosino told an interviewer that he "did not want to get into a shouting match with CAMERA. My feeling is that CAMERA makes its living by attacking people. I spent three years on the film and I thought it was important and constructive. CAMERA has made statements about the film that I consider libelous. In my opinion, Alex Safian is not an objective analyst."[39]

In fact, CAMERA possessed documents demonstrating that Ambrosino knew his film was false in relation to at least one other charge it contained: that, in 1992, Israel was preventing Gaza citrus from reaching Europe. Not only did newspaper accounts report the Gaza citrus trade as of 1990, Ambrosino admitted in a 1993 memo to *Frontline* producer

David Fanning that "in 1987 . . . the prohibition on direct export was lifted." But in his film Ambrosino pretended that the ban on direct exports was still in effect.

Meanwhile, CPB had recorded thousands of telephone complaints about the anti-Israel bias of the program in response to the CAMERA newsletter's account of the case. By law, the CPB has the authority to ensure the integrity of the public broadcasting system by penalizing stations that air fraudulent material or by commissioning programming to set the record straight. CAMERA asked its members to complain directly to local stations when action from CPB was not forthcoming.

Hearing nothing from PBS regarding his report on "Journey to the Occupied Lands," Safian presented copies of it to members of Congress.[40]

In response to CAMERA's request, Congressman Peter Deutsch, a Florida Democrat, wrote to PBS president Ervin Duggan asking why there was no fact-checking department at the federally funded network when such a division is a normal part of news operations at ABC, CBS, and NBC. He had not received a reply as of January 1995. Then, Democratic congressman Ed Markey of Massachusetts assigned one of his top staffers to investigate CAMERA's concerns, and the group was invited to submit written testimony in September 1994 to his oversight committee detailing their problems with the *Frontline* show.

Following a phone and letter campaign and Safian's in-person congressional testimony in January 1995 to Congressman John Porter's (R-IL) appropriation subcommittee, there was some movement. On April 3, 1995, WGBH's Peter McGhee issued a joint statement with PBS executive Kathy Quattrone that its "internal review is now completed, and has resulted in a report that is being shared with CAMERA."[41] Safian was shocked at the results, however. The study accepted Ambrosino's claim not to be aware of the satellite photo deception and blamed the photo laboratory. Safian argued that the report "never addresses the fact that Mr. Ambrosino was caught in a lie" and objected to WGBH's conclusion that "nothing in the CAMERA report warrants their view that 'Journey to the Occupied Lands' is fundamentally flawed." Safian called the findings "palpable nonsense, as demonstrated by the unprecedented actions [recommended] at the conclusion of [the] report." These "unprecedented actions" included making corrections, for the first time in two years, and *Frontline* agreed to do so.

Most of all, Safian was distressed that WGBH had lied to CAMERA about its investigation. The unnamed "former staff member" who conducted it had actually been a WGBH insider: Louis Wiley, executive editor of *Frontline*. "[Wiley] was responsible for the original 'fact-checking' of the film prior to broadcast. . . . [H]e could hardly be characterized as disinterested or independent," Safian protested.[42]

But a partial victory was better than no victory at all. Alex Beam, an irreverent columnist for the *Boston Globe,* recorded the outcome from an outsider's perspective. He wrote, "A long and indecorous slanging match over bias and factual errors in the 1993 'Frontline' documentary 'Journey to the Occupied Lands' has ended with WGBH publicly admitting several mistakes in the piece, and offering to replace all videotapes in retail or commercial distribution with a more accurate version." Beam was full of praise for Safian's tenacity and powers of analysis and even managed to persuade McGhee to embarrassingly disclose his self-serving rationale for choosing an investigator whose name appeared in the film's credits. "McGhee explains that he chose Wiley 'because we would not have exposed our outtakes to an outsider.' "[43]

On June 12, 1995, *Frontline* issued a statement responding to four of CAMERA's complaints about the film.[44] However, as in the case of *Frontline*'s maiden episode on the death of NFL owner Carroll Rosenbloom, the producers did not apologize, did not admit any wrongdoing, and stood by their now-discredited story. "We believe that 'Journey to the Occupied Lands' was a thoroughly researched, fair, and journalistically sound program as originally broadcast," *Frontline* declared, although the document went on to list its corrections. *Frontline* also aired a brief, half-hearted "correction" announcement at the conclusion of one of its episodes; it included a clip of Safian testifying to Congress.

However, WGBH never did produce a full-length program to counter Ambrosino's anti-Israel propaganda.

Rather than taking the elementary steps needed to set the record straight, the producers, WGBH, PBS, and the CPB stonewalled, delayed, prevaricated, insulted, and ignored CAMERA, leaving the group no alternative but to raise their concerns in Congress. CAMERA spent two years and approximately $100,000 on the effort, resources not available to most parties.

By contrast, when the same group complained about an anti-Israel documentary on cable's Discovery channel, they were swiftly granted a meeting with a senior vice president, who immediately aired balancing programming. The reason? He was worried about losing sponsors, he told the delegation from CAMERA. Apparently, angry viewers were cutting up credit cards advertised on the program and sending pieces to the sponsor. The sponsor got the message, called Discovery, and Discovery set the record straight.

Yet in public broadcasting, no one felt compelled to investigate CAMERA's complaints, determine whether they were justified, and respond accordingly within a reasonable period. Instead, the complainants were subjected to dismissive condescension. As a result of its experience with *Frontline,* CAMERA is urging its members to reconsider their personal financial support for public broadcasting.

6

The Case of "Liberators"

Troubling as *Frontline*'s biases and inaccuracies might be, perhaps no single incident casts more doubt on PBS's credibility than an episode of *The American Experience,* a series that has enjoyed a solid reputation for its presentation of American history since its premiere in the fall of 1988. The series is a legacy of the Reagan administration, an outgrowth of a bitter fight among board members of the Corporation for Public Broadcasting that led to the resignation of CPB president Edward Pfister in May 1985.

The proximate cause of the dispute was the cancellation of CPB sponsorship for a planned trip by public broadcasting executives and directors to the Soviet Union. When Sonia Landau, who had been appointed to the CPB by President Reagan in 1981 and was elected chairman of the board in 1984, learned of the staff's plan to exchange programs with Russian radio and television in the spring of 1985, she was aghast. Landau mobilized her friends on the board to put a stop to what she saw as at best a junket wasting the taxpayers' money.[1]

At the May 16 board meeting in San Francisco, the board voted six to four to withdraw its support for the Moscow journey, prompting the CPB president to quit. Edward Pfister said he had wanted to travel to Moscow "to bridge walls and create better communications between our two countries" and his resignation was "a matter of important principle." The *Washington Post* reported the announcement and trip cancellation as "the most dramatic events yet in a Reagan administration campaign to politicize the CPB and give it a more conservative profile."

Landau responded that the CPB was intended to serve as a heat shield against political pressures of all sorts, "and we should probably include the Kremlin in that." When the *Post* reporter challenged Landau with the assertion that she was moving CPB to the right, she answered defiantly, "From where? To the right of George McGovern? Yeah."[2]

The late September trip had been arranged by David Stewart, a former Ford Foundation staffer who had been among the first employees hired by CPB in 1968. He had organized the expedition in order to "learn more about Soviet television and radio" and then establish "long-term program relationships" between American public broadcasters and Russia's official Gostelradio.[3]

Soviet broadcasting meshed with the political goals of the Communist Party. Landau could not understand why American public broadcasters would want to purchase programming that was well known to be "dull." As Elisa Tinsely had noted in a 1985 report from Moscow, Russian television had not changed much since it first went on the air in the late 1940s. She concluded, "There's only one sponsor here, and its message is the official ideology of the Soviet government."[4] Other journalists as well had noted that "glorification of the Communist system" was the purpose of the enterprise.[5]

The trip had come about as the result of Stewart's earlier participation on behalf of the CPB in the Raduga ("Rainbow") program contest held in Moscow in January 1985. At that time Stewart had been invited by his Soviet hosts to return with a group of American public broadcasters for the "Intervision" television fair, a five-day exhibition of Eastern European and Asian programming held in Moscow in late September and early October.

Many public broadcasters were eager to attend, and some stations began working with Gostelradio on programming prior to the event. WGBH, Boston, had agreed to coproduce *The Russians* (a series on Russian history) with the Soviets. KPBS, San Diego, had created a "space bridge" (a two-way television hookup) with Moscow to commemorate the fortieth anniversary of v–e day on May 7, 1985. Several other "space bridge" programs had also been produced at public broadcasting stations around the country.[6]

Landau's victory in getting the CPB to cancel funding for the trip was somewhat pyrrhic. After the CPB pulled out, PBS took over as underwriter and the trip to Moscow went ahead. The guest list read like a Who's Who of American public broadcasting. PBS chairman Alfred Stern, an investment banker and trustee of WNET, New York, led the group, along with PBS senior vice president in charge of programming Suzanne Weil. CPB board members Sharon Rockefeller and Lloyd Kaiser, then president of WQED, Pittsburgh, joined station executives Gerald Slater, then executive vice president of WETA, Washington; Stephen Kimatian, then executive director of Maryland Public Television; William Kobin of KCET, Los Angeles; Robert Kotlowitz, then editorial director of WNET, New York; David Liroff, WGBH's station manager; Nebraska Educational Television general manager Jack McBride; then–NPR chairman Donald Mullally, general manager of WILL, Urbana, Illinois. Each broadcaster paid travel expenses for its representative.[7] This PBS group had thumbed its nose at Landau.

Among the steps Landau took as chairman to respond to the political tilt of public broadcasting was having the board review programming decisions made by the CPB staff. She personally sat in one panel meeting where grants were reviewed.

In June 1985, Richard Brookhiser, an editor of William F. Buckley's *National Review* and another Reagan appointee to the CPB board, suggested that the CPB commission a review of its programming to see whether it fulfilled the mission of public broadcasting to be objective and balanced.[8] Brookhiser had recommended social scientists Stanley Rothman and Robert Lichter, authors of *The Media Elite,* to conduct a content analysis of documentaries appearing on PBS. But the study was dropped after objections from public broadcasters and Congressman John Dingell, the powerful Democratic chairman of the House Subcommittee on Oversight and Investigations.

Hearing of the proposed inquiry, Dingell sent a letter to the CPB demanding copies of all documents and memoranda related to a "legal justification for conducting a content investigation" and questioning "to what extent CPB has the authority to conduct such a study." The tone threatened congressional inquisitions of CPB if Brookhiser's proposal were to be enacted.[9] One week later, CPB president Martin Rubenstein wrote Dingell informing him that Brookhiser had asked him "not to issue the request for proposals (RFP) for a content analysis."[10]

Even without the content analysis, Landau and fellow Reagan appointee R. Kenneth Towery (a Pulitzer Prize–winning Texas newspaperman) knew that public television favored current affairs programming at the expense of American history. So, as their alternative (and with the support of Donald Ledwig, who replaced Pfister as CPB president) the Reagan contingent on the CPB board urged public broadcasting to make American history a priority. Sonia Landau was outspoken on the topic, calling for "more programming of a historical nature on topics such as the American Revolution and fewer documentaries on current affairs."[11] So was Ken Towery, who decided to attempt to "move as much money and as much interest and as much everything else into that general area of activity."[12] Towery used board meetings to remind the CPB staff, including Ron Hull (who had been hired as director of the CPB program fund), about his interest in history. The result of this agitation for American history by Reagan's board members, says former CPB chairman Howard Gutin, who was one of them, was PBS series such as *Eyes on the Prize, The Civil War,* and *The American Experience.* "What we had done was say that the history of this country as interpreted by Americans, not by the British or by somebody else, is one of our priorities."[13]

The American Experience became a reality when Ron Hull offered $3 million to WGBH's national programming director, Peter McGhee, to create a regularly scheduled history program in 1987. Through the cunning of public broadcasting, the conservative concept would be executed by bona fide liberals. McGhee hired two of Bill Moyers's former producers at CBS, Judy Crichton (who retired in 1996) and Margaret Drain.

Crichton, wife of novelist Robert Crichton, had produced Moyers's controversial attack on anti-Castro Cubans titled "The CIA's Secret Army" while at CBS. She had later produced two documentaries critical of Israel for ABC News, "Fortress Israel" in April 1982 and "Tell the World What Happened . . ." in September 1982, which blamed the Jewish state for attacks by Christian Phalange soldiers on Palestinian camps in Lebanon. "We said at the outset that we'd try to do for history what 'Nova' did for science," Crichton told the *New York Times.*[14] They did.

Crichton's number two, Margaret Drain, had begun her career with Fred Friendly at the Ford Foundation, then worked for CBS on *The American Parade* and *Our Times* and for PBS on *Bill Moyers' Journal*. Historian David McCullough, a veteran of the United States Information Agency in the Kennedy administration who had anchored the PBS series *Smithsonian World,* was selected as host.[15] Aetna Insurance was the first corporate underwriter.

However, as the series unfolded it became clear that the producers were inserting left-of-center ideological revisions of history among more straightforward accounts. The opening broadcast in fall 1988 was about an act of God, "The San Francisco Earthquake." But it was quickly followed by "Radio Bikini," about the first atomic tests in the Pacific—and how the inhabitants of the island "had no say about the decision to turn their idyllic island into an atomic test site." "Indians, Outlaws, and Angie" told of an Oklahoma historian who had written about "a statewide conspiracy to rob the Indians of their oil-rich land." "Eric Sevareid's Not So Wild a Dream" celebrated the CBS news commentator, stressing his early pacifism. "The Life and Times of Rosie the Riveter" gave a feminist twist to the story of the home front during World War II. "Kennedy v. Wallace" presented the civil rights struggle as a stark choice between John F. Kennedy and George Wallace in cinema verité style. "Geronimo and the Apache Resistance" celebrated the Indian warrior. "Let Us Now Praise Famous Men, Revisited" reminded viewers of the horrors of the Depression. "That Rhythm, Those Blues" recalled Jim Crow and segregation as a background to the life of blues singer Ruth Brown. "The Radio Priest" attacked Father Charles Coughlin as a fascist. "Hearts and Hands" celebrated the cooperative nature of quilting bees. "Views of a Vanishing Frontier" followed nineteenth-century German painter Karl Bodmer and naturalist Prince Maximilian of Wied into the American West, where they befriended the Indians. "The World That Moses Built" attacked New York city planner Robert Moses for declaring "Bulldozing is exactly what the ghettos need" when he built Lincoln Center.

While in later years the series presented excellent straightforward accounts of the Battle of the Bulge, D-Day, America and the Holocaust,

Thomas Edison, John Philip Sousa, George Washington, Richard Nixon, and the Kennedy brothers, a politically correct sensibility lingered over the series like a mist.

Among the more striking later episodes were yet another account of the quiz show scandals, a hagiographic portrayal of Malcolm X, a nostalgic look at "Chicago 1968," and a paean to a miners' strike. "Love in the Cold War" in the 1991–92 season deserves special mention for its sympathetic portrayal of what the producers called "a family's struggle to survive as communists in a country openly hostile to their beliefs."[16] The country was the USA.

Howard Gutin, who with his fellow Reaganites helped bring these historical programs to public broadcasting, said that one of the advantages historical shows have over the current affairs series on PBS is that time has passed and a record has been built up that can be consulted. "With public affairs programs, there was no way a viewer could check if what he saw on PBS was true," Gutin said. "At least with historical shows, you can look it up."[17] This was a step in the right direction, Gutin believed, because even a flawed historical account would lead to a greater interest in finding out what really happened.

One program provides a good case study for Gutin's thesis. Even before it aired on November 11, 1992—Veterans' Day—to a national audience of 3.7 million,[18] "Liberators: Fighting on Two Fronts in World War II" had inititated a disturbing controversy that persists to this day; a controversy that revealed the extent to which PBS producers worked against the historical truth.

The "Liberators" project must have garnered instant approval when first presented to *The American Experience* staff. The film's subject, the liberation of Jewish concentration camp prisoners by black soldiers during World War II, was a natural for public broadcasting. It was apparently an untold story—even better, a seemingly *suppressed* story—that resonated with the history of two oppressed groups. It was, as the filmmakers put it, the story of "one persecuted people helping another."[19] The only problem was, it didn't happen as the film depicted it.

"Liberators" was a clever blend of fact and fiction. The filmmakers' announced intention was to document the experience of African-American soldiers during World War II, which, in a way, it did rather effectively. But the film was really two stories in one. In addition to giving a fairly accurate account of segregation in the armed services, the film told the story of the all-black 761st Tank Battalion, known as the Black Panthers. According to "Liberators," the members of the 761st were the first American soldiers to arrive at the Nazi concentration camps at Buchenwald and Dachau. By all other accounts, however, they were not.

"Liberators" was produced for *The American Experience* by William Miles and Nina Rosenblum, who had enjoyed long associations with PBS. Miles's official résumé describes him as "the only African-American independent producer based at WNET/Thirteen in New York"; African-American history was, in fact, a specialty of his. The shows he produced at WNET for PBS include *I Remember Harlem,* which won a DuPont award in 1982 for its depiction of the New York neighborhood; *Men of Bronze* (1977), the story of black soldiers in World War I; *The Different Drummer: Blacks in the Military* (1983), a three-part series; and *Paul Robeson: Man of Conscience* (1986) and *James Baldwin: The Price of the Ticket* (1989), both profiles of prominent black artists. Miles also produced *Black Stars in Orbit* (1990), about African-American astronauts. None of his previous works generated the controversy that would engulf his World War II project.

Nina Rosenblum, however, was used to controversy. Among the titles listed in her credits are a number of issue-oriented projects, including *Inside Rikers* (1991), an exposé of conditions in a New York prison; *Women's Rights History* (1990), made for the National Park Service; *Through the Wire* (1989), the story of "an isolation unit for women political prisoners in the Federal Correctional Institution, Lexington, Kentucky"; *America and Lewis Hine* (1984), about the social-issues photographer; *Their Lives' Sweat* (1979), a film funded by a labor union; *El Salvador: Another Vietnam/Seeds of Liberty* (1981), a pro-guerrilla account of that conflict; the Hollywood feature film *Reds* (1980), for which she served as assistant to director Warren Beatty; and *Compassionate Ally:*

A Photographer in the South Bronx (1978), a documentary about her photographer father, who had been active in leftist politics. In 1987 Rosenblum was awarded a National Endowment for the Humanities development grant with the title "Let Truth Be the Prejudice."

"Liberators" had a gala screening sponsored by Time-Warner at Harlem's Apollo Theater in January 1993, which was attended by both the black leadership of New York and a number of prominent Jewish businessmen, such as Felix Rohatyn, a noted liberal Democratic financier, and Lewis Rudin, active in New York's real estate industry. Also in attendance was the Reverend Jesse Jackson, who embraced a Hasidic rabbi on the stage.[20] The screening was a nakedly political event: Mayor David Dinkins, the city's first black mayor, was in trouble with the Jewish community over his seeming indifference to a series of anti-Semitic incidents, notably the riots in the Crown Heights section of Brooklyn and the stabbing death of a Jewish graduate student, Yankel Rosenbaum. "Liberators" was intended to smooth over black–Jewish friction. As Jeffrey Goldberg wrote in the *New Republic,* it was intended to be "an important tool in the rebuilding of a black–Jewish alliance."[21]

But instead of improving black–Jewish relations in New York or at PBS, the controversy surrounding "Liberators" succeeded in driving a wedge between public broadcasting and its supporters. Indeed, the 1992 broadcast—and the failure of PBS to correct its errors on-air (or apologize)—can be seen as having played a role in congressional cuts in the PBS budget amounting to more than $100 million since the show was aired. (The controversy over the program has been discussed in congressional testimony and floor speeches on both sides of the aisle.)

Jim Dingeman, host of a weekly program about military history on the Pacifica public radio station WBAI in New York and the son of a career military officer, had checked with the commanding officer of the 761st when he heard "Liberators" was coming out and was told the filmmakers had never interviewed the officer and the units had in fact not liberated Buchenwald.[22] Dingeman contacted WNET and *American Experience* executives at WGBH to share his concerns. He talked with Fred Noriega, the WNET vice president who was responsible for all documentary programming, yet Noriega did nothing about the inaccuracies, even after Dingeman warned him that the troops in the film could not have liberated Dachau and Buchenwald. As a Pacifica host, Dingeman was part of the public broadcasting family and was therefore surprised to be ignored. So he also talked to series producers. Dingeman said he spoke to Judy Crichton, warning her that "Liberators" was not accurate and urging her to avoid embarrassment by correcting the problem before airtime. His protests had no effect.[23]

Tipped off by a friend, Melvin Rappaport, a captain in the 6th Armored Division that had actually liberated Buchenwald, had also called WNET some three weeks before the show was aired to protest its inaccuracies and had alerted Colonel James Moncrief (Ret.), the senior surviving officer of the 6th Division, who wrote to WNET some ten days before the broadcast as well. But WNET ignored all of the warnings.[24] One public broadcasting insider said the letters were probably dismissed because the authors were old soldiers, and PBS staffers are generally unsympathetic to complaints from the military as a hangover from the Vietnam War days.

Shortly after "Liberators" aired on *The American Experience* in November 1992, articles appeared in the press questioning the film's claim that the 761st Tank Battalion had liberated Buchenwald and Dachau. The first reporter to expose deficiencies in the film was Christopher Ruddy, then of the *New York Guardian,* sister publication of the *Washington Times.* His December 1992 article carried the headline "PBS Documentary Lies About Liberation of Concentration Camps: Black Vets, Jewish Survivors Angry with PBS: Black Units Did Not Liberate Buchenwald and Dachau." Ruddy's reporting was confirmed by Jeffrey Goldberg, then New York bureau chief of the *Forward,* who published an exposé in the widely respected Jewish weekly. Goldberg tracked down the 761st battalion commander, Paul Bates, and the C Company captain, Charles Gates, who said the claim of liberating Dachau was "totally inaccurate."[25]

Later *American Experience* coproducer Margaret Drain said that the film had been approved by a panel of academic advisers and that the series staff had been assured by the film's producers that the film was accurate. *The American Experience* has its own panel of academic advisers, which included at the time Alan Brinkley, a professor at Columbia University; David Kennedy of Stanford; Nancy F. Cott of Yale; and Leon

Litwack of Berkeley. But they were little more than window dressing for the production, since no action was taken to investigate questions of accuracy before the broadcast. "We can't have a group of fact-checkers going over everything," Drain said. "There's not enough money." Neither did the producers inform host David McCullough that the film he would introduce had been flagged as fraudulent prior to its premiere and enable him to check his historical library. "He's called the host," Drain said. "He does not participate in research."[26]

After "Liberators" aired, an upset Dingeman made setting the record straight a priority of his radio program. Over subsequent weeks, he devoted more than a half-dozen shows to discussing errors and misrepresentations in the film. He felt that he owed it to the veterans of World War II to help correct the historical record and felt a special responsibility as the host of a show on a network that was part of public broadcasting.[27]

Yet Miles and Rosenblum brushed off complaints that their film was "underdocumented," claiming they relied on the "oral testimony" of several former soldiers of the 761st and 183rd to construct their story. (There are documents available that would establish conclusively the exact location and deployment of the 761st and 183rd throughout the war.) Some of the ex-soldiers were flown to Europe for filming. No officers, who had the responsibility for administration, deployment, and resupply of the troops of the battalions, were quoted in the film. Many members of the 761st, including one who is quoted in the film, have denied being at Buchenwald or Dachau.[28]

In the face of what was fast becoming a journalistic onslaught, WNET—without having conducted a thorough investigation—issued a press release signed by executive Karen Salerno stating,

> Thirteen/WNET, WGBH, and *The American Experience* have absolute confidence in the veracity of this outstanding film. Scrupulously researched and based on unimpeachable eyewitness testimony, it vividly recounts an unjustly ignored part of our country's history. It is because historical accuracy is so essential that we believe films like "Liberators: Fighting on Two Fronts in World War II" must be made and broadcast.[29]

In its February 8, 1993, issue, the *New Republic* carried Jeffrey Goldberg's "Exaggerators," which quoted E. G. McConnell, one of the black soldiers featured in the film: "It's a lie. We were nowhere near these camps when they were liberated." Nina Rosenblum responded that Mc-Connell, a central spokesman in her film, was "severely brain-damaged."

Two days later, the American Jewish Committee released a report by Kenneth Stern, a specialist on anti-Semitism and extremism, which declared that the program made the "factually erroneous" claim—among other mistakes—that the all-black 761st Tank Battalion had liberated Buchenwald.[30] The next day, WNET announced in a press release that the station and *The American Experience* had withdrawn the film pending its own investigation. WNET apologized for its role in the production and broadcast of the film, asking that stations not show the film again until the errors could be rectified, but adding, "Thirteen and the producers of *The American Experience* make absolutely no retreat from the essential thesis of the documentary that black American soldiers played a role in the liberation . . ."[31] The statement neglected to mention that the film was not being withdrawn from the home video market.

Miles and Rosenblum, however, did not agree with the team's findings. They accused WNET of censorship and issued their own response expressing their "disappointment," declaring that they remained "committed to telling the truth" and taking "strong exception to your assertion . . . that our credibility is now beyond redemption." They concluded with an ad hominem swipe at the American Jewish Committee's Kenneth Stern, charging "your own credibility, in many matters, cannot always be taken for granted."[32]

Six months later came a report by Morton Silverstein, a documentary producer who led a team of researchers paid by WNET to evaluate the charges of fraud. The three investigators concluded that "the review team can not substantiate the presence of the 761st Tank Battalion at Buchenwald on its day of liberation, April 11, 1945, nor during the 48-hour period" following its discovery by Allied troops. The report concluded that the Third Army's 6th Armored Division, 4th Armored Division, and 80th Infantry Division deserve credit for the liberation of the camps.[33]

Three weeks later, WNET's Karen Salerno issued another press release about the film from WNET, concluding that Silverstein's study confirmed allegations that some portions of the film contain factual inaccuracies. Thirteen/WNET has determined that research for this documentary was not as diligent and comprehensive as basic documentary practice would require, and that the producers' panel of expert advisers was inadequately utilized to monitor the factual content of the film. Thirteen/WNET will continue to withhold public television station broadcasts until the documentary is corrected.

The statement added that WNET had asked the production company to remove the channel's name from the credits. However, WNET did not ask for its money back and still did not insist that the videocassettes and companion book be withdrawn from bookstores, schools, libraries, and museums.[34]

That same day, producers Miles and Rosenblum issued a statement blasting WNET's report.

We do not feel that WNET has conducted an independent assessment of the program. We continue to object to PBS censorship. We feel it is dangerous to limit historical inquiry, especially in light of recent revelations concerning the role of black troops in the military. A continuation of this dialog is counter productive and only serves to denigrate the courageous concentration camp survivors and their heroic Liberators.[35]

Miles and Rosenblum hired the high-powered public relations firm of Clein and White to argue their case in an attempt to garner an Academy Award; they succeeded in winning a nomination, but not the prize, manifestly because of the cloud that hung over the production.

To date, neither of the filmmakers nor any PBS executive has admitted responsibility for errors in "Liberators." Preserving the integrity of the public broadcasting system is the legal duty of the Corporation for Public Broadcasting, yet the CPB declined to investigate the matter and discipline those responsible. Nor has the CPB seen fit to commission its own production to set the record straight. Needless to say, no PBS, CPB, WGBH, or WNET official has been publicly disciplined or held accountable for the errors in the program. Despite the ample warnings of inaccuracy ahead of time, public broadcasting officials at all levels approved the show for airing—yet were not criticized by those conducting the analysis of what went wrong. The facts of the case clearly show that public broadcasting bears responsiblity for airing the program, responsibility it cannot escape by pinning the blame on Miles and Rosenblum alone, especially since they have conceded nothing.

The actual liberators of Buchenwald have continued their efforts to preserve the story of what really happened. In every issue of the division newsletter, *The Super Sixer,* published since the broadcast of "Liberators" there has appeared an article by Colonel James Moncrief demanding correction of what he calls "the Big Lie" and calling on fellow veterans to write their congressmen and senators. Moncrief has also sent numerous letters of complaint to public broadcasting officials. He says that while he has gotten polite letters back, they have not responded to the specific complaints about the film's falsehoods, nor about the actions of PBS since the airing of the program.

Among those who have responded to Moncrief and his comrades, however, has been Congressman Greg Laughlin (then a Texas Democrat, now a Republican), who made a passionate speech on the House floor in the summer of 1996, denouncing "Liberators" as "a grave injustice to the millions of veterans of our great nation."[36] Colonel Moncrief also submitted testimony to Congressman Edward Markey's House Subcommittee on Telecommunications in September 1994.[37] It makes sobering reading:

> The film, seen by millions, contained *many* falsehoods and distorted statements concerning military history. Among others, it depicted the 761st Tank Battalion as liberating both Buchenwald and Dachau, as well as several other erroneous claims (spearheading Patton's Army, relieving the 101st Airborne in Bastogne, etc) involving the 761st and the 183rd.

Because Moncrief only wished to discuss matters he knew about personally, he restricted his testimony to the issue of the liberation of Buchenwald and its "false representation" in the film:

> On April 11, 1945, Buchenwald was discovered by a patrol of the 9th Armored Battalion, an organic unit of the 6th Armored Division. The patrol was commanded by Captain Fred Keffer, who later became the head of the Physics Department at the University of Pittsburgh. Keffer died in early 1992 without having knowledge of the controversial "Liberators."

As G-1 (Personnel Officer) of the Division Commander's Staff, I went to Buchenwald and was there within two to three hours following its reported discovery by Keffer's patrol. I was able to conduct a cursory inspection of the horrible conditions and the need for immediate large-scale relief measures from higher headquarters, General Patton's 3rd Army. My immediate and urgent radio message brought some assistance from the limited capabilities of my division, but more importantly, resulted in prompt action by 3rd Army's more abundant resources.

My allegation that the award-winning, overzealous authors, with little or no organized and scholarly research, created or rewrote history to satisfy their own agenda has never been refuted. In a letter to me, the authors claimed "exhaustive research" of the Archives in "Sutland, Va." Actually, the Military Reference Branch of the National Records Center is at Suitland, Maryland. It is apparent that WNET and PBS accepted and aired the film as produced without any investigation into its accuracy.

The 761st did play a role in the liberation of a concentration camp at Gunskirchen. Again, my allegation that the scene was switched from little-known Gunskirchen to the high-profile Buchenwald and Dachau because such change would sell more tickets and books in America was never refuted.

As an eighty-two-year-old man and, I believe, the senior-ranking living officer with the 6th Armored Division in combat, I have an obligation to those 15,000 men, more than 1,200 of whom perished in combat, and several thousand others who can no longer speak for themselves. Additionally, mine is one small voice speaking for the millions of young men of the forties who willingly left their home and loved ones to represent our country overseas in combat. Thousands of those same young men lost their lives. They paid dearly for the military victory which our country achieved. Those of us who survived also take some credit for contributing to that military victory. We were and are very proud of our achievement. The country was, and I like to believe is, proud of all those brave young men.

Speaking for all those young men, we made the history of the United States during the period between 1940 and 1945. That is our history. We have enormous pride in our respective contribution to our history. We resent some "Johnny-Come-Lately" dysfunctional historian rewriting and distorting our history merely to suit his personal whim. Likewise, we resent that false representation being broadcast to millions of Americans as true history. If that course of action can be permitted a mere fifty years later, there is no way that our history can be preserved in centuries to come.

Soldiers don't make much money. Soldiers are compensated in direct proportion to their achievements, and to the self-satisfaction gained from having performed well. A soldier's pride in himself and his unit, his esprit de corps, his staunch and everlasting friendships with fellow soldiers generated in training and cemented in combat, the recognition given him by his fellowman, and his love for his country are his rewards. I cannot, and will not, stand idly by and watch while any soldier is denied any of those priceless rewards.

PBS, by its actions in relation to "Liberators," has violated the pride of the American veteran, and has not been honest and forthright with the American people. Until PBS displays some action in relation to "Liberators" to earn the respect of the American citizens, and not merely to "depend" upon them, I suggest that federal funds for PBS's use be eliminated or reduced considerably.[38]

The fight to correct the historical record has indeed become the last mission for these veterans. The 1994 annual reunion of the 6th Armored Division, which drew some three hundred survivors to Minneapolis, was called "The Last Battle of World War II" in the *Star-Tribune* account of the proceedings. Reporter Chuck Haga noted, "The longest battle the 6th Armored Division fought wasn't the siege of Brest, the relief of Bastogne, or the run-and-gun race across Germany at the end of World War II. That all took less than a year. The 6th Armored's battle with the Public Broadcasting Service started almost two years ago, and the shells are still flying."[39]

To this day, Moncrief and the surviving members of his division continue their lonely quest to set the record straight. Asked why he persists in his quixotic struggle against the public broadcasting bureaucracy, Mel Rappaport, who served with Moncrief, notes, "It was a sea of blood. We still owe something to the guys who didn't come back."

What really happened at Buchenwald? According to those who were there, the 9th Armored Infantry Battalion of the 6th Armored Division of General George Patton's 3rd Army reached Buchenwald on April 11, 1945. Captain Fred Keffer led the patrol that first arrived at the camp in the late morning. A second team of soldiers, led by Sergeant

Milt Harrison, himself Jewish, set an explosive charge on the camp's gate and entered around the same time. Soon, additional troops arrived from the 80th Infantry Division and the 4th Armored Division. Captain Melvin Rappaport, also Jewish, who was present at the liberation of Buchenwald, said, "We liberated Buchenwald. I was there. I saw no black troops."[40] *The American Experience* has yet to announce the broadcast of a documentary on the real liberators of Buchenwald and Dachau.

As Moncrief says: "If they can lie about history in my lifetime, what can they do when I'm gone?"[41]

7

Conservatives on Trial

The debate over liberal bias in public broadcasting predates the establishment of PBS in 1969. In 1966 National Educational Television, with 112 stations in its network, could reach two-thirds of the American population. Among the programs on its schedule was *The Radical Americans,* produced by Donald Fouser at Boston WGBH, which looked at conservatives such as Milton Friedman alongside left-wing representatives. In 1967 Fouser interviewed William F. Buckley, Jr., for a follow-up series on radical journals of ideas on both the left and right. The message was clear: Conservatives were as extreme as the SDS. The liberal position was the political center.

Such efforts—especially insofar as they lumped editors like Buckley and economists like Friedman in the same category as those seeking to overthrow the American free enterprise system (sometimes by violence)—did little to change an internal problem NET was facing. The fledgling network of college and school district stations had been called "liberal" by many of its affiliates outside the Eastern seaboard, and the tag stuck—uncomfortably. John F. White, NET's president, felt he had to make a public statement.

Speaking to an affiliates' meeting in April 1966, White announced that NET was "neither conservative nor liberal" and rejected "any ideology." After his declaration, however, some local stations continued to

161

refuse certain programs produced in New York, especially those concerned with issues such as civil rights and poverty. In June 1966,
NET vice president for administration Edwin R. Bayley cautioned that a
perception of liberal bias threatened NET's unique relationship with its
affiliates.[1] In an unpublished outline for his memoirs, White responded
to the charge in a section he called "The Eastern Liberal Establishment."
"This well-worn accusation against many institutions and causes
haunted NET and was the excuse used most often in seeking to curtail its
influence," he wrote, noting in rebuttal that of the six top executives at
NET, one came from the South, two from the Midwest, and three from
the West.

Nevertheless, perhaps because of what White admitted was the
"pre-eminent financial role" of the liberal Ford Foundation, headed by
former Kennedy and Johnson adviser McGeorge Bundy, and the de
facto power of Fred Friendly over network offerings, the perception of
bias did not fade with time. As an olive branch to its critics, NET presented nine commentators to discuss President Johnson's State of the
Union message in January 1968 (in 1967 NET had broadcast the speech
without this wraparound). The analysts were William F. Buckley, Jr.,
Milton Friedman, economist Walter W. Heller, columnist James J. Kil-
patrick, *Newsday* publisher Bill Moyers, Harvard professors Daniel P.
Moynihan and Edwin O. Reischauer, historian Arthur M. Schlesinger,
Jr., and Cleveland mayor Carl Stokes. The wide selection was praised by
TV Guide, which at that time was a leading voice against bias in the
news media under proprietor Walter Annenberg's direction. NET
reprinted an excerpt from the *TV Guide* review in its annual report as
evidence of its ongoing commitment to presenting "conflicting viewpoints, and . . . a genuine dialog."[2]

But the gesture was not sufficient. When White spoke to an affiliates' meeting in New York on April 22, 1968 (shortly after the assassination of Martin Luther King), he found that two years had not lessened
member stations' concerns about bias. While he acknowledged that "differences do exist between us—between NET and the stations, and
among the stations themselves," White remained defiant in the face of
his critics. He said King's death and the riots that followed had vindi-

cated his programming decisions over the previous year and that instead of fewer politically charged telecasts, "we should have done more."

White then went on to address continuing concerns about a liberal bias on the network, admitting "we present more liberals than conservatives in our programs," yet declaring that NET had given more time to conservatives than any other network had, and that the reason more liberals than conservatives had appeared was not bias but that "those who would change the status quo are more provocative and more openly persistent in presenting their views than those who would preserve it." White once again stated "categorically" that NET did not have any "collective bias, liberal or conservative." He contended that the balance question was being used to confuse the issues. "Surely you would agree," he told the assembled broadcasters, "that you cannot balance bigotry and tolerance, hate and understanding, racism and freedom, wealth and poverty, justice and injustice, the rights of free men anywhere with the interests of the authoritarian, whatever his disguise."

He concluded that NET would become "a major force" only if "we spoke truth and spoke it boldly and performed a valuable public service not available in any other place," and not if the schedule were "quiet and balanced." He concluded that he would not compromise with the critics of NET, because "you cannot compromise with prejudice or ignorance or apathy."[3]

But the NET president's ringing speech was not enough to defuse the issue, especially since he was essentially saying those who were not liberals were in favor of bigotry, hate, racism, injustice, and authoritarianism. The affiliates continued to object to bias, especially after the election of Richard Nixon in November 1968. In March 1969 eight of the larger stations (WNDT, New York; WQED, Pittsburgh; WTTW, Chicago; WHYY, Philadelphia; WGBH, Boston; KQED, San Francisco; KCET, Los Angeles; WETA, Washington) proposed that Fred Friendly's *Public Broadcasting Laboratory,* which had featured Robert MacNeil's attacks on the Johnson administration's Vietnam policy, be replaced with a "less controversial" cultural series.[4]

Although White had not initially supported PBL, he understood the message from the "big eight" stations was in part a repudiation of his policy for NET of defiance on the balance question. (White had been opposed to federal funding because he felt it would lead to government influence on programming, and now his fears were being realized.) He resigned suddenly on March 12, 1969, to assume the presidency of Cooper Union, an art and engineering school in New York City, surprising NET's by then 150 affiliate stations.[5] James Day, the former head of San Fransisco's KQED and White's NET successor, was "blithely unaware that NET was being used as a bargaining chip in political games being played out in Washington," in which the Corporation for Public Broadcasting and the Ford Foundation would eventually shut down the "dangerously liberal" network, National Educational Television, to please the Nixon administration and Congress—and replace it with PBS.[6] After NET merged with WNET, Channel 13, Day was one of two NET affiliate members to vote against abolishing NET in 1970. The other was Robert Chitester, head of the Erie, Pennsylvania, educational station, who went on to produce Milton Friedman's *Free to Choose* in 1980.

Following Nixon's inauguration in January 1969, a major switch in programming priorities was made. In place of *PBL*, the Ford Foundation paid NET to distribute a series of twenty-six one-hour episodes of the BBC serial *The Forsyte Saga* to fill what had been the first of *PBL's* two hours. (This hour would be filled in 1971 by Mobil's *Masterpiece Theatre*.) The second hour of *PBL's* time slot would go to a new public affairs program designed specifically to address the concerns over balance. It was called *The Advocates* and was produced by Boston's WGBH and Los Angeles's KCET, two of the stations that had signed the *PBL* protest.

At least one WGBH producer did not think the station should host the new debate program. Donald Fouser had produced the first shows examining conservatives for WGBH, had set up the black current affairs program *Say, Brother,* and by 1969 was in charge of *The Nader Report,* a weekly program hosted by consumer advocate Ralph Nader, the author of *Unsafe at Any Speed,* which—in Fouser's words—"held corporate America up to ridicule."

Fouser made his opposition to *The Advocates* known at the station. "I objected because *The Advocates* was another yap-yap talk show, and it would absorb a lot of resources that we couldn't give to young people, blacks, or the community," he recalled. Money spent on *The Advocates* "was money we could not put into other things."

Fouser argued that *The Advocates* was symbolic of the cultural change that took place when president Hartford Gunn left WGBH in 1969 to become head of the newly formed Public Broadcasting Service. He was succeeded first by Stanford Calderwood, a Polaroid executive who brought *Masterpiece Theatre* to the station and departed after six tumultuous months because of opposition to his corporate ties from Fouser and other producers. Calderwood was followed by David O. Ives, a former *Wall Street Journal* reporter who had been a longtime WGBH executive. "The new management cowered when Nixon and Agnew came in; they were just afraid," Fouser said. Instead of promoting radical change with Ralph Nader, the new station executives tossed him and his audience overboard in favor of fund-raising opportunities. According to Fouser, "Radicals don't give money and suburban people do," so WGBH sought to attract "the sweet gray-haired ladies in the suburbs who spent their time talking about their flower gardens, the self-satisfied middle class—because those are the people who give to PBS." Fouser says *The Advocates* had a very loyal following among WGBH donors. Disgusted, he left the station in 1969 to work for Alvin Perlmutter on *The Great American Dream Machine* and *VD Blues* at WNET in New York. (Fouser, still personally committed to his radical principles, ended his public broadcasting career as producer of *3-2-1 Contact!,* a nonpolitical science show, for the Children's Television Workshop.)[7]

Like *PBL*, *The Advocates* was designed as a live broadcast to showcase the advantages of network interconnection and carry out Ford Foundation consultant Fred Friendly's vision of a national network rather than a loose coalition of local college stations. To demonstrate its national scope, it was produced both at KCET, Los Angeles, and at WGBH, Boston. *The Advocates* was structured as a trial, using lawyers to present cases with witnesses for both sides on an issue of the day. It had been the brainchild of Roger Fisher, a Harvard law professor who taught negotiation. Born in Winnetka, Illinois, Fisher was a graduate of Harvard University and Harvard Law who had served as a diplomat administering the Marshall Plan in Paris in 1948, with the Justice Department in the Eisenhower administration, and at the London School of Economics as visiting professor of international relations from 1965 through 1966.

Fisher started his television career in 1968 by appearing on a WGBH panel show about Vietnam, where "all we did was tell the people they were too stupid to understand." This frustrated him. He told WGBH general manager Michael Rice that he did not want to return under those conditions. In reply, Rice asked Fisher to come to work for WGBH to develop new television formats. Fisher accepted the offer and became a consultant while remaining on the Harvard faculty.

Together, Rice and Fisher developed a local show called *It's Up to You,* which began airing in February 1969. Fisher said the purpose of the show was "to serve up yes-able, decidable questions, to have a real question facing the state or federal government rather than an abstract discussion." A decision maker in the studio would hear the presentation of pro and con arguments. Toward the end of each program, viewers could call in to vote about the issue posed to the decision maker: It's up to you. Fisher may have become familiar with this format during the year he spent teaching in England, where the BBC had a similar program on its schedule, *Your Witness,* hosted by Ludovic Kennedy. When *The Advocates* went into preproduction in 1969, teams of producers, advocates, and researchers were taken to a resort hotel to meet with Fred Friendly, plan the program, and watch a tape of the British show. Like many other popular PBS series, *The Advocates* was of British origin.

Fisher supervised a half-dozen episodes of *It's Up to You,* including one with Republican Senator Edward Brooke of Massachusetts about American aid to Biafra, and another with scientists from the Massachusetts Institute of Technology about stopping the production of MIRVed nuclear weapons. The series was considered lively and provocative. One of the most memorable episodes of this local predecessor to *The Advocates* asked the question "Should Boston City Hospital permit abortions where legal?" At the time, Boston maintained a no-abortion policy in its municipal medical facilities out of consideration for the city's sizable Catholic population—although the procedure was legal in the state of Massachusetts. As editor of the WGBH debate, Fisher recalled, he "rigged it a little" by having the hospital's director, who was upset about the rule and wanted the city to change it, as his in-studio decision maker. A Catholic Boston College faculty member argued against abortions, while another lawyer without clear religious affiliation argued for them.

Also present was a "medical expert" to answer questions. That made the lineup at least two-to-one for permitting abortions (if the "medical expert" had been neutral, as Fisher claimed). After twenty minutes of discussion, Fisher opened telephone lines to callers for reaction. The station had counters on two lines, one pro and the other con. While the discussion continued, the hospital director could look at the totals and craft his statements accordingly.

It's Up to You was a success as a format and became the pride of WGBH's programming department. When the Ford Foundation agreed to replace *PBL* and Fred Friendly asked WGBH executives Hartford Gunn and Michael Rice for a proposal for a live weekly public affairs show, they thought of *It's Up to You* and asked Fisher to "dress it up" for a national proposal, which was written by Austin Hoyt, a former *PBL* producer on the WGBH staff. Fisher, Hoyt, Rice, Gunn, and KCET president Jim Loper—who had been included at Friendly's suggestion—went to New York to meet with Friendly at Ford Foundation headquarters. According to Fisher, everyone was aware of the need for the program to demonstrate balance, although the issue was not discussed during the meeting.

Friendly said that if Fisher were there "to make it work," he could persuade McGeorge Bundy to approve the project. There can be little doubt that Bundy's career as dean at Harvard University made him think of Fisher as a "safe pair of hands" the Foundation could rely on. In addition to his Harvard credentials, Fisher had Republican political experience from his tour of duty in the Justice Department, where he had argued cases before the Supreme Court for the Eisenhower administration. Friendly announced, "If Gunn and Loper can persuade Fisher to take a year off from Harvard to run the program, I'll give you $3 million."

Fisher applied for a year's leave from Harvard on June 28, 1969. On July 1 he became executive editor for *The Advocates,* responsible for the legal side of the program. WGBH staff producer Greg Harney, who had produced *Tennis at Longwood* for WGBH, became the executive producer. Running the "idea department" was Peter McGhee (who went on first to succeed Harney and then to supervise *Frontline* and *The American Experience* as WGBH's program manager for national productions).

Instead of phone calls, viewers were invited to send cards and letters to vote on the proposition being debated (after an aborted attempt at regional focus groups).

"Roger's model was that the show was about issues, not advocates, though it was called *The Advocates,*" recalled Lisle Baker, one of the original on-air lawyers. Therefore, each show unfolded as the trial of a proposition, complete with opening arguments, testimony from witnesses, cross-examination, rebuttals, and conclusions—presenting each case in about ten minutes. Initially, Fisher had insisted that each advocate restrict his arguments to two lines of seventeen characters on a blackboard. "Roger thought that if the Supreme Court could decide cases in thirty minutes, we could condense our argument to two lines," Baker remembered. It was highly theatrical and often emotionally charged television.

The first year was not constructed as a liberal–conservative joust, and there was no mention made of the politics of the attorneys involved. Russell Morash (who produced *The French Chef* and *This Old House*) was the studio producer in Boston. The West Coast producer was Tom Burrows at KCET. The first year *The Advocates* was aired live in both Boston and Los Angeles, at 10 P.M. Eastern time and 7 P.M. Pacific, which added to the tension and excitement. Fisher and Harney would fly back and forth the first year between KCET on alternate Sundays. The three original Boston lawyers, Baker, Joseph Oteri, and Evan Semerjian, had been chosen after taped auditions by Fisher and Harney. Baker was twenty-eight years old, one year out of Harvard Law School. Although he sometimes argued the conservative side, he "was not a conservative," said Fisher. "We were never identified as conservative or liberal," Baker recalled. "We were supposed to be ambidextrous." Fisher remembers Oteri, however, as a "wild, liberal-radical type guy." He was middle-aged and had an independent criminal law practice. Semerjian was in his forties and a partner at Hill and Dorr, known at the time for partner Joseph Welch, who had confronted Senator Joseph McCarthy during the televised Army–McCarthy hearings in 1954 with the line "Have you no decency?" Semerjian became host of the series for its final season in 1973.

According to Baker, "the issues were cutting edge for our time." Among the first year's topics were supersonic transport, legalizing football gambling, workfare, no-fault divorce, placing doctors on salary instead of fee-for-service, and banning Christmas presents. Michael Dukakis was invited onto his first *Advocates* program by Baker as an expert witness on behalf of no-fault auto insurance. Alan Dershowitz was invited by Baker as an expert witness for automatic expulsion of disruptive college students. One of the production assistants who traveled around the country screening the program at remote public television stations was the son of musician Hoagy Carmichael.

The first moderator was Victor Palmieri (although Roger Fisher occasionally filled in). He was from Los Angeles, where he had been president of the Janss Company, developers of Westwood Village and the San Fernando Valley. But he was known to Fisher and his Boston associates for his work as staff director for the Kerner Commission, put together by President Johnson to study America's race problem in the aftermath of the 1965 Watts riots. In that capacity he had become acquainted with Fred Friendly, who had served Kerner as a media consultant. Palmieri had done a lot of public speaking around the country and readily accepted Fisher's offer to host. He moderated the program until 1972, when he was replaced by Dukakis, who had been a repeat expert witness. Palmieri said the television series had been a logical outgrowth of his work for Lyndon Johnson on Great Society initiatives, an example of "what [Columbia sociologist] Herb Gans told me on the Kerner Commission, that if you want to interest the general public in policy issues, the only way to do it was to translate it into drama." *The Advocates* gave the audience "complex political and social policy issues placed into dramatic form, a cross between a trial and a debate, that had precisely the impact of a dramatic series. People looked forward to the next fight," Palmieri recalled.[8] While moderating the show, Palmieri kept up his career as a businessman, supervising the reorganization of the Pennsylvania Central Railroad during bankruptcy. Occasionally Palmieri would be replaced by what Fisher called "a decision maker," usually a public official facing a controversy with which the show was concerned.

In Los Angeles, the cases were argued by Max Greenberg and Howard Miller, two Southern California attorneys. Miller soon emerged as the most persuasive and became a regular with a loyal following among liberals. Thirty-two years old and a professor at the University of Southern California Law School, he had seen an advertisement for the show, answered a casting call, auditioned for Fisher and Harney, and got the job.

Fisher occasionally argued cases himself. One marked a turning point for the program. In June 1970 the question posed was "Should the United States sell Phantom fighters to Israel?" Fisher took the negative. He said the reason was that it was "a side no one wanted to take." In fact, sources close to the production say that no one else was seriously considered. Among the reasons Fisher (who is not Jewish) might have chosen the Arab side was that as a lawyer working in the field of international relations he stood to benefit from making a strong case on American television. Fisher indicated to the well-known, well-liked, and experienced Howard Miller (who is Jewish) that he did not want him to advocate the pro-Israel position on the show, although Miller had wanted to do so. Miller later debated Northern Ireland with Fisher without incident, taking the side of unionists against Fisher's pro-IRA position. Fisher maintained that it was unfair to have a Jewish advocate for Israel when the Arab side was not represented by an Arab. Although the broadcast was to take place in Los Angeles at KCET and therefore Miller should have been an advocate, he reluctantly agreed to step aside, since as executive editor Fisher was his boss.

But instead of choosing a non-Jewish advocate to argue Israel's case, Fisher picked Alan Dershowitz, at that time a thirty-one-year-old Harvard professor, junior to Fisher on the university faculty. Although Dershowitz had been a guest witness on *The Advocates,* he had never argued a case on a live coast-to-coast broadcast, something Miller had done for a year. While producer Austin Hoyt said Dershowitz had been chosen because he was "the best," according to a source close to the program the reason Fisher chose Dershowitz was precisely his inexperience with the television medium in general and *The Advocates* format in particular. The one thing everyone involved in the show knew was that it was very rough to do live television. To bring in someone who had seldom done it before was to guarantee that his side would have problems. And the man running the series had chosen the topic, opted to be an advocate for one side, and then selected as his own opponent a young and inexperienced attorney without the required television experience. It was to be Dershowitz's trial by fire.

Perhaps unkown to Dershowitz, Fisher had edited a volume of scientific papers in 1962 originating at a summer conference on applying behaviorial science techniques to international relations (Harvard had long been known for a psychology department dominated by B. F. Skinner, developer of "operant conditioning" and author of *Beyond Freedom and Dignity*).[9] Years later, Fisher would distill his scientific and psychological approach to negotiations further, most remarkably in a 1994 volume with the curious title *Beyond Machiavelli: Tools for Coping with Conflicts.*

Now famous for his successful defenses of O. J. Simpson and Claus Von Bulow, Dershowitz still remembers Fisher's Machiavellian intrigues unhappily after almost a quarter of a century. "*The Advocates* was not balanced at all," he said. "There was a very real anti-Israel bias." He added that he was especially disappointed in what he perceived as his second-class treatment by Fisher during the production. "I was unhappy with it because I'd had no reason to believe that we wouldn't be equal in one way or another." Yet he soon found out that he did not have a choice of producer. Austin Hoyt was assigned to Dershowitz by Fisher, who picked Molly Geraghty, one of Dershowitz's law students (after the show's run ended, she joined Fisher at Harvard Law School as an admissions officer) and Peter McGhee, head of the "ideas department," as his producers. Dershowitz soon felt uncomfortable with the arrangement. "These are all Roger Fisher's people," he realized midway through the preparation of his case. "My producer could be hired and fired by Roger Fisher," who was arguing against him. "I was very unhappy with the whole slant," he said.

But there was more to disturb Dershowitz when actual preproduction began. The show involved filmed testimony from Egypt, Israel, and Jordan in addition to cross-examination of witnesses in the WGBH studio. "We had been told originally that each of us would be doing each of our own cases separately," he said. Dershowitz would do his interviews with the Israeli side and Fisher with the Arabs. Once production was under way, Dershowitz learned that Fisher had changed the rules.

Fisher showed up unannounced during Dershowitz's interview with Golda Meir in Israel. "Roger had a major advantage. He was able to come with me during my interview of Golda Meir. He was an advocate and executive producer and he insisted on coming with me when I interviewed Golda Meir," he said. Dershowitz's producer, Austin Hoyt, remembered the session as friendly and informal. "During the filming in Israel, Golda Meir picked up my cigarette during the reel changes to light hers," he said.

But Dershowitz had not been permitted to interview Gamal Abdel Nasser with Fisher. Dershowitz recalled, "He said no, Egypt wouldn't allow Jews. I was not allowed to go with him when he interviewed Nasser because I was Jewish. I didn't think it was right for the show to accede to that kind of anti-Semitism—and it gave him an enormous advantage. Both sides had full access to the Israelis, but only his side had access to the Egyptians. You want to be there when the witness is interviewed." What's more, says Dershowitz, by taking only non-Jews to Egypt, the show incorporated anti-Semitism into the production process, causing a division between Jews and non-Jews. There were very few Jews on WGBH's original production staff for *The Advocates*. Dershowitz was practically alone. He was also kept out of interviews conducted in Jordan.

At that point, Dershowitz said, "A number of us got the slant that the whole production was pro-Arab." Dershowitz noticed some strange things about the production that suddenly made sense. "In Jerusalem, I was stuck in the American Colony Hotel, which is owned by Arabs and a place where pro-PLO people gather. And the producers are all working for Roger Fisher. And they are calling the shots—who I can interview and who I can't."

Hoyt said that the young Harvard Law professor was scared and his complaints unjustified. "Fisher went to Cairo. I don't remember it being a big issue with Dershowitz; maybe Fisher does. I don't think the success of the program rested on that kind of stuff," he said. "If he didn't want to stay in the American Colony Hotel, he sure as hell wouldn't want to stay in Cairo." There was no pro-Arab tilt in the choice of hotel, nor any intention to undermine Dershowitz's performance, Hoyt said. "I chose the American Colony Hotel because a friend had said it was the most charming hotel. It was a beautiful hotel. East Jerusalem was more interesting. The restaurant was better. I was aware after several days there that Dershowitz was getting spooked," Hoyt continued. "Some Arab cab-drivers badmouthed Jews. There were some bullet holes in the walls and curtains, and he got spooked." But Hoyt disagrees with Dershowitz's view that the WGBH team was pro-Arab. "It wasn't a conspiracy against Dershowitz. The case for Israel was very, very powerful."

Fisher and his crew conducted a long interview in Cairo with Nasser of which Fisher is proud to this day. "I got Nasser to say things he'd never say before," Fisher remembered. "He said he'd accept the 1967 borders if Israel would, and he would accept Israel as a Jewish state in spring 1970." One member of the *Advocates* team joked that Fisher was so contented with his footage he would have sold it frame by frame. Dershowitz was unimpressed, however. "The tape was edited and nobody could really figure out what Nasser was saying," he said. "Whatever he said to this audience, he certainly backtracked at home." Dershowitz had not been permitted in the editing room, although Fisher, as executive producer, supervised the cutting of both Nasser's and Golda Meir's interviews.

There was yet another development that reflected the atmosphere of distrust around Fisher and the production. Instead of a live broadcast, Fisher decided the second part of the program would be recorded at KCET in Los Angeles in advance, to air around Israel's Independence Day. The pro-Israel argument would be live, with maximum tension. The anti-Israel case would be taped, and subject to review. Fisher was covering all his bases. "We taped two programs together and broadcast one one week and one the next, contrary to our standard policy," Fisher recalled. Such a format, of course, gave Fisher yet more control as exec-utive editor. If it had not turned out to his liking, it could have been fine-tuned in postproduction (and using taped interviews permitted very little opportunity for live cross-examination by Dershowitz or Fisher, one of the highlights of the program's usual format). However, in addition to the prerecorded interviews with Golda Meir, King Hussein, and Nasser, there were two live witnesses in the studio when the taping finally took place in Los Angeles.

Representing the pro-Israeli side was Yehosephat Harkabi, head of Israel's intelligence services. On the other was a man who claimed to be a guerrilla, wearing the combat dress of an Al Fatah fighter. According to Fisher, "The Palestinian said, 'Let's discuss this reasonably.'" In his mind, Fisher won the debate by goading Dershowitz into an emotional cross-examination of his star witness, a sympathetic revolutionary using a *nom de guerre* of "Abu Omar." According to Hoyt, the occasion was of historic importance. "Peter McGhee found him through Molly Geraghty. He was the first Al Fatah member to face an American audience." Fisher said when the pro-Israel side tried to cross-examine the Palestinian, "Dershowitz lost his cool." Hoyt said the evening caused quite a stir in diplomatic circles. "The transcript reads brilliantly, but it did not come across on television," he said. "The Israelis felt their case had been lost. The Israeli consul suggested they'd been set up."

However, Dershowitz remembers the debate differently. "Roger's memory may be a little self-serving," he said. While admitting "I really let this guy have it," he argues "there's a difference between saying I lost the debate and I lost my cool." In the end, Dershowitz says, "I was pretty satisfied." The reason for this satisfaction? According to Dershowitz, the reputed Al Fatah fighter had been a complete fraud cooked up to make Fisher's case. "He put up a phony guy. He put him in a guerrilla uniform," Dershowitz said. In fact, "Abu Omar" was an American-educated academic. "The guy never had been in a guerrilla uniform, and I exposed him. My recollection is that I just asked: Have you ever worn a guerrilla uniform?" The supposed hero could not answer. Dershowitz said his witness for the pro-Israeli side, Harkabi, "loved our performance, and he gave me the information that this guerrilla type was a phony." To resolve the dispute over who won that debate is easy, said Dershowitz, noting that the show was nominated for a Peabody Award. "Just get the tape, look at the tape."[10]

Unfortunately that is not easy to do in 1996. Fisher said the tapes were destroyed accidentally after the broadcast. And Hoyt remarked, "One of the great regrets of my life is that episode of *The Advocates* was erased. . . . The FBI and immigration officials came around afterwards."[11] They were looking for the supposed Al Fatah fighter operating under the alleged *nom de guerre,* whose visage and actual identity is now lost to the ages. The producers received some 45,000 cards and letters commenting on the broadcast.

So Fisher's first year as executive editor of *The Advocates* came to an end. It was also his last although he would remain a consultant and occasional guest for the show. He returned to Harvard Law School. Hoyt said the reason for Fisher's departure was a generalized "tension" at the station. "The WGBH promotion people came up with the 'fight of the week' slogan; Roger didn't like that." Fisher said he left because "they kept calling it a show and I kept calling it a program" and because he was "a professor, not a television producer."[12]

When *The Advocates* returned to the air sans Fisher in 1971, it had a new executive editor, Peter McGhee, who reported to executive producer Greg Harney. Fisher's freewheeling structure was gone. The program now featured two regular advocates: Howard Miller for the liberal side and William Rusher for the conservative. Both sides were provided with equal teams of producers and researchers. In addition, the executive editor's "idea department" had a staff of five researchers who worked out the issues to be debated. Austin Hoyt was named producer of the conservative side. Molly Geraghty, who had handled the anti-Israel assignment for Fisher, became producer for the liberal team. And Dershowitz was repeatedly invited on the broadcast to substitute for Miller when he was unavailable to plead a case. This period of *The Advocates,* from 1971 to 1974, is the one best remembered by public television viewers.

In 1972, Fisher said, he "persuaded Mike Dukakis to be the moderator and taught him to be balanced and cool." (Fisher jokes that he wrote to Dukakis when he was running for President and said, "Don't be so cool. Forget everything I taught you.") Dukakis, at the time a state legislator, became a media celebrity because of his appearances on *The Advocates* beginning in the fall of 1970 and was launched on the road to the governorship of Massachusetts in 1974 and his 1988 Democratic bid for the presidency.

Dukakis recalled, "Politicians were our best witnesses and invariably academics were the worst." He liked the chemistry of the program. "The Miller-Rusher combo was terrific to work with," he said.

Conservative advocate William Rusher was born into a Republican family in Chicago in 1923 and was raised in New York City as a moderate supporter of Wendell Willkie, to whom he dedicated his Princeton senior thesis. A graduate of Harvard Law School, Rusher was a charter subscriber to the *National Review* in 1955, served as counsel to the Senate Internal Security Subcommittee from 1956 to 1957, then joined the *National Review* as publisher (a job he would hold until 1988). He was one of the leaders of the 1964 "Draft Goldwater" movement. In 1969 he was approached by the producers of *The Advocates* as someone to balance Howard Miller, who in Rusher's words had been "shellacking a series of conservatives." The choice of Rusher came a few months after Vice President Spiro Agnew's November 13, 1969, speech (written by Patrick Buchanan) attacking television news as controlled by an Eastern establishment with a liberal bias. Rusher recalls, "I myself felt the impact of the Agnew speech in the number of invitations to appear on the media I got. They felt they were vulnerable. Maybe it helped *The Advocates* stay on."

Howard Miller remembers the change Rusher's arrival meant for the show. "The first year there was no conservative," he said. "The second year, after the show had been funded [by CPB as well as Ford], we got this liberal–conservative thing. One of the benefits of having a conservative spokesman was that people could say we're having a fair shake in discussing issues."

Rusher felt the program had a liberal slant but was grateful for the opportunity to present a conservative case to the American public on prime-time television. Although his fee was $1,000 per broadcast, he also enjoyed the lavish production budget for the series, which he estimated at $10 million per year at its peak. "You'd be surprised at how expensive it can be when you're working on somebody else's money," he said. Duplication and waste were built into the process. "We did two shows back to back at WGBH in Boston and two back to back at KCET in Los Angeles. Because Ford wanted to build up production facilities, there were identical sets and identical staffs on both coasts. The rule was that the show's director and two advocates flew first class when flying on *Advocates* business." Each advocate had a producer, two researchers (usually lawyers), and an assistant on each coast. "The money was impressive," Rusher said. "I loved it. Money makes the mare go, as LBJ said, and boy, does it." While he appreciated the added income, Rusher felt the program could have been done without the cross-country travel, double staffing, and identical sets. In its final year, the program was consolidated at Boston's WGBH.

Although Rusher enjoyed the perks, he, like Dershowitz on the Israel show, noted a stacked deck. Not only were the questions biased, Rusher said, but so were the chief decision-making personnel for the series, such as the liberal Fred Friendly of the Ford Foundation. And at the station level a similar situation was obtained. "The overall editor was Peter McGhee and the overall producer was Greg Harney, both liberals." This was reflected in the setup for each debate, which Rusher saw as favoring the left's agenda. "The absolute rule of the directors of the programs was that each question litigated had to be a proposal for some new federal government action," he said. "We wouldn't just discuss 'Are hummingbirds desirable?' but question: 'Should the federal government outlaw hummingbirds or subsidize hummingbirds?'"

The result of liberal sponsorship and liberal producers? Rusher was often forced by the design of the show to take the negative position. Luckily, he said, this attempt to make him look like a spoilsport did not hurt his debating effort in the slightest. "I happened to come along at a time when public opinion was running more to the conservative. At the time, this was not appreciated in Massachusetts."

Indeed, in October 1971 PBS had commissioned a study by Willard Rowland (now dean of the University of Colorado School of Journalism) to analyze Rusher's unexpected ability to convince even the liberal PBS audience of the rightness of his cause.[13] During the 1970–71 season the series covered thirty-four different issues. One-fifth were about foreign affairs and the rest about domestic problems. Rusher and Miller faced each other twenty-seven times. A look at the list confirms Rusher's views of the programs as liberal and generally favoring government action of some kind. But the analysis showed a "disbalance" *(sic)* in favor of Rusher that could not be explained. In other words, he was winning too many debates. Rusher never realized this was a problem, however. When asked about his performance on the series, he was straightforward. "The reason I kept winning was they were proposing all these lunatic federal programs. I would only argue things I would believe in."

In 1970 the season opener began with the question "Should colleges reschedule classes so that students get two weeks off to work in political campaigns?" Rusher's negative position was supported by 67 percent of the viewers who responded. But the next question was a loser for the conservative position. When asked, "Should the federal government subsidize all campaigns for federal office?" PBS watchers answered in the affirmative 75 to 20. Other debates in 1970 took place over school vouchers (about evenly split), prohibiting police from keeping intelligence files on political dissidents (53 against to 45 in favor), the federal government's registering voters for presidential elections (split), import quotas on shoes and textiles (about split after cards from an organized campaign were removed), the President's Report on Pornography and Obscenity (65 percent against), conscientious objector status for draft evaders (59 percent in favor), a guaranteed minimum income (75 percent against), two shows on forming a coalition government in Saigon (split), and two shows on apartheid in South Africa (about 60 percent against on each).

Among Miller and Rusher's favorite shows was a December 1, 1970, debate over the guaranteed minimum income plan proposed by the Nixon administration. Among the expert witnesses were Barbara Jordan, then a Texas state senator, and Ronald Reagan, then governor of California. "Miller thought he was going to make his fame and fortune by demolishing Ronald Reagan," Rusher recalled. Interestingly, the White House paid close attention to this broadcast before it aired, for different reasons.

On November 25, 1970, CPB president John Macy wrote to President Nixon's domestic policy advisor, Daniel Patrick Moynihan, author of the plan, to call his attention to the program.[14] On learning of the upcoming broadcast, Moynihan immediately became upset and wrote a "personal and confidential" reply to Macy. "I am not only not pleased by your letter," Moynihan said, "I am genuinely troubled by it. It seems to me yet another example of a persistent pattern of biased treatment of the administration by public television. I would not say this to many persons, but I would say it to you."

Moynihan complained that at the moment the Nixon bill for guaranteed minimum income had passed the House and was facing the Senate, public broadcasting chose Roger A. Freeman, an economist who had once served in the Nixon administration, to oppose Nixon's plan. He objected to the rest of the cast as well because the White House was not allowed to make its case. "Your audience will be liberal to left in its politics. They will be for the Guaranteed Income. They will see it opposed by an appointee of President Nixon's and defended by an appointee of President Johnson's [Barbara Johnson]. A Reagan Republican will side with the Nixon man [Ronald Reagan himself], and a Minnesota liberal [Theodore Marmor, a professor at the University of Minnesota] will side with the Johnson lady." Moynihan understood what was going on: The deck had been stacked.

Because of this configuration—Republicans against the Nixon plan and Democrats for it—Moynihan felt the broadcast would hurt the chances of the guaranteed income bill in the Senate. The setup indicated little Republican support even after passage in the House. Despite Moynihan's protest, no administration spokesman had been included to speak in favor of the President's bill. Moynihan concluded his letter somberly: "I leave profoundly uncertain of the moral and intellectual capacity of institutional liberals to defend the standards of liberal enquiry."[15] This angry letter was a powerful factor in the Nixon administration's decision to confront public broadcasting in the coming years, especially after the Senate killed Moynihan's guaranteed income plan.

Moynihan was furious. He sent a copy of this letter to H. R. Haldeman with an angry memorandum attached, which asked, "We have men on that [Corporation for Public Broadcasting] Board. Why aren't they looking out for the President's perfectly legitimate interests? Why are federal funds being spent (as I assume they are) to distort the facts of this situation?"[16] Haldeman then passed Moynihan's complaint to White House director of communications Herb Klein, counselor Leonard Garment, and Peter Flanigan, the Nixon aide responsible for public broadcasting issues. He asked, "Do we have any control over the choice of participants in something like this? If so, how did we allow an ex–Special Assistant to oppose one of our bills? Please look into this and give me a report so that when the situation arises again, we can make sure that our side is strongly defended by one of our own people."[17] Two days later Flanigan sent Haldeman's note to Clay Whitehead in the Office of Telecommunications Policy with his own comment. "It is my understanding that *The Advocates* is an NET program and therefore not run by the Corporation for Public Broadcasting," he said, asking Whitehead to investigate the matter and report back.[18]

Four days later, Whitehead wrote to Haldeman that although *The Advocates* was cosponsored by the Corporation for Public Broadcasting, the administration had "no direct control over the choice of participants," and although the CPB often asked the White House to suggest participants for programs, "that procedure was not followed in this case." Whitehead added that the White House had no control over former employees and that there should be a more active contact with the CPB to avoid surprises on future programs. He concluded that Moynihan's complaint was not unforeseeable, since "public television producers and directors have a rather unsubtle liberal bias," and called upon the CPB board of directors to "exert a strong influence to see that a sound mix of programming viewpoints is provided in spite of that bias." Whitehead said that he would meet with CPB directors to discuss the bias issue and that he would have "some suggestions" after Nixon filled a Republican vacancy on the board, which could "tip the balance to a Republican majority."[19] The Moynihan memo had put public broadcasting on the White House radar.

Rusher and Miller knew little of Moynihan's frenzy over the broadcast when they were preparing their show. But Miller agreed with Rusher that the *Advocates* debate on the guaranteed income proposal was among the most memorable because of Ronald Reagan's participation. "He was very, very good on the air," Miller said. The liberal advocate had been told by his researchers and producers that Reagan "needed four-by-six cards" and therefore should be forced to ad-lib during the cross-examination. To his surprise, Miller found that "for all his reputation, he knew what he needed to know, when he needed to know it. He was very prepared on the particular subject. And he knew how to handle the unstructured cross-examination very well. He didn't know what the questions would be." Rusher still remembers the occasion with glee. When Miller asked Reagan whether he thought the government had an obligation to the poor, "Reagan said, 'I always thought the federal government should promote the general welfare, not provide it.' And down went Howard Miller." Thanks to PBS, Ronald Reagan had helped defeat Daniel Patrick Moynihan's welfare reform legislation.

On January 5, 1971, *The Advocates* debated another administration program opposed by conservatives when they debated wage–price controls. The expert witnesses opposing the administration plan were Milton Friedman and William F. Buckley, Jr. "I joked that I had to put in for combat pay," Miller said. The program was quite timely. "We did that one in a week turnaround," he remembered. "Nixon had just put in price controls." Arguing against Friedman on Miller's side was economist John Kenneth Galbraith, a friend of Buckley's and an antagonist of Friedman's. Miller noted that "Galbraith and Friedman had a long-standing professional disagreement." This disagreement would resurface a few years later in two PBS miniseries, Galbraith's *Age of Uncertainty* (1977) and Friedman's *Free to Choose* (1980).

The program veered further to the left. On April 20, 1971, *The Advocates* hosted a remarkable broadcast in which neither Miller nor Rusher chose to participate. Roger Fisher returned to argue the negative on the proposition "If you oppose the war, should you answer the call for massive civil disobedience?" Arguing the affirmative was radical lawyer William Kunstler. Kunstler lost the write-in vote 41 to 55.

Until its cancellation in 1974, *The Advocates* remained the flagship public affairs program on PBS. Miller and Rusher acquired a devoted public following and even took the program on the road, appearing at public events as an odd couple. They became close friends.[20] But the attention of the Nixon administration and flurry of memos at the White House following Moynihan's complaint led to another effort at placating conservatives in 1971, after Republicans had, as Whitehead suggested, seized control of the board of the Corporation for Public Broadcasting. Conservatives wanted a program of their own on PBS. And in 1971, they got it. William F. Buckley, Jr., would host the first show on PBS run by a conservative.

8

Buckley and the Triumph of Tokenism

When New York senator Daniel Patrick Moynihan, who had been President Nixon's adviser on domestic policy, changed his mind about the administration's guaranteed income plan in 1978, he did not announce it on *The Advocates,* for the show had been off the air for four years. Moynihan, now as senator from New York (having replaced James Buckley in 1976), announced his change of heart in a letter to William F. Buckley, published in the *National Review.* "And so you turn out to be right," he concluded, adding as a personal touch the comment, "In addition, your recipe for apple soup works."[1]

Perhaps no conservative figure looms so large in public broadcasting as William F. Buckley, Jr., author of *God and Man at Yale,* founder and editor of the *National Review,* and "patron saint of the conservatives," in the words of his biographer, John B. Judis. Since 1966 Buckley has been host of *Firing Line,* a weekly talk show that moved to PBS from its commercial slot on RKO stations in 1971. When liberals seek to refute charges that public broadcasting is biased against the conservative point of view, they point to Buckley's show. And in the minds of many, Buckley is as closely associated with public broadcasting as Big Bird or Bill Moyers is. He is a mainstay of the institution and has come to serve as an ambassador of conservative thought to Americans interested in ideas.

As soon as President Nixon was inaugurated in January 1969, public broadcasters realized they would need to take steps to ensure continuing federal appropriations for the recently formed Corporation for Public Broadcasting. One effort resulted in *The Advocates* (discussed in Chapter 7). But there was more. Public broadcasters invited Chester Finn, Moynihan's staff assistant, to attend a June 1969 public television conference in Wisconsin. The young aide (later to become Assistant Secretary of Education in the Reagan administration) came back impressed with the "good ideas" he had heard. He wrote a memorandum outlining what he saw as an opportunity for the Nixon administration to "put its stamp on public television" and help it "really flourish."[2] At first, the administration followed Finn's advice.

That month the Nixon administration began circulating a proposal for an earmarked tax on radio and television sets, an income source public broadcasters had wished for since the release of the 1967 Carnegie Commission report. By August, the administration had set up a "working group" to review other possibilities for "permanent financing" for the CPB.[3] In September the Bureau of the Budget began circulating its draft bill for a three-year reauthorization of the CPB.[4]

The Advocates had premiered on October 5, 1969, as an attempt by public broadcasters to ingratiate themselves with the new President, from whom they hoped to receive the permanent endowment suggested by the tax proposal. But the changes represented were in some sense simply cosmetic. *The Advocates* appeared balanced but was actually still a liberal program.

NET was also trying to woo the administration in an even more obvious fashion with a weekly series of half-hour profiles of Cabinet officers, including Attorney General John Mitchell and Secretary of State William Rogers, broadcast under the title *The President's Men*. This series had started in the Johnson era and seemed a useful tool to curry favor with Nixon. In addition to reminding the administration of broadcast times for *The President's Men,* CPB president John Macy alerted the White House to other specials designed to appeal to the President, including complete coverage—during prime time—of the 1969 White House Conference on Food, Nutrition, and Health featuring presidential adviser Dr. Jean Mayer.[5]

To further bolster political support for the new network, the CPB set up an Advisory Committee of National Organizations composed of major Washington lobbies, including the AFL-CIO, the Boy Scouts of America, the National Catholic Office for Radio and Television, the American Jewish Committee, the U.S. Chamber of Commerce, the Consumer Federation of America, the National Association for the Advancement of Colored People, and the National Education Association. Two months later, John Macy complained to President Nixon that the administration had reduced the CPB's federal funding by 57 percent (from a requested $35 million to $15 million) for 1971. He noted "the development of any important alternative to commercial broadcasting will be slowed." Macy argued that if Nixon were not to increase funding for public broadcasting, "the success of recent programs such as . . . THE ADVOCATES . . . will not be sustained." The CPB was trying to use the debate series as a hostage in the struggle for greater federal funding.[6]

Some in public broadcasting realized that *The Advocates* was not going to offer enough to appease conservatives. Among them was Henry Cauthen, then president of South Carolina Educational Television. One of the pioneers in noncommercial broadcasting and a bit of a lone ranger, he had connected schools and junior colleges by cable to a state instructional network before broadcast channels became available.[7]

Wishing to preserve the educational focus of his system's television services, Cauthen had written Carnegie Commission chairman James Killian protesting the name change to "public broadcasting" in 1967, to no avail.[8] His pragmatic approach in South Carolina was in marked contrast to the liberal idealism rampant in Boston, and Cauthen and his ideas would come to play an important role in public television. He served as a member of the board of PBS, the National Council for the Arts, the 1978 Carnegie Commission on the Future of Public Broadcasting, and the CPB. Cauthen was elected chairman of the CPB in 1995.

As a Southern Democrat whose state was represented in the Senate by former Dixiecrat Strom Thurmond, one of the first converts to Republicanism in Nixon's "Southern strategy," Cauthen was attuned to the sensibilities of conservative viewers (SCETV was one of the public television stations that declined to show the sexually explicit *Tales of the City* and *Tongues Untied* in the 1990s). As a Carolinian from an old family, Cauthen also knew that William F. Buckley's family maintained a summer estate in Camden, South Carolina. As an educational broadcaster, he was a friend of Fred Friendly, powerful consultant to the Ford Foundation, and knew that Ford was looking to further decentralize the system to demonstrate that public broadcasting was something different from NET.

Cauthen was alert to the political climate in 1971 surrounding PBS. "I had the feeling we needed a respected conservative voice on public broadcasting which simply wasn't there," he said, aware that the Nixon administration had not yet settled on a public broadcasting policy. "I had no idea how [Buckley] felt about it. I thought public broadcasting needed him, and he was right for our audience. The type of people who watch public broadcasting are thinking people who would listen to an in-depth discussion of important issues." Buckley was the thinking man's conservative, and as Cauthen put it, "public broadcasting needed not only a conservative voice, but serious discussion of serious issues."

So in 1971 Cauthen approached Buckley—whom he did not know—directly. "I just called him cold and told him I'd like to talk to him about coming to public broadcasting," he recalled. Buckley invited Cauthen to New York to explain his notion that public broadcasting could reach more people nationally than Buckley's existing syndication by RKO. Cauthen was prepared with visual aids showing the location of public television transmitters to help sway the young editor of the *National Review*. "I went up to his apartment and literally laid out the maps on his apartment floor and made the best case I could. He said he'd like to think about it. Three weeks later I heard from his producer, Warren Steibel, and he said how would you like to coproduce a debate at the Cambridge Union?" The show would be taped in conjunction with the BBC.

The 1971 debate was Buckley's third at the Cambridge Union, the traditional arena for conflicting ideas at the British university (he lost to James Baldwin on the question of civil rights in 1965 and won against John Kenneth Galbraith regarding the free market in 1970). This time the question on the table was feminism. Buckley's opponent was Germaine Greer, the renowned Australian writer. Buckley found the occasion so remarkable he wrote about it in his memoirs of *Firing Line*.

He said Greer took control of the proceedings early on by demanding to approve in advance the question to be debated (a similar strategy to that of *The Advocates*). In the spirit of fair play, his Cambridge hosts, unlike the WGBH producers, contacted Buckley. "There was a period of progressive suspense as Ms. Greer refused one after another resolution as suggested by the Cambridge Union," he recalled. "In desperation, the president of the Union called me in New York." Buckley's suggestion was "Resolved: The women's rights movement is at the expense of women." Greer rejected it as "preposterous." Buckley, "knowing the formulation was suicidal," then suggested "Resolved: This house supports the women's liberation movement." That wording "proved eminently satisfactory to Miss Greer."[9]

Cauthen attended in person, traveling with Buckley. "It was a fascinating debate. I don't think he was prepared for what he faced," he remembered. Buckley later wrote of the match, "Nothing I said, and memory reproaches me for having performed miserably, made any impression or any dent in the argument. She carried the house overwhelmingly. She could have won on 'Resolved: Man should be abolished.' "

Cauthen shared Buckley's analysis of the outcome but was not troubled by the poor showing by the *National Review* publisher in his PBS debut. "We went back to London and the next day we went to breakfast and he said, 'We've got a deal if you agree to represent me personally,' "Cauthen recalled. Cauthen agreed to handle the negotiations with the system to add *Firing Line* to its core schedule.

Of course, Buckley's loss to Greer would not bother liberal public broadcasters, who liked to see conservatives lose. "I immediately called [CPB president] John Macy and he was very willing and excited to do it and put together the funding package," Cauthen said. One factor that might have helped was Buckley's friendship with Fred Friendly, who was then funding alternative production centers to supplement NET. According to Buckley, "They gave the money to SECA [Southern Educational Communication Association] to finance *Firing Line* because the Ford Foundation's preceding ventures had been grants to Los Angeles and Boston" (for *The Advocates*). Buckley continued living at his Stamford, Connecticut, home; in a sense, the South Carolina base was an "administrative abstraction. That is just where they did the paperwork. It was never suggested there would be any Southern, let alone Carolinian, orientation in the coverage of *Firing Line.*" Indeed, many of the programs were taped in New York City.

Cauthen said *Firing Line* was not a hard sell to the PBS stations. "Bill brought a lot of conservative and Republican voices into the arena of public debate that would not have gotten there otherwise," he noted. "His show was so well known and so popular it negated the need to have much additional effort in that direction. He could get anybody on the program, any world leader, any level of life, except a few who were scared to go on there to debate with him."

Buckley had launched *Firing Line* on RKO's WOR-TV in New York after he ran for mayor of that city in 1966 and discovered he was quite telegenic. His assistant at the time was Neal Freeman, who had worked on his campaign and at the *National Review.* Freeman recalled that Buckley had "captivated the media in New York. He went from being an obscure columnist to being a visible public figure, and that is how the *Firing Line* show started."

Freeman later became a member of the PBS family along with Buckley, serving as a consultant to *The Advocates* and producer of public broadcasting's *Technopolitics, American Interests,* and *Crisis in Central America*—a four-part 1986 *Frontline* special—and a documentary entitled *Mexico.* On both of the Latin programs he worked with *Advocates* producer Austin Hoyt (apparently WGBH's ambassador to conservatives). Freeman was appointed to the board of the Corporation for Public Broadcasting by President Nixon in 1972.

Like *The Advocates, Firing Line* had originally been billed as a "fight of the week" in which a caustic and confrontational Buckley would square off against representatives of the ruling liberal orthodoxies on the issues of the day. Freeman recalled the shows were "real mix-'em-ups, very feisty, almost who can stay two rounds with the kid, Buckley. Even then he was very much the *enfant terrible,* and most of the liberal opponents were older, establishmentarian, and better known, such as columnist Jimmy Wechsler of the *New York Post.* It was an incendiary, unmoderated debate—one-on-one."[10]

Of the first seasons Alistair Cooke said, "I myself was worried in the early days, because he seemed to be setting himself up each time as a prosecutor almost more than a moderator." The reason was that, as Cooke noted, Buckley enjoyed his role as *enfant terrible*, "the gadfly of the liberals," who, "even in introducing them, put them on the defensive from the start."[11] Neal Freeman told Buckley's biographer, John Judis, that some station managers were "appalled by the level of intensity of the shows" and that after a number of Buckley's guests had been "carried out on a stretcher," for a time it became difficult to recruit liberals to appear. When Robert Kennedy declined an invitation, Buckley quipped, "Why does baloney reject the grinder?"

After the first eight shows in the first year, the show's new producer, liberal Democrat Warren Steibel, changed the format, removing Buckley as moderator and replacing him with Steibel's lawyer, C. Dickerman Williams. Though Buckley remained the dominant personality, Steibel described himself as a counterweight to Buckley. "I'm totally opposite Bill," he said. "He has a producer who is totally unconservative. I call myself a liberal, very much so. I don't think the other conservatives would have a liberal anywhere near them on their show, so Bill should get gold stars for that point."[12] Steibel said he put professional obligations to balance ahead of his personal feelings in the selection of guests. "I try to agonize on both sides to get the best people on both sides," he said. "Even if I hate them I ask them. I've asked Pat Buchanan about ten times and I find him repugnant."

Buckley took the early criticism of his aggressive style to heart. "I am a very nice man, but I have a lot of enemies because my tone isn't right," he wrote to Freeman in 1967.[13] As time went by, Buckley mellowed, developing, as Alistair Cooke points out, "a newfound benevolence, indulging even the more intemperate arguments of his opponents with an almost Churchillian grace."[14] Milton Friedman, who had appeared on the show in 1968, 1972, and 1986 to champion free-market issues, took the opposite view. "Buckley's *Firing Line* was at its best in early years," he said.[15] (Friedman had appeared with Buckley on the January 5, 1971, episode of *The Advocates* to confront John Kenneth Galbraith on the question of wage and price controls.)

Running for a full hour during prime time, *Firing Line* soon developed a loyal and devoted following—especially among liberals, who admired Buckley's command of the English language, elegant style, and

Kennedyesque glamour as he engaged in gladitorial combat with their champions. In many ways the Buckleys were a Republican version of the Kennedys and their Camelot: politically active, rich, Ivy League, good-looking, Anglophile Irish Catholics. And in demand. Buckley recalls, "I was the original commentator on *60 Minutes* for the first four or five shows, what is now done by Andy Rooney." He would rewrite his syndicated column for the TV show, but it didn't quite work, and so he was dropped. As a solo talking head, he may have been in the wrong format, for he thrived on intellectual conflict, as *Firing Line* producer Warren Steibel points out. "Bill's whole essence is to argue," he said. "Bill Buckley is best when you pit him against liberals."

Henry Cauthen used his mastery of the arcane bureaucracy of public broadcasting to secure a slot for *Firing Line* in 1971. According to Buckley, Fred Friendly committed the Ford Foundation to "simply back any talk show that gets at least forty votes in the annual election that was in those days held by PBS stations." Those votes were gathered by Cauthen for Buckley, and Ford agreed to pay the tab in cooperation with the Corporation for Public Broadcasting. Buckley remembered a private commitment of "a comprehensive endowment by the Ford Foundation to CPB for five years" to pay for the program. "The Ford Foundation came in first, then CPB gave part of the budget based on votes in the general election."[16]

Friendly wanted more public affairs on PBS, said Buckley. "The idea was to pay the cost of news explorations with two intentions in mind: Convince PBS management that people could be interested in news analysis, and expose viewing audiences to news analysis at something less than the hectic rate of commercial television." He added that Friendly liked the one-hour format because it was rare on commercial television. And Friendly was generous: Buckley received a $3,000 personal fee and $8,000 in production expenses per program.

Buckley remembered he was treated well at first, with the program "sent out at six or seven o'clock on Thursday by the PBS satellite, with a local option on when to air it." Usually, although he had no say in scheduling, he was on prime time.[17] Indeed, WGBH put Buckley in *The Advocates'* time slot when that show folded at the end of the 1974 season.

For Cauthen, the most memorable *Firing Line* was one taped in Saigon on January 18, 1972, as one stop in an around-the-world journey. The trip started in Los Angeles, where the team taped a program with then-governor Ronald Reagan, Buckley's brother James (then a senator), and a lineup of conservative thinkers discussing a variety of financial and political topics. From there Cauthen and the crew proceeded to Vietnam, but Buckley and his brother took a quixotic detour, which impressed on the South Carolina public broadcasting executive the fact that Buckleys are not like ordinary people and *Firing Line* more than an ordinary chat show.

"Jim and he went down to the South Pole," Cauthen recalled. "When we met back up in Vietnam the first morning, we had breakfast at the Caravelle Hotel rooftop restaurant. They had killed a couple of Vietcong in the streets outside the hotel the first night." Cauthen was concerned for the production and asked the hotel staff whether such fighting was normal. "The manager said don't worry about it. They won't touch this hotel because they love the press—and besides, we pay them off." Then William F. Buckley came in to meet Cauthen and had a surprise. "He saw his brother across the room—and neither had mentioned to the other they were going to Vietnam. That is a level of living I am not used to. Apparently they didn't think it important enough to tell each other." This nonchalance, according to Cauthen, is part of Buckley's charm. As they proceeded to prepare their television show, Buckley showed great personal courage as well.

"It was supposed to be a program with President Thieu and Ambassador Ellsworth Bunker, but the Vietcong blew up part of the studio facilities thirty minutes before the program was supposed to start. It killed three of the Vietnamese crew. [Producer] Warren Steibel was there, and Bill and I were on our way over when it happened. President Thieu did not show up after that, but Bunker did, and we got three newsmen. It was fascinating to do a show in Vietnam. After that, we went straight to Israel to do [Jerusalem mayor] Teddy Kollek and Golda Meir."

The most remarkable thing about *Firing Line*'s host, according to Cauthen, is his decency. "Watching him over the years, I can't remember one program where the guest didn't go away respecting and usually liking Bill Buckley. People felt they had been in a fair fight, and a lot of friendships were built up with people who had different views. People who go into combat together usually end up mortal enemies, but not with Bill. He's one of the most thoughtful people I've ever met, always thinking of the other person. He always tries to have a fair fight. He always wants to win—and usually he does."

For Buckley's producer, Warren Steibel, the *Firing Line* debate over the Panama Canal treaty in 1978 was the most memorable program because it pitted Buckley against Ronald Reagan. On Reagan's team were Admiral John McCain (father of Arizona senator John McCain), Georgetown professor Roger Fontaine, and Patrick Buchanan. "Bill believed we should give it back and Reagan believed we shouldn't," Steibel recalls. "It was quite a good debate." Arguing with Buckley were the same Ambassador Ellsworth Bunker from the Vietnam show, who had negotiated the treaty, former senator Sam Ervin of Watergate fame, *National Review* editor James Burnham, Admiral Elmo Zumwalt, and columnist George Will. Buckley felt that it was of "major consequence" that he divided the conservatives and thus allowed the sale of the canal to pass through the Senate.[18]

Steibel remembers that Buckley had been personally solicited to take up the treaty by Ambassador Sol Linowitz, President Carter's chief negotiator. "Linowitz wanted Bill to fight for giving away the Panama Canal, and [Buckley] became enamored of the idea of giving it back to Panama," Steibel said. Buckley believed if the treaty had not passed the Senate, which it might not have done if the conservative opposition had been hegemonic, uprisings in Central America during the 1980 campaign might have frustrated Reagan's presidential campaign.[19] Reagan joked with Buckley at the start, "Well, Bill, my first question is, Why haven't you already rushed across the room here to tell me that you've seen the light?" When Reagan was greeted with laugher and applause, Buckley riposted in kind, "I'm afraid that if I came any closer to you, the force of my illumination would blind you."[20] The American people agreed with Reagan, and two years later they elected him over the President who gave away the Panama Canal.

Buckley's commitment to fair play has been remarked upon by none other than Alan Dershowitz, who has enjoyed appearing on *Firing*

Line to debate the death penalty, the Patty Hearst trial, separation of church and state, the rights of accused Nazis, the exclusionary rule, and, more recently, the O. J. Simpson case. Among his televised visits with Buckley, Dershowitz appeared on a notable 1976 *Firing Line* in a discussion of pornography, as attorney for Harry Reems, the male star of *Deep Throat*. Dershowitz brought the performer along to the taping, much to Buckley's consternation. Buckley felt that Reems was "a sex exhibitionist" who could "ply his wares and make the case for doing so elsewhere, say on the [Phil] Donahue program." So when Reems talked, the erudite and sophisticated host ignored him, "addressing not one word to him throughout the hour." Buckley felt it was important to separate the legal conflict from the person involved and that Reems merited "the ostracism anyone deserves who makes his living by exhibitionistic obscenity."

In 1985 Buckley debated Dershowitz over a proposal to tattoo with an identifying mark those infected with the AIDS virus and got Dershowitz to admit that the military should be permitted to test its soldiers. In debating the "scarlet letter" suggestion, Dershowitz said it would lead to mandatory testing for the entire population—to which Buckley had been opposed. The debate was apparently a draw, but it attracted such interest that Dershowitz and Buckley were invited to publish their views in side-by-side essays in the *New York Times*.[21]

In contrast to his experience on *The Advocates,* Dershowitz has nothing but praise for his appearances with Buckley. "I liked [*Firing Line*] a lot," he said. "It is a great show. Buckley is very fair. He is one of the fairest talk show hosts in television. Compare him to any of those today. He has his point of view, but he allows you to express yours."[22]

Buckley himself says he makes an effort to be fair and balanced. "It is substantially correct to say the program is balanced," Buckley noted, although he is quick to point out, "We often have conservative guests to explore a conservative position." Nevertheless, Buckley is committed to being as straightforward as possible and not serving as a platform for slanted propaganda. He bristles at the characterization of the program as purely conservative. "People who list it as a conservative show are trying to get away with something," he declared. While "I'm always there presenting the conservative position and therefore people get exposed to it, there are liberal guests as well as conservative ones." Among Buckley's left-of-center visitors have been organizer Saul Alinsky, folk singers Joan Baez and Theo Bikel, leftist scholar Richard Barnett, actor Orson Bean, British Labour MP Tony Benn, Watergate journalist Carl Bernstein, civil rights leader Julian Bond, California governor Edmund G. (Pat) Brown, Kennedy staffers McGeorge and William Bundy, Carter Secretary of Health, Education, and Welfare Joseph Califano, author Truman Capote, Carter State Department spokesman Hodding Carter, New York art powerhouse Schuyler Chapin, MIT linguistics professor and leftist crackpot Noam Chomsky, Johnson administration Attorney General Ramsey Clark, Black Panther Eldridge Cleaver, environmentalist Barry Commoner, *Saturday Review* editor Norman Cousins, lawyer Lloyd Cutler (later President Clinton's White House counsel), leftist documentary filmmaker Emile de Antonio, antiwar activists David Dellinger and William Sloane Coffin, Berkeley congressman Ronald Dellums, Massachusetts governor Michael Dukakis, feminist Andrea Dworkin, Pentagon Papers celebrity Daniel Ellsberg, McCarthyism opponent John Henry Faulk, author Frances FitzGerald, feminist Betty Friedan, Ford Foundation consultant Fred Friendly, liberal economist John Kenneth Galbraith, ACLU head Ira Glasser, Kennedy aide Richard Goodwin, Senators Albert Gore Senior and Junior, union leader Victor Gotbaum, consumer activist Mark Green, NAACP legal defense fund head Jack Greenberg, and the list goes on.

The lineup reflects producer Warren Steibel's influence as well as Buckley's (it does not, after all, look like the *National Review* masthead). "The show was balanced ever since I came along," said Steibel. "He didn't care what my ideology was. I care very much that the program is fair." Steibel adds that he, not Buckley, controls the roster of guests.[23]

For a number of years Buckley shared his platform with liberal questioners in addition to booking liberal guests, putting him in the minority on his own program as conservative advocate. He sometimes had a panel of "three bright young guys, which I would bring in later or sooner," depending on how the program was going. If the show was boring, the questioners would be introduced sooner, although always for the last ten to twenty-five minutes of the broadcasts. Among the panelists Buckley selected was a young liberal Harvard Law School graduate named Michael Kinsley, then a journalist at *Harper's* and *The New Republic* magazines. When the program shrank to a half-hour in 1985, the panel vanished and Steibel proposed that Kinsley introduce Buckley and ask questions for the last five minutes. Kinsley so impressed the *National Review* editor that Buckley chose him to moderate the two-hour *Firing Line* debate specials. "We have done a lot of big debates, two-hour specials, and he does not know who is on the other side. Michael Kinsley is the basic moderator; you cannot be fairer than that since ideologically he is on the left," Steibel said.[24] In a sense Buckley's *Firing Line* can be seen as a predecessor to CNN's *Crossfire,* which Kinsley also hosted, although as Buckley notes, "*Crossfire* is relatively recent. Back then it was different, and I think for a while I was the only conservative on television. And for fifteen years there was not any other regularly scheduled conservative television show on PBS."

Another media superstar who served with Buckley on *Firing Line* is ABC News commentator Jeff Greenfield, who Buckley said did "about a hundred shows with us as a panelist before he and ABC plighted their troth." Other liberal regulars on *Firing Line* included the late Allard Lowenstein—instrumental in Eugene McCarthy's 1968 presidential campaign, later American delegate to the United Nations commission on human rights—and feminist lawyer Harriet Pilpel.

In addition to his duty as *Firing Line* regular, Buckley assumed Alistair Cooke's role for the presentation of "Brideshead Revisited" by WNET in 1982 after Mobil's *Masterpiece Theatre* rejected the series. When New York's Channel 13 bought the miniseries for Exxon's *Great Performances*, it needed a conservative host because the frank treatment of homosexuality in the adaptation of Evelyn Waugh's novel had raised concerns. With Buckley as presenter, there would be little chance of a firestorm.

"They just called me and asked me if I would do it," Buckley recalls.[25] He tried to telephone Alistair Cooke to seek his advice but could not reach him. "Having made the decision, I was glad of it," he later wrote, "and all the more glad . . . on seeing it whole, inasmuch as it seemed to me to have a most fearfully anti-Catholic impact." Buckley would use his commentaries to try and undo what he viewed as Waugh's literary attempt to make the Catholics "personally insufferable."[26] "It was all taped in a day and a half, pretty hectic. Part of it had to be improvised, depending on how much time was left at the end of a program." Buckley's introduction was scripted, but the discussion afterward with guests was not. Buckley described the taping as "done under melodramatic circumstances. I arrived eleven A.M., started watching tapes till nine P.M., wrote an introduction to all thirteen episodes in one evening, didn't enjoy that, had to time the guest discussion outros to the second." Buckley was allowed to pick his own discussants. He chose American critic Wilfrid Sheed, "who'd been to Oxford"; Peter Grenville, a British movie director who had collaborated with Waugh on a proposed film version, "both a Catholic and Oxonian"; and *National Review* literary critic Hugh Kenner, "a Catholic convert."

Just as Buckley's role in *Firing Line* had been as an envoy to political conservatives by the liberal mandarins of public broadcasting, his role on "Brideshead" was as PBS's emissary to Catholics and cultural conservatives. Buckley himself summed up his paradoxical feelings about the hosting job in his book *Overdrive,* where he reprinted the judgment of a nineteen-year-old college student as documented by *San Francisco Chronicle* columnist Herb Caen. "What is this," he wrote, "a kind of preppy *Roots?*"

Indeed it was. "Brideshead" was an immense hit for public broadcasting, and Waugh became a major influence for a generation of conservatives on college campuses because of his attitude toward order and tradition. Journalist Christopher Hitchens discovered the legacy of the broadcast when he attempted to deconstruct the conservative movement and chose as an example Benjamin Hart's *Poisoned Ivy,* a 1984 volume reminiscent of Buckley's own *God and Man at Yale,* to which Buckley had contributed an introduction. Hitchens found several paragraphs that were almost identical to "Brideshead" and confronted Hart (the son of *National Review* editor Jeffrey Hart), who told Hitchens that "Brideshead" was "the stylebook upon which my generation modeled itself" and conceded that "some of his generation were going less by the novel than by the television series." Hitchens thought there was irony in "Hart and his cohort of moralistic young 'family values' warriors modeling themselves on the doings of a fictional group of English upper-crust bisexual alcoholics at the close of the First World War."

Hitchens did note, however, that Waugh had been a contributor to the *National Review.*[27]

No matter how much he may appear to have moderated his positions over the years he has appeared on PBS, Buckley has kept a consistent commitment to fairness, to the rights of the underdog, and especially to victims of communism. When asked which show he finds most memorable, Buckley referred to a 1976 documentary special on Aleksandr Solzhenitsyn produced by the BBC. "I got a phone call from Malcolm Muggeridge," Buckley recalled, "saying he'd seen the most entrancing forty-five minutes he'd ever seen in his life, but that he couldn't sell it to PBS." So on March 10, 1976, Buckley devoted his program to the writer who had been banned in the Soviet Union and then kept off the PBS national schedule.

PBS has presented other programs of a conservative nature from time to time, but they are exceptions that prove the rule of tokenism, including Ben Wattenberg's *In Search of the Real America,* which aired 1976–78. Wattenberg is a conservative, probusiness Democrat who had served as a speechwriter for Lyndon Johnson before becoming a columnist and author. With Richard Scammon he had written *The Real Majority* in 1970 and *The Real America* in 1974, taking an upbeat view of America. "Ben is the only person I know who believes in Big Government, Big Business, and Big Labor," remarked Austin Hoyt, his WGBH producer. The program featured neoconservatives such as Norman Podhoretz and Irving Kristol. Hoyt's favorite episode, "There's No Business Like Big Business," had Wattenberg walking through a graveyard of dead industrial giants that had been highlighted in *Forbes* magazine. "It was hysterical," Hoyt recalled. "Ben paused at every one, giving a eulogy" for the traction companies and trusts of yesteryear.

Wattenberg went on to become a regular presence on PBS, hosting specials such *America's Political Parties* in 1988 and 1992, produced by Michael Pack, a young conservative who had made *Hollywood's Favorite Heavy* (1987), hosted by Eli Wallach; *Campus Culture Wars* (1991), attacking political correctness and hosted by Lindsay Crouse; and *Inside the Republican Revolution* (1994), hosted by *Washington Times* columnist Donald Lambro. In 1994 Wattenberg established his own version of *Firing Line,* called *Think Tank*. Like Buckley's Ford Foundation–supported show, it is sponsored, in this case by Amgen Inc. Like Buckley, Wattenberg features at least 50 percent liberal guests and topics. Unlike Buckley, Wattenberg endorsed President Clinton in 1992.

John McLaughlin's *The McLaughlin Group*, which went on the air in 1981, is sponsored by a private corporation, General Electric, and has a perfectly balanced cast of characters, with two liberal journalists such as Jack Germond, Eleanor Clift, or Clarence Page facing off against two conservatives such as Fred Barnes, Morton Kondracke, or Pat Buchanan. The program, which is also syndicated to commercial stations, made a star out of Clift, who often drowns out her antagonists. And McLaughlin has not always been considered as conservative as he is today. A former liberal Jesuit priest who testified to Congress on behalf of the Public Broadcasting Act of 1967 and edited *America,* McLaughlin went to work for Buckley's *National Review* as Washington editor after working in the Nixon and Ford administrations as a White House aide.[28]

Typical of the way PBS treats conservatives is the case of Reed Irvine's response to WGBH's thirteen-hour series *Vietnam: A Television History* (1983), which he believed was filled with "inaccuracies, a lot of errors, and distortions." (Two hours of this thirteen hour program were produced by the ubiquitous Austin Hoyt, on the Tet offensive and Lyndon Johnson.) As head of Accuracy in Media, a conservative media watchdog, Irvine asked to be permitted to offer a rebuttal documentary on PBS. In June 1984 then–National Endowment for the Humanities chairman William Bennett granted Irvine's group $30,000. By contrast, Irvine pointed out that the NEH had given WGBH $1.2 million for its program. Grateful even for the token contribution, however, Irvine pieced together the funds for his film from individual donors and persuaded historian Peter Rollins to serve as producer. Charlton Heston agreed to narrate the program. In the end, Irvine's show cost $100,000.

Television's Vietnam: The Real Story premiered on December 13, 1984, before an audience gathered at the White House that included Heston, Assistant Secretary of Defense James Webb, and John Agresto,

Bennett's special assistant at the NEH. PBS announced that former Carter administration State Department spokesman Hodding Carter's short-lived PBS show *Inside Story* would produce a companion roundtable discussion of the film. It marked a breakthrough for the network, the first time "a mechanism of response" had been found, in the words of *New York* magazine's Edwin Diamond. However, Peter McGhee, WGBH's executive-in-charge, declined to participate in the debate over the accuracy of this production, saying, "I simply wouldn't want to be judged on the basis of what some amateur TV performers were able to muster in a panel show."[29]

When *Television's Vietnam* aired on June 26, 1985, Irvine found himself at the center of a maelstrom. He pointed out that unlike WGBH's Vietnam series, his show hadn't received a penny of CPB or PBS money, and none had been offered. Furthermore, *Television's Vietnam* was not permitted to stand alone but was surrounded with critical interviews and commentary. Irvine was not allowed to suggest alternative reading material to compete with the PBS companion volume to the WGBH series, written by Stanley Karnow.

WGBH's McGhee denounced Irvine's program as "a piece of vicious intellectual vandalism"—yet declined every invitation to debate the merits of both productions on the air. WGBH producer Richard Ellison likewise refused to debate Irvine, declaring, "They are skilled polemicists and propagandists. I'm not. I think they'd cut me to ribbons."[30]

If PBS had been serious about its commitment to balance, it would have insisted that the producers debate Irvine's critique of their program on the air. The failure to insist on this indicated that PBS was not, in fact, concerned with the accuracy of the WGBH production.

Boston Globe columnist David Chanoff had an explanation for the refusal of WGBH personnel to debate Irvine. They had something to hide because their *Vietnam: A Television History* "does not qualify as an honest piece of work." In fact, Irvine was right and "WGBH did indeed produce a biased series," Chanoff wrote, pointing out that author Al Santoli had given producer Richard Ellison evidence of how the Vietcong had waged a murderous war of their own with callous disregard for the peasantry, yet Ellison had ignored him. "I thought he was out to etch in stone the mythology of the sixties," Santoli said. Chanoff himself, who had assisted former Vietcong minister of justice Truong Nhu Tang in writing his memoirs, had offered to put Ellison in touch with these Vietnamese dissidents, former Vietcong who had second thoughts in light of the boat people and the carnage in Cambodia, but Ellison showed no interest. In the finished documentary Chanoff found a "great deal . . . about American savagery and errors, little or nothing that showed that side of the Vietcong or North Vietnamese. The result was a distortion of what happened."[31]

Taking up the cudgels for WGBH and PBS, author Peter Boyer went on CBS *Morning News* to chastise PBS for showing Irvine's film, declaring the network "will have to go a ways before it makes another decision so wrongheaded" and that it should not have shown the rebuttal because "Reed Irvine is not a journalist." CBS had disinvited Irvine from that very program, so he was not allowed to defend his reputation. The result of the outcry against Irvine was that PBS president Bruce Christensen and vice president for news and public affairs Barry Chase rejected AIM's request that their film be shown when *Vietnam: A Television History* was aired. And when Irvine completed a second hour to further rebut the WGBH program the next year, Chase and Christensen refused to show it on the PBS national schedule (although PBS did agree to air *Witness to Revolution: The Story of Anna Louise Strong,* a portrait of a promoter of Chinese communism).[32]

Stymied by the PBS bureaucracy, Irvine arranged for his colleague Deborah Lambert to call every public broadcasting station in the country and offer them a free copy for airing—a form of syndication. To promote his second rebuttal, Irvine again previewed the production at the White House. His efforts were successful, to an extent. Although AIM's film had been kept off the national feed, more than 150 PBS affiliates agreed to air it.

However, PBS's treatment of him made Irvine realize that it was not willing to even attempt to balance its schedule. "Through more than five years of the Reagan administration," Irvine wrote in a 1986 *Wall Street Journal* op-ed titled "Give Up on Public Broadcasting," "it has grown increasingly obvious that the public broadcasting establishment cannot be depoliticized." Programs featuring conservatives, such as Bill Buckley's *Firing Line,* were "tokens that can be cited to disarm critics" and nothing more.[33]

Since 1986 PBS has been presented with some solid proposals to balance the schedule, such as Michael Pack's proposal for an investigative documentary about the Whitewater scandal (made to CPB in 1996), best-selling author Dinesh D'Souza's offer to host a documentary based on his controversial *The End of Racism,* or best-selling author David Horowitz's suggestion that he be permitted to present a rebuttal to PBS's *Making Sense of the Sixties* (which championed the rise of the counterculture in response to his and Peter Collier's *Destructive Generation*). PBS's response has been the same as that given to Reed Irvine: the cold shoulder.

As William Rusher has pointed out, "Bill Buckley's weekly *Firing Line* has served, for over two decades, as the token conservative presence on the PBS television network."[34] And since 1989, the weekly version of *Firing Line,* like Reed Irvine's Vietnam rebuttal, has not received a penny from either the Corporation for Public Broadcasting or PBS.

Buckley is not unaware of his second-class status in public broadcasting. "Somebody speaking with the accents and the emphases of Bill Moyers is acceptable" to PBS executives, he said, "in the sense that someone speaking with those of a Milton Friedman or me would not be. I don't think there is any denying the fact that the establishmentarian thought is liberal, and Moyers is acceptable in the sense that us types are not; that is, Moyers is tolerated in the sense that we are not."[35] Most noticeable to Buckley is evidence that he is not accepted as an equal in what Ken Burns has called "the PBS family"—after twenty-five years of providing programs. In contrast to the treatment given Moyers, whose publications are promoted as pledge bonuses and highlighted in station program guides, Buckley pointed out that "New York station WNET never ever mentions *National Review* in any of its promotional literature. I've called it to their attention and they have not rectified it."[36]

9

Four Legs Good, Two Legs Bad

Science and nature shows rank among the most popular programs ever broadcast on the public television network. The excellence of such series as *Nova, Nature,* and the *National Geographic* specials is undeniable, and they fill an important niche for a large constituency. Yet, even here, politics and public policy are frequently as central as the activities of scientific researchers and investigators.

The immense appeal of PBS's science and nature shows should not be surprising. The natural human interest in science and technology was fed by the network broadcasts of the manned space program during the 1960s. When that wound down, there was a niche to be filled. CBS offered Walter Cronkite's *Twenty-First Century,* which focused on technological change. Animal films, too, could be found on commercial stations. *Mutual of Omaha's Wild Kingdom* was among the longest-running programs on television. Disney's *Wonderful World of Color* featured wildlife pictorials as well. In some measure, PBS's science and nature shows should be considered commercial programs that have migrated (they tend to have commercial underwriters).

In 1992, PBS confirmed the popularity of its science and nature shows by compiling a list of its most-watched programs, which it distributed to television critics. The top five were all *National Geographic* specials:"The Sharks" (1982, 24.1 million viewers); "Land of the Tiger" (1985, 22.4 million); "The Grizzlies" (1987, 22.3 million); "Great Moments with National Geographic" (1985, 21.3 million); and "The Incredible Machine" (1975, 19 million). Indeed, six out of the ten top shows were *National Geographic* specials, as were eighteen out of the top twenty-five.[1]

Besides being the most watched of the PBS science and nature offerings, the *National Geographic* series is one of its most critically acclaimed; it has won 44 Emmys. Producer David Wolper introduced the programs in 1965 on CBS, where they enjoyed considerable popularity during their eight-year run.

Wolper is famous today for producing the miniseries *Roots,* which became the highest-rated program in television history in 1977, and *The Thorn Birds* and for popular situation comedies of the 1970s like *Welcome Back, Kotter* and *Chico and the Man.* But in the 1960s, Wolper was known as the biggest name in television documentary production. He had begun his career in the late 1950s with *The Congressional Investigators,* a program he produced for ABC. *Race for Space,* another show Wolper produced, independently in 1959, included original material from the Soviet space program. Unable to place it with the networks, which rejected outside productions, Wolper called on individual television stations and sold the program to one station manager at a time; he made 120 sales that way. The *New York Times* ran a front-page story about Wolper's efforts, headlined "Fourth Network Formed by Documentary Filmmaker." Three years later, Wolper was the largest independent documentary producer in the country. His high-powered production team included CBS and NBC veterans of such prestigious series as *The Twentieth Century, Project XX,* and *CBS Reports;* by 1962, he had 200 employees. Over the next thirty years, Wolper's production company made documentaries for all three commercial networks.

In 1960 Wolper purchased the rights to Theodore H. White's *The Making of the President 1960,* which told the story of the election of John F. Kennedy as the first Catholic President of the United States. Although he was able to convince Xerox to sponsor the film, at first none of the networks would broadcast it. Finally the then-fledgling ABC network bought the film in 1962. It won an Emmy and thus began a longtime relationship between Wolper and ABC. Within two years,

ABC bought twelve Wolper productions turned down by other networks. Such was Wolper's gratitude that ABC got first option to air *Roots, The Thorn Birds,* the 1984 Olympics, and *Liberty Weekend* (a salute to the Statue of Liberty). In 1969, Wolper returned to the Kennedy theme with *The Journey of Robert F. Kennedy,* which he produced for ABC.

Wolper also conceived and produced *The Undersea World of Jacques Cousteau,* which first aired on ABC in 1967. He later recalled that he got the idea while looking at some oceanic scenes on his television and thinking, "A TV screen looks like a fish tank."[2] Cousteau agreed to participate in twelve programs, and Wolper outfitted Cousteau's boat, the *Calypso,* with a helicopter pad and closed-circuit televisions, as well as a fresh coat of paint. The series was sponsored by Encyclopedia Britannica and DuPont.[3]

Unlike network producers, Wolper was a true independent, with loyal sponsors dedicated to his productions. His *National Geographic* specials were produced in conjunction with the society. When he set about putting together his first *National Geographic* specials, he lined up his corporate sponsors first, then went to CBS, where he placed four programs for the 1964–65 season.

The programs were produced in the style of *National Geographic* magazine, with exceptionally fine photography documenting the wonders of the world and the discoveries of scientists, provided by the society itself. Celebrity narrators, including Orson Welles, Leslie Nielsen, and Alexander Scourby, contributed their voices to the program.

Among Wolper's most memorable *National Geographic* specials produced for CBS were those dealing with the discoveries of anthropologist Dr. Richard Leakey at Olduvai Gorge in Africa. *Dr. Leakey and the Dawn of Man* explored the work of a dedicated scientist pushing back the known origins of humankind. Another memorable episode was *Miss Goodall and the Wild Chimpanzees,* about primatologist Dr. Jane Goodall's research into the socialization of chimps.

Under Wolper's direction, the CBS *National Geographic* specials maintained a scrupulous journalistic standard. Marshall Flaum, a line producer for the Goodall episode, provides some sense of this. In attempting to fill in the sound track during a beach scene, he recalled, he used dialogue from another activity as a voice-over. But the *National Geographic* executives questioned Flaum about the overdubbing. "I admitted I simply dubbed in the words she said somewhere else during the filming to remove the dead feeling on the screen," Flaum said. "It was removed, and when the documentary was finally shown, it appeared with no dialogue, just dead air."

However, Wolper was not always as careful with other programs as he was with *National Geographic*. In 1966, Wolper produced a show for CBS called "Wall Street: Where the Money Is." Narrated by the late Harry Reasoner, the show drew objections from CBS News executive Richard Salant. Salant complained that the program, which was sponsored by Xerox, had given right of approval to Wall Street firms discussed on the air and to the National Association of Securities Dealers. Wolper responded that although the companies profiled had purchased newspaper ads promoting the show, and some had actually purchased advertising during the commercial breaks, they had not had any say in the editing; the conflict quickly died down.

After Wolper stopped producing *National Geographic* in the early seventies, Metromedia Producers Corporation took over the contract, but ratings began to dip. Some critics think Wolper's personal touch was missed by audiences.

In 1973, the *National Geographic* series moved to ABC for one year. That season's lineup included "The Big Cats" (about lions and tigers), "Bushmen of the Kalahari," "Wind Raiders of the Sahara," and "Journey to the Outer Limits." Although ABC had rehired Wolper, ratings were not satisfactory. In 1974, Wolper produced three *Smithsonian* specials for CBS. The first, "Monsters! Mysteries or Myths?," was the top-rated documentary for the season. It featured reports on the Abominable Snowman, Bigfoot, and the Loch Ness Monster, complete with dramatizations. Like the *National Geographic* series, the *Smithsonian* programs would eventually migrate to PBS.[4]

National Geographic moved to PBS in 1975. Gulf Oil paid for Pittsburgh's WQED to serve as the program's "station of entry" into the PBS system and ultimately sponsored the program. The Gulf sponsorship was part of a move by oil companies to improve a public image damaged by the energy crisis of the 1970s. This and other oil company sponsorships (notably Mobil's) prompted observers to label PBS "the petroleum broadcasting service."

National Geographic was an instant success on PBS. It was a commercial show from a commercial network with a commercial sponsor. Resolutely picturesque and apolitical, the series brought new visibility and new audiences to public broadcasting. The success of the *National Geographic* series was further evidence that nature and science programming constituted a strong niche market—a niche that would be a natural for PBS to fill.

Since it first went on the air in March 1974, promising "science adventures for curious grownups," *Nova,* produced by WGBH, Boston, has also enjoyed enormous popularity.

The idea of putting a science series on WGBH was first suggested by BBC executives in 1971 to then-president Stanford Calderwood, who had traveled to London to arrange the original deal for *Masterpiece Theatre.* BBC executive Robin Scott suggested that he also look at the BBC's massive backlist of science and nature programming. Calderwood made a note of Scott's suggestion but left WGBH before following up on it.[5]

Scott's suggestion was pursued in 1974 by WGBH executive Michael Ambrosino, who had worked at the BBC in 1973 in an exchange arrangement, attaching himself to the BBC's Horizon unit, which produced science programs. At Ambrosino's urging, WGBH soon agreed to coproduce a science series with the BBC, supplying in a barter deal half the productions.[6]

To this day, *Nova* relies on the British for programming and personnel. Because WGBH had little production expertise in science documentaries, the station took it upon itself to hire BBC producers to work out of its Boston studios on the joint productions. Thus, although officially American, the coproduced *Nova* episodes were put together in large part by British filmmakers and BBC alumni. In effect, *Nova* was a British series housed at WGBH.

Among the British producers on the *Nova* staff were Graham Chedd and John Angier, who went on to make *Scientific American Frontiers;* Adrian Malone, who produced *The Ascent of Man* and *Cosmos;* and Robin Bates, who produced *Dinosaurs.*

Nova proved to be more than just a television series for WGBH; in recent years, the program has branched out into online services, interactive video, educational materials, publishing, and other video programming. (The *Boston Globe* recently carried a review of two *Nova* children's books. It reported that *Garbage,* written by Evan and Janet Hadingham, paints a realistic picture of the enormous amount of trash we produce, of the health and environmental problems it causes, and of practical suggestions for children who want to help stop pollution. Certainly as scary as any Grimm's fairy tale.)

Les Brown, former *New York Times* television columnist, described *Nova* as a program that "concerned itself with the effects on society of new developments in science."[7] The producers of *Nova* saw it as distinct from "blockbuster" productions like Jacob Bronowski's *Ascent of Man* or Carl Sagan's *Cosmos* precisely because of its social conscience. This attitude was reflected in a 1981 *Boston Globe Magazine* piece, which gushed:

> *Nova* advertises itself as "science adventures for curious grownups" (Ambrosino says it's for people who are "ignorant but not stupid"). It promises the equivalent of informed consent through films that vary from the life of dinosaurs to the disposal of toxic wastes—films that, more often than not, put science into a social context to examine the multiple ways it touches our lives and public policy.[8]

Of course, not all the programs in the series were solemn analyses of weighty moral issues connected to science. Among the more popular of those was one aired in 1991 called "Sex, Lies and Toupee Tape." Hosted by the notably bald actor Alan Rachins of *L.A. Law,* the show provided an irreverent and humorous look at the phenomenon of baldness and the various medical treatments available to cure it. The program was, however, a notable exception to the typical *Nova* style. But there have been others.

"Iceman," for example, was a fascinating 1992 account of the accidental discovery in the Italian Alps of a mummified Stone Age man and his mostly intact clothing and gear. In 1994, *Nova* aired a compelling episode about a thirteen-year-old girl whom hospital researchers at first believed to be a "wild child." Examinations by psychologists eventually revealed her simply to be retarded and severely abused, which resulted in the termination of the study. Subsequently, her mother sued the hospital and psychologists for damaging the child's life.[9] (Both of these episodes were from the BBC.) Other 1994 programs followed the pilots of the United States Acrobatic Team[10] and life aboard the aircraft carrier USS Independence.[11]

Nova has indeed shown a social conscience in its coverage of science. A review of the last twenty years of programs makes it clear that ideology is at least as important to series producers as science is. The series has tended to follow the trendier issues in science and society, with programs covering the greenhouse effect and global warming, the threat to the rain forests, animal rights, chemical and nuclear weapons, and the Soviet space program.

In August 1974 British Nova producer John Angier asked WGBH's Michael Ambrosino to "commission the design of an atomic weapon, and then take it to Sweden to have it tested," for a program called "The Plutonium Connection." Ambrosino approved the project and Angier hired an MIT student to draft plans for the bomb. The New York Times commented, "that such a project was dreamed up and carried out at WGBH should not surprise regular viewers of public television."[12] The producers have tried their hands at diplomacy as well as bomb-making. Ten years after "The Plutonium Connection," Nova hosted "Space Bridge to Moscow," a special hookup linking Soviet and American scientists.

Unfortunately, this social approach to science has led to some lapses in reporting. During the 1980s, for example, the greatest growth in scientific discovery was probably in the fields of molecular biology and genetic engineering. Indeed, in recent years the courts have ruled that new species of plants and animals may be protected by patent, and new agricultural and pharmaceutical industries have blossomed. Yet, surprisingly, only one Nova episode ("The Gene Engineers," aired in 1977) has dealt specifically with this research. That episode focused on the vague possibility of disaster due to a genetic mishap. Nova producers are not cheerleaders for American biotechnology.

To be fair, Nova has covered the medical applications of interferon and has presented several programs on clinical medicine, including shows featuring visits to practitioners in Nigeria and Tanzania who combine Western medicine with native rituals and Chinese "barefoot doctors" who worked with an American group of ophthalmologists. The Tanzania program ("The New Healers," 1977) was a glowing account of "alternative health care" in that country and similar practices in America. However, *Nova* was critical of American insurance companies that did not recognize such unusual procedures. "The Doctors of Nigeria" (1981) showed traditional and modern methods working together in a highly favorable presentation designed to affirmatively answer the question "Is the fagara root a match for the stethoscope?"

A review of *Nova*'s medical programs turns up quite a few that emphasize the dangers and drawbacks of high-tech medicine. In "The Beersheva Experiment" (1979), the *Nova* team visited both England and Israel to show general practitioners at work, seeming to imply that their efforts were somehow more important than cutting-edge research. "Make My People Live: The Crisis in Indian Health" (1984) focused on the failure of the Indian Health Service to provide adequate care for American Indians living on reservations. One of the health problems faced by the Indians was, according to *Nova*, poverty. "Child Survival: The Silent Emergency" (1985) addressed the "worldwide health crises facing children." In 1978 the series had even run a sympathetic docudrama based on a lawsuit against heart surgeon Dr. Denton Cooley, raising questions about "the practice of modern medicine."

When pharmaceuticals are the topic, *Nova* seems to emphasize the problems. For example, "The Overworked Miracle" (1976) was an entire show devoted to the growing problem of antibiotic-resistant infections; overuse of antibiotics by doctors was blamed. One of the series's first programs, "Are You Doing This for Me, Doctor, or Am I . . . for You?" (1974), criticized the use of human volunteers for drug research. NBC's Jane Pauley presented a two-part *Nova* special on experimental cancer drugs in 1988. A 1987 ode to natural cures called "The Hidden Power of Plants" sang the praises of herbs and vegetable extracts.

What emerges from such coverage is an image of modern medicine as troubled or impotent. Interestingly, the contemporaneous health coverage of the commercial news media tended to hail medical break-throughs, even when not fully tested.

Another important difference between *Nova*'s coverage of medical news and issues and that of the commercial networks is in the area of drug abuse. In 1992 alone, Journal Graphics, a company that provides transcripts of television programs, recorded over 200 stories in the main-stream media about drug abuse, including stories on heroin, cocaine, and marijuana.[13] That same year, *Nova* did not run a single program on drug abuse; the closest the series seems to have come to the subject was a 1984 episode dealing with alcoholism ("Alcoholism: Life Under the In-fluence"). One cannot but wonder at these omissions; watching *Nova,* viewers might conclude that there was no such thing as drug abuse and that psychopharmacological research was unimportant.

Similarly, twenty years of *Nova* programming has produced only one show on aging. In 1982, the series presented "Aging: The Methuselah Syndrome," which dwelled on the use of plastic surgery by the elderly in a futile attempt to stop life's inevitable decay. Again, *Nova* failed to inform viewers about important ongoing scientific research into, for example, Alzheimer's disease. Indeed, a keyword search of the online Journal Graphics database yielded not a single entry for Alzheimer's in the *Nova* listings; that omission stands in stark contrast to over 160 list-ings under "aging" for the commercial networks in 1992 alone and nine references to Alzheimer's disease in that same year. Aging research is among the most heavily funded fields in medicine today.

Judging from their program offerings, the producers of *Nova* seem to have an agenda more in keeping with technophobes than techno-philes. While many programs are expertly produced and deal with interesting subject matter, they often emphasize risks over benefits. Coverage of medical issues is not the only area in which this agenda is apparent. As mentioned earlier, *Nova* has repeatedly taken a position against nuclear weapons (despite their proven deterrence of a third world war and defeat of the Soviet Union), against preparing for nuclear defense, and against the development of germ warfare countermeasures.

Nova has also often looked at computer technology as science fraught with peril, a somewhat Luddite perspective in the age of the Internet and World Wide Web. "Computers, Spies, and Private Lives"

(1981) and "We Know Where You Live" (1990) argued that computer databases were a threat to the American citizen's right to privacy. "Talking Turtle" (1983) raised the specter of schoolchildren "programmed" by computerized instruction. In 1990, the series presented "The KGB, the Computer, and Me," which told the story of how an unemployed Berkeley astronomer named Cliff Stoll exposed a spy network in Hanover, Germany, and raised fears, again, about the evils of computers. The menace of computerized weaponry was examined in a show called "Killing Machines," aired in 1990, just prior to America's decisive victory over Iraq in the Gulf War. Spectacularly wrong in retrospect, the program was advertised by WGBH with the tagline "questions whether their proliferation may spell an end to superpower invincibility."

Which is not to say that computers have always fared badly at the hands of *Nova* producers. In 1978, "The Mind Machines" provided a straightforward account of the status of computing; "Artists in the Lab" (1981) featured artists who used high-tech equipment; and "Finding a Voice" (1983) was about computerized help for the disabled. "The Chip and the Chess Master" (1991) took a humorous look at chess master Garry Kasparov's match with the "Deep Thought" computer. But overall, the picture *Nova* has painted of computers over the last twenty years has been of an emerging threat to the American way of life.

Again, a comparison to the mainstream media in this regard is revealing: In 1992, over 200 references to "Computer Hardware and Software" appeared in the Journal Graphics index of commercial television programs. These programs dealt with a wide range of subjects, including the rise of new corporations like Microsoft and Intel and the troubles of old mainframe giants like IBM. There were listings for shows about using computers to make movies and of a profile of Intel chief Andy Grove. There were stories about e-mail, voice mail, fax machines, robotics, "battery powered gizmos," a computer network for Alzheimer sufferers, robot submarines, check scanners, computerized film processing, computer-assisted stone carving, computers in the courtroom, laptop developments, carpal tunnel syndrome, and CD-ROM software. Little of this subject matter seems to have been suitable for *Nova*.

Despite its ideological slant, *Nova* has been a successful program by PBS standards because Americans are interested in gadgets, medicine, and scientific advances. Since its second year on the air, *Nova* has enjoyed corporate sponsorship, currently by Lockheed Martin and Johnson & Johnson.

No account would be complete without mentioning one accusation against *Nova* relating to the 1992 broadcast of "This Old Pyramid," a ninety-minute special featuring stonemason Roger Hopkins from *This Old House* and Egyptologist Mark Lehner. The charge was made by Margaret Morris, an assistant to chemist Joseph Davidovits, author of *The Pyramids: An Enigma Solved* (1988). Davidovits is an expert in high-strength cements who had determined one possible chemical process involving dissolved limestone that might have been used by the ancient Egyptians to pour the six-ton bricks on site, as in modern construction.

Morris said she had sent Davidovits's book to *Nova* producers, who interviewed him and then attempted to discredit his hypothesis, claiming instead that the pyramids were carved from solid stone blocks and telling viewers that *Nova* had successfully built a pyramid using only this ancient method. Instead, Morris claimed, the *Nova* team "cheated with modern tools and a front-end loader! Only the two or three blocks shown being raised on camera were moved by hand."

After WGBH producer Michael Barnes declined to respond to her complaints, Morris, who lives in Michigan, contacted the office of Senator Donald Riegle, whose staff assistant, Tom Hester, obtained a verbal promise that *Nova* would add a disclaimer admitting that the pyramid shown in the broadcast had not been constructed in completely ancient fashion. He told Morris not to worry about any damage to Davidovits's scientific reputation because "*Nova* is basically nothing more than an entertainment program about science."[14]

The popularity of science and nature programming with viewers soon led PBS to establish another slot for what insiders jokingly refer to as "fur and feather" shows. Developed in 1980, *Nature* brought even more animal life to the PBS screen. *Nature* is produced by George Page, who had been a PBS public relations executive before coming to WNET, New York, in 1972 to serve as the station's director of science and natural history programming. Since there was no dialogue involved, it was easy for Page to go about acquiring a great deal of animal footage from foreign broadcasters, including the British, the Germans, and the French. Page would record his own voice-overs and do his own stand-ups, creating the impression to the casual viewer that he had something to do with stalking the animals he presented. In essence, *Nature* was yet another repackaged foreign program.

George Page had come to public television after covering the civil rights movement for Atlanta television stations and, later, the Vietnam War for NBC News. He served as producer of such major PBS series as *The Brain* and *The Mind* (the BBC and WNET settled a multimillion-dollar lawsuit regarding contractual dispute between these two series), *Childhood, Travels,* and *Medicine at the Crossroads.* Among his other credits are a series of tributes he commissioned, including *The Spencer Tracy Legacy: A Tribute by Katherine Hepburn, Fred Astaire: Change Partners and Dance, Jukebox Saturday Night, New World Visions,* and *Fred Astaire: Putting on His Top Hat.* Many of the latter shows were run during pledge weeks, a reminder of Page's earlier calling as a public relations man with a knack for fund-raising.

Nature has won two Emmy awards and still reigns as prime-time television's longest-running weekly natural history program. But one would be mistaken to conclude that the series has no political agenda.

Just as *Nova* dwells on the perils of science, *Nature* often warns of the danger the "white man" poses to the harmony of the planet. For example, in 1991, the series presented "Land of the Eagle," a miniseries about the flora and fauna of the United States, described by Page as "one of the most popular presentations in *Nature's* long history." The premise of the show can be summarized as follows: Before the white man came, America was a garden of Eden where Indians lived in balance with nature, tending to the needs of Mother Earth. Then the greedy white man brought his so-called Western civilization and destroyed the natural goodness the Indian maintained. Although claiming to be a natural history series, "Land of the Eagle" was really an indictment of the opening of the North American continent to European settlement. Part one used the intellectually fashionable term "encounter" to describe the discovery of America, called "The Great Encounter."

The eight-hour series, which aired over four nights around Thanksgiving (no accident, no doubt), failed to mention that the Indians practiced slash-and-burn agriculture, stampeded buffalo off cliffs to their deaths and processed them into pemmican in Stone Age factories, and waged in intertribal warfare, leaving death and suffering in their wake. Nor did Page's series mention that the practice of modern agriculture has enabled the land to support far more native people than their nomadic hunting practices had. Multiculturalism was apparently Page's guiding principle; facts that interfered with his premise were not reported. Rousseau's noble savage had been uncritically recycled once more.

In 1993, *Nature* aired another miniseries. This one was called "Land of the Russian Bear." Amazingly, the Russian white man seems not to have been as bad as his American cousin, and the Russian bear seems to have dominion over a land in which no humans were ever persecuted, much less tortured and killed by the millions in gulags located near the lovely Siberian villages the filmmakers visited. The series was filmed with the cooperation of the Soviet authorities over a period of years— indeed, the show originally was put together by Soviet crews for Soviet television in the last days of the Soviet Union. They presented a beautiful paradise, indeed, even in a land devastated by rampant industrialization and nuclear contamination from accidents like Chernobyl.

In 1994, *Nature* broadcast "The Nature of Sex," which featured animals fighting and mating. Unlike David Attenborough's spectacular *Trials of Life,* which appeared on the TNT cable network, "The Nature of Sex" offered little in the way of zoological explanation. Rather, it was a peeping Tom approach to animal husbandry, with Page ululating about "these magnificent creatures" in between sex scenes. Needless to say, ratings were high, and PBS president Ervin Duggan, an erstwhile opponent of smut on commercial television as FCC commissioner, scheduled repeat broadcasts of the program on PBS.

In 1995, *Nature* presented a five-part miniseries called "Nomads of the Wind" that featured a visit to the islands of Polynesia, described by Page as "paradise on Earth." Like many other *Nature* shows, this series was developed as a coproduction with the BBC. Coproductions actually allow PBS to "pre-buy" a show before a competing cable channel can make a bid.

Peter Crawford of the BBC's Bristol science unit, a specialty production facility known for nature films, spent three years in the South Seas producing the series. Again, intellectual fads dominated the context in which nature was being presented. Crawford told a PBS press conference that his purpose was to show that Captain Cook had not "discovered" the islands, but that they had their own proud five-thousand-year history prior to the landing of Europeans.

One of the stars of the series was a witch doctor who took Crawford around the islands in his boat. He tells Crawford that Polynesians sail against the wind so that they can always "go back." That is, the wind will enable them to turn around if they get into trouble on their voyage. This gave Crawford the concept for this series: that Thor Heyerdahl, the explorer who recreated ancient sailing routes for his classic *Kon-Tiki,* was wrong and that the Polynesians sailed, not with the prevailing trade winds, but *against* them. This too was Crawford's mission: "to go against traditional historical accounts"—that is, to subvert traditional history as such.[15]

Onscreen, Crawford objects to the notion that "history started when the Europeans arrived" and says his storyline was "based on what we've learned . . . from Polynesians themselves." Yet the Polynesians have no written records of ancient times. There is no recorded Polynesian history to compare to the European version. What Crawford relies upon instead is myth, legend, and imagination. While perhaps making an entertaining program, they are not a good guide for historical analysis.

Nature's attitude is consistent with the revisionist multiculturalism found in fashionable intellectual circles today, displaying a relativism in relation to progress and civilization that former National Endowment for the Humanities chairmen Lynne Cheney and William Bennett, among others, have labeled political correctness.

When asked at a PBS press conference why a program called *Nature* was dealing with the human history of the Polynesian islands, Page responded, "You really can't do a natural history film anymore without some acknowledgment of the role of human beings in the particular ecological system that you're dealing with." This would be news indeed to David Attenborough and other naturalists and filmmakers who have managed to do precisely that.

Despite the revisionism and political correctness of *Nature,* and the antipathy toward Western science and progress of *Nova,* public broadcasting's science and nature programs continue to be enormously popular among viewers. But this popularity has annoyed some television critics, who seem to begrudge the public network its high ratings. In 1986 *Boston Globe* columnist Ed Siegel damned with faint praise this most successful strand of the PBS lineup. "One certainly can't fault PBS," he wrote, "for failing to fill the network void in science and nature series. One certainly can ask, however, if—after *Nova* and *Nature* and *Discovery* and *National Geographic* and *Smithsonian World* and the BBC series—PBS isn't as interested in appeasing a mass audience (these are the most popular programs on PBS) and corporate angels [as] are the commercial networks. Documentaries on continental drift and tropical fossils in the Antarctic don't offend anybody and are extremely attractive to the likes of IBM."[16]

What is the secret of the appeal of nature and science programming? George Page has said that one factor is their sheer drama and action, perhaps more sex and violence than might be available from MacNeil/Lehrer, Bill Moyers, or Charlie Rose. "There's a lot of sex and violence in nature," Page told reporters. "We don't try to exploit the sex and violence in *Nature*, but you know, occasionally it is unavoidable."

In addition to the sex and violence, Page said he felt that environmental awareness was another factor in the success of PBS's science and nature programming. Audiences, he said, "are fascinated with the complexity and the diversity of life on our planet and realize the importance of keeping this planet for not only future generations of human beings but future generations of plants and animals. And so I think, and would like to hope, that we've helped raise consciousness about the importance of environmental issues."[17] However, WGBH's *Race to Save the Planet* (1990), a multipart exploration of the environmental movement based on the Worldwatch Institute's State of the World Reports, was a ratings flop, indicating that it might well be the sex and violence (as well as the cute and cuddly critters) that attract the viewers.

In the end, the politically correct attitude toward nature, science, and technology is what separates science and nature programs on PBS from coverage elsewhere. With the exception of the *National Geographic* specials, whose editorial control is maintained by the National Geographic Society under strict standards, and the occasional program that slips through the editorial process, *Nova* and *Nature* and their cousins have been consistent with the general approach of the rest of the programs on the PBS network.

The *Wall Street Journal* noted this tendency in an editorial-page item headlined "Nova Finds Paradise," which discussed promotional material the paper's editors had received from WGBH in connection with *Nova's* "Little Creatures Who Run the World," hosted by Harvard sociobiologist Edward O. Wilson. "According to the politically resonant publicity release, the show will provide an intimate portrait of two forms of life whose members labor exclusively for the good of the community. 'Unselfishness is the rule,' the release informs us, adding, 'For them, socialism works.' The two species are ants and cockroaches."[18]

10

This Old How-To

Every year PBS station managers from around the country come together at an annual meeting to see what is on the schedule for the year ahead. In June 1994 the delegates gathered at the Marriott Orlando World Center Resort, near Walt Disney World. The location is a favorite of PBS executives because their spouses and children can enjoy a day at Disney while they deal with the details of station management and finance. Also present at this meeting were PBS producers and their stars, eager to sell shows to stations around the country. Among those who turned up to pitch their programs were Ken Burns, touting *Baseball;* David Frost, plugging his interviews; Bill Kurtis, promoting his adventure series *The New Explorers;* Lily Tomlin, selling her educational *Magic Schoolbus* cartoons; and a gaggle of puppets from *The Puzzle Place.*

The assembled programmers were treated to screenings of upcoming episodes of *Nature, The American Experience,* and *Frontline* and a birthday tribute to Bill Moyers on videotape (since he was in the hospital recuperating from heart surgery). There was a banquet and an awards ceremony.

At the Orlando meeting, incoming PBS president Ervin Duggan had decided to present a new scheme for enticing local stations to run more of his core programming and fewer cooking shows like Julia Child's. To do this, PBS would impose financial penalties—in essence, fines—on stations that did not carry the national feed. He was greeted with hostility by the managers present, who did not want to take orders from Washington about what to show on their stations. The atmosphere grew so unpleasant that PBS called an unscheduled meeting with the managers in which Duggan quickly backtracked from his plan. Given a choice between the French Chef and anything out of Washington, D.C., the preference was crystal clear.

The highlight of the convention, for many of those present, was a chance to meet—and be photographed with—Julia Child herself. She was in Orlando to introduce her new series, *Cooking with Master Chefs,* a coproduction of Maryland Public Television and a private company, A La Carte Communications. Maryland Public Television was highlighting its new relationship with the star best known for her work with WGBH, Boston. Raymond Ho, then president of the state network, had lured her away for her new series by outbidding the competition (though the finances were kept private). To celebrate the quarter-century on the air, Maryland Public Television sent out silver invitations reading "25th Anniversary: Fulfilling the Promise" to everyone in attendance. "Join us at the marketplace [the exhibit area for the convention] to celebrate our 25th anniversary!" it gushed. "Talk with Julia Child about her next 'Cooking with Master Chefs' series and enjoy the wine and food tasting."

Maryland Public Television had paid for an elaborate buffet of international delicacies (chosen to reinforce the theme of the program) artistically displayed in the Palms Ballroom of the hotel. There were silver chafing dishes at four stations, one for each direction on the compass, with finger foods ranging from eggrolls to quiche and carving stations with hot meats served on good china. Red and white wine flowed freely, served to the station managers in fine crystal.

In the center of the ceremonies was a small tent, with a little counter, a couple of stools, and a pile of books. On one of the stools sat the eighty-one-year-old Julia Child. The guests were herded into a receiving line and one by one led up to shake hands with the legendary PBS cooking star, have their books signed, and have a photo taken. After a few words were exchanged, the excited executives were moved along to make room for the next. The line snaked through the entire ballroom. There were speeches praising Child, and Maryland Public Television president Ho paid tribute to her continuing contribution to public broadcasting—and the American palate. And not so subtly, he sold his latest program to the assembled PBS managers.

Since public broadcasting is both a network and a loose system of affiliated stations, each station has the option of purchasing its own programs. For many people in America, and certainly for those at the Marriott that night, Julia Child is what PBS is and has been all about for thirty years. In 1965 WGBH reported the French chef was "the major drawing card in all [educational television]."[1]

Child has remained on the air these many years because the national core schedule known as the PBS feed fills only a small portion of the time stations are on the air: Sunday through Thursday nights from 8 to 11 P.M. The rest of the airtime is their own to use as they see fit. They may also present programs of their own choosing at times of their own choosing, preempting the national schedule to better meet local preferences. (In New York City, for example, Mystery! was shown for many years on Saturday nights, while in the rest of the country it was carried on Thursday nights.)

In 1996 Land O' Lakes butter announced that it would sponsor a new series of baking programs on PBS—hosted by Julia Child. The series, called Baking at Julia's, features twenty-six different pastry chefs demonstrating recipes for cakes and breads. Child declared, "Our new series is designed to help the home cook. We have wonderful chefs who are the best in their field. Our viewers will see how it's done in a home situation so they'll be able to bake the recipes themselves in their own kitchens."

As she had been with the Boston Gas Company over thirty years ago, and with Safeway and Polaroid, Child is grateful to her underwriter for paying the bills related to her most recent venture, stating, "I'm delighted Land O' Lakes could join us as a sponsor." For Julia Child, at least, there is no conflict between education, salesmanship, and sponsorship—and there never has been, for it has been her lifelong task to popularize the finer things in life to the largest possible audience. She was, is, and forever will be an anti-snob, and that is one secret of her successful syndication to PBS stations and the tremendous demand for her books, videos, and CD-ROMs.

This and other PBS cooking shows, such as those of Jacques Pépin, Jeff Smith *(The Frugal Gourmet),* Cajun cook Justin Wilson, health-conscious Jane Brody, the midwesterner Marcia Adams, and Martin Yan *(Yan Can Cook),* demonstrate that educational and instructional fare can flourish without federal subsidy. They were available before the Corporation for Public Broadcasting was created in 1967 and would continue to be available were it to fade from the scene, because they fulfill a genuine need of the American television audience.

Without a doubt, some of the most successful programs to emerge from the PBS experiment are its "how-to" shows, which teach viewers how to cook, fix up a house, perform yoga, sew a quilt, or master woodworking techniques. Aimed at a middle-class audience interested in self-improvement, these straightforwardly instructional programs have attracted enormously loyal followings. Cheap to produce and possessing long shelf-lives, the shows are self-sustaining from sponsorships, receive no federal tax dollars, and even make a profit; more than a few of them sell books by the millions. What's more, they're produced according to *commercial* principles. They are conceived in conjunction with the associated books and merchandise, funded by sponsors, and then sold to stations just as commercial programs are sold by syndicators to independent television stations. They go to PBS simply because that's where the eyeballs are for such niche programming. (Until founding CNN executive Reese Schoenfeld recently set up the Food Channel, PBS was in this area without serious competition.)

PBS how-tos are typically produced by local stations. Indeed, each of the very successful WGBH shows examined in this chapter began as a local venture utilizing local talent. WGBH president Henry Becton says the success of such series is rooted in a Yankee spirit of self-reliance. But the popularity of the WGBH how-tos was probably better explained in a *Boston Globe* article, which pointed to the Boston-based station's "reverence for money." "[Money] is the fuel that propels the station's creative engine," the *Globe* asserted. "And it is money that the station's talented producers—both in-house and the independents—fight over."

Or, as author Edwin Glick concluded in his 1970 history of the station, "Any viewer of WGBH's programs or any reader of the station's annual reports will realize that 'underwriting' or 'sponsorship'—call it what one will—is a major fact of life at WGBH, and [is] one of the reasons so many of its major productions have shown the quality which has become a hallmark of so much of the station's output."[2]

The first truly national star to rise from public television was the host of a how-to program, and she has remained PBS's most enduring and most widely recognized personality. Julia Child, longtime hostess of *The French Chef* and its many sequels and spin-offs, has come to represent the most popular genre of PBS programming. The WGBH handbook *On Air* states, "*The French Chef* launched our reputation as the major PBS producer of 'how-to' shows." Many other PBS how-tos have been on the air almost as long as Child's, but hers was the original, and it remains the best.

Julia Child was not always a French chef. She was born Julia McWilliams in Pasadena, California, on August 15, 1912, to John and Julia Carolyn (Weston) McWilliams. After graduating from Smith College in 1934, she moved to New York, where she worked in the advertising department of W & J Sloane.

At the start of World War II, Julia McWilliams moved to Washington, D.C., where she found a job in the file room of the head of the Office of Strategic Services (predecessor to the Central Intelligence Agency), General William "Wild Bill" Donovan. Her talents were quickly recognized, and the young file clerk was soon assigned by the OSS to intelligence work in Ceylon (now called Sri Lanka), of strategic importance because it was near vital shipping lanes off the coast of India between the Arabian Sea and the Bay of Bengal. There, in 1943, she met Paul Child, an American working as a visual presentations specialist under Britain's Lord Mountbatten. Child, whose father had been head of the Smithsonian's Astrophysics Laboratory, had a reputation for brilliance among his colleagues and associates. The couple spent 1944 and 1945 working together as a team on intelligence projects in Kungming, China. After the war ended, they married. After retiring from his government career, Paul Child would collaborate with his wife on her television shows and cookbooks as photographer and designer.

When they first married, the now world-famous television chef reportedly wasn't much of a cook. In his obituary, the *Boston Globe* quoted Paul Child, who remembered his wife's pre–Cordon Bleu efforts in the kitchen as distinctively non-gourmet: "I was willing to put up with all that awful cooking to get Julia."

Switching from the OSS to the Foreign Service after the war, Paul Child was posted to Paris during the height of McCarthyism in the United States from 1948 to 1952, and Marseilles from 1952 to 1954, on assignment for the United States Information Agency, a federal organization responsible for disseminating American propaganda. Julia, of course, accompanied her husband to France. He had lived in Paris before World War II and befriended Ernest Hemingway and Gertrude Stein, among others.

She ate her first French meal in the city of Rouen in 1948. "I never, never turned back after that," she later told an interviewer. "I just fell in love with French food from the first bite."[3] With her husband's encouragement, Child entered the Cordon Bleu cooking school in Paris in 1949. Julia Child later said she learned to cook "for the same reason every woman gets flour up to her elbows. To please a man."[4]

During this period Julia Child met the two women with whom she would collaborate on the book that would change her life and the course of American cuisine. Her encounter with the two Frenchwomen, Simone Beck and Louisette Bertholle, took place at a cocktail party. They were already working on a cookbook and hoping to sell it in the United States, but their American collaborator had died. Julia Child agreed to step in, and the trio set to work.

In 1952, Child opened a cooking school in Paris with Beck and Bertholle. They called it Ecole des Trois Gourmandes: the School of the Three Hearty Eaters. She joined the select Le Cercle des Gourmettes. Between cooking classes, the three women worked on their cookbook. It took them ten years to complete the manuscript. Today, *Mastering the Art of French Cooking* is considered a classic. The dedication reads: "To La Belle France, whose peasants, fishermen, housewives, and princes—not to mention her chefs—through generations of inventive and loving concentration have created one of the world's great arts."

It was the right book in the right place at the right time. America was changing. After the middle-class and middle-American tastes of Mamie Eisenhower, "Camelot" was bringing a stylish new sensibility to

Pennsylvania Avenue. First Lady Jacqueline Bouvier Kennedy, an avowed Francophile who spoke French fluently, had made all things French appealing to ordinary American women. And at the end of the affluent fifties, American women were interested in taking steps to improve their quality of life. They needed what Child had to offer, a book that took the snobbery (and some mystery) out of continental cuisine. What had once been the perquisite of high society would become the dinner fare of the suburbs.

This democratic dissemination was the author's intention. Child told interviewers her book was designed "to take a lot of the la-dee-dah out of French cooking." She objected to "the one-upsmanship and We Happy Few and all that" which had surrounded haute cuisine. *Mastering the Art of French Cooking* was for "the servantless American cook who can be unconcerned on occasion with budgets, waistlines, time schedules, children's meals, the parent–chauffeur–den mother syndrome, or anything else which might interfere with the enjoyment of producing something wonderful to eat." Child suggested that an alternate title might be "French Cooking from the American Supermarket." In a sense, she offered "snobbery made easy" by combining a plummy accent and a love of French food with a typically American do-it-yourself approach.[5]

Child's first television exposure came when she appeared on a commercial American network during her book tour, demonstrating how to prepare her recipes. Shortly after she and her husband moved to Cambridge in 1961, a town known for its hospitable intellectual climate as home to Harvard University and MIT, a friend invited Child to appear on WGBH and discuss her book on the program *I've Been Reading*. Child cooked an omelet before the cameras to demonstrate a recipe from her book in a specially constructed demonstration kitchen at the Boston Gas Company. The producer, Russell Morash, had Child take a balloon whip and beat some eggs in a copper bowl. Morash was amazed by what Child did with her simple demonstration, later telling a reporter, "I thought to myself, who is this mad woman cooking an omelet on a book review program?"[6]

According to David M. Davis, then a WGBH executive, Child's first *French Chef* broadcast, on February 11, 1963, provided her first opportunity to demonstrate her now famous unflappability. "Julia was twenty minutes into her first show," he recalls, "and the elevator bell rang. I was in the remote truck, and I thought, 'What are you going to do?' Julia was whipping away at something. She said, 'Oh, somebody's at the door but I'm much too busy.' We knew we had something."[7]

Three episodes of *The French Chef* were produced in the gas company kitchen. They were an instant success and led to a full series of twenty-six programs for which Child was paid $50 each. They were first aired on the seven stations of the Eastern Educational Network based at WGBH and were soon offered to other affiliates of National Educational Television as Child gathered a following. *The French Chef* was picked up almost at once by a hundred educational stations and became one of the most popular programs on NET. Child told a reporter later that the name of the show was an accident. "I'm not French," she said. "I'm not really a chef. But when I started on television, someone said we had to pick a title that fitted on one line in *TV Guide*."

Once her series began, Child worked twelve-hour days, taping four weekly shows. Editing was reduced to a minimum to keep costs down. The theme of each show was honest cooking. Paul Child, who worked closely with his wife, overseeing almost every detail, told an interviewer the rules were "no fakery, no pretense, very free, natural, the same off-screen as on." The democratic spirit and evangelical mission to spread the gospel of French cuisine that had inspired her cookbook continued to infuse her television work.

Child was charming and enthralled her growing viewership. She proved to be, according to her husband, "a natural clown."[8] This appealed to audiences up and down the social spectrum. A less highbrow critic, Ted Holmberg of the *Providence Sunday Journal,* wrote, "My favorite is Julia Child. . . . I couldn't be less interested in cooking, except for the results, but I can watch Miss Child prepare a leg of lamb, which I detest, and remain fascinated for half an hour. She'll grab a hipbone (the lamb's, of course, this *is* educational television) and describe it as a 'great big complicated thing,' and then drop her glasses. She'll pick up a huge cleaver and start hacking at some leftover bones with more glee than such a task deserves. All the while, she's chattering away in a kind of

Boston accent, which has a touch of mashed potato about it." This apparently self-deprecating approach to cooking with a sense of humor (and a glass of wine or two) has been the secret to Child's lasting appeal.

But as popular as Child was with American viewers and critics, her unique style did not at first translate overseas. *The French Chef* was turned down by the BBC after one test broadcast resulted in a host of viewer complaints. The bewildered English wondered "what on earth a drunken or demented American woman was doing"[9] on their network. British viewers were much more responsive to Child's later series, however, which were aired in Britain as *From Julia Child's Kitchen.* Yet the very qualities that alienated the British helped make Julia Child an American star.

In the States, the certified hit was first sponsored by Safeway Stores of California, as well as Boston Gas. Later, the Polaroid Corporation would come aboard as an additional sponsor. To this day, Julia Child's programs continue to be as popular with sponsors as they are with audiences.

In 1973, *The French Chef* ended its eleven-year run. Public demand for Child continued, however. Five years later, in 1978, *Julia Child and Company* debuted on WGBH, and Child has been a constant presence ever since. In 1984, her series *Dinner at Julia's* invited legendary gourmet James Beard and trendy Spago chef Wolfgang Puck, among others, to prepare her supper. This was followed by *Cooking with Master Chefs.* The interaction between Child and the other chefs provides a unique theatrical element that makes these programs more than ordinary cooking shows. They are like a visit to a wonderful old friend, or a doting, eccentric aunt. One waits to see her reaction. In a sense, the guest chefs are auditioning to see who might succeed Julia Child, clamoring for the chance to be the one to whom the toque is passed.

Jacques Pépin comes closest to being Child's successor as interpreter of French cuisine for an American audience, though he will never replace her unique personal qualities (much as Russell Baker has taken the chair from Alistair Cooke to introduce British drama on Mobil's *Masterpiece Theatre* without fully matching Cooke's assurance and aplomb). Pépin's three PBS series, *Happy Cooking, Good Life Cooking,* and *Today's*

Gourmet, have sold thousands of cookbooks. But where Child is resolutely American and began her career as an amateur, Pépin is very
definitely French, and a professional chef from a line of restaurateurs.

The success of *The French Chef* allowed Child's producer, Russell
Morash, to carve out a niche for himself as unit producer of specialized
how-to programming at WGBH. In 1975, Morash began producing a
program called *Crockett's Victory Garden,* hosted by gardener James Un-
derwood Crockett. The show was originally taped in a forty-foot-square
section of the WGBH parking lot that had been torn up to create a vegetable patch. Though it had been envisioned as a local show and tailored
to the climate and soil conditions of New England, within a year *Victory
Garden* was being syndicated nationally to PBS stations. Crockett himself
unfortunately died of prostate cancer after only three seasons.

"Jim had great charisma," Morash recalled. "He was instantly
beloved. And he was a great storyteller. There was no editing. You'd turn
on the camera and let it rip. It was like filming a baseball game." Like
Julia Child, Crockett was a natural screen presence who was in the right
place at the right time. His program appealed to ex-hippies who wanted
to return to the land, as well as to older PBS viewers who remembered
World War II and their actual Victory gardens. As interest in organic
foods and self-sufficiency spread through the general population in the
1970s, this public broadcasting program was perfectly positioned for this
growing niche market of baby boomers and retirees. About the same
time, organic food chains like Bread and Circus, catering to this demo-
graphic group, began to make their appearance.

"The history of *The Victory Garden* is a mirror of the changing
movement it helped create," the *Boston Globe* reported. "Jim Crockett
[an offscreen junk-food junkie who didn't much like vegetables, according to Morash] convinced viewers that they could actually grow delec-
table carrots and peas in their back yards, even if they were three
generations removed from the farm and didn't know hoes from hoses."
Crockett excited PBS viewers with the prospect of growing their own
food, and they dug in by the thousands. Unfortunately, they learned all
too quickly that gardening took an enormous amount of effort. Many
viewers reared in urban environments and unfamiliar with the drudgery
that is a part of agriculture decided that the vegetables they bought at

the supermarket were a real bargain after all. So, after a few years, viewers hung up their trowels and the show's ratings slipped.

Meanwhile, as *The Victory Garden* struggled to find a new image with substitute hosts in 1979, Morash began preparing another how-to series, *This Old House,* hosted by Bob Vila and master carpenter Norm Abram. Claiming to be inspired by his own experience rehabbing his home, Morash persuaded WGBH to purchase a Victorian house in the unfashionable Boston neighborhood of Dorchester for $17,000. His idea was to renovate the structure on camera, then resell it for $55,000 at the WGBH on-air auction. Though the auction sale never took place, the week-by-week video record of the renovation set all-time ratings highs and the station found itself with another hit. Within a few years, *This Old House* had some 12 million viewers.

Bob Vila, original host of the show, tells a different story about the program's genesis. In a 1987 interview with *Playboy* magazine he said he had been renovating his new home when a newspaper reporter appeared in his driveway and asked to do a story about the renovation. "It was a further coincidence," Vila recalled in the interview, "that a TV producer saw the article, came out, and asked if he could shoot some videotape and interview me and then called back six months later to ask me to host a new show."

Whatever the origin of *This Old House,* it was a hit.

One WGBH staffer told the *Boston Globe* that the secret of the program's success is that it shows process. "You don't have to be a do-it-yourselfer," he said. "You can get into it even if you don't know how to drive a nail. You say, 'Oh, so that's how you do that.' People are fascinated by process. The program follows a project from beginning to conclusion. . . . It shows a major project, a serious renovation, an addition to a house, and how you can accomplish it from day one."

Like *The Victory Garden, This Old House* began as a local show. But by 1980, it was distributed nationally to a growing audience of loyal viewers. By 1982, the series took a detour from straightforward historic renovation, first with an 1851 Greek Revival house in the Boston suburb of Arlington, to which the producers added an exercise room, a redwood deck, a Jacuzzi, a sauna, a steam shower, an expanded kitchen, a greenhouse, and a wine cellar. By this time WGBH had stopped trying to flip the properties (that is, buying them, fixing them up, and selling them) and instead looked for private owners whose renovations might be documented by the series.

Morash gave his reasons for the change to a reporter: "After the first four episodes, it became clear that we shouldn't own the house. It was too cut-and-dried without the homeowner trying to stay ahead of the construction project, being a part of the project." By the second season, the cost of a *This Old House* renovation had reached $100,000.

When *This Old House* chose a 1950s ranch house in Woburn, Massachusetts, for a renovation, it marked a move into a contemporary vein of little interest to preservationists, but perhaps more appealing to the average homeowner—and PBS viewer. The *Globe* reported the details:

> Russ Morash, the show's producer, did not want to buy a house and be left holding the bag trying to sell it. So, through a broker friend, he located a young couple, Doug and Sara Briggs, who had bought the little ranch last September for $64,000. Briggs leased the house to WGBH for $1 a month while host Bob Vila and carpenter Norm Abram have their way with it. The lease is good for seven months, up to April 1. The Briggses won't spend a cent for the renovation, which has a $20,000 budget. They do, however, have to continue paying the mortgage and taxes during the lease time, which works out to be a lot cheaper than $20,000. The Briggses also agreed that they would not have any direct say in the planning or design of the renovation. That will be all Channel 2's doing. The Briggses, however, will help with the actual work.

In other words, WGBH had come up with a thrifty Yankee trader's solution to its cost problems. No more risk of being stuck with a white elephant.

Owens-Corning Fiberglas sponsored the renovations of the home, which featured liberal use of Fiberglas insulation and the first actual product promotion noticed by the *Globe*—but certainly not the last. In the next season, Morash actually changed the name of the series temporarily to *The All New This Old House,* because, in collaboration with Boston Edison, the producers were building a new, energy-efficient, solar home: the so-called "state-of-the-art Impact2000 House." Whatever one thought about it, the program gave evidence that sponsors were eager to reach the public television audience.

Following this little more than a program-length commercial, the producers tackled yet another ranch house, adding a second story to the structure. Thus the project was not, strictly speaking, either new construction or a renovation. It was an addition that changed the character of the home. Perhaps feeling wanderlust, and flush with money from the sponsors whose products were featured on the programs, the *This Old House* team traveled to Tampa, Florida, beginning a series of shows in remote locations, from Arizona to England to Hawaii to even New York's Trump Tower—a location that is neither old nor a house.

By this time, complaints were beginning to surface that the show's producers were not being honest with homeowners about the estimated costs of their renovation projects. In one case, the *Wall Street Journal* referred to a 200-year-old farmhouse as a "money pit," noting that the owner accused Morash of underestimating the actual restoration costs by $100,000 when he was pitching the project to secure his cooperation with the show. WGBH responded that the owner of the house did not understand the "sweat equity" involved in the program. Morash claimed participants were told up front that the homeowner is expected to "be a full partner in the project and not just sit around waiting." Serious tensions were beginning to develop between the producers and the hapless homeowners.

In 1989, more unhappy homeowners came forward. According to *Boston Globe* business reporter Alex Beam, William and Cynthia Dromgoole were miserable with the 1987 *This Old House* renovation job of their Benjamin Weatherbee house. The project, the Dromgooles claimed, was supposed to cost $200,000; it ended up costing $440,000, and WGBH did not cover the increase. In an attempt to make ends meet, the couple was forced to take in boarders. But they were unable to meet the payments on their $325,000 mortgage—which they had taken out in desperation, they said, to pay for their share of the restoration project. The Dromgooles said they would be listing their house for sale for around $700,000. "We're disappointed we can't stick with the house," William Dromgoole said. "But the debt service is becoming a bit heavy."

Needless to say, the news that construction costs had bankrupted one of their model homeowners, who had lost their dreamhouse, was not carried on broadcasts of *This Old House*.

Meanwhile, host Bob Vila had troubles of his own. On April 4, 1989, WGBH announced that it had terminated his contract after the program's national sponsor objected to his moonlighting endorsements of products and services not displayed on the show. In other words, the station did not object to commercial exploitation, just commercial exploitation that they did not control. Vila had been making an estimated $500,000 doing extracurricular plugs for Time-Life Books home repair series, American Electric Power, Rickel Home Centers, and Boyle-Midway Household Products. Home Depot, a competitor to Rickel Home Centers, was a local sponsor of *This Old House* in twenty markets and a big customer of Weyerhauser, *This Old House*'s $1 million-a-year national sponsor. Home Depot complained to Weyerhauser, which complained to WGBH and discontinued its funding for *This Old House*.

After the controversy became public, Vila accused producers of the supposedly noncommercial *This Old House* of promoting products by exposing their brand names to the camera in exchange for payment—in other words, for accepting "plugola." Vila's published accusations seemed to prompt WGBH to adopt a policy it claimed would end the practice (however, brand names are still mentioned by some contractors on the program to this day). WGBH executive David Liroff told the *Boston Globe,* "A lot of people won't admit the obvious, that funders determine what shows get produced or not. Why? Because the next question is, Do funders also determine what's in these shows? And the answer, here anyway, is absolutely not. If that's on the table we walk away." But despite (or perhaps because of) WGBH's protests, the show came under a cloud of scandal. Adding fuel to the fire was a statement from Chris Ridley, another WGBH executive, arguing that Vila was axed from *This Old House* because he had "cast a shadow on the show's credibility."

The sacking of Vila raised questions about the commercial nature of PBS how-to programs in general. In discussing Vila's fate as a sacrificial lamb, the *Globe* pointed out that Julia Child made money from sales of cookbooks and videos, noting some 500,000 of her latest were in print.

It noted that the then-host of *The Victory Garden,* Bob Thompson, owned a commercial nursery and made personal appearances at home and garden shows, thereby cross-promoting his business with his television show on supposedly noncommercial PBS. But Vila had embarrassed WGBH and the others had not, and so he had to go (while the practice of cross-promotion continued).

In 1990, Vila began hosting a commercially syndicated home improvement show called *Bob Vila's Home Again,* sponsored by Sears. He also made a guest appearance playing himself on the network sitcom *Home Improvement,* which was largely based on *This Old House.* Vila also continues to write books, such as *Bob Vila's Tool Box.*

The departure of Vila did not go unnoticed. It provoked comment even from leading journals of opinion such as the *New Republic:* "The problem wasn't that Vila was too commercial. The problem was that Vila's efforts were interfering with public television's own efforts to get underwriting from rival companies. . . . Out went Mr. Vila, a martyr to non-commerce."[10] Or, as WGBH's David Liroff told the *New York Times,* "It had become clear that [Vila] was showing up in enough places in the commercial marketplace that there was almost no direction in which we could turn to get funding." Of course, that may not have been the case, either. *This Old House* has found other funders and continues successfully to this day.

Vila's replacement was a WGBH insider. In contrast to Vila, who is Hispanic, Stephen Thomas is a quintessential white Anglo-Saxon protestant, the grandson of an Episcopalian missionary to Alaska who had retraced his Arctic journeys for the WGBH documentary series *Adventure.* The young Thomas was chosen over some 400 applicants, despite the fact that he had little prior experience with home renovation, unlike Vila, who had a home contracting business before becoming a TV star. It was unlikely that someone as uncomfortable with manual labor as Thomas appeared to be in his broadcasts would be hired to plug any chain of hardware stores. In a sense, Thomas resembled Julia Child. Just as she had been an unlikely French Chef, since she was not French and was not a professional chef, Thomas was an unlikely carpenter. This, perhaps, allowed the amateurs in the PBS audience to identify more readily with him.

And producer Russell Morash admits that Thomas was chosen not for his expertise but because "the screen test went really well." The then-bearded Thomas would still have to make some personal compromises to secure the host role. "When we looked at [Thomas and cohost carpenter Norm Abram] together, with their beards and glasses, they looked like the Smith Brothers," Morash said. "I thought they looked so much alike that people would think it was a cruel joke." It was Thomas, the newcomer, who shaved off his beard to land the role.[11]

At first, the critics were quick to attack the weaknesses of Vila's replacement. Ed Siegel wrote in the *Globe*, "Now we have Abram and Thomas beginning the show like Mr. Wizard and one of his high school students, but gradually evolving into Batman and Robin the Boy Wonder. Thomas actually looks more like Clark Kent . . . here he's cast as an innocent, if not a virgin. 'I'm scared,' he declares at the beginning. 'Well,' asks Abram toward the end, 'how did you like the first experience?'"

But soon even Siegel had adjusted to Thomas, concluding that same article, "Once Abram and Thomas get these opening, amateurish scenes out of the way, they establish an intriguing, if overdone, relationship. Thomas plays the cockeyed optimist, singing the praises of every old post and beam in sight, while Abram plays the grizzled realist . . . the new *Old House* still has the same old pleasures."[12] And it remained the highest-rated half-hour program on public television, with sponsors eagerly lining up for underwriting credits and product placement.

While Thomas was settling in as the new host of the series, WGBH gave Norm Abram a carpentry series of his very own, *The New Yankee Workshop*—perhaps part of a deal to keep him with *This Old House* after Vila's departure. "The basic idea was to showcase Norm," says Victoria Devlin, a WGBH fund-raising executive. "We had hundreds of calls a year from do-it-yourselfers wanting more Norm."

But while viewers may have been clamoring for an Abram-hosted show, sponsors were not so eager to fund the untested program. Abram's first sponsor was all but blackmailed into funding the series. The Parks Corporation, which sells wood stains, wood finishes, and paint removers nationwide under the Parks and Carver Tripp brand names, had long wanted to sponsor *This Old House,* but WGBH executives had shrugged and told the company that others had gotten there first (there actually was a waiting list). When *The New Yankee Workshop* was in development, Devlin met Parks executives and they agreed to sponsor the show, no doubt as price of entry to underwriting *This Old House*. Parks funded the program for a year, then WGBH allowed Parks to come in on *This Old House* as well. After four years, Parks dropped *The New Yankee Workshop*.

While its audience is not as large as that commanded by *This Old House, The New Yankee Workshop* does have a devoted following, and Abram has become a celebrity, earning over $300,000 a year; WGBH's magazine has called him "the most famous carpenter since Joseph." Abram's father was a carpenter, and at age fifteen, young Norm joined him in the family business. He worked as a contractor until 1979, when Morash hired him for *This Old House*. (Abram had built a barn for the WGBH producer on his property.)

Abram says of his role, "I'm probably the most visible carpenter in the country. That doesn't mean I'm the best. I just got back from a carpenters' convention in Seattle, and people told me that they thought I represented the trade very well. That means a lot."[13]

Abram's modesty aside, PBS how-tos such as *The French Chef* and *This Old House* serve as examples of both the power and profitability of educational programming, the raison d'être of public broadcasting. WGBH, in particular, has shown that high-quality educational programming put together with an eye to the bottom line simply doesn't need the government to thrive. Indeed, the pretense that these extremely successful commercial vehicles are noncommercial has caused—in the case of *This Old House*—embarrassment that need not have occurred if WGBH had simply admitted that the program was, in fact, dependent on sponsorship. Whether the sponsor of a particular program is the federal government or a tool company is, in the end, a distinction without a difference.

As one WGBH producer told William Hoynes, a professor of sociology at Vassar College who conducted an elaborate survey of station attitudes for his book *Public Television for Sale:* "There is a certain amount of whoring that goes on, and that pervades everything we do. The shows are designed around who will fund them. So there's a constant compromise around doing shows, and shows that will be funded." As Hoynes found out in his study of the Boston station, many of his informants saw little difference between what public broadcasters insist on calling "underwriting" and what everyone else in America recognizes as advertising.[14] Clearly the lasting success of *The French Chef* and *This Old House* without government funding is a phenomenon worth considering by public broadcasting.

11

Mobil's Masterpiece

Few programs are more readily identified with America's public broadcasting system than the very British *Masterpiece Theatre*. For almost a quarter-century the series has offered a weekly visit to a peaceful little corner of England; a civilized respite for the cultured viewer from a turbulent America. Mobil's *Masterpiece Theatre* and its sister series, *Mystery!,* are also some of the best examples of the dependence of PBS on British programming. For many years, the series served as the primary outlet for the British "Heritage Industry" seeking new customers in the United States. Interestingly, *Masterpiece Theatre* and *Mystery!* were and are commercial enterprises, sponsored by a Fortune 500 corporation in the tradition of the "Golden Age" of 1950s network television. The continuing success of *Masterpiece Theatre* and *Mystery!* (which spun off in 1980) challenges the contention by public broadcasters that quality television programming depends on a noncommercial environment. If anything, the lesson of *Masterpiece Theatre* is that commercial sponsorship improves television drama.

Masterpiece Theatre premiered on PBS on January 10, 1971. A few years later, during the height of the OPEC oil boycott and the consequent gasoline shortage, the Mobil Corporation canceled all its product advertising and turned over the company's entire advertising budget to Herb Schmertz, Mobil's vice president for public relations. A labor lawyer specializing in arbitration and mediation who had worked for Mobil since 1966, Schmertz was also a prominent Democrat with extensive experience in national political campaigns; he had been an advance man and adviser for John F. Kennedy in 1960, for Robert Kennedy in 1968, and for Edward Kennedy in 1980.

Of the Mobil decision, Schmertz recalls: "I got the entire ten million dollars to spend." No executive of any American corporation had ever before had such personal authority to spend such a large sum of money.[1] Schmertz had developed a new confrontational public relations strategy for Mobil, which he called "Good-bye to the low profile." It helped transform the company's image from that of a good, gray, Republican institution happiest out of the headlines into a scrappy fighter taking on politicians and environmentalists on television and in newspapers. Schmertz also employed what is known in PR circles as "affinity-of-purpose marketing" through sponsorships of the arts and cultural projects that would have a "halo effect" on the company's image. Public broadcasting, which reached an elite audience of opinion makers, was a crucial element of Schmertz's campaign.

In 1970 Stanford Calderwood, the new president of WGBH, Boston, who had succeeded Hartford Gunn when Gunn moved to head PBS in Washington, told Schmertz he wanted more high-quality programs for his station and thought English television was a bargain. Calderwood said Mobil could purchase thirty-nine hours of BBC programming for $390,000, from Time-Life television, the BBC distributor at the time. "That was an absurdly low figure for television," Schmertz says, and he agreed to have Mobil serve as sole sponsor.

Masterpiece Theatre's first producer was Christopher Sarson, a WGBH staffer who had created the children's series *Zoom*. Sarson, himself English, met with Calderwood, Schmertz, and Mobil television consultant Frank Marshall to decide on a series host for the anthology format. Only one candidate was seriously considered: the respected British journalist Alistair Cooke. His public stature as a literary celebrity and host of CBS's *Omnibus*, the Ford Foundation's cultural initiative of the 1950s, would give the show a special cachet. If Cooke had not accepted their invitation, the producers were prepared to use "visual essays" instead; no one but Cooke would do.[2]

The first series was, appropriately enough, "The First Churchills," a *Forsyte Saga*–style look at the historical ancestors of Sir Winston and Princess Diana. *Masterpiece Theatre* quickly won a substantial audience. The lineup for the series's first two years, drawn from the vast programming archives of the BBC, resembled the reading list for a freshman world history and literature survey course. "The Spoils of Poynton," "The Possessed," "Père Goriot," "Jude the Obscure," "The Gambler," "Resurrection," "Cold Comfort Farm," "The Six Wives of Henry VIII," "Elizabeth R," and "The Last of the Mohicans" made up the 1971–72 season. "Vanity Fair," "Cousin Bette," "The Moonstone," "Tom Brown's Schooldays," "Point Counterpoint," and "The Golden Bowl" were on the schedule for 1972–73.

The decision to air the commercial London Weekend Television series "Upstairs, Downstairs" changed this complexion in the 1973–74 season—but not without a fight. It was Mobil versus PBS and WGBH, and when the dust cleared, Mobil had won.

Producer Christopher Sarson joined his station's management and PBS's Washington staff in opposing the acquisition of "Upstairs, Downstairs." They argued that as a soap opera it was not appropriate for their high-minded series. Also, it was more expensive than the BBC offerings had been. Allowing other suppliers such as London Weekend Television to enter the market would change the "special relationship" between the BBC and PBS, driving up the prices for British programs. A flurry of memos swirled between PBS in Washington and WGBH in Boston to try to prevent "Upstairs, Downstairs" from airing and thus weaken Mobil's influence on programming decisions.[3] Herb Schmertz and Mobil chairman Rawleigh Warner, whose wife had seen the program in England, wanted it on *Masterpiece Theatre* and threatened to pull Mobil's support if it were not aired. Mobil agreed to make extra payments directly to the British for "Upstairs, Downstairs" in a way that would not appear on WGBH's books.

When the dust had settled, WGBH station manager Michael Rice announced an important personnel change: Sarson would be replaced as *Masterpiece Theatre* producer by Joan Sullivan (later Wilson), a WGBH producer who had no problem with showing "Upstairs, Downstairs."[4] (Sarson's voice is still heard in the introductory credits; he is the one telling viewers that *Masterpiece Theatre* is "made possible by a grant from Mobil Corporation.")

Joan Sullivan Wilson had started at WGBH in 1967, producing *Elliott Norton Reviews,* a weekly theater criticism program, as well as two women's programs: *Kitchen Sync,* featuring feminist films, and *Growing Up Female,* a coming-of-age documentary with a woman's point of view.[5] Wilson would also produce *Classic Theatre: The Humanities in Drama, Piccadilly Circus,* and *Mystery!,* all British anthologies acquired by WGBH through grants from Mobil. Mobil would deal with its own WGBH team, or no one at all.

The personnel changes led to a friendlier working relationship between WGBH and Mobil. Schmertz describes Mobil's association with WGBH as "very collegial" after "Upstairs, Downstairs." He cannot recall a single case after WGBH's acquisition of the miniseries in which he insisted on broadcasting a program and WGBH refused.[6]

Wilson would coordinate her activities with Frank and Arlene Goodman, Mobil's New York–based public relations consultants. Their mom-and-pop company had represented NBC shows, Hollywood films, and Broadway spectaculars. Genuinely creative show business veterans, they closely supervised the packaging, promotion, and other aspects of *Masterpiece Theatre,* reporting to Herb Schmertz at Mobil. Among their other contributions, the Goodmans recommended Diana Rigg for the hostess slot on *Mystery!*

The WGBH acquisition of "Upstairs, Downstairs" marked the birth of a relationship with producer John Hawkesworth, who became a favorite of Schmertz, Marshall, and Wilson. *Masterpiece Theatre* would run every major Hawkesworth production, whether for London Weekend Television, the BBC, Thames Television, or other Independent Television (ITV) companies. Hawkesworth eventually produced four series of "Upstairs, Downstairs" and a half-dozen other programs for *Masterpiece Theatre.* Along with "Upstairs, Downstairs," he was responsible for "The Duchess of Duke Street," "The Flame Trees of Thika," "Danger UXB," "By the Sword Divided," and "The Tale of Beatrix Potter." And those who had worked with him on "Upstairs, Downstairs" would find continuous representation on the schedule, as well.

"Upstairs, Downstairs" followed an Edwardian upper-class London family and their servants through the changes in British society over two generations. It had been inspired by the success of *The Forsyte Saga* based on John Galsworthy's novels—but differed in one crucial respect: it would devote as much attention to servants' lives as to their masters'. It could appeal to two PBS audiences at once: upper-middle-class Americans nostalgic for the days when employing servants was the norm and less well off citizens who enjoyed the spectacle of a fragile and dependent ruling class.

Masterpiece Theatre host Alistair Cooke made explicit the social conflict he felt "Upstairs, Downstairs" embodied. He said:

> It was a triumphant time for a small, rich and immensely powerful minority that owned the land, the factories, and, for that matter, the reins of government. But below them was the mass of British men and women who formed the second, and very much the larger, of what Disraeli called "The Two Nations" . . . the Bellamy household staff formed a complete little society of its own, a downstairs society called upon by God—so its betters thought—to minister for life to upstairs society.[7]

"Upstairs, Downstairs" was brilliantly executed, with first-rate performances, authentic-looking sets and costumes, and literate scripts. Its success led to an almost permanent place on *Masterpiece Theatre* for Edwardian costume drama.[8] Under Joan Wilson's stewardship, with Mobil's approval, contemporary social issues such as feminism, class conflict, and imperialism would be dealt with in Edwardian period settings. A Goodman press release quoted Wilson comparing the Edwardian era to 1970s America: "The death of Edward VII was [a] symbolic ending. . . . Never again was there this elegance, this luxury, this leisure and class distinction. . . . I think we are at the end of an era too. We're being forced to go back to the days of candlelight and bicycles . . . because of the energy crisis."[9]

During the 1973–74 season, in addition to the continuing saga of the Bellamy family (which included episodes written by feminist novelist Fay Weldon), *Masterpiece Theatre* presented under the anthology "The

Edwardians" popular adaptations of two of Dorothy Sayers's Lord Peter Wimsey mystery novels, "Clouds of Witness" and "The Unpleasantness at the Bellona Club"; a thriller, "The Man Who Was Hunting Himself"; H. E. Bates's short story "The Little Farm"; and a series of four BBC docudramas about Prime Minister David Lloyd George (starring Anthony Hopkins), automobile moguls Charles Stewart Rolls and Henry Royce (played by Robert Powell and Michael Jayston, respectively), Arthur Conan Doyle (played by Nigel Davenport), and music hall comedienne Marie Lloyd (played by Georgia Brown). For the 1974–75 season Wilson produced a new opening credit sequence that featured British flags waving in the wind, emphasizing the show's origins. With more money available from Mobil, and the addition of mysteries and serial melodrama in the form of "Upstairs, Downstairs," the 1973–74 season showed significant growth in viewership over the previous season. "Upstairs, Downstairs" got the highest prime-time ratings of any PBS show since "The Six Wives of Henry VIII" (1971), with a series average of 1.39 million households. The second series of "Upstairs, Downstairs" put all previous numbers to shame. It had an average rating of 2.5 million. The programming policies of Wilson, Marshall, and Schmertz, combined with promotion by the Goodmans, were delivering larger audiences than public television was accustomed to receiving.[10]

The 1975–76 season began with "Shoulder to Shoulder," a BBC–Warner Bros. coproduction about the Pankhurst family and their struggle for women's suffrage in England. Since Wilson was an ardent feminist, one might guess that the series was her idea. However, she did not commission or even select it. The series, sponsored by Mobil, was originally intended for CBS. According to Herb Schmertz, the decision to run the show on CBS was consistent with his philosophy of putting "better-quality" material on commercial television "that would enable us to have a vehicle for advertisements we wanted to run."[11] However, CBS ultimately rejected "Shoulder to Shoulder" when Mobil found it was impossible to cut the original six-hour version to an acceptable four-hour network length.[12] Warner Bros. Television had sold the show directly to Schmertz, so he was stuck with it.[13]

Wilson was happy to run "Shoulder to Shoulder" on PBS as the *Masterpiece* season opener, and although the project had fallen into her lap, it came to symbolize her style as executive producer. The Goodmans sought to place an article profiling Wilson in *Ms.* magazine in order to promote the broadcast. The draft of their solicitation letter highlighted Wilson's commitment to female emancipation:

> I'd like to nominate for a piece in *Ms.* an unusual young woman named Joan Sullivan [Wilson], who's responsible for this season's focus on women on PBS's *Masterpiece Theatre*. She's the WGBH, Boston, producer of the series—which this year might easily be re-named Mistress-piece Theatre. . . . As you know, the current . . . season [opened] with "Shoulder to Shoulder," then came "Notorious Woman," the story of George Sand's break with restrictive conventions of her time . . . and "Sunset Song," beginning April 25, is the emancipation of one "ordinary" woman. All this is no accident. Joan Sullivan planned the season that way. . . .[14]

A PBS press release noted that "Shoulder to Shoulder" "dramatizes the parallels to many vital social issues, such as violence vs. nonviolence, prison reform, women's rights, class struggles, 'conspiracy' trials, and many other problems at large today in the United States."[15] The official PBS Screening Report records that Alistair Cooke announced "Shoulder to Shoulder" was being presented "in salute to International Women's Year."[16] In a public relations coup for the series, the *New York Times's* Sunday Arts and Leisure section assigned Susan Brownmiller—feminist author of *Against Our Will: Men, Women and Rape* (1975)—to write up "Shoulder to Shoulder." Invoking the benchmark show against which all other *Masterpiece Theatre* presentations would be judged, Brownmiller noted " 'Shoulder to Shoulder' . . . is no 'Upstairs, Downstairs,' although it owes a schematic debt to that earlier fictional import."[17]

Although the *Times* article was favorable, the PBS establishment was stirring itself against Mobil once again. Prior to the broadcast, PBS executive Karen Thomas had circulated an internal memo: "What with the advent of 'Shoulder to Shoulder,' I think PBS and Mobil can expect some, perhaps minimal, press reaction. The question will be raised as to why public broadcasting must import programming on the history of women's suffrage from Great Britain rather than producing a more germane series on the suffrage effort in the United States." Thomas went on to call attention to a series in development by a former WGBH staffer, Mary Feldhaus-Weber, which had received some money from the National Endowment for the Humanities for "scripts and treatments." She thought that perhaps Mobil could be shamed into funding the American effort, called *The Stanton Project*.[18] She was wrong. There was no shame for Mobil, only pride. "Shoulder to Shoulder" got a very respectable Nielsen household average of 1.25 million and the highest single-night tune-in to date, 1.66 million. *Masterpiece Theatre* was on its way to becoming a public broadcasting institution, impervious to the whims of the PBS bureaucracy in Washington.

For the 1975–76 season of "Upstairs, Downstairs," Wilson replaced Alistair Cooke's heavy social-historical "Edwardian Essays" with lighter fare: short music hall numbers taped on the stage of the Player's Theatre in London. Wilson taped 28 different music hall turns, featuring such numbers as "Daddy Wouldn't Buy Me a Little Bow-Wow," "The Honeysuckle and the Bee," and "She Was Poor but She Was Honest."

Wilson said she felt quite strongly about the social significance of these musical numbers. "Now 'Don't Dilly Dally' is an example," she explained in an interview when the fillers were in production. "[T]hat grew out of the fact that people couldn't afford to pay their rent, you know, this great mass of poverty-stricken people, so they'd skip out at night."

However, Wilson was not the only person involved in choosing the programs for *Masterpiece Theatre*, which, at this point, was a fact Herb Schmertz, Frank Marshall, and, no doubt, WGBH were happy to keep quiet, because PBS claimed that sponsors were forbidden to have any influence on programming—a fiction perpetrated for political purposes.

Masterpiece Theatre soon faced domestic PBS competition for the first time in the miniseries genre. In 1976, WNET produced *The Adams Chronicles*, a thirteen-hour history of America's earliest political and cultural dynasty. Members included Revolutionary War leader Samuel Adams and Presidents John Adams and John Quincy Adams. The saga was not new ground for television. *Omnibus* had also aired a dramatization of the lives of the Adamses. One account of the rationale for the remake concludes that WNET "aspired to create a dramatic series equal in scale and quality to those imported from the BBC"—in other words, programs of the quality of *Masterpiece Theatre*.[19] *The Adams Chronicles'* budget of $5.2 million was raised from the National Endowment for the Humanities, the Andrew Mellon Foundation, and the Atlantic Richfield Company. The production was so expensive, however, that it led to the near-bankruptcy of WNET, and the station never again tried its hand at the dramatic miniseries. PBS itself did not produce another such period drama until WGBH's presentation of *The Scarlet Letter* in 1979, also an expensive disappointment.

The 1976–77 season was the last one for "Upstairs, Downstairs." Perhaps because of its success, *Masterpiece Theatre* had expanded to a fifty-two-week-a-year schedule. So important to public television was the finale of the unprecedentedly successful series that it was the occasion of a pledge special, called "'Upstairs, Downstairs' Farewell . . . A Million-Dollar Party." The title alone indicates the value of the show to PBS. The attention given to this special by the top brass makes it worth a closer look, for its minutiae reveal the successful commercial nature of the PBS system even in its early days.

This pledge program featured PBS president Larry Grossman, WGBH president David Ives, and Alistair Cooke as cohosts. The principal cast members from the series were present, including Jean Marsh and Simon Williams, who had also been booked on the *Today* show to publicize the fund-raising special.[20] Earlier, as part of a publicity blitz, the Goodmans had flown the "Upstairs, Downstairs" cast to Boston via New York's La Guardia airport, which was filled with photographers when the cast changed planes. In Boston, the actors rode from the airport to the Ritz-Carlton Hotel (where Cooke stayed when he recorded his commentaries) in a parade of Rolls-Royce convertibles supplied by local car dealers. The group proceeded to the hotel's Adams Room for a press tea; strains of the *Masterpiece Theatre* theme played in the background. There, the cast was greeted by a crowd of sixty reporters and their guests, who, according to the *New York Times*, "broke into spontaneous applause." After the press event, the celebrity group continued on to WGBH to screen the last "Upstairs, Downstairs" episode in the station's boardroom before going on camera to participate in the telethon.[21]

The format of the pledge show was straightforward: The last episode carried three minutes over into the ten o'clock time slot. Alistair Cooke did a voice-over "tease" while the credits rolled. The cameras came

up on " 'Upstairs, Downstairs' Farewell . . . A Million–Dollar Party."
Cooke did the introductions, followed by a station breakaway for local
pledging. Then Grossman and Ives gave their "punch" (slang for
begging). Series stars Simon Williams (son James Bellamy: Upstairs) and
Jean Marsh (parlormaid Rose: Downstairs) then came out to explain a
contest gimmick: Viewers were invited to vote either "Upstairs" or
"Downstairs" with their pledges to see which had more fans. Local stations were asked to report numbers of phone calls and numbers of
pledges every ten to fifteen minutes. Following this came brief interviews, breakaways, and excerpts from past shows intercut with contests
and "content"—namely, more pledging. The program concluded with
"thank yous/toasts/bye byes" and finally the PBS logo. There were three
areas of the set: a living room used for interviews designed to match
Alistair Cooke's normal set; a tote board to keep tally of national results; and phone banks with phone operators and guests in black tie. PBS
president Grossman served as scorekeeper, and WGBH president Ives was
"the official pitchman."

The script called for nine station breakaways, for a total of thirty-
eight minutes of local pitching. It noted, "While you are pitching locally,
the talent will be pitching (generically) for those stations who choose
'not' to pitch locally. . . . The lower third of the screen will remain free
for local use during the entire two-hour program. You may want to take
advantage of this space for supering . . . your phone number, membership categories, premium information, slogans, etc."[22] Designed to garner $1 million in pledges, the special proved the loyalty of *Masterpiece
Theatre* viewers to PBS. It raised $1.735 million.[23]

Herb Schmertz said he found the spectacle of using *Masterpiece
Theatre* for PBS fund-raising amusing. "They'd say that if you don't
give money, *Masterpiece Theatre* isn't going to run. I used to complain
and say, you won't need any money from pledge week for *Masterpiece
Theatre* because *Masterpiece Theatre* doesn't get any money out of
pledge week. . . . For you to make the statement that it's because of
Masterpiece Theatre that people should give money to public television
is a lie. It's not truth in advertising."[24] Nonetheless, the pitches have
continued.

If reaching the opinion leaders who read the *New York Times* was one of Schmertz's reasons for sponsoring *Masterpiece Theatre,* there could be no better result than the one he achieved with "Upstairs, Downstairs." Not only did the series get four years of good reviews from *Times* critic John J. O'Connor, many companion profiles ran in the news and arts sections of the paper. The series established *Masterpiece Theatre* as more than mere television programming. It was now a serious cultural phenomenon worthy of comment by the most famous names on the paper's masthead. "Upstairs, Downstairs" became the subject of a Russell Baker "Sunday Observer" column, in which the humorist detailed how he would replace Hudson, the Bellamy family's butler, with Bunter, late of Lord Peter Wimsey.[25] In a lengthy (and lavishly illustrated) *New York Times Magazine* feature titled "Did Rose Live Happily Ever After?: Alistair Cooke Updates 'Upstairs, Downstairs,'" the show's urbane host wrote himself into the tale, having an affair with Rose. Several weeks later, the magazine printed letters responding to Cooke's imaginings.[26] A solemn tribute was paid by columnist Anthony Lewis, the *Times*'s Boston-based pundit who was an influential liberal opinion leader and a frequent critic of the oil companies. Not only did Lewis salute "Upstairs, Downstairs," defending it as socially redeeming drama against the charge of "snob appeal," he even wrote glowingly about the success of the pledge-drive special.[27] And in fall 1993, *New York Times* columnist Russell Baker replaced Alistair Cooke as host.

With the 1978–79 season opener, "The Duchess of Duke Street," *Masterpiece Theatre* introduced a new opening sequence, the one it still uses today. *Masterpiece Theatre* was beginning to recycle itself; the new opening reflected this by taking a nostalgic look at the bric-a-brac of its own past programs. The Union Jacks were removed, perhaps in response to the U.S. bicentennial. That revolutionary spirit was somewhat hostile to the quantity of English imports on PBS. The network also had a new president, Larry Grossman, who announced his goal was to bring more domestic productions and public affairs programming to the system.[28] The Carnegie Commission on the Future of Public Broadcasting (known as "Carnegie II") was holding hearings, receiving testimony from hundreds of public television officials, and preparing its report. The Commission's findings, issued in 1979, called for a drastic restructuring of CPB. One reason given by the Commission for this recommendation was the perception that British programming dominated the PBS lineup.[29]

However, Joan Wilson did not refer to the sentiment against things English in her public explanation of the need for a new opening sequence. Instead she argued that the segment was designed to make it clear that *Masterpiece Theatre* was based on great literature and historical personalities and only incidentally British. Wilson's stated concept for the new opening was to create "everyone's ideal library," with "elegant, beautiful volumes of great literature of the world, and memorabilia from *Masterpiece Theatre* presentations." Among her selections were pictures from the upcoming "Lillie" (a biopic about the nineteenth-century British actress Lillie Langtry) and "Love for Lydia" (based on H. E. Bates's novel), as well as miniatures representing "The Six Wives of Henry VIII" and "Elizabeth R." Wilson included items from her own personal collection, such as the photo album used for displaying the Bellamys and their "Upstairs, Downstairs" servants. Wilson rented $40,000 worth of antiques for the shoot, including Lalique bookends to hold books by Bates and Coppard and a model sailing ship to stand for "Poldark." The martini glass was added as a "joke" to be "Wimsey-ish," a reference to the Dorothy Sayers hero. The little metal snake represented "I, Claudius."[30] Leather-bound books were borrowed from the Princeton University library. The sequence was filmed in a Princeton, New Jersey, studio used for network television commercials; the director was a veteran of Coca Cola and Oldsmobile spots. The footage was shot with a snorkel camera (also called a butterfly camera), one of two in the world at the time.

John Hawkesworth's BBC production "The Duchess of Duke Street," the story of Rosa Lewis, a kitchen maid who climbed from obscurity to own a hotel and become a mistress to Edward VII, was one of many subsequent attempts to recapture the success of "Upstairs, Downstairs." His success in America enabled him to obtain funding from Mobil. He says the BBC made "a special case" for his "Duchess" deal and gave him "a big budget." Hawkesworth says the series originated at a lunch with Shaun Sutton, the BBC's head of drama, who told him, "We want another 'Upstairs, Downstairs.'" Hawkesworth recalls:

I said, "Do you mean just the same?" He said, "Just the same." And I said, "I don't want to do anything just the same." And he said, "Well, you can change it a bit, perhaps make it a part-German family or something." I said, "I really don't want to do it. I've had five or six years of it. I'd rather do something completely different." So he said, "Go away and think."

So I thought, well, television series are about a group of people under pressure . . . a small group of people you get to know very well. So I thought, well, quite different to a house in Eaton Place, if we had a kooky kind of hotel, with this mad Cockney woman running it like a dictator. Which is very much like the Cavendish Hotel was. This would make a good basis for a television series. So I put this to the BBC and they said yes. So that's what we did. And it was a big effort to make it completely different to "Upstairs, Downstairs," because we were going over the same ground, the same period really.[31]

Joan Wilson was not enthusiastic at first. She told WGBH program manager Henry Becton, "I guess I would have to say that I'm least excited about this series of all in next season! Probably because I've had so much Up/Down!—and although sometimes it being a tougher, more realistic presentation of Edwardianism makes it more interesting, the characters, for me, are not nearly as sympathetic or captivating."[32] But the *New York Times* ran a favorable notice, commenting that it continued the *Masterpiece Theatre* formula, providing "at least a glimpse of the gritty underside of Edwardian life by way of contrast to the gleam of the diamonds, the pop of champagne corks and the glow of warm female flesh."[33] This socially conscious Edwardianism from Hawkesworth was clearly a Schmertz (and Mobil) signature. First, Schmertz and Marshall had triumphed over WGBH's Christopher Sarson to get "Upstairs, Downstairs" on the series. And now, Schmertz had overcome Joan Wilson's doubts about "The Duchess of Duke Street." Again, it was clear that Schmertz, Marshall, and Mobil were in charge.

Mobil's hand was evident once more in the last production of the 1979–80 season: the venerable British film producer Lew Grade's docudrama "Disraeli." It was the brainchild of Herb Schmertz, who tells this version of its origins:

I'd never met Lew Grade. I was in my hotel room [in London] about six o'clock in the morning, and [Grade called and] said, "My boy, I can see you as soon as possible." I said, "How about six-thirty?" "Ah," he said, "That's fine." I go on over there about six-thirty, quarter of seven. I had never met him before. He gave me a huge cigar and said, "My boy, I want to make a show on George the Third." I said, "Fine. Would you like to buy some scripts? I have a whole set of scripts." He said, "What do you mean?" I said, "About two years ago we considered doing a show on George the Third. I paid for a bunch of scripts. They weren't worth doing. Very dull subject. No big audience interest in the United States." . . . "Is that right?" "Yeah," I said. "You won't get any audience for it in the United States." "Oh," he said. "What would you do?" I said, "Disraeli's very popular in the United States; you ought to do a show on Disraeli." "Fine." Gets the phone, calls Cecil Clarke, his top producer. "Cecil, come in here." Cecil walks in. He says, "Cecil, I've been doing research. George the Third is not popular in the United States, but Disraeli's very popular. We're going to do 'Disraeli.' " And that was the deal. True story. Exactly that way. And Cecil went off and made "Disraeli." Good show.[34]

Schmertz, the first Jewish member of the board of directors of the Mobil Corporation, may have identified with the Jewish prime minister. (Disraeli had been among President Nixon's favorite historical figures as well.)

The *New York Times*'s John J. O'Connor used the broadcast of "Disraeli" to defend *Masterpiece Theatre* against "certain critics [who] have grown fond of taking pot shots at [it], evidently considering its very existence an elitist and negative comment on the viewing habits of the great masses who obviously prefer 'Flo' or 'Real People.' " This spirited broadside was a rebuttal to the recommendations of the Carnegie Commission on the Future of Public Broadcasting to reduce the amount of British product on PBS. O'Connor's polemical defense went on to explain that "the series represents the best of a particular British product, carefully screened and chosen from dozens of candidates by executives of Boston's WGBH, the producing station, and of Mobil Oil, the underwriter."[35]

It is ironic that the example the *Times* chose to illustrate how carefully and judiciously *Masterpiece Theatre* made its selections was actually produced by Lew Grade as a commercial presale to Schmertz, a fact confirmed by Grade in his memoirs.[36] Schmertz had the power to green-light a project for *Masterpiece Theatre* all by himself—because he controlled the funding. The summer after "Disraeli" aired, Joan Wilson sent a memo to Schmertz and to WGBH president Hentry Becton that listed properties currently under consideration for *Masterpiece Theatre*. That Wilson was reporting to both Mobil and her WGBH superior indicates the central role of the sponsor in the selection process.[37]

It is evident that Mobil consultant Frank Marshall was also an important contributor to *Masterpiece Theatre* programming decisions. He received scripts before Wilson did. Mobil was funding script *development*, which meant input from the oil company at a very early stage of the creative process. One can argue that by 1980, shows were being made to order for Mobil by British producers based on Schmertz's suggestions. The large number of ITV suppliers mentioned in Wilson's memo reveals that 1980 was a year of significant change for *Masterpiece Theatre*. The BBC had ended its distribution contract with Time–Life Television, and instead of dealing with another commercial distribution company, it had signed an exclusive agreement with Rockefeller Center Television (RCTV) to provide programming for their new cable service (which later became A&E). This was reported as being "of grave concern to both the Public Broadcasting Corporation [*sic*] and Time–Life's TV division" by *Adweek*, which noted that "PBS has long depended on BBC series to lure their viewers and attract their financial contributions." As a result of this deal, it seemed that *Masterpiece Theatre* would no longer have any access whatsoever to BBC shows. Although *Masterpiece* had found alternative sources of supply in the ITV companies, the agreement still made scheduling a full season of material a challenge for the series.[38] In 1980–81, all the *Masterpiece Theatre* selections, with the exception of John Hawkesworth's "Danger UXB," had been from the BBC, including "Crime and Punishment," "Pride and Prejudice," "Testament of Youth," and "Thérèse Raquin." How would Mobil cope?

Meanwhile, consultant Frank Marshall and Herb Schmertz had started stockpiling English mystery stories. The genre had vanished from *Masterpiece Theatre* after the 1977 season, reemerging in 1980 as *Mystery!* Unsurprisingly, Joan Wilson was named producer of this companion Mobil series. Originally hosted by American film critic Gene Shalit, later by horror-film star Vincent Price, and currently by British actress Diana Rigg, 1980 marked the second time around for *Mystery!*

Mobil had first aired a season of what it called *The Mobil Mystery Theatre* as a limited series within *Masterpiece Theatre* during the fall of 1973. At the time, this title outraged Sam Holt, an influential PBS executive, who called it "a disastrous piece of publicity." PBS executive vice president Gerry Slater was asked to "contact Herb Schmertz and tell him that this sort of nonsense has got to stop or we will jeopardize both PBS and Mobil's relations with the stations. But, more importantly, we run the risk of upsetting all of our government relations. . . ."[39] Mobil temporarily agreed to put the mystery series on hold.

Alistair Cooke was disappointed that he was not permitted to keep British mysteries on his program. He suggested *Mystery!* was taken from him because of Joan Wilson's romance with British actor Jeremy Brett. "Joan was completely happy with *Masterpiece Theatre* and then she met Jeremy Brett. And Jeremy Brett was dying to come here and do something similar to the thing I did. Well, they got married. And she was the one who initiated the whole idea of *Mystery!* She thought *he* would do that [host the introductory segments]," Cooke recalled. "And I remember at the beginning saying to Herb Schmertz, 'Well, I hope this doesn't mean we're going to lose the Wilkie Collins and the Dorothy Sayers and so on [from *Masterpiece Theatre*].' Of course it meant we did."[40]

The revived *Mystery!* enjoyed great success, featuring, among others, Jeremy Brett as Sherlock Holmes, David Suchet as Hercule Poirot, Leo McKern as Rumpole of the Bailey, and John Thaw as Inspector Morse. *Mystery!*'s ratings soon surpassed those of *Masterpiece Theatre.*

In addition to getting the new *Mystery!* series on the air, Wilson was simultaneously choosing product for a twenty-two-week *Masterpiece Theatre* rerun season billed as a "Festival of Favorites" to commemorate the series's tenth anniversary in 1981. Mobil helped with Alfred A. Knopf's publication of Alistair Cooke's book *Masterpieces,* a companion volume to this lineup. In some sense, the book was one outcome of a suggestion from Marshall and Schmertz in 1971 for a *Masterpiece Theatre* library. (The series had also been regularly running "book-tags," short advertisements promoting editions of works dramatized by the series.)

Publicity efforts for the "Festival of Favorites" were extremely success-ful, with *TV Guide* devoting a special five-page picture feature to "A Decade of Masterpiece Theatre."[41] The *New York Times* ran commemora-tive articles, and WNET aired a special titled "Uniquely Masterpiece: A Personal Retrospective," which featured film clips, Alistair Cooke's com-ments, sales pitches, and a segment with PBS star Bill Moyers interviewing Huw Weldon, a BBC executive legendary in British broadcasting.[42] To have a well-known liberal journalist like Moyers (who had been a mem-ber of the second Carnegie Commission that had recommended reduc-ing the number of English shows on PBS) as a part of a salute to a series "made possible by a grant from Mobil" was the sort of endorsement Herb Schmertz had in mind when he first funded *Masterpiece Theatre*.

Still, with the BBC temporarily out of the picture, *Masterpiece Theatre* needed an alternative supplier. They found one in Australia. The 1981–82 season began with "A Town Like Alice," based on Nevil Shute's novel, cowritten by Rosemary Anne Sisson (of "Upstairs, Downstairs") and costarring Gordon Jackson (Hudson on "Upstairs, Downstairs"). Mobil sponsored a press party to introduce the producer, Henry Craw-ford, and stars Helen Morse and Bryan Brown, to the American media.[43]

The show's provenance was vividly brought home to viewers by Al-istair Cooke's introduction to the first installment. He was seen in a strangely shuttered room, with a golden light playing all around him. On a table next to his simple wooden chair was a globe. After Cooke's customary greeting, he announced dramatically:

> Tonight for the first time, we don't go to Britain for our drama. We are delighted to introduce our first Australian dramatic series. . . . You know, forty, fifty years ago, Australians of marked talent, actors, singers, writers especially, tended to move to England and become English. Not anymore. For the past quarter century, the Australians have been enjoying a new deal in the arts. Now they stay home, and establish an indentity that is nothing but Australian.[44]

Cooke, in his signature this-won't-hurt-a-bit style, attempted to put the audience at ease in unfamiliar territory. He pointed to the globe sitting next to him, helpfully indicating the locations of Malaya, Thailand, In-donesia, and Australia for the benefit of viewers. He reminded the audience that it would see "a familiar face" in the person of the heroine's Scottish lawyer, Gordon Jackson.[45] What Cooke did not tell his audience was that there would be a great deal more Australian (and Canadian) product coming along, unless some way were found to get around the exclusive BBC–RCTV deal.

But it wasn't long before Schmertz and his team discovered a loophole. Mobil had years of direct personal relationships with individual producers, BBC staffers as well as independents. Schmertz learned that "if we could make the deal with the independent producer, or even with the BBC for a specific producer, that was a way to beat the RCTV deal." Today, Schmertz is full of admiration for the people at BBC Enterprises who worked out the RCTV contract in such a way that he could continue to supply his series on PBS: "The BBC are very shrewd negotiators. No question about it. [They] took RCTV to the cleaners."[46] Within a year after announcing its deal, RCTV was out of business.

Although BBC material would in fact remain available to WGBH, the scare resulted in a 1981–82 season of *Masterpiece Theatre* without a single BBC program, perhaps because Mobil wanted to show the BBC that they could tough it out. Indeed, the season consisted of several outstanding productions. After "A Town Like Alice" came Thames's "Edward and Mrs. Simpson." There was an obvious Anglo-American appeal to the Cinderella story of the Baltimore divorcée who almost became queen of England. There was also an almost allegorical correlation to the resignation of President Richard Nixon after the Watergate revelations. Like Watergate, the abdication of Edward VIII was a constitutional crisis. That series was followed by John Hawkesworth's spectacular African adventure, "The Flame Trees of Thika," another Thames offering, based on Elspeth Huxley's memoir of life in British colonial Kenya. Filmed on location in Africa, and featuring remarkable footage of wild animals, it was also a reunion of sorts for Hawkesworth and the series's star, Hayley Mills, who had appeared in the first Hawkesworth film, *Tiger Bay* (1959). "Flame Trees" was *Masterpiece Theatre*'s highest-rated program to date, commanding an estimated audience of 9.8 million households.[47]

Thanks to the exit clause Schmertz had found in the RCTV contract, the BBC was back in the lineup for the 1982–83 schedule. The opener was "To Serve Them All My Days," an adaptation of R. F. Delderfield's novel about a teacher at a British boarding school in the years between the World Wars. It was, to that date, the second-highest-rated series in the history of *Masterpiece Theatre,* with a total viewership of 9.7 million households.[48]

In 1984 "The Jewel in the Crown," from Granada Television, attracted the same sort of cult following as "Upstairs, Downstairs." It was profiled on the cover of the Arts and Leisure section of the *New York Times,* a rare event indeed—under the headline "'Jewel in the Crown'—Superb Drama." The prose was purple: "Viewers in search of indisputable quality are advised to set aside their Sunday evenings, brooking no interruptions for 'The Jewel in the Crown' over the next three months."[49] And set them aside they did. When the Broadway musical *Grind* was in rehearsal, legendary producer–director Harold Prince would stop all activity on Sundays at nine sharp to watch the program on a small television in the back of the theater. When the episode ended, he would resume rehearsals.

The Goodmans coordinated a full-scale publicity blitz and even flew Granada chairman Sir Denis Forman to New York. Forman was glowingly profiled in the *New York Times,* as was Art Malik, who played Hari Kumar in the series. In his introduction, Alistair Cooke emphasized the social issues that underpinned the narrative. Wearing a white tropical jacket, on a set designed to look vaguely Indian, Cooke announced:

> Now, what we're going to look at is a prolonged study of two class systems, the Indian and the British, the British abroad. Raj meant rule. And the Raj meant every resident Briton in India. Down from the viceroy, who's the king's representative, down through the army, to the civil service, the top and the lower layers, down to merchants and insurance men and traders and the like. All of whom had very well understood relations between each other. Then India, this huge subcontinent of one and a half million square miles, two long opposed religions, the Hindus and the Muslims, of princes who were secure in their independent kingdoms, of Indian officers of high rank, Indians who had been knighted, millions of untouchables, and millions more of every degree of servitude.[50]

In other words, Cooke was presenting "The Jewel in the Crown" as "Upstairs, Downstairs" on an epic scale.

At the end of *Masterpiece Theatre*'s 1984–85 season, on the Fourth of July, 1985, Joan Wilson died of cancer. In her obituary, the *Boston Globe* summed up her contribution: "She leaves a record of bringing quality television to this country that is quite possibly unsurpassed by anyone in the history of the industry."[51] On September 30, WGBH chief Henry Becton assigned Rebecca Eaton to replace Wilson as producer. The decision changed the balance of power within the administration of the series. Eaton, although a fourteen-year veteran at WGBH, was an outsider to Mobil. But she was considered friendly to business, having had produced numerous documentaries for *Enterprise,* WGBH's business magazine show. Her one connection to *Masterpiece Theatre* was that she had secretly been reading *Masterpiece* scripts for Henry Becton during the last year of Joan Wilson's life.[52]

Eaton recalls that when she was appointed,

> *Masterpiece Theatre* was fifteen years old, and you had to be pretty blind not to realize that things had changed in broadcasting in Britain and this country in fifteen years. That there were different people who were producing the programs, writing the programs, broadcasting the programs in England. And it was folly to keep looking for the same kind of "Upstairs, Downstairs," "Poldark" material—the real studio costume drama. Because they weren't making that anymore.[53]

Eaton proceeded to look cautiously for contemporary material to add to the series, in contrast to Schmertz, who seemed interested only in period pieces. Her contribution to the series would be the successful transition to contemporary British drama.

Eaton's first season, 1986–87, began with "Paradise Postponed," an original, contemporary story by John Mortimer, author of the Rumpole novels adapted on *Mystery!* Produced by "Rumpole" veteran Jacqueline Davis, "Paradise" was about the postwar political climate of England and the rise of a toadying working-class Thatcherite politician into conservative circles of power. Ed Siegel of the *Boston Globe* noted the significance of the piece: It was "the first *Masterpiece Theatre* to take place later than the '40's."[54] This series was followed by a return to the past, "Goodbye, Mr. Chips," a BBC–MGM coproduction starring Roy Marsden, known to viewers from his appearances in *Mystery!* The program emulated the popular "To Serve Them All My Days" and also belonged to the clearly developed *Masterpiece* subgenre of Hollywood remakes. Showing his commitment to period drama, the *New York Times*'s John J. O'Connor praised this production highly, calling it a "fail-safe classic."[55] The season's closing series, "Love Song," another modern drama, was based on a story by the popular novelist Jeffrey Archer about two Cambridge students whose competition leads to marriage.

Eaton's influence was now being felt, as was a shortage of British period costume drama. Herb Schmertz was on record as wanting to keep contemporary material to a minimum. He told a reporter, "I don't see any shift to contemporary material. [Fewer] classic novels are being [adapted], but the audience of *Masterpiece Theatre* has expectations. There is no shortage of contemporary material elsewhere." But Schmertz would soon be gone. His *Masterpiece Theatre* swan song was "The Bretts."

This pre–World War II period piece about a family of London theater fold was a backstage drama whose episodes used many of the plot and character elements found in other *Masterpiece* series. The screenplay's authors were "Upstairs, Downstairs" alumna Rosemary Anne Sisson and Mobil's Frank Marshall. Herb Schmertz today complains that WGBH's Henry Becton wouldn't give him an onscreen credit though the program had been his idea. "I was too identified in the public's mind with Mobil, and it would look like Mobil was controlling things. I said, 'What about Marshall? He works for me.' 'Well, he's not identified in the public's mind, so he can have a credit.'" Schmertz insisted that his role in the production "didn't violate [WGBH's] guidelines. They could have given me a credit." Schmertz said the episode convinced him that in public broadcasting, "they were more concerned with appearances than reality."[56] But this lost battle for credit also reflected the precariousness of Schmertz's position at Mobil. His reduced influence on the show was a direct result of a change in management at the company. When Mobil chairman Rawleigh Warner retired in 1988, Schmertz's days were numbered. After "The Bretts," Schmertz and Marshall left Mobil's employ, though Marshall would later independently produce "A Piece of Cake" for *Masterpiece Theatre*.

Schmertz's replacement as Mobil's executive for public affairs, Peter A. Spina, announced that he would leave day-to-day management of television programming to WGBH. Although many of the series broadcast in 1988, 1989, and 1990 were developed under the reign of Schmertz and Marshall, some control over programming decisions was allowed to revert to the Boston PBS station.[57] Taking advantage of the post-Schmertz relationship with the oil company, Eaton sought to make her personal mark as series producer right away. On January 15, 1989, *Masterpiece Theatre* presented the radical and extremely contemporary (in fact, set in a not-too-distant mythical future) "A Very British Coup," from Britain's Channel Four, about an English prime minister overthrown with the collusion of the CIA. The next season, Eaton aired "Traffik," a *Miami Vice*–style thriller about the international drug cartel. And in 1991 came "House of Cards," about the overthrow of a prime minister by his trusted friend, Francis Urquhart. In it, the Americans were depicted as an unwelcome force in English politics; one villain was an Americanized Rupert Murdoch–type international media tycoon speaking in a thick American accent. The contemporary political thriller was a new genre for *Masterpiece Theatre,* one that would become extremely successful. "House of Cards" spawned two riveting sequels, "To Play the King" and "The Final Cut." Ian Richardson's portrayal of a ruthless Conservative prime minister—a transgendered tribute to Margaret Thatcher—will long raise a chuckle among PBS viewers.

But there was a link to past *Masterpiece* traditions as well. For one thing, political dramas had always been part of the series—Churchill, Edward VII, Edward VIII, Disraeli, Lloyd George, Mountbatten had all been subjects. And the star of "House of Cards," Ian Richardson, was an old trouper from the *Masterpiece Theatre* stock company. The producer, Ken Riddington, had made the highly rated "To Serve Them All My Days." So despite Schmertz's departure, the contemporary dramas were in keeping with the overall pattern he had established.

In the midst of the shift from Schmertz to Spina at Mobil, and Wilson to Eaton at WGBH, these contemporary political thrillers, with their themes of conspiracy and revenge, might well have reflected the unsettled atmosphere at two institutions. In the fall of 1993, Russell Baker replaced Alistair Cooke as *Masterpiece* host, and Mobil announced that it would no longer fund *Mystery!,* which would have to seek support on its own. No one doubted, however, that loyal PBS audiences would ensure the survival of what had become twin pillars of the public broadcasting schedule.

12

And Now for Something Completely Different

U pstairs, Downstairs" is not the only program that has grown to be almost synonymous with public broadcasting despite its initial rejection by PBS executives and the fact that it never received any money from the Corporation for Public Broadcasting. In the early 1970s, Ron Devillier, a programming executive at PBS, was a frustrated *Monty Python's Flying Circus* fan. The PBS bureaucracy would not consider running the offbeat BBC comedy in its core schedule, and Devillier felt that Time-Life Films, the BBC's distributor in the United States, was not able to market it successfully. Gambling on the appeal of the then little-known troupe, Devillier opened his own distribution agency. He went on the road, showing cassettes to local PBS station managers and selling the program market-by-market in exchange for a commission.

Today the affable, middle-aged television agent is a rich man because of his lifetime interest in *Monty Python's* American distribution, a concession bestowed on him by the grateful Pythons themselves. His office in northwest Washington, D.C., is at the end of a hallway graced by *Python* posters. These days most of Devillier's business is in cable television, but the resounding success of his promotion of British comedy has ensured a continuing solid demand for imported comedies from local public television stations and the identification of the once exclusively educational public television network with British comedy in the minds of most Americans.[1]

Former President Richard Nixon once grumbled about public television and its financing that commercial network executives "can watch taxpayer subsidized ballet and British sitcoms when they go to the Hamptons for the weekend."[2] Nixon, like most viewers, did not realize that a federal subsidy for the British sitcoms was provided only in the most general sense. While ballet was indeed part of national arts programming distributed in the PBS core schedule through series like *Dance in America, Great Performances,* and *Live from Lincoln Center,* "Britcoms" are not carried on the national PBS feed. They are still syndicated on a commercial basis and acquired locally to meet audience demand, a legacy of Devillier's bold move. Stations use them to attract pledges from viewers and increase audiences. Thus many British comedies have attained immortality of a sort. Long after their runs in Britain, they are endlessly aired by American PBS stations.

At PBS, even after Devillier's departure, the bureaucracy remained wary of comedy—to the extent that former PBS programming czar Jennifer Lawson once called it the "humor-impaired network." PBS did try its hand at producing its own comedy in the mid-1980s with a series called *Trying Times.* It flopped. When Lawson became PBS's executive in charge of programming in 1989, she hired former NBC executive Brandon Tartikoff to develop more appealing comedies for the network. However, shortly after Lawson resigned from the network in 1995, PBS president Ervin Duggan canceled comedy development in order to devote PBS's resources to a political series he called *The Democracy Project.*

Devillier's first success in getting *Monty Python* on the U.S. airwaves came on a warm July evening in 1974, on Dallas's KERA. American television viewers had never seen a comedy show quite like it. Five unknown British actors and an American expatriate animator were doing and saying things that had never been done or said on American television before. Their irreverent, disjointed sketch-comedy show roamed unfettered by taste or convention over a range of outrageous topics that would have gotten performers booted off the commercial networks: venerable high-court judges revealing Madonna-esque bustiers and spike heels under their black robes; a Hungarian tourist using an altered

English phrasebook in which the translation of "Where is the tobacconists?" read "My nipples burst with delight"; a funeral director convincing a bereaved gentleman that, rather than disposing of his dead mother's remains, they might very well consider eating them.

The show was nihilistic, vulgar, profane, and sexually explicit—and to nearly everyone's surprise, instantly and phenomenally popular in the States, especially with younger viewers. Within a few months of its initial airing on KERA—and while the just-released feature film *Monty Python and the Holy Grail* was filling theaters across America—more than 130 PBS stations had individually purchased the show for late-night airings. As television historians Harry Castleman and Walter Podrazik note, "Much to the surprise of everyone, the show took off and became one of public TV's highest rated programs. Viewers simply ignored the occasional inscrutable allusion to obscure British interests and enjoyed the fresh, daring insanity."[3] Soon, the Ministry of Silly Walks, "Nudge, nudge, wink, wink, know what I mean?", the Dead Parrot sketches, and "The Lumberjack Song" had become part of the American lexicon, and *Monty Python's Flying Circus* had thrust PBS before an audience it had all but ignored.

Produced by the BBC, *Monty Python* first aired in Great Britain in 1969 as a substitute for a low-rated Sunday religious interview program hosted by essayist Malcolm Muggeridge (William F. Buckley's favorite *Firing Line* guest),[4] which was moved to Tuesday nights.

The Pythons were John Cleese, Michael Palin, Terry Jones, Eric Idle, and Graham Chapman, who wrote and acted in the show, and American animator Terry Gilliam, who supplied the trademark cartoon sequences. Cleese, Chapman, and Idle were Cambridge pals who had already performed together as undergraduates with the Footlights Revue, while Palin and Jones were Oxford men, in the rival Oxford Line Revue. The British members of the troupe had actually met through a man who was to become prominent in both public and network broadcasting in the United States, as well as a pillar of the broadcasting establishment in Britain: David Frost. While perceived by American audiences as a serious interviewer, Frost began his career as a stand-up comedian, arriving in the wave of madcap postwar British comedy that gave rise to *The Goon Show* and Peter Cook and Dudley

Moore's *Beyond the Fringe* revue. The five future Pythons were brought together on *The Frost Report,* a comedy show that aired on British television in 1966 and 1967. Chapman, Palin, Idle, and Jones were among Frost's writers.[5] Cleese's first job in television had also come from David Frost. Just out of Cambridge, Cleese had been a staff writer for Frost's satirical program *That Was the Week That Was.*[6] That show premiered on the BBC in November 1962 and was brought to the United States as an NBC special in November 1963. British imports were actually not uncommon on American commercial networks. For example, *The Prisoner,* starring Patrick McGoohan, ran from 1968 to 1969 on CBS as a sequel to the British *Secret Agent,* which had appeared on CBS from 1965 to 1966.

That Was the Week That Was (known as *TW3*) was an instant hit; the American version would be carried on NBC until 1965. Frost would fly to New York from London each week to host both shows, the start to his career as a transatlantic television personality. Like *Monty Python,* *TW3* flaunted an irreverence toward established institutions, and like *Python* its format featured sketch comedy, blackout humor, and ersatz news broadcasts. Unlike *Python,* which was shown unaltered on PBS, NBC's version of *That Was the Week That Was* was adapted to American tastes, commenting on American politics and finding its own talented humorist in former mathematics professor Tom Lehrer, who performed his own compositions such as "Smut" and "The Vatican Rag."[7]

In 1967 Idle, Jones, Palin, and Gilliam collaborated on the BBC's madcap series *Do Not Adjust Your Set,* a *Python* precursor. Gilliam, the American animator in the troupe, had worked with Cleese in New York two years earlier, doing a photo-comic book called *Help!* for cartoonist Harvey Kurtzman, the founder of *Mad* magazine. (It featured a love triangle between an executive, his wife, and his daughter's Barbie doll.) Gilliam's friendship with Cleese led to the BBC job. Cleese had also worked with Palin and Chapman on a British television special called *How to Irritate People* the next year.

It was veteran BBC script editor Barry Took who decided to take a gamble and put the group of young writers together to create a new, cutting-edge comedy show. One of the show's influences was America's groundbreaking comedy series *Rowan and Martin's Laugh-In,* which aired on NBC from 1967 to 1973, pushing the comedy envelope as far as any show to date. Within two months of its debut, *Laugh-In* was the highest-rated program in the United States.[8] The success of *Python* with younger audiences was also in keeping with that of another American show of the time: *The Monkees*. NBC's American "TV Beatles" had cavorted impishly—and, in retrospect, rather innocently—across the little screen from 1966 to 1968, inspired by the big-screen antics of John, Paul, George, and Ringo in *A Hard Day's Night* (1964) and *Help!* (1965).

The humor of *Monty Python* featured the unpredictable, relying on shock for effect. A sixteen-ton weight would crash onto the set to end a scene, a huge animated boot would crush people, characters would explode. *Monty Python's* transitional announcement, "And now for something completely different," captured the kaleidoscopic frenzy of the series.

Despite its eventual success on both sides of the Atlantic, *Monty Python* was not immediately appreciated by the Establishment in Great Britain. After its 1969 debut, the *Daily Telegraph* complained about the loss of Malcolm Muggeridge in the time slot: "Is this a sufficient reason for dropping that program with glee, and substituting comedy shows which the BBC announces as 'Nutty, zany and oddball'? Is this not yet another instance of the BBC's desire to forget, as far as it can, its subsidized status and its duty to maintain high standards, in order to compete for audience ratings with ITV?" The government-funded BBC was seeing the newly established commercial broadcasters such as ITV (Independent Television) eat into its audiences. No doubt the temptation to out-Frost the master of British television comedy, who had departed for London Weekend Television—and to do it using alumni from his own show— proved irresistible to BBC executives at the time.

The head of BBC Features Group for Television, Aubrey Singer, said at a staff meeting in 1970 that he found bits of the show "disgusting." Paul Fox, the BBC program controller, said the show "was continually going over the edge of what was acceptable." The head of BBC Arts Features, Stephen Hearst, complained "the values of the program were so nihilistic and cruel." Bob Reid, the chief of BBC Science Features, commented that the Pythons "seemed often to wallow in the sadism of their humor." And naturalist and presenter David Attenborough, then Director of Programs for Television, noted that the Pythons "shied away from responsibility."[9] Some in the press said that *Monty Python* was too commercial in its appeal, that it was comparable to *Laugh-In* and therefore not suitable for government-supported broadcasting. In other words, *Monty Python* was just too lowbrow for the BBC.

The downmarket sensibility was intentional. "We made progress," Terry Jones has said, ". . . in pushing back the barriers of what is considered 'good taste.' There were things the BBC thought one couldn't do before we started doing them; we were often able to do them purely because the BBC didn't really like us very much and didn't pay much attention to us to begin with."

Even though it continued to air the program, the BBC did little to improve the fortunes of the Pythons. The show ran late at night, with scant promotion. According to British critic Robert Hewison, "audience appreciation distinctly faded out above the age of thirty-five."[10]

Competition from ITV companies such as London Weekend Television was keen enough, however, that the BBC executives wanted to keep the show on the network—especially since, despite the BBC's neglect, it was growing in popularity. BBC executives tried to rein in the Pythons, censoring a reference to masturbation here, a four-letter word there, but they remained unrepentant and determined to do the show their way.

"When executives did begin to read the scripts," Jones recalls, "a few little disputes did break out, but by then, we usually had a precedent to point at. For instance, we could say that we said 'shit' in program two, and they would then have to go back and check and find out that we had in fact said 'shit' in program two, and that no one had written in to complain. Therefore, they would allow us to say it once in this program, but not the three times that we wanted."

Flush with success, John Cleese left the program after the 1973 season to produce and star in his own TV series, *Fawlty Towers.* It was the beginning of the end for *Monty Python's Flying Circus,* but not for the Pythons, who were now a worldwide phenomenon. The weekly series was canceled by the BBC in 1975, and the Pythons went on to work on other projects. Among those projects were two more series-related movies, *Monty Python and the Holy Grail* and *The Life of Brian,* both of which were produced by former Beatle George Harrison, a longtime Python fan. (He went on to produce *Privates on Parade, The Missionary,* and *Time Bandits* with former Pythons.) In 1983, the Pythons reunited for the big-screen *Monty Python's The Meaning of Life;* John Cleese and Michael Palin worked together on the 1988 American comedy film *A Fish Called Wanda.* Terry Gilliam directed a number of films, including *Jabberwocky, Time Bandits, Brazil, The Fisher King,* and, most recently, *Twelve Monkeys.* Terry Jones and Michael Palin collaborated on a "Boys' Own" television adventure series called *Ripping Yarns,* which lasted only one season. Palin would appear again on public television in reruns of popular BBC travel shows *Around the World in Eighty Days* and *Pole to Pole,* in the 1990s. Eric Idle, perhaps the loner of the group, did a series called *Rutland Weekend Television,* and then wrote, produced, and starred in an NBC special called *All You Need Is Cash,* one of the first "mockumentaries," a spoof of the Beatles. Some see this television show as the inspiration for the American film *This Is Spinal Tap.*

The Pythons had actually been available to American audiences prior to their first appearance on public television: their 1970 feature film, *And Now for Something Completely Different,* had already developed something of a cult following. That's where PBS vice president Ron Devillier first encountered the Pythons and became a fan. Devillier believed that their series belonged on PBS, which had established itself as the Anglophile channel in the United States.

Devillier thought that the success of *Masterpiece Theatre* demonstrated there was a niche market for British programming on American television. Since PBS had established itself as a major provider of English drama, comedies would be a logical complement. This was, in Devillier's opinion, a fulfillment of the legal mandate that the network serve underserved audiences and provide alternatives to commercial television shows.[11]

But some people within the public broadcasting system believed then, and still believe today, that the scheduling of comedy on PBS conflicts with the serious mission of public broadcasting as an educational outlet dedicated to uplift instead of entertainment. Al Vecchione, retired president of MacNeil/Lehrer Productions, is a longtime critic of the practice of airing comedies on PBS, saying it diverts money, time, and audiences from serious and educational shows. And indeed, his point of view is consistent with the intentions of the original Carnegie Commission report of 1967, which concluded that public broadcasting should not spend its money on programming that could survive with advertiser support. Yet, Devillier's point to PBS executives in 1974 had been precisely that commercial support for the Pythons did not and could not exist, that their brand of comedy was anathema to advertisers.

Actually, the commercial networks did take note of the popularity of PBS's comedy programming from across the pond. But rather than importing successful British series, they preferred to remake them for American audiences. Thus, the British situation comedy *Til Death Do Us Part* became CBS's *All in the Family*, and *Man About the House* became ABC's *Three's Company*. And the success of *Monty Python* on public television also increased commercial opportunities for British imports. *The Benny Hill Show*, with its more traditional English music hall variety of comedy, soon appeared on syndicated commercial television nationwide. The youthful audiences attracted by the Pythons encouraged NBC to launch *Saturday Night Live* in October 1975.[12] The similarities did not go unnoticed by the audience. TV historians Harry Castleman and Walter Podrazik described SNL as "deliberately outrageous, sometimes even tasteless, in the style of the increasingly popular BBC import *Monty Python's Flying Circus*."[13]

Also in 1975, ABC attempted to adapt *Monty Python* as part of a series called *ABC Wide World of Entertainment*. If NBC had the imitation, went the logic, why couldn't ABC broadcast the original? But the effort soon collapsed into a nasty lawsuit when the Pythons objected to changes made by ABC to their original scripts to remove profanity and sexual references. Only one program was ever broadcast because the Pythons had forced the network into court. One interesting aspect of this lawsuit was the argument at the time against the Pythons by ABC's attorney Charles Fried that standards of decency "are much more rigid as far as commercial [broadcasting] is concerned" than at PBS.[14]

This, then, is one example of the paradox of public television. What is the educational benefit to the American citizen if local public television stations are airing vulgar fare like *Monty Python* instead of children's and educational programming one might expect? And yet shows like *Monty Python* are without a doubt among the best programs ever aired on PBS, far superior to the supposedly educational product supplied by the national network and among the reasons Americans love and support public broadcasting and donate to their local stations.

Even though *Monty Python's Flying Circus* was purchased on the commercial market by each PBS station that aired it (and even some commercial television stations, such as KPRC in Houston), it has come to symbolize the educational network's comedic identity in much the way *Masterpiece Theatre* came to be seen as the signature PBS drama series. The success of *Monty Python* showed local PBS stations that British comedy had a ready viewership they could serve, and the local stations went after that viewership with a vengeance.

Following the success of *Python*, John Cleese's *Fawlty Towers* soon began appearing on American public television schedules. Shortly thereafter, a host of other, more conventional, comedies followed, among them: *Yes, Minister; Yes, Prime Minister; No Job for a Lady; Are You Being Served?; To the Manor Born; The Bounder; Dad's Army; May to December; 'Allo, 'Allo; The Two Ronnies; The Fall and Rise of Reginald Perrin; The Darling Buds of May; The Good Neighbors* (called *The Good Life* in England); *Waiting for God;* and *Keeping Up Appearances.*

Britcoms mix high and low comedy, and include references to classical antiquity and to the latest British fad, but a few generalizations can be made about the shows that have reached public broadcasting stations. They reflect PBS's traditional dependence on the BBC for programming and also the fact that PBS is the place Americans tune to watch the English at play. Most recently, *One Foot in the Grave* has been Americanized and converted into a vehicle for Bill Cosby by CBS. The original, shown on PBS stations, features British character actor Richard Wilson railing against the insanity of contemporary life and driving all around him mad, a comedy of exasperation not usually seen on network television but a frequent theme of PBS Britcoms.

Among the most appealing to highbrows has been *Fawlty Towers,* John Cleese's first effort after *Monty Python.* Like the protagonist of *One*

Foot in the Grave, the leading man of *Fawlty Towers* is an exasperated individual at war with the world around him. In *The Logic of the Absurd,* his study for the British Film Institute, critic Jerry Palmer calls *Fawlty Towers* "one of the best British television farce series." Indeed, the comedy captured the existentialist spirit of playwrights like Stoppard, Beckett, Ionesco, and Sartre. *Fawlty Towers* ran two seasons in Great Britain, and reruns are still shown on PBS stations. Much of the appeal was generated by its aristocratic star, who conveyed the image of all that was decent and traditional in the English gentleman. Cast against type, which heightened the comic effect, the tall and angular Cleese (*Monty Python's* Minister of Silly Walks) played Basil Fawlty, rude and henpecked proprietor of a small English inn. British comedienne Prunella Scales played Mrs. Fawlty, and Cleese's real-life American-born first wife, Connie Booth, played the maid.

The show was based on a real hotel called the Gleneagles outside the resort of Torquay, where Cleese and other Pythons had stayed during *Flying Circus* filming. "The manager was just wonderfully rude," Cleese recalled. "He was like Basil, but much smaller, a skinny little guy about five foot four inches, with a large wife who dominated him. We reversed the sizes." The Pythons moved out after one night of terrible service. "An old friend of mine said to me, 'There's a series in that hotel,'" Cleese said. "The extraordinary thing was, he was absolutely right. When Connie and I sat down three years later, it was the second or third idea that came into our minds." With the premiere of *Fawlty Towers,* a new PBS comedy cult was born. As with *Python,* there were some growls from the British Establishment. Among those not amused was Christopher Price, a member of Parliament, who complained the comedy was based on insult humor and "jokes about dagoes and wops." But Jerry Palmer's BFI review of the program maintained that it carefully walked the line between humor and embarrassing insult, "probably one of the reasons for its ecstatic reception."[15] In any case, it did not hurt Cleese's career. After the second season, he set up his own production company, Video Arts, specializing in comedic industrial training videos. Cleese sold his company in 1993 for $70 million. Among his partners was Tony Jay, who served as consultant to economist Milton Friedman's 1980 PBS special *Free to Choose* and wrote *Yes, Minister* (which ran in Britain from 1980 to 1984) and its sequel, *Yes, Prime Minister* (1986–87).

These two political series were as sophisticated and dry as *Fawlty Towers* was vulgar. Yet they shared the same absurdist sensibility. The *Minister* series embodied the spirit of the Thatcher era as *Monty Python* had done in the previous decade. Where *Python* had been wild and wacky, characterized by the youthful energy and irreverence typical of its era, *Yes, Minister* took place in a more grownup milieu appropriate to the businesslike 1980s. Indeed, Milton Friedman says that Jay drew many of his *Minister* plots from topics they discussed together after working on *Free to Choose*.[16] A class act in all respects, the writing team had experience both in politics and show business. Jay had covered politics as a correspondent for the BBC's nightly news and, like the Pythons, as a writer for *The Frost Report*. His coauthor, Jonathan Lynn, had run his own company as a director at the National Theatre.

Both *Yes, Minister* and *Yes, Prime Minister* featured Nigel Hawthorne as Sir Humphrey Appleby, a career civil servant who shrewdly manipulates Minister of Administrative Affairs James Hacker, played by Paul Eddington—usually away from whatever political goal he might have had in mind at the beginning of the episode and eventually into the prime minister's job. Reviewing the new series, the London *Evening Standard* declared that "Mssrs. Lynn and Jay have created something as immortal as P. G. Wodehouse's Bertie Wooster and Jeeves." And indeed the theme was similar to that of *Masterpiece Theatre's* "Jeeves and Wooster" and "Upstairs, Downstairs," with masters completely dependent on their servants.

In a feminist twist on *Yes, Minister,* Penelope Keith played a Labour version of Margaret Thatcher in *No Job for a Lady* (1989–91). Each episode cut between Keith's busy leftist parliamentary office and her topsy-turvy home, where her husband resentfully tried to get her attention. Keith had become known to PBS audiences as the star of two more conventional situation comedies, *The Good Neighbors* (1975–79; called *The Good Life* in England) and *To the Manor Born* (1979–81). *The Good Neighbors* was a comedy of self-sufficiency in which Keith played Margo Leadbetter, the very proper suburban neighbor of Tom and Barbara Good (Richard Briers and Felicity Kendall), who had abandoned the rat race for the joys of home gardening and organic living. Margo's husband, Jerry, played by Paul Eddington (later the minister of *Yes, Minister*), was still the striving executive who looked askance at the commune next door. Each episode featured a confrontation between the formidable Margo and her more back-to-nature neighbors.

In *To the Manor Born*, Keith moved up a rung on the social ladder, playing Audrey fforbes-Hamilton, a downwardly mobile aristocratic widow forced to sell her ancestral home to a noveau-riche food magnate based on the real-life James Goldsmith, played by Peter Bowles, and move into the gatekeeper's cottage. Keith takes it upon herself to train the brash and rakish businessman in the finer points of etiquette. The subtext is romance motivated by cool calculation: Keith wants to move back into the family manse. The show had a spinoff for Bowles, *The Bounder* (1982–83, later picked up by PBS stations).

Another middlebrow program about a businessman was *The Fall and Rise of Reginald Perrin* (1976–79). It depicted the trials and tribulations of a middle-class Everyman figure, played by Leonard Rossiter, who tries to escape his station as a mid-level executive at Sunshine Desserts. His luck changes in the second season when he opens the Grot Shop, which sells useless junk at high prices. He becomes immensely successful and sets up a commune. No question about it, *The Fall and Rise of Reginald Perrin* was a commentary on the seventies, one of the tackiest decades in history.

But not all of the Britcoms aspired to high status. *'Allo, 'Allo* was an essay in low comedy out of the music hall tradition, basically one long vaudeville sketch about two British airmen who lie low in France during the Second World War at René's Café, a Resistance hideout. The plot was a variation of the 1960s American sitcom *Hogan's Heroes*. It first aired in England in 1984 and is still running on PBS stations today. *Dad's Army* is a similarly low comedy about civil defense crews on the home front. *The Two Ronnies* features music hall performers whose material resembles that of Benny Hill (whose program was shown on commercial American channels). Dame Edna Everedge, played by Australian drag comedian Barry Humphries, was another music hall act picked up by PBS stations. He was so well liked by some viewers that he was briefly rewarded with his own NBC specials in 1991 and 1992. Less than tasteful, too, has been *Waiting for God,* set in an English nursing home. Half the jokes in this series are about the Grim Reaper. While it is doubtful any commercial American program would deal with this subject matter in quite the same way, it is curious that those critics who denounced the vulgarity of network comedies like *The Golden Girls* have voiced no criticism of the more outrageous British counterparts when shown on PBS stations.

Are You Being Served? has been among the longest-running British sitcoms and is another favorite of PBS station managers. The show ran from 1972 to 1985 in England and was revived as *Grace and Favour* from 1992 to 1993 (*Are You Being Served? Again!* on PBS). Based on the 1940 Ernst Lubitsch film comedy *The Shop Around the Corner,* the sitcom version centered on the interpersonal conflicts and rivalries among the sales force of a department store. It closely resembled a 1970s American sitcom such as *The Mary Tyler Moore Show* in structure, though not in style, relying on sexual innuendo and crude puns. It has been immensely popular among PBS donors, who cite broadcasts of the program as among the reasons they watch PBS.

Another more vulgar comedy of manners is *Keeping Up Appearances* (1990–95). Like *Are You Being Served?,* it features crude jokes, often of a sexual or scategorical nature. The setting here is a home rather than a shop, in which a bossy, pretentious, middle-class housewife and her henpecked husband living in a fashionable London suburb interact with—and try to avoid being embarrassed by—her relatives, who live in a housing project and survive on the dole. Each episode cuts between the squalid conditions in the projects and the more salubrious surroundings of the garden suburb.

Less vulgar are two Britcoms frequently seen on PBS. *The Darling Buds of May* is a 1991 British comedy-drama set in the 1920s detailing some of the silliness of the flapper era. *May to December* tells the story of a sixty-something suburban lawyer and his twenty-something wife, a local gym teacher. His daughter from a previous marriage doesn't approve. The situation has the potential for seamy jokes yet is handled in a rather more wholesome manner.

One series defies easy categorization. *Blackadder* (1984–89) combines vulgar low comedy with wit and sophistication and features a streak of sadism in the vein of *Monty Python.* Rowan Atkinson played the Blackadder, a nasty operator who had to deal with the idiocracies of both upper-class twits and lower-class morons. The program featured episodes of human frailty recurring across different historical time periods: medieval, Elizabethan, Regency, and the First World War. Dark and cynical, Atkinson was often hysterically funny as he negotiated in exasperation between two poles of the British class system. He later created a silent comedy called *Mister Bean,* which was carried by PBS stations after its initial 1992 Home Box Office run.

This is certainly not a complete account of all the British comedies shown on PBS stations since 1969, but it is an overview of the more popular series shown in this country. Each station in each market makes its own decisions on what programming to buy from the back lists of British broadcasters. Despite the fact that the network is readily identified with British situation comedies, PBS still does not carry such sitcoms in its national program feed. But that feed only lasts a few hours each night, exclusive of the *NewsHour,* which leaves plenty of time for stations to fill with programming targeted to local viewers; and the Britcoms have served well in this capacity. For example, WETA in Washington, D.C., has frequently rerun episodes of *Yes, Minister* and *Yes, Prime Minister,* no doubt due to local appeal. Similarly, KCET in Los Angeles has been showing *May to December,* perhaps because of the city's high divorce rate and the number of trophy wives of rich, older men among the viewership. The series casts a widower-husband and a down-to-earth, anything-but-a-golddigger woman—in, perhaps, appealing contrasts to L.A. stereotypes.

There are several commercial vendors of Britcoms in addition to the American-owned Devillier-Donegan Associates, which has the *Monty Python* franchise: BBC-Lionheart, London Weekend Television, Richard Price Television Associates, Inc., Thames Television, and other ITV companies. They maintain sales forces that contact each station individually about programming. A local station usually buys a particular comedy because there is a demand for it in the community. It is a purely market-driven mechanism; during pledge week, station managers evaluate which programs are the most popular with donors, and those are the ones they buy.

The Britcoms are part of a highly lucrative secondary commercial market in public broadcasting. It is clear that exposure on PBS stations was the key to the phenomenal success of *Monty Python's Flying Circus.* "Monty Python" is now a household name in the United States, and the brilliant comedians who created the show are millionaires. Kim Johnson, author of *The First Twenty Years of Monty Python,* notes, "It was only when the TV series began to catch on in America in 1974–5 that *And Now for Something Completely Different* surfaced again [the film had first been released in the U.S. in 1972] and now is a perennial favorite on campuses and on cable, and in revival houses."[17] The ancillary merchandising of Python records, books, live shows, films, videos, and other spin-offs demonstrated the value of the public broadcasting niche market to British comedy and the value of British comedy to PBS stations.

There can be no question but that *Monty Python* is one of the most successful programs ever to air in the United States, giving promotional value worth millions to the Pythons. It also demonstrated the influence PBS might have on the networks, as the producer of *Saturday Night Live* admitted that the Pythons inspired his show. The *Python* shows did, indeed, contain more graphic and scatological humor than commercial programs and did indeed "push the envelope" for what commercial broadcasters were prepared to show. In this sense, the phenomenon fits Senator Daniel Patrick Moynihan's model of "defining deviancy down": the changing of social norms to accept as permissible behavior that had formerly been censured.

Today, PBS does face some competition in the British comedy market. Comedy Central is now home to *Absolutely Fabulous,* an outrageous BBC comedic descendant of the Pythons, which has been "fabulously" successful for the cable network. Rude, lewd, and crude, *"AbFab"* exhibited the same irreverence the Pythons tapped, and the same shocking caricatures making a mockery of British life and institutions—this time from a feminine perspective in the persons of Patsy and Edina, two fashion-world denizens who find their decadent '60s lifestyles in conflict with the traditional values of Edina's daughter Saffron. In the 1970s *Absolutely Fabulous* would have been a natural for local PBS stations, though today some of the most cutting-edge British comedy programs have migrated elsewhere due to competition. Nevertheless, local PBS stations are still the places to tune in for many Britcoms.

Ironically, the case of the Britcoms shows that American audiences want high-quality entertainment and that they make contributions to their public television stations to allow them to see and hear something completely different.

13

Free to Choose

In addition to its regularly scheduled series, PBS broadcasts at least one prestigious "blockbuster" miniseries each year. Many of them are released on videocassette and sold to libraries and schools; they are also available through bookstores and catalogs, providing, in a sense, a national curriculum. Originally these productions were British in origin, but by the 1990s some prominent American-made miniseries had reached the PBS schedule.

One early example of the genre was Kenneth Clark's *Civilisation* (1970), which set the tone for the format as one of uplift and which fit the cultural and educational mission behind the establishment of PBS; Jacob Bronowski's *Ascent of Man* (1974) related the evolutionary history of *Homo sapiens* to that of science. Carl Sagan's *Cosmos,* the highest-rated PBS program of 1980, was the first such PBS miniseries hosted by an American (although produced by a Briton, Adrian Malone, who had also made *Ascent of Man*). Among the American-made miniseries that followed have been Ken Burns's *Civil War* (1990) and *Baseball* (1994); Henry Hampton's *Eyes on the Prize* (1987), *The Great Depression* (1993), and *America's War on Poverty* (1995); and Ken Burns's and Stephen Ives's *The West* (1996).[1]

These and other PBS blockbusters have been accompanied by coffee table books that became best-sellers due in part to the promotional value of the television exposure, making rich men of the authors and producers. For example, Carl Sagan's book version of *Cosmos* reportedly sold

750,000 copies.[2] Knopf is said to have sold some 750,000 copies of Ken Burns and Geoffrey Ward's companion book to *The Civil War* at $50 each, grossing approximately $37 million. Time-Life Video reportedly sold more than 250,000 *Civil War* cassettes for home viewing, and PBS Video sold thousands of institutional cassettes, grossing in excess of $12 million.[3] So PBS special programming is valuable not only to PBS in terms of enhanced prestige and increased pledges, but also to the program producers and talent, who earn literally millions in sales because PBS's target audience is composed of literate, upscale, educated book-buyers.

Yet in at least one case, PBS aired a blockbuster miniseries unwillingly, a program it neither purchased, funded, nor commissioned, and which it fought to keep off the national schedule every step of the way—as it had with the Mobil *Masterpiece Theatre* production of the similarly successful "Upstairs, Downstairs." The year was 1980, the same year *Cosmos* aired, and the program was Milton Friedman's ten-part documentary miniseries *Free to Choose: The Importance of Free Markets to Personal and Political Freedom*. Despite its scheduling problems, the series was extremely successful. The companion volume by Friedman and his wife, Rose, was on the *New York Times* best-seller list for a year and was the best-selling nonfiction book of 1980. The sales, which made Friedman a millionaire, did much to expose American audiences to economic ideas that were crucial to understanding what would be called the Reagan Revolution.

At first glance, the miniseries might have seemed a natural for PBS, which at that time also carried programs such as Louis Rukeyser's *Wall Street Week* and later added *Adam Smith's Money World*. These were simply business shows, however. They did not try to preach the superiority of the free enterprise system or explain the basic economic and historical principles of capitalism. Most certainly, they did not attack, head on, the Keynesian principles undergirding American economic thinking since the end of the Second World War. Although Friedman had appeared as a guest on PBS programs, including *The Advocates* and *Firing Line,* he had never before been permitted to present his monetarist economic analysis in lecture form. *Free to Choose* was different. It was explicitly ideological. And the ideology was robustly free market.

But doing *Free to Choose* for PBS was not Milton Friedman's idea. The program originated as a suggestion by Allen Wallis, an economist serving as chancellor of the University of Rochester who had been appointed to the board of the Corporation for Public Broadcasting by President Gerald Ford. In 1977 Wallis was elected CPB chairman as a "compromise candidate" between the Republican and Democratic appointees. He resigned in 1978, "disgusted" at the system's mismanagement—"CPA firms were certifying statements which were absolutely not valid," Wallis said—but not before he had persuaded the CPB to fund a series of the complete Shakespeare plays produced by the BBC (cosponsored by Metropolitan Life, on whose board Wallis sat) and set the wheels turning for Milton Friedman's *Free to Choose*.[4]

Wallis and Friedman had been graduate students together in the University of Chicago's economics department in the 1930s. Wallis was eager to have his former schoolmate, a leading spokesman for free enterprise, appear on PBS to rebut John Kenneth Galbraith's *Age of Uncertainty,* a 1977 BBC production that presented his defense of Keynesianism. To Galbraith, the trouble with capitalist economies was their unpredictability and lack of security. Galbraith's 1958 book *The Affluent Society* argued that one problem with the American economy was too much emphasis on private consumption and not enough attention to public interests. Like many PBS programs, *The Age of Uncertainty* was supported in part by the Ford Foundation.[5]

Like Friedman, Galbraith had been a familiar face on PBS prior to his series. The Harvard professor of economics and Kennedy administration ambassador to India had appeared on *The Advocates* arguing against Friedman's criticism of President Nixon's wage and price controls in January 1971. Galbraith, too, had been a repeat guest of William F. Buckley on *Firing Line* and shared skiing vacations with Buckley in Gstaad, Switzerland, where they both had second homes.

As economist Thomas Sowell has noted, Galbraith and Friedman represent two conflicting visions, which he calls "unconstrained" and "constrained." Galbraith's "unconstrained" vision holds that it is within the capabilities of man to control the exercise of power and limit it to socially desirable results.[6] Galbraith's solution to economic problems is to increase the power of the state.[7]

The PBS broadcast of Galbraith's series had upset Robert Chitester, station manager of WQLN in Erie, Pennsylvania. A libertarian and a free spirit, Chitester had sided with NET president James Day in voting against the dissolution of National Educational Television and its replacement by PBS. "I was kind of a hippie element at PBS," he said. "I was a nonconformist. I refused to wear a necktie for ten years, anywhere. I was leftist to the degree that I didn't understand what it meant. I had actually campaigned for McGovern because I was livid over what I saw as Nixon's attempt to throttle the free press in the United States."[8]

However, Chitester was a libertarian, not a collectivist, committed to individualism and freedom. He knew Wallis both as an economist who believed in free markets and as chairman of the Corporation for Public Broadcasting. In the spring of 1976, Chitester drove to Rochester to have lunch and ask for Wallis's help producing a response to Galbraith. Wallis was "surprised and pleased" to find a PBS station manager with a free-market perspective.

"We commiserated on the Galbraith series," Chitester recalled. "It was basically a socialist tract, redistributionist, big government. Allen and I were both wringing our hands over the fact that this was going on. True to form, PBS had made no effort to do anything other than to tack on three- to five-minute counterstatements with people like Clay LaForce, then dean of the business school at UCLA. So Galbraith would go on for 55 minutes and then these respondents would get a fraction of that."[9]

At the time, public broadcasters considered Galbraith "a middle-of-the-road person," which troubled Wallis.[10] In the 1950s, Galbraith had been a cold-war liberal and participated in seminars organized by the anti-Communist Congress for Cultural Freedom. In the mid-1960s he defended the organization against charges that it was a CIA front.[11] But Galbraith's opposition to the Vietnam War had pushed him steadily to the left. By 1981 he was described by sociologist Paul Hollander as a "sometime admirer of Mao's China," who saw capitalism as "a source of economic irrationality and wastefulness."[12] Wallis was appalled that someone like Galbraith had been given thirteen hours by PBS to put forward his call for central planning.

While Galbraith was seen as a moderate by PBS, Friedman, who called himself a liberal and who advocated laissez-faire free-market policies, was viewed as an extremist. "The public broadcasting people regarded Friedman as a fascist, an extreme right-winger," Wallis said. "They didn't want to have anything to do with him."[13] Friedman agrees: "From the point of view of the people who were running PBS, Galbraith's series was politically correct and mine was incorrect."[14]

Chitester recalls, "I told Allen I was very keen on producing something that was a counter to Galbraith. He said, 'I know the person who should host that show.' And I said, 'Who?', and he said, 'Milton Friedman.' And I'd have to say that I didn't know who he was talking about." Friedman, however, was not totally unknown to the American public at that time. He had been writing a column for *Newsweek* since 1966 and was a professor in the prestigious economics department at the University of Chicago.

Wallis recalled, "I gave [Chitester] a copy of *Capitalism and Freedom* and he read it. He said 'Are you serious about making a Friedman television series? Would you be willing to give me an introduction?' " Wallis was happy to help.

In the fall of 1976, Chitester put together his PBS proposal. Wallis met with him again and contacted Friedman. "That was the year in which Milton won the Nobel Prize," Chitester recalled. "Allen told me Friedman said he couldn't meet with me before he went to Stockholm, Sweden, retired from the University of Chicago, and moved to San Francisco."

Once Friedman had collected his Nobel Prize, Chitester traveled to San Francisco. The two met in the second week of January 1977 at Friedman's apartment. They had two meetings that week, amounting to ten hours of discussions. One month later, Chitester came back. "I showed him the shows I'd produced. I guaranteed Milton the shows would accurately present his point of view and when it came to the mechanics of creating the show, the actual creative process would be undertaken by the best in the world—and in my view the best documentary producers in the world today are in Britain."

Friedman was not easily convinced. "I was reluctant to do it," he said. "You really have to give my wife credit for persuading me." Finally, after a fourth meeting, Friedman agreed to work with Chitester. But Rose Friedman was not the only one who thought the program a good idea. Chitester recalled: "I showed up that night, and Milton said, 'Bob, it's been an interesting day. I've decided to go ahead with the project.

This morning I received a call from Chuck Lichtenstein at PBS, to say that he had been advocating that PBS should do something counter to Galbraith.'" Lichtenstein, then a vice president of PBS, had known Friedman from his work for Barry Goldwater and Richard Nixon. A former assistant to FCC chairman Dean Burch in the Nixon administration, Lichtenstein was the only Republican executive then at PBS. Chitester recalled that Friedman was happy to report that PBS said "Go ahead" and they offered half a million dollars as startup.

But there was a problem. Chitester felt that PBS wanted him out, or at least moved aside. "Chuck told Milton that I was the manager of a very small station who had no experience doing these things and PBS would be uncomfortable if I were producer. Chuck said, 'We'd like to introduce you to someone at NET, a station with more experience.'" But Lichtenstein's understandable questioning of Chitester's qualifications had bonded Friedman to the entrepreneurial producer from Erie, Pennsylvania. Friedman remained loyal to Chitester, who shared his free-market outlook. He would not do the program without him.

Chitester believed that the resistance to him came from PBS president Larry Grossman and his vice president for programming, Chloe Aaron, both liberal Democrats. "I think Larry Grossman and Chloe Aaron worried that they had no control over me. That was their primary concern, but they couldn't say that to a brash young radical, and I *was* known as a bomb-throwing radical by the people at PBS. I was a radical individualist from the moment I came on this earth. I had no strong party affiliation," he said. Chitester credits his own stubbornness as enabling him to triumph over Grossman's lack of interest. "I didn't convert Larry. I went ahead because I was young and ignorant. I assumed the concept of the program was so powerful and Friedman such a presence that he could not be denied. There was no way PBS could walk away from it. I was coming in as a PBS station, a member station which created a documentary with a Nobel laureate." And Chitester's presence gave Friedman an ally in confronting the PBS brass he might not have had at a more liberal station such as New York's WNET.

"It is my firm belief that they never would have shown [*Free to Choose*] if it had not been that they had shown Ken Galbraith's series. Having shown that, it was difficult for them not to show ours," Friedman recalls, noting, "At the time, remember, Allen Wallis was a member of the governing body [CPB], and our series was closer to his views than Galbraith's."

The next step was to meet personally with PBS executives. In early March 1977, Chitester came to Washington. "I had a one-hour meeting in D.C. with [PBS president] Larry Grossman, [vice president for programming] Chloe Aaron, and Chuck Lichtenstein. The general tone was one of polite and slightly disguised prodding about my abilities to carry off such a project, followed by a growing concern about the approach to the programs. They asked how I intended to have balance in the program. And I said I don't intend to have any balance, in the light of the thirteen hours by Galbraith."

In the end, Friedman and Chitester did preempt criticism by incorporating it into the program format. Nine of the ten episodes consisted of a half-hour presentation by Friedman at locations around the world, followed by a half-hour debate in which he defended himself against a panel of critics, which included self-identified socialist economists such as Robert Lekachman and Frances Fox-Piven as well as free-market advocates like Thomas Sowell. The final hour featured a cross-examination by Lawrence Spivak of NBC's *Meet the Press*. The discussions were included at Friedman's insistence, according to his wife, Rose, who said it was his idea to "have half of the people on his side and half on the opposite." Indeed, during one broadcast Friedman permitted Fox-Piven to attack him on the air for traveling to Chile after Pinochet had deposed Allende in a coup. He later noted that he never met with protests for attending conferences in China, which has a far worse human rights record.[15]

The $500,000 startup money that PBS had earlier mentioned to Friedman "disappeared from the face of the earth," Chitester said. "I heard nothing more from PBS until I had raised a million or more dollars. Then PBS fund-raising people started to call me after they were aware I was being successful, and they told me they were very excited by this project. They asked me, 'Would I be willing to help them?' I didn't get back to them. I didn't tell them 'Go to hell,' but I ignored them."

Despite Chitester's friendship with Wallis, the CPB did not give the project any money, either. "I didn't ask the CPB for money," Chitester said, "because I didn't want any obligation to the establishment, and I had no doubt that I could raise the money myself." Chitester ultimately put together $4 million for the project. The first grant he received was from the Sarah Scaife Foundation for $500,000. The program eventually had over a dozen underwriters, among them the Olin Foundation and Lily Endowment and Firestone, Bechtel, General Motors, Hallmark, and *Reader's Digest*. "The money that came to the show came from people who endorsed Friedman's ideas," Chitester recalled. "We caused a legal semi-crisis at PBS because they had never confronted a show that had so many underwriters. The credits go by so fast you can hardly read them. But the underwriters didn't much care about credit, they just wanted Friedman's ideas to spread."

Meanwhile, PBS kept its distance. "I never got anything from them," Chitester said. "I never got a letter, even one of those worthless pieces of paper saying they are 'interested' in a project, that has nothing whatsoever to do with if a show would get on the air. But there was no way they could deny the program."

Chitester decided to ingratiate his series with the network executives while he was working on it in London. "As soon as we went into production, I brought the PBS programming people into the process on my terms. I put up the money to fly [PBS executives] Chloe Aaron and Barry Chase to London. I treated them royally. So they could see rough cuts of the show, I paid for their trip. They accepted. I provided them with first class airfare to London, I believe, in order to go into the cutting room, to preview, to talk to the producer and myself. As we began to show them the episodes, they critiqued them, they gave notes, and I had the sense that they were going to be as tough on this project as they could possibly manage to be."

At an early stage Milton Friedman contacted Ralph Harris, the founder of London's Institute for Economic Affairs, a free-market think tank, to suggest possible producers. Friedman had known Harris for years, for Friedman was among the original members of the Mount Pelerin society, founded by Nobel Prize–winning economist F. A. von Hayek in 1947 to promote free-market liberalism. Among the organizations that developed from this society was the IEA, to whose journals Friedman became a contributor. By the mid-1970s he had become "the Institute's most celebrated exponent of monetary stability, or what was called monetarism."[16] Harris called Tony Jay, who had been a cocreator of David Frost's *That Was the Week That Was* and later producer of *Yes, Minister* and *Yes, Prime Minister.* Jay was one of the founders and principals of Video Arts, a private television production company specializing in business training videos.

Chitester recalled, "We got in touch with Jay, and he said, 'I don't feel comfortable working with you as an individual, but would with my partners at Video Arts.'" The company's partners included John Cleese (of *Monty Python* and *Fawlty Towers*), BBC veteran Michael Peacock, and Bob Reid, who had been in charge of BBC science programs when Jacob Bronowski had made *The Ascent of Man* there. This suited Chitester perfectly. "I used *Ascent of Man* as a model for what we should create," he said. Video Arts, in turn, lured Michael Latham away from the BBC, where he was a staff producer. It was Latham who came up with the title *Free to Choose.* Rose Friedman recalled, "The title was originally suggested by our producer as the title for our segment on consumers. We thought it was a good title for our series and he agreed." Milton Friedman recalled Latham's expertise. "Two years before the show was on the air, he set down a detailed time schedule, and we ended on the day he had said."

Before the filming began, Friedman delivered fifteen lectures to a number of different audiences. These talks were videotaped, and the texts and tapes were distributed by Harcourt Brace Jovanovich, which had paid for the recordings. William Jovanovich, the publisher, had personally approved the $100,000 expense. The transcripts were used by Friedman as the basis of the scripts for *Free to Choose* and for the companion book written with his wife, Rose, and published in 1979, also by Harcourt Brace Jovanovich.[17]

Production filming took place around the world in 1978 and 1979, from Hong Kong to Las Vegas to Wall Street to Thomas Jefferson's home, Monticello, in Virginia. Friedman's theme was simple. "My god is freedom," he declared. And the free-market system, which respected private property and voluntary exchange, was the best guarantor of that freedom, he believed. The first episode contained perhaps the most persuasive example of how the free market can create cooperation through voluntary exchange for the benefit of mankind.

Friedman held up a simple no. 2 pencil and explained that there was no single person in the world who knew how to make one. The wood came from a tree in Northern California, the graphite from Sri Lanka, the brass ferrule from copper and zinc mines in far-flung locations, and the rubber eraser from Indonesia. Its manufacture involved thousands of people who did not know one another, could not communicate with one another, and did not want to make a pencil. "No one sitting in a central office gave orders to these thousands of people," Friedman noted. "The price system is the mechanism that performs this task without central direction, without requiring people to speak to one another or to like one another." This process illustrated Adam Smith's insight that many people, each seeking his or her own interest, could create the unintended consequence of cooperation in order to make everyone better off.[18] It was a clear and easily understood reply to Galbraith's indictment of capitalism.

The documentary episodes were edited in April and May 1979 in London; the discussions were recorded in Chicago in September. When Friedman went to London to record his voice-over narration, Chitester began talking to PBS about when *Free to Choose* would be scheduled. In June 1979, the network finally decided the broadcasts would start in January 1980, two years after production had begun. "We had hoped to be on the air much earlier," said Chitester, "but as it turned out, that time period was congenial, for it was the beginning of the 1980 presidential campaign. We could not be accused of trying to influence the election, but it made the subject matter relevant and the show would get more attention." Friedman was among presidential candidate Ronald Reagan's economic advisers.

Chitester was unprepared for what came next, however. The PBS executives who controlled scheduling were not willing to give what they perceived as a Reaganite approach to economics the same prime-time slot Galbraith had enjoyed. Chitester assumed he would have precisely the same time slot as Galbraith, based on the principle of balance. "Milton and I were both aware that Galbraith had appeared on Tuesdays at nine in the core PBS schedule. I was brazen enough to say our show would go in the core schedule." But he was wrong. Friedman remembered, "Chitester had one heck of a time even getting a firm commitment when they would show it."

PBS's initial time slot was Friday evening at 10. Friday was a low viewership night, because many people went out to movies and social events; and all of Friday night was outside the core PBS schedule. "Milton was livid, partly at me, because he thought I'd misled him," Chitester said. "So what we did was a full-court press." Chitester and Friedman alerted their friends, among them Allen Wallis. "I have no idea what was done, but in my direct discussions with PBS the compromise we came to was nine o'clock, but on Friday night, so it was still not a high sets-in-use night. Therefore there was no legal incentive for stations to carry the program as fed."

Rose Friedman remembered, "PBS did not cooperate. In New York they showed it opposite the Super Bowl. But after complaints from contributors, they showed it again." After three weeks of giving it Sunday-afternoon slots and receiving viewer protests, Channel 13 scheduled repeats on Tuesday nights at 10. "We were ecstatic," said Chitester. The program was sold to television stations all over the world. Videotapes were made available to schools and colleges throughout the United States. Milton Friedman became a household name. While his 1962 book *Capitalism and Freedom* had not been reviewed by a single non-technical publication except *The Economist,* the book version of *Free to Choose,* with its TV tie-in, was widely reviewed in newspapers and magazines. It was impossible to ignore. "I believe *Free to Choose* had a larger audience than *The Age of Uncertainty*," Friedman modestly noted, "despite all of the best efforts of the PBS bureaucracy."[19]

Allen Wallis said, "I wasn't particularly aware of it at the time, but I do know now that it had a tremendous influence, because I often run into people who say how much it had influenced them." The broadcast of *Free to Choose* brought the ideas of one of Ronald Reagan's principal economic advisers to a larger audience than ever before and might even have played a role in his winning the 1980 election.

However, the experience left Friedman deeply skeptical of PBS. "There is no doubt that the PBS bureaucracy would have been happier if they had never aired the show," he said. "Having accomplished their purpose of demonstrating their evenhandedness by showing me as well as Galbraith, PBS has since been unreceptive to ideas." After the fall of the Berlin Wall, PBS refused to update four original *Free to Choose* episodes with a special half-hour featuring new discussions and a fifth program filmed in Poland and Hungary.

"You have to know what people's incentives are," Friedman explains. At PBS, "they are not running a for-profit enterprise, they are running an ideological enterprise. Ideology is the foremost consideration. I have been very impressed by the way that PBS has tried to show critics [that it is balanced] by showing conservative programs with no ideological content. No one who saw them would be persuaded to convert to conservatism." On the other hand, he notes, unlike the nonideological "conservative" programs on PBS, "A large fraction of left-wing programs they show are highly ideological attempts to change people's attitudes. The real objection to *Free to Choose* was that it was directed toward changing people's ideas. It was full of ideological content."[20]

Milton Friedman's experience with public television provides a fitting conclusion to a study of PBS. In *Capitalism and Freedom,* Friedman explains the principle whereby the market protects those who wish to advocate unpopular ideas. "The suppliers of paper are as willing to sell it to the *Daily Worker* as to the *Wall Street Journal,*" he notes. "In a socialist society, it would not be enough to have the funds. The hypothetical supporter of capitalism would have to persuade a government factory making paper to sell to him, the government printing press to print his pamphlets, a government press office to distribute them among the people, a government agency to rent him a hall in which to talk, and so on."[21]

In a sense, this is what Friedman had to do with *Free to Choose.* He succeeded only because the PBS network existed within the framework of a larger capitalist society. For Friedman depended on market forces and private sponsors to get his program on the air against the wishes of the network executives. The series never appeared in the national core schedule. It received not a penny of federal funding. It was a privately sponsored, commercial enterprise that gave Friedman his freedom to speak to the PBS audience.

But this experience surely did not surprise him. Friedman was aware of the dangers to freedom that systems such as PBS represented even when he published *Capitalism and Freedom* in 1962. In it he chillingly described the precedent of Winston Churchill:

> From 1933 to the outbreak of World War II, Churchill was not permitted to talk over the British radio, which was, of course, a government monopoly administered by the British Broadcasting Corporation. Here was a leading citizen of his country, a Member of Parliament, a former cabinet minister, a man who was desperately trying by every device possible

to persuade his countrymen to ward off the menace of Hitler's Germany. He was not permitted to talk over the radio to the British people because the BBC was a government monopoly and his position was too "controversial."[22]

Time and personal experience have not changed Friedman's analysis that "the groups in our society that have the most at stake in the preservation and strengthening of competitive capitalism are those minority groups which can most easily become the object of the distrust and enmity of the majority."[23] It is for this reason, among others, that Friedman remains adamant in his view that a free market is a necessary condition for a genuine marketplace of ideas. The Nobel Prize–winning host of what was, undoubtedly, among the most special of PBS specials is in favor of abolishing federal funding for PBS. Friedman's principle is clear: "I do not believe that the government ought to be in the position of using other people's money to try and change people's values."[24] His own experience is evidence for the rightness of this judgment.

The best possible future would be for PBS to recognize that freedom of expression is strengthened, not weakened, by the dynamics of the marketplace. A nonprofit, nonmarket system ruled by bureaucratic whim in response to political pressures—a fair description of the current status of PBS—reduces the range of possible programming available to viewers. If one truly values freedom, especially freedom of speech, one must honestly recognize that a free marketplace of ideas cannot possibly exist in an intellectual and administrative environment hostile to the very concept of the free market itself.

Notes

Chapter 1

1. Letter from Joseph Iseman, Esq., to Newton Minow, July 26, 1962, Newton Minow Papers, State Historical Society of Wisconsin (SHSW), Madison.
2. "Inaugural Program of Channel 13," script, Minow papers, SHSW.
3. NET press release, September 6, 1962, National Educational Television (NET) papers, SHSW.
4. "Inaugural Program of Channel 13."
5. "Opening Night at WNDT," *Saturday Review*, September 29, 1962.
6. John Witherspoon and Roselle Kovitz, *The History of Public Broadcasting* (Washington: Current Publishing, 1989), pp. 7–8.
7. Witherspoon and Kovitz, *A Tribal Memory of Public Broadcasting,* unpublished manuscript, Corporation for Public Broadcasting (CPB), Washington, D.C., July 1986, p. 14.
8. Witherspoon and Kovitz, *History of Public Broadcasting,* p. 8, and *Tribal Memory,* p. 15.
9. Witherspoon and Kovitz, *Tribal Memory,* p. 21.
10. Jim Robertson, *Televisionaries* (Charlotte Harbor, Fla.: Tabby House, 1993), p. 66.
11. James Day, *The Vanishing Vision: The Inside Story of Public Television* (Berkeley: University of California Press, 1995), p. 20.
12. Witherspoon and Kovitz, *Tribal Memory,* p. 24.
13. Les Brown, *Encyclopedia of Television* (New York: Zoetrope, 1982), p. 345.
14. Frederick Jauch, *A True Fourth Network: Why and How* (New York: NET, 1962), John F. White Papers, National Public Broadcasting Archives (NPBA), University of Maryland.
15. John F. White papers, NPBA.

16. Barbara Delatiner, "NET President Quits to Head University," *Newsday,* March 13, 1969.

17. "Whatever Happened to 'Educational Television'?," *Change,* May 1972.

18. An account of this from Day's perspective can be found in *The Vanishing Vision,* pp.193–197. This account is drawn from the John F. White papers, NPBA.

19. Jack Gould, "FCC to Study NBC Motive in $100,000 gift to Channel 13," *New York Times,* April 29, 1963.

20. Jack Gould, "No Terms Tied to WNDT Gift, Dr. Gould and NBC Maintain," *New York Times,* April 30, 1963.

21. Robertson, *Televisionaries,* p. 203.

22. Minow papers, SHSW.

23. David M. Stone, *Nixon and the Politics of Public Broadcasting* (New York: Garland, 1985), p. 61.

24. Ibid., p. 10.

25. Ellen Condliffe Lagemann, *The Politics of Knowledge: The Carnegie Corporation, Philanthropy, and Public Policy* (Middletown, Conn.: Wesleyan University Press, 1989), pp. 222–26.

26. Doris Kearns, *Lyndon Johnson and the American Dream* (New York: Harper & Row, 1976), p. l00.

27. Lagemann, *Politics of Knowledge,* p. 223.

28. Interview with Douglass Cater, Montgomery, Ala., October 19, 1992.

29. Interview with Jack Valenti, Washington, D.C., 1992.

30. Cater interview.

31. Stone, *Nixon and the Politics of Public Broadcasting,* p. 23.

32. Day, *Vanishing Vision,* p. 137.

33. For a full account of this period, see Stone's *Nixon and the Politics of Public Broadcasting.*

34. Interview with Clay T. Whitehead, McLean, Va., December 17, 1991.

35. Stone, *Nixon and the Politics of Public Broadcasting,* p. 56.

36. Interview with Alistair Cooke, New York, June 19, 1990.

37. Stone, *Nixon and the Politics of Public Broadcasting,* p. 28.

38. Ibid., p. 55.

39. Day, *Vanishing Vision,* p. 220.

40. Valenti interview.

41. Telephone interview with Peter Flanigan, 1992.

42. Leonard Goldenson, *Beating the Odds* (New York: Scribners, 1991), p. 339.

43. Stone, *Nixon and the Politics of Public Broadcasting,* pp. 104–5.

44. Witherspoon and Kovitz, *Tribal Memory,* pp. 103–53.

45. Stone, *Nixon and the Politics of Public Broadcasting,* pp. 178–80.

46. Interview with David M. Davis, Los Angeles, January 12, 1991.

47. Interview with Ralph Rogers, Dallas, Tex., March 11, 1992.

Chapter 2

1. Jeanne Marie Laskas, "What Is Essential Is Invisible to the Eye," in *Mister Rogers' Neighborhood: Children, Television, and Fred Rogers,* Mark Collins and Margaret Mary Kimmer, ed. (Pittsburgh: University of Pittsburgh Press, 1996), p. 20.
2. Ibid., p. 31.
3. Ibid., p. 28.
4. Interview with John F. White, Washington, D.C., May 14, 1993.
5. Interview with Lloyd Morrisett, New York, December 30, 1991.
6. Interview with Joan Ganz Cooney, New York, May 10, 1994.
7. Interview with Lewis Freedman, Chicago, May 23, 1992.
8. Cooney interview. Also see Gerald S. Lesser, *Children and Television: Lessons from Sesame Street* (New York: Vintage Books, 1974), pp. 186–7.
9. Cooney interview.
10. Morrisett interview.
11. Cooney interview. Also James Day, manuscript, "More Than Meets the Eye: America's Reticent Affair with Public Broadcasting" (New York: Publivision, 1990), National Public Broadcasting Archives (NPBA), University of Maryland.
12. Cooney interview. Also see Lesser, *Children and Television.*
13. Day, "More Than Meets the Eye," p. 221.
14. Morrisett interview.
15. Day, "More Than Meets the Eye," p. 192.
16. Cooney interview.
17. Ibid.
18. Ellen Edwards, "The Kids Crusader: Peggy Charren, Still Plugging Away at the Horrors in TV Land," *Washington Post,* August 2, 1993, p. B1.
19. Interview with Monica Sims, London, April 10, 1996.
20. Kay Hymowitz, "On *Sesame Street* It's All Show," *City Journal,* Autumn 1995, pp. 60–69.
21. John C. Wright and Aletha C. Huston, "Effects of Educational TV Viewing on Lower Income Preschoolers," Center for Research on the Influences of TV on Children, Department of Human Development, University of Kansas, Lawrence, May 1995.
22. Billy Tashman, "E-Z Street: 25 Years and Still Counting," *The Village Voice,* November 23, 1993, p. 56.
23. Lesser, *Children and Television,* pp. 186–7.
24. Cy Schneider, *Children's Television* (Chicago: NTC Business Books, 1987), p. 174.
25. Interview with Charles Lichtenstein, Washington, D.C., June 15, 1993.
26. Cooney interview.
27. Elizabeth Jensen, "Barney and Friends: Public TV Prepares for Image Transplant to Justify Existence," *Wall Street Journal,* January 13, 1994, p. 1.
28. Damon Darlin, "Highbrow Hype," *Forbes,* April 12, 1993, p. 126.

Chapter 3

1. Jon Katz, "Why Bill Moyers Shouldn't Run for President," *New York Times,* March 8, 1992.
2. Frank Donner, *The Age of Surveillance* (New York: Knopf, 1980), pp. 216–7.
3. Telephone interview with Morley Safer, June 14, 1996.
4. Morley Safer, *Flashbacks: On Returning to Vietnam* (New York: St. Martin's Press, 1990), pp. 148–51.
5. Andrew Ferguson, "The Power of Myth," *New Republic,* August 19 and 26, 1991.
6. Bill Moyers, "An Open Letter to the Editor from Bill Moyers," *New Republic,* September 2, 1991.
7. David Halberstam, *The Best and the Brightest* (New York: Random House, 1972), p. 437.
8. Bill Moyers, Memorandum to the President, August 1–15, 1965, Handwriting File, Box 9, Presidential Papers, Lyndon Baines Johnson Library, Austin, Texas.
9. Safer, *Flashbacks,* pp. 148–51.
10. Merle Miller, *Lyndon: An Oral Biography* (New York: Ballantine, 1980), p. 586.
11. Michael Good, "Bill Moyers Fights the Good Fight," *OnAir* magazine (KPBS, San Diego), June 1994, p. 20.
12. Robert F. Keeler, *Newsday: A Candid History of the Respectable Tabloid* (New York: Arbor House, 1990), p. 387.
13. Donner, *Age of Surveillance,* p. 351.
14. Keeler, *Newsday: A Candid History,* p. 387.
15. Halberstam, *The Best and the Brightest,* p. 40.
16. Keeler, *Newsday: A Candid History,* p. 387.
17. Miller, *Lyndon,* p. 410.
18. David Halberstam, *The Powers That Be* (New York: Knopf, 1979), p. 531.
19. Doris Kearns, *Lyndon Johnson and the American Dream* (New York: Harper & Row, 1976), p. 240.
20. Halberstam, *The Powers That Be,* p. 543.
21. Nicholas Katzenbach, Memo regarding the death of President Kennedy, Box 55, office files of Bill Moyers, LBJ Library.
22. Miller, *Lyndon,* p. 626.
23. Associated Press, "Capital Festivity: He Objects to Dancing Till Dawn by Top Officials," *New York Times,* May 12, 1966.
24. Halberstam, *The Best and the Brightest,* pp. 220, 497, 626.
25. Keeler, *Newsday: A Candid History,* p. 390.
26. Harry F. Guggenheim papers, Library of Congress, Washington, D.C.
27. Keeler, *Newsday: A Candid History,* p. 389.
28. Ibid., p. 391.
29. Miller, *Lyndon,* p. 586.
30. Keeler, *Newsday: A Candid History,* p. 392.
31. "Moyers Hospitalized Before Johnson Rites," *New York Times,* January 26, 1973.
32. Keeler, *Newsday: A Candid History,* p. 394.

33. Bernard Weinraub, "Moyers to Shun Role in Politics," *New York Times,* February 16, 1967.

34. Keeler, *Newsday: A Candid History,* p. 400.

35. Ibid., p. 414.

36. John H. Davis, *The Guggenheims: An American Epic* (New York: Shapolsky Publishers, 1988), pp. 26–7.

37. Joseph Goulden, *Fit to Print: A. M. Rosenthal and His Times* (New York: Lyle Stuart, 1988), p. 149.

38. Keeler, *Newsday: A Candid History,* p. 457.

39. Ibid., pp. 461–2.

40. Henry Raymont, "Newsday Employees Seek to Block Sale of Paper," *New York Times,* March 13, 1970.

41. Keeler, *Newsday: A Candid History,* pp. 471, 476.

42. Halberstam, *The Best and the Brightest,* pp. 32–4.

43. Alexander R. Hammer, "Technology Concern Weathers Shift in Politics," *New York Times,* July 6, 1969.

44. Jane Chekenian, "Bill Moyers Now Enjoying Pace of Suburban Living," *New York Times,* October 28, 1973.

45. John J. O'Connor, "TV: Away from Rigidity," *New York Times,* March 16, 1972.

46. "Econometrics—Making It Pay for the Founding Fathers," *New York Times,* October 31, 1976.

47. James Day, *The Vanishing Vision: The Inside Story of Public Television* (Berkeley: University of California Press, 1996), p. 249.

48. Don Hewitt, *Minute by Minute* (New York: Random House, 1985), p. 111.

49. Halberstam, *The Powers That Be,* p. 734.

50. Ed Joyce, *Prime Times, Bad Times* (New York: Doubleday, 1988), p. 35.

51. Reed Irvine, Accuracy in Media (AIM) Report, 1978.

52. Gary Paul Gates, *Air Time: The Inside Story of CBS News* (New York: Harper & Row, 1978), p. 418.

53. Carey Winfrey, "Moyers: A Regular Audience Is Better Than a Big One," *New York Times,* February 1, 1979.

54. Tony Schwartz, "Moyers Returns to CBS," *New York Times,* May 2, 1981.

55. Joyce, *Prime Times, Bad Times,* pp. 103–04.

56. Van Gorden Sauter, fax to author, September 26, 1996.

57. Joyce, *Prime Times, Bad Times,* pp. 187–88, 236.

58. Ibid., p. 344.

59. Ibid., p. 356.

60. Ibid., p. 392.

61. Alan Bernson, letter to Bill Moyers, May 11, 1991. Copy in possession of author.

62. Letter, *Comint,* 1994, vol. 4, no. 3, pp. 12–5.

63. Paul Berman, "Gas Chamber Games: Crackpot History and the Right to Lie," *The Village Voice,* June 10, 1981.

64. Werner Cohn, *The Hidden Alliances of Noam Chomsky* (New York: Americans for a Safe Israel, 1988), p. 57.

65. Bill Moyers, *A World of Ideas: Conversations with Thoughtful Men and Women about American Life Today and the Ideas Shaping Our Future,* ed. Betty Sue Flowers (New York: Doubleday, 1989), p. 57.

66. Personal comment to author on background, Washington, D.C., 1993.

67. Moyers, *A World of Ideas,* pp. 20, 23.

Chapter 4

1. Robert MacNeil, *The Right Place at the Right Time* (Boston: Little, Brown, 1982), p. 30.

2. Les Brown, *Encyclopedia of Television* (New York: Zoetrope, 1982), p. 208.

3. Interview with Robert MacNeil, New York, May 19, 1993; MacNeil, *Right Place.*

4. See MacNeil's confessional account in Todd Gitlin's *The Sixties: Years of Hope, Days of Rage* (New York: Bantam, 1987), p. 278.

5. Jon M. Huntsman, Memorandum for Peter Flanigan, September 23, 1971, National Public Broadcasting Archives (NPBA), University of Maryland.

6. James Day, *The Vanishing Vision: The Inside Story of Public Television* (Berkeley: University of California Press, 1995), p. 142.

7. Interview with Jim Karayn, Washington, D.C., April 9, 1994.

8. Jim Lehrer, *A Bus of My Own* (New York: Putnam, 1992), p. 113.

9. MacNeil, *Right Place,* p. 281.

10. Ibid., p. 282.

11. Interview with Al Vecchione, Washington, D.C., November 2, 1992.

12. MacNeil, *Right Place,* p. 286.

13. Ibid.; MacNeil interview.

14. Vecchione interview.

15. Lehrer, *A Bus of My Own,* p. 114.

16. Ibid., pp. 112–21.

17. MacNeil, *Right Place,* p. 287.

18. Lehrer, *A Bus of My Own,* p. 121.

19. MacNeil, *Right Place,* p. 288.

20. Lehrer, *A Bus of My Own,* p. 112.

21. Ibid., pp. 124–25.

22. MacNeil, *Right Place,* p. 289.

23. Lehrer, *A Bus of My Own,* pp. 126–28.

24. Ibid., p. 132.

25. MacNeil, *Right Place,* p. 307.

26. Mary Marshall Clark, *Interviews with Charlayne Hunter-Gault* (Washington Press Club Foundation, 1994), pp. 37, 42.

27. Lehrer, *A Bus of My Own,* p. 230.

28. Susan Jane Labaschin, *Towards a Unified Field Theory of Television News,* doctoral dissertation, New York University, UMI, 1987.

29. Marshall Clark, *Interviews,* p. 53.

Chapter 5

1. *"Frontline: A Brief History,"* press materials, WGBH, Boston, 1991.
2. Don Kowet, "Frontline: Fanning Flame of Controversy; Cameras Focus on Chic, Radical Point of View," *Washington Times,* February 20, 1990.
3. Peter Johnson, "Staffers Grade the Newsmags," USA *Today,* August 19, 1993.
4. Interview with Lewis Freedman, Chicago, April 23, 1992.
5. Ibid.
6. James Day, *The Vanishing Vision: The Inside Story of Public Television* (Berkeley: University of California Press, 1995), p. 268.
7. Kowet, "Frontline."
8. Ed Siegel, "Can This Network Be Saved?" *Boston Globe,* July 11, 1990.
9. Robert Levey, "Discussion to Be Aired After 'Princess': WGBH Plans to Televise Controversial Movie Despite Saudi Arabia's Protest," *Boston Globe,* May 10, 1980.
10. Associated Press, "Ch. 2 to Air 'Princess'; Mobil Suggests Review," *Boston Globe,* May 8, 1980.
11. Interview with Larry Grossman, New York, May 19, 1993.
12. Interview with Henry Becton, Los Angeles, January 12, 1991.
13. Conversation with William Cran, Los Angeles, January 12, 1991.
14. Tom Jory, Associated Press, " 'Frontline' Controversy Preceded Debut," *Boston Globe,* January 17, 1983.
15. Associated Press, "Ch. 2 to Air 'Princess.' "
16. Peter J. Boyer, Associated Press, "A Film's New Controversy," *Boston Globe,* May 19, 1980.
17. Patricia Brennan, " 'Frontline': A Decade of Prize-Winning Documentaries," *Washington Post,* October 13, 1991.
18. Alanna Nash, *Golden Girl* (New York: HarperCollins, 1996 ed.), pp. 351–53.
19. Ibid., p. 365.
20. Ibid., p. 364.
21. William Taafe, "Unfounded Findings," *Sports Illustrated,* January 31, 1983.
22. Michael Kernan, " 'The Russians Are Here' on WETA: Meeting the Dark Side of Freedom," *The Washington Post,* June 13, 1983.
23. Jack Thomas, "Here's Looking at You, Tube," *Boston Globe,* December 30, 1983.
24. Ibid.
25. Ed Siegel, "An Eye on the Shallow," *Boston Globe,* April 9, 1988.
26. Howard Kurtz, "Media Notes: 'Frontline' Repeat Pulled," *Washington Post,* February 19, 1991.
27. Telephone interviews with Austin Hoyt and Neal Freeman, July 1996.
28. Brennan, " 'Frontline.' "
29. Thomas B. Edsall, " 'Defunding' Public Broadcasting: Conservative Goal Gains Audience," *Washington Post,* April 15, 1995.
30. David Muska, " 'Frontline': Conservatives Need Not Apply," unpublished manuscript (Alexandria, Va.: Media Research Center, 1993).
31. Ibid.

32. Jess N. Hordes, Statement of the Anti-Defamation League before the Corporation for Public Broadcasting, Washington, D.C., December 12, 1994. Corporation for Public Broadcasting (CPB), Washington, D.C.

33. Conversations with Andrea Levin, Boston and Washington, D.C., 1995.

34. David Bar-Ilan, "Public TV Makes Commercial Networks Look Benign," *Jerusalem Post,* August 12, 1994.

35. Alex Safian, "PBS and Israel: A Pattern of Bias: The Case of 'Journey to the Occupied Lands,'" unpublished monograph, CAMERA, Boston, August 1994.

36. Letter from Donald Quayle to CAMERA, 1995.

37. Jerrold S. Auerbach, "Journey to Fantasy Land," *The Jewish Advocate,* February 5–11, 1993.

38. Sandy Heberer, letter to Alex Safian, February 7, 1994, copy in possession of author.

39. Robert Israel, "CAMERA Charges Fraud in PBS Doc," *The Jewish Advocate,* July 29–August 4, 1994.

40. Statement of Alex Safian, Hearing Before the Subcommittee on Telecommunications and Finance, U.S. House of Representatives, September 12, 1994; and Statement of Alex Safian, Hearing Before the Subcommitteee on Appropriations, Labor, Health, and Human Services, January 19, 1995.

41. K. Quattrone, "To: General Station Manager and All PTV Stations, Subject: 'Journey to the Occupied Lands' and CAMERA," PBS DACS message, April 3, 1995.

42. Alex Safian, "Frontline's Internal Review of 'Journey to the Occupied Lands': A Brief CAMERA Response," CAMERA, Boston, 1995.

43. Alex Beam, " 'Frontline' Admits Mideast Missteps," *Boston Globe,* April 28, 1995.

44. "Memorandum to All Past Purchasers of Videocassettes or Transcripts of 'Journey to the Occupied Lands,' from *Frontline,*" June 12, 1995, WGBH, Boston.

Chapter 6

1. Telephone interview with Sonia Landau, January 20, 1995.

2. Tom Shales, "Pfister Resigns CPB Post, Political Interference Cited in Decision," *Washington Post,* May 17, 1985.

3. David Stewart, "Memorandum to U.S. Public Broadcasting Delegation to Russia," March 28, 1985, Corporation for Public Broadcasting (CPB), Washington, D.C.

4. Elisa Tinsley, "Russian TV in a Nutshell: Dull: Government Ideology Dominates Programming," *Electronic Media,* February 28, 1985.

5. Los Angeles Times Syndicate, "Soviet TV Mostly Propaganda," *Ottawa Citizen,* February 19, 1985.

6. David J. Brugger and David Stewart, "Memorandum to CPB Board of Directors, Re: International Activities Review," May 9, 1985, CPB.

7. Stu Kantor, "Report to Managers," September 9, 1985, PBS.

8. Minutes of the Missions and Goals Committee, Board of Directors, CPB, June 27, 1985.

9. Hon. John Dingell, letter to Martin Rubenstein, CPB president, July 10, 1986.

10. Martin Rubenstein, letter to Hon. John Dingell, July 18, 1986.

11. Ralph Engelman, *Public Radio and Television in America: A Political History* (Thousand Oaks, Calif.: Sage Publications, 1996), p. 189.

12. Interview with R. Kenneth Towery, Austin, Tex., March 13, 1992. Also see R. Kenneth Towery, *The Chow Dipper* (Austin, Tex.: Eakin Press, 1994), pp. 380–405.

13. Interview with Howard Gutin, San Antonio, Tex., March 12, 1992.

14. William Grimes, "Following the Flow of America's Narrative," *New York Times,* August 4, 1996.

15. Ibid.

16. WGBH Website, July 1996.

17. Telephone interview with Howard Gutin, July 1996.

18. Richard Bernstein, "Doubts Mar PBS Film of Black Army Unit," *New York Times,* March 1, 1993.

19. William Miles and Nina Rosenblum, "Liberators: Fighting on Two Fronts in World War II" (Santa Monica, Calif.: Direct Cinema Limited, 1992); Lou Potter with William Miles and Nina Rosenblum, *Liberators: Fighting on Two Fronts in World War II* (New York: Harcourt Brace Jovanovich, 1992).

20. Jeffrey Goldberg, "Exaggerators: Black Soldiers and Buchenwald," *New Republic,* February 8, 1993, pp. 13–4.

21. Ibid., p. 13.

22. Telephone interview with Jim Dingeman, n.d.

23. Ibid.

24. Correspondence and interviews with Colonel James S. Moncrief, Jr., 1994–96.

25. Moncrief, letter to Ervin Duggan, August 14, 1996. Copy in possession of author.

26. Telephone interview with Margaret Drain, n.d.

27. Dingeman interview.

28. Moncrief correspondence and interviews.

29. WNET press release, February 2, 1993.

30. Kenneth S. Stern, " 'Liberators': A Background Report," American Jewish Committee, February 10, 1993.

31. WNET press release, February 11, 1993.

32. William Miles and Nina Rosenblum, "The Filmmakers' Response to Kenneth Stern's Report to the American Jewish Committee," March 5, 1993.

33. Morton Silverstein, et al., "Findings of the Review Team: An Examination of 'Liberators: Fighting on Two Fronts in World War II,' " WNET, August 19, 1993.

34. WNET press release, September 7, 1993.

35. John Carmody, "Report on a Controversy," *Washington Post,* September 8, 1993.

36. Hon. Greg Laughlin, letter to author and enclosures, June 7, 1994.

37. Col. James S. Moncrief, Jr., prepared statement, Hearing Before the Subcommittee on Telecommunications and Finance, U.S. House of Representatives, September 12, 1994.

38. Ibid.

39. Chuck Haga, "The Last Battle of World War II: Sixth Armored Division Wants Credit for Liberating Buchenwald," *Minneapolis Star Tribune,* September 16, 1994.
40. Telephone interview with Mel Rappaport, 1994.
41. Moncrief interview.

Chapter 7

1. Stephen B. Jones and Willard D. Rowland, Jr., NET *Programming: A History and Appreciation of the Programming Service of National Educational Television, 1952–1970,* Contract #A86-31, February 16, 1990, p. 58, Library of Congress, Washington, D.C.
2. NET, *A Progress Report 1967–68,* "Specials," p. 9, Library of Congress, Washington, D.C.
3. John F. White, "A Report to the Affiliates," Statler Hilton Hotel, New York, April 22, 1968. John F. White papers, National Public Broadcasting Archives (NPBA), University of Maryland.
4. Jones and Rowland, NET *Programming,* p. 86.
5. Lawrence Laurent, "President of NET Resigns," *Washington Post,* March 13, 1969.
6. James Day, *The Vanishing Vision: The Inside Story of Public Television* (Berkeley: University of California Press, 1995), p. 170.
7. Telephone interview with Donald Fouser, July 1996.
8. Telephone interview with Victor Palmieri, July 1996.
9. Roger Fisher, ed., *International Conflict and Behavioral Science: The Craigville Papers* (New York: Basic Books, 1964).
10. Telephone interview with Alan Dershowitz, July 1996.
11. Telephone interview with Austin Hoyt, July 1996.
12. Telephone interview with Roger Fisher, July 1996.
13. W. D. Rowland, "Analysis of Pro and Con Topic—Vote and Popularity Poll Data for The Advocates, 1970–71," unpublished research paper, 1971, PBS. Copy in possession of author.
14. John Macy, letter to Daniel Patrick Moynihan, November 25, 1970, NPBA.
15. Daniel Patrick Moynihan, letter to John Macy, November 30, 1970, NPBA.
16. Daniel P. Moynihan, memorandum for H. R. Haldeman, November 30, 1970, NPBA.
17. H. R. Haldeman, memorandum to Peter Flanigan, Leonard Garment, and Herbert Klein, "Subject: Televised Debates," December 2, 1970, NPBA.
18. Peter Flanigan, memorandum for Clay Whitehead, December 4, 1970, NPBA.
19. Clay Whitehead, memorandum for H. R. Haldeman, December 8, 1970, NPBA.
20. WGBH, *The Case for The Advocates,* Boston, 1973.

Chapter 8

1. Peter Steinfels, *The Neoconservatives* (New York: Touchstone, 1979), p. 159.
2. Chester Finn, "Memorandum to Daniel P. Moynihan, Concerning: Public Television," July 1, 1969, National Public Broadcasting Archives (NPBA), University of Maryland.
3. Clay T. Whitehead, "Memorandum for Mr. Flanigan," August 7, 1969, NPBA.
4. Richard P. Nathan, "Memorandum for Clay Whitehead, Subject: Corporation for Public Broadcasting," September 25, 1969, NPBA.
5. Bill Duke, "Memorandum to Pete Flanigan re: 'Programs of Particular Interest,' " November 26, 1969, NPBA.
6. John Macy, letter to the President, December 18, 1969, NPBA.
7. Jim Robertson, *Televisionaries* (Charlotte Harbor, Fla.: Tabby House Books, 1992), pp. 121–24.
8. Telephone interview with Henry Cauthen, July 1996.
9. William F. Buckley, *On the Firing Line* (New York: Random House, 1989), pp. 56–7.
10. Telephone interview with Neal Freeman, July 1996.
11. Alistair Cooke, foreword to *On the Firing Line*, p. xiii.
12. Telephone interview with Warren Steibel, July 1996.
13. John Judis, *William F. Buckley: Patron Saint of Conservatives* (New York: Touchstone, 1990), pp. 267–8.
14. Cooke, foreword to *On the Firing Line*, p. xiv.
15. Telephone interview with Milton Friedman, July 11, 1996.
16. David M. Stone, *Nixon and the Politics of Public Television* (New York: Garland, 1985), p. 120.
17. Telephone interview with William F. Buckley, Jr., July 1996.
18. Buckley, *On the Firing Line*, pp. 56–7.
19. Ibid., pp. 362–86.
20. Ibid., p. 366.
21. Ibid., p. 205.
22. Telephone interview with Alan Dershowitz, July 1996.
23. Steibel interview.
24. Ibid.
25. Buckley interview.
26. William F. Buckley, *Overdrive* (New York: Doubleday, 1982), p. 122.
27. Christopher Hitchens, *Blood, Class and Nostalgia* (New York: Farrar, Straus, 1990), pp. 41–2.
28. Richard Sandomir, "Just Another Talk Show, Wronnnggg!!!" *New York Times,* December 6, 1992.
29. Reed Irvine, "Notes from the Editor's Cuff," *AIM Report*, March-B, 1985.
30. Ibid., July-A, 1985.

31. David Chanoff, "Biased Series on Vietnam," *Boston Globe,* June 25, 1985.
32. Irvine, "Notes from the Editor's Cuff," November-A, 1985.
33. Reed Irvine, "Give Up on Public Broadcasting," *Wall Street Journal,* March 28, 1986.
34. William Rusher, *The Coming Battle for the Media* (New York: William Morrow, 1988), p. 113.
35. Buckley interview.
36. Ibid.

Chapter 9

1. "The Most-Watched PBS-Distributed Programs (as of August 1992)," *Facts About PBS* (Alexandria, Va.: PBS, January 1993), p. 12.
2. David Marc and Robert J. Thompson, *Prime Time, Prime Movers* (Syracuse, N.Y.: Syracuse University Press), p. 290.
3. Les Brown, *Encylopedia of Television* (New York: Zoetrope, 1982), pp. 470–1.
4. Charles Montgomery Hammond, *The Image Decade* (New York: Hastings House, 1981), p. 156.
5. Interview with Stan Calderwood, Boston, 1991.
6. Telephone interview with Michael Ambrosino, 1995.
7. Brown, *Encyclopedia of Television,* p. 310.
8. Marcia Smilack, "The Truth About Murder," *Boston Globe Magazine,* February 15, 1981.
9. "Secret of the Wild Child," *Nova,* broadcast November 18, 1994.
10. "Daredevils of the Sky," *Nova,* broadcast February 1, 1994.
11. "Aircraft Carrier!" *Nova,* broadcast April 19, 1994.
12. Andy Merton, "What Makes WGBH Crackle with Creativity," *New York Times,* August 15, 1975.
13. *1992 Broadcast Television Index* (Denver, Col.: Journal Graphics, 1993), pp. 629–44, 857–71.
14. Margaret Morris, letter to the author, January 14, 1995; Margaret Morris, letter to Michael Barnes, August 14, 1994. Copies in possession of author.
15. *Nature* press conference transcript, PBS, 1995.
16. Ed Siegel, "PBS Lineup: Too Many Valleys, Too Few Peaks," *Boston Globe,* January 19, 1986.
17. George Page, press conference, PBS Press Tour, Los Angeles, Calif., July 1994.
18. "Nova Finds Paradise," *Wall Street Journal,* January 11, 1995.

Chapter 10

1. Edwin Glick, *WGBH-TV: The First Ten Years,* doctoral dissertation, University of Michigan, UMI, 1970.
2. Ibid., p. 152.

3. Jewell Fenzi and Carl L. Nelson, "Bon Appetit Julia Child. From Foreign Service Wife to French Chef," *Foreign Service Journal,* November 1992, pp. 40–3.

4. Edgar J. Driscoll, Jr., "Paul Child. At Age 92, Was Artist and Retired Foreign Service Officer" *Boston Globe,* May 14, 1994.

5. Julia Child, *Mastering the Art of French Cooking* (New York: Knopf, 1961), p. vii.

6. Glick, *WGBH-TV,* p. 111.

7. Jim Robertson, *Televisionaries* (Charlotte Harbor, Fla.: Tabby House Books, 1993), p. 49.

8. Betty Harper Fussell, *Masters of American Cookery* (New York: Times Books, 1983), p. 47.

9. Ibid.

10. "Broadcast Views," *The New Republic,* October 2, 1989, p. 8.

11. "A New Master of Renovation on 'Old House,'" *New York Times,* August 10, 1989.

12. Ed Siegel, "Slight Rehab on 'Old House,'" *Boston Globe,* October 12, 1988.

13. "Talking Shop with Norm Abram," *WGBH Magazine,* February 1991, pp. 14–5.

14. William Hoynes, *Public Television for Sale: Media, Market, and the Public Sphere* (Boulder, Colo.: Westview Press, 1994), p. 98.

Chapter 11

1. Interview with Herb Schmertz, New York, N.Y., March 15, 1991.

2. For a more detailed account, see Laurence Jarvik, *'Masterpiece Theatre' and the Politics of Quality: A Case Study,* doctoral dissertation, University of California, Los Angeles, UMI, 1991.

3. Interview with Herb Schmertz, New York, March 15, 1991.

4. Michael Rice, "Memo to PBS, CPB, & Mobil," August 2, 1973; Sam Holt, "Memo to Gerry Slater, Re: Masterpiece Theatre," August 7, 1973.

5. Evelyn Kaye, "More of Those Masterpieces from England on Ch. 2 List," *Boston Globe,* July 7, 1974.

6. Schmertz interview.

7. Alistair Cooke, "Essay One," *Edwardian Essays,* Mobil, 1973.

8. Schmertz interview.

9. Press release draft, Frank Goodman Associates, n.d.

10. WGBH, memo to Frank Goodman, unsigned, undated, "Re: audience ratings for Masterpiece Theatre [1972–76]." The memo cites Allen Cooper in the statistics department of WGBH as the source. It does not specify whether the numbers represent individuals or households. It would be commonly assumed that it is a measurement of households.

11. Schmertz interview.

12. "Memo to All Member Stations, Subject . . . Shoulder to Shoulder," *Public Information,* February 3, 1975, PBS.

13. Interview with Frank Marshall, Key West, Fla., 1991.

14. Letter to *Ms.* magazine, draft, Frank Goodman Associates, n.d.

15. Memo, *Public Information,* February 2, 1975, p. 2, PBS.

16. John A. McKinley, "PBS Screening Report: Masterpiece Theatre: Shoulder to Shoulder, #101," November 1, 1977, PBS Archives.

17. Susan Brownmiller, "TV Series Exalts British Feminists," *New York Times,* October 19, 1975.

18. Karen Thomas, "Memo to Jack Crutchfield, Frank Little," September 23, 1975.

19. Les Brown, *Encyclopedia of Television* (New York: Zoetrope, 1982), pp. 20–1.

20. Susan Fergenson and Ron Devillier, "Memo to Development Directors, Program Managers, PI Directors, Re: Upstairs, Downstairs Farewell . . . A Million-Dollar Party," April 14, 1977.

21. Carey Winfrey, "Reunited Cast Bids Last Adieu to Eaton Place," *New York Times,* May 2, 1977.

22. Fergenson and Devillier, "Memo."

23. Anthony Lewis, "Reality in Romance," *New York Times,* May 9, 1977.

24. Schmertz interview.

25. Russell Baker, "Sunday Observer," *New York Times,* January 30, 1977.

26. Alistair Cooke, "Did Rose Live Happily Ever After?" *New York Times Magazine,* March 8, 1977; "Letters," *New York Times Magazine,* May 29, 1977.

27. Lewis, "Reality in Romance." This reaction contrasts with WGBH producer Christopher Sarson's original view that the series was too "commercial."

28. Telephone interview with Larry Grossman, May 6, 1991.

29. Carnegie Commission on the Future of Public Broadcasting, *A Public Trust* (New York: Bantam, 1979), p. 163.

30. "Masterpiece Theatre Gets New Opening Look," press release, n.d.; unpublished interview with Joan Wilson, "New Masterpiece Theatre Logo," Frank Goodman Associates, n.d.

31. John Hawkesworth, Simon and Goodman interview transcript, Frank Goodman Associates, n.d., tape 10, pp. 24–5.

32. Joan Wilson, memo to Henry Becton, June 19, 1977.

33. Tom Buckley, "TV: Duke Street Duchess," *New York Times,* December 2, 1978.

34. Schmertz interview.

35. John J. O'Connor, "Disraeli: More Evidence of the British Skill at Characterization," *New York Times,* June 1, 1980.

36. Lew Grade, *Still Dancing: My Story* (London: Fontana, 1988), p. 280.

37. Joan Wilson, memo to Henry Becton and Herb Schmertz, "Re: Masterpiece Theatre Potential Properties," June 16, 1980.

38. "RCTV Shakes Up Time-Life TV," *Adweek,* December 15, 1980.

39. Hartford Gunn, memo to Norm Sinel and Gerry Slater, "TLF Quarterly and Holt's memo to Sinel of 8/17/73," August 24, 1973.

40. Interview with Alistair Cooke, New York, June 16, 1990.

41. "A Decade of Masterpiece Theatre," *TV Guide,* January 17, 1981.

42. John J. O'Connor, "TV Weekend," *New York Times,* March 13, 1981; "A 10th Birthday for Masterpiece Theatre," *New York Times,* September 21, 1980.

43. "Mobil Bankrolls Aussie-Produced 'A Town Like Alice' for PBS Air," *Variety*, September 23, 1981.

44. Transcription of Alistair Cooke's introduction, "A Town Like Alice," episode one, UCLA Film and Television Archive.

45. Ibid.

46. Schmertz interview.

47. Patricia Harris, "Table 1: Highest Rated Masterpiece Theatre Programs," unpublished data, WGBH Research, n.d.

48. Ibid.

49. John J. O'Connor, "TV View," *New York Times*, December 16, 1984.

50. Transcription of Alistair Cooke's introduction, "The Jewel in the Crown," episode one, UCLA Film and Television Archive.

51. Ed Siegel, "A Jewel in the Medium's Crown," *Boston Globe*, July 11, 1985.

52. Interview with Rebecca Eaton, Boston, January 9, 1991.

53. Ibid.

54. Ed Siegel, "Ch. 2 Plans Updated Masterpiece," *Boston Globe*, May 1, 1986.

55. John J. O'Connor, " 'Goodbye, Mr. Chips' Is Welcome Once More," *New York Times*, January 4, 1987.

56. Schmertz interview.

57. Interview with Peter A. Spina, Fairfax, Va., 1991.

Chapter 12

1. Interview with Ron Devillier, Washington, D.C., 1992.

2. Richard Nixon, *In the Arena* (New York: Simon and Schuster, 1990), p. 257.

3. Harry Castleman and Walter Podrazik, *Watching TV: Four Decades of American Television* (New York: McGraw-Hill, 1982), p. 273.

4. William F. Buckley, *On the Firing Line* (New York: Random House, 1989), p. 453.

5. Kim Johnson, *The First Twenty Years of Monty Python* (New York: St. Martins, 1989), p. x.

6. Francis Wheen, *Television* (London: Century, 1985), pp. 53, 211.

7. Tim Brooks and Errol Marsh, *The Complete Directory to Prime Time Network TV Shows* (New York: Ballantine, 1988), p. 781.

8. Castleman and Podrazik, *Watching TV*, p. 259.

9. Robert Hewison, *Monty Python: The Case Against* (London: Methuen, 1989), p. 8.

10. Ibid.

11. Devillier interview.

12. Johnson, *The First Twenty Years*, p. xvi.

13. Castleman and Podrazik, *Watching TV*, p. 273.

14. Hewison, *Monty Python*, p. 52.

15. Jerry Palmer, *The Logic of the Absurd: On Film and Television Comedy* (London: British Film Institute, 1987), pp. 115–40.
16. Telephone interview with Milton Friedman, July 11, 1996.
17. Johnson, *The First Twenty Years*, p. 198.

Chapter 13

1. For a personal account, see Bruce Cumings, *War and Television* (London: Verso, 1992).
2. Les Brown, *Encyclopedia of Television* (New York: Zoetrope, 1982), p. 110.
3. David Horowitz and Laurence Jarvik, *Public Broadcasting and the Public Trust* (Los Angeles: Second Thoughts Books, 1995), p. 263.
4. Telephone interview with Allen Wallis, July 1996.
5. John S. Friedman, "Underwriting the Right: Public TV's CIA Show," *The Nation*, July 19–26, 1980, p. 77.
6. Thomas Sowell, *A Conflict of Visions: Ideological Origins of Political Struggles* (New York: Quill, 1987).
7. Ibid., p. 128.
8. Telephone interview with Robert Chitester, July 1996.
9. Ibid.
10. Wallis interview.
11. Peter Coleman, *The Liberal Conspiracy: The Congress for Cultural Freedom and the Struggle for the Mind of Postwar Europe* (New York: Free Press, 1989), pp. 9–12, 223.
12. Paul Hollander, *Anti-Americanism: Critiques at Home and Abroad, 1965–1990* (New York: Oxford University Press, 1992), pp. 55, 401.
13. Wallis interview.
14. Telephone interview with Milton Friedman, July 11, 1996.
15. Ibid.
16. Richard Cockett, *Thinking the Unthinkable: Think-tanks and the Counter-revolution, 1931–1983* (London: Fontana, 1995), p. 149.
17. Milton Friedman and Rose D. Friedman, *Free to Choose* (New York: Avon Books, 1981), p. x.
18. Ibid., p. 5.
19. Friedman interview.
20. Milton Friedman, *Capitalism and Freedom* (Chicago: University of Chicago Press, 1982 ed.), p. 18.
21. Ibid., p. 19.
22. Ibid., p. 21.
23. Friedman interview.
24. Ibid.

Acknowledgments

P_{BS}: *Behind the Screen* has taken many years to develop and I've been helped by many people in many ways. The Heritage Foundation gave me the chance to come to Washington as a Bradley Resident Scholar and begin this book, for which I'd like to thank Chuck Heatherly, Burt Pines, and Ed Feulner. While at Heritage I had the assistance of Jennifer Gately, John Slye, Melissa Reynolds, Amy Ricketts, Mary Ann Bradfield, Jeff Dickerson, Richard Odermatt, Meg Hunt, Karen Miller, Betsy Hart, Ed Hudgins, John Gregory, Dani Doane, Brigitte Wagner, Scott Hodge, Tom Atwood, Maureen Beckman, Hugh Newton, Herb Berkowitz, Joe Loconte, Stuart Butler, Dan Mitchell, Adam Meyerson, Kate O'Beirne, Dave Mason, Robert Rector, Bob Huberty, Hadley Arkes, David Forte, Nancy Bord, John Addison, and the late David Osterfeld, who introduced me to Thomas Sowell's *Knowledge and Decisions*.

David Horowitz and Peter Collier subsequently gave me the chance to help edit *Comint: A Journal About Public Media* at the Center for the Study of Popular Culture, an excellent platform from which to observe PBS and work on this book. At the Center, I had help from Alison Warner, Bill Cerveny, Lisa Maguire, Steve Morton, Joe Piechowski, Maura Whelan, Sherri Annis, Craig Hymowitz, Elizabeth Larson, Allyson Tucker and John Howard. Roger Ream of the Fund for American Studies provided me with two helpful summer interns, Jeff Watts and Dan McConchie. My current employer, Capital Research Center president Terrence Scanlon (who did some of the paperwork for the Corporation for Public Broadcasting in the Johnson administration) also deserves thanks, along with his staff, Tara Wheeler, David Wood, Gary Ross, Lorraine Overbeck, Bob Pambianco, Jill Lacey, Dan Oliver, Natasha Clerihue, Austin Fulk, Shayna Cook, Anne Marie Temple, and Bob Huberty once more.

William Bennett invited me to luncheons with Richard and Cynthia Grenier and a dinner with Rush Limbaugh, for which I am grateful. Ben Wattenberg was kind enough to ask me onto a panel at the American Enterprise Institute to debate American culture with Judge Robert Bork and Michael Medved. Pat Aufderheide included me in a session at the International Communications Association with PBS president Bruce Christensen. Sanford Ungar hosted an American University forum with myself and Action for Children's Television head Peggy Charren. And MacNeil/Lehrer Productions' Al Vecchione invited me to a Washington luncheon for the Twentieth Century Fund report with Ervin Duggan, Vartan Gregorian, and Richard C. Leone. The late Erwin Glikes encouraged me to write this book and even edited kind words about my research in George Will's *Restoration*. Don McNeil and Tom Connors and the staff of the National Public Broadcasting Archives at the University of Maryland were extremely helpful and considerate. Bill Voegeli and Jim Piereson of the Olin Foundation were personally helpful, as was Heather Higgins of the Randolph Foundation. I also received assistance from the staffs of the State Historical Society of Wisconsin, the Library of Congress, the Lyndon Baines Johnson Library, the Jimmy Carter Library, and the Richard Nixon presidential papers collection in the National Archives.

Though doubtless she disagreed with my editorial viewpoint, Sharon Rockefeller, president of WETA, Washington, saw to it that my information requests to her station were answered promptly and in full, which I appreciate. Former CPB chairmen Howard Gutin, Ken Towery, and Sonia Landau were extraordinarily helpful, as was former CPB director Vic Gold and former CPB president Donald Ledwig. Among those who opened their files were Alex Safian and Andrea Levin at the Committee for Accuracy in Middle East Reporting in America; Brent Bozell, Brent Baker, and Tim Graham at the Media Research Center; Reed Irvine, Joe Goulden, and Debbie Lambert at Accuracy in Media; and Robert

Lichter at the Center for Media and Public Affairs. I am also grateful to Allen Wildmon, Bob Knight, Rod Dreher, Karen Bedford, Steve Behrens, Janine Aversa, Jeff Kole, Brooks Boliek, George Archibald, Walt Riker, and Thomas W. Forrest, whose coverage of the PBS story in different ways has enriched this book. I have had the help and support of dozens of people inside public broadcasting and outside, literally too many to mention here (some, I am sure, would rather not be named). They know who they are, and I am grateful for their assistance.

I have been lucky to have financial support from the Lynde and Harry Bradley Foundation of Milwaukee, Wisconsin, headed by Mike Joyce. Diane Monroe Sehler was an understanding friend as well as a patient program officer, and I am grateful for the interest of Hillel Fradkin and Dan Schmidt. The Fieldstead Institute came through with a lifesaving full-time research assistant, Wendy Nentwig, in addition to financial support for myself, and I am grateful to Howard and Roberta Ahmanson as well as Steve Ferguson and Victor Porlier.

I'd like to express my gratitude to Carol Mann, my agent, and her assistant Gail Feinberg, my attorney Michael Remer and his assistant Marilyn Gilhuley, and my patient and dedicated editors at Prima Publishing, Steven Martin and Betsy Towner. I am thankful for the understanding and support of Alice Goldfarb Marquis, Mary Abbe, Tom Satterwhite, and Mark Horowitz, who put up with me.

I'm especially indebted to my wife, Nancy, whose contributions are beyond measure.

Any errors, of course, are my own.

Index